Indigenous Courts, Self-Determination and Criminal Justice

In New Zealand, as well as in Australia, Canada and other comparable jurisdictions, Indigenous peoples comprise a significantly disproportionate percentage of the prison population. For example, Maori, who comprise 15% of New Zealand's population, make up 50% of its prisoners. For Maori women, the figure is 60%. These statistics have, moreover, remained more or less the same for at least the past thirty years. With New Zealand as its focus, this book explores how the fact that Indigenous peoples are more likely than any other ethnic group to be apprehended, arrested, prosecuted, convicted and incarcerated, might be alleviated. Taking seriously the rights to culture and to self-determination contained in the Treaty of Waitangi, in many comparable jurisdictions (including Australia, Canada, the United States of America), and also in the United Nations Declaration on the Rights of Indigenous Peoples, the book makes the case for an Indigenous court founded on Indigenous conceptions of proper conduct, punishment, and behavior. More specifically, the book draws on contemporary notions of 'therapeutic jurisprudence' and 'restorative justice' in order to argue that such a court would offer an effective way to ameliorate the disproportionate incarceration of Indigenous peoples.

Dr Valmaine Toki is an Associate Professor in Law based at the Faculty of Law University of Waikato, New Zealand. Dr Toki was the first New Zealander appointed an Expert Member of the United Nations Permanent Forum on Indigenous Issues.

Indigenous Peoples and the Law

Series editors
Dr Mark A. Harris, *University of British Columbia, Canada*
Professor Denise Ferreira da Silva, *University of British Columbia, Canada*
Dr Claire Charters, *University of Auckland, New Zealand*
Dr Glen Coulthard, *University of British Columbia, Canada*

For information about the series and details of previous and forthcoming titles, see https://www.routledge.com/law/series/INDPPL

"He tohu tenei rakau mo te whanaungatanga me te kotahitanga i mua i te kōtanga"
"This tree is a unique metaphorical representation of relatedness and strength in the face of adversity"

A GlassHouse book

Indigenous Courts, Self-Determination and Criminal Justice

Valmaine Toki

Routledge
Taylor & Francis Group

LONDON AND NEW YORK

First published 2018 by Routledge

2 Park Square, Milton Park, Abingdon, Oxfordshire OX14 4RN
52 Vanderbilt Avenue, New York, NY 10017

Routledge is an imprint of the Taylor & Francis Group, an informa business

First issued in paperback 2020

British Library Cataloguing in Publication Data
A catalogue record for this book is available from the British Library

Library of Congress Cataloging in Publication Data
Names: Toki, Valmaine, author.
Title: Indigenous courts, self-determination and criminal justice / by Dr Valmaine Toki.
Description: Abingdon, Oxon ; New York : Routledge, 2018. | Series: Indigenous peoples and the law | Based on author's thesis (doctoral - University of Waikato, 2016) issued under title: A case for an indigenous court – a realisation of self-determination?
Identifiers: LCCN 2017043374 | ISBN 9780815375524 (hbk) | ISBN 9781351239622 (ebk)
Subjects: LCSH: Maori (New Zealand people)–Criminal justice system. | Customary law courts–New Zealand. | Criminal justice, Administration of–New Zealand. | Maori (New Zealand people)–Legal status, laws, etc. | Therapeutic jurisprudence–New Zealand.
Classification: LCC KUQ3478 .T65 2018 | DDC 345.93/0108999442–dc23
LC record available at https://lccn.loc.gov/2017043374

ISBN: 978-0-8153-7552-4 (hbk)
ISBN: 978-0-367-40442-0 (pbk)

Typeset in Baskerville
by Taylor & Francis Books

Contents

Acknowledgments

The journey for this book has been driven by an unforgiving criminal justice system that continues to rupture the very fabric of our indigenous community. This challenging journey, however, has been tempered by supportive and encouraging colleagues, whanau and friends, both here in Aotearoa, New Zealand and internationally whom I would like to acknowledge, in particular the inimitable indigenous scholar Professor John Borrows.

My *whanau* Kiri, Tama, Taumata and Steve remain my greatest inspiration. My *hapu*, Ngati wai ki Aotea, *iwi*, Ngapuhi, my source of connectedness and my Mum and Dad, Freda and Arthur Toki, my spiritual security.

He aha te mea nui o te Ao? He tangata he tangata he tangata!

In this book I draw on some articles that I have previously published and I would like acknowledge the following:

"Are Domestic Violence Courts Working for Indigenous Peoples?" (2009) *Commonwealth Law Bulletin* 35(2), 255–286

"Are Parole Boards Working or is it Time for an Indigenous Re Entry Court?" *International Journal of Law, Crime and Justice* 39 (2011), 230–248

"Therapeutic Jurisprudence and Mental Health Courts for Maori" (2010) 33 *International Journal of Law and Psychiatry*, 440–447.

Foreword

This book discusses the importance of applying Māori law in contemporary settings in Aotearoa. Professor Toki shows how this could be done in at least two ways: through the extension of an existing forum, such as the Māori Land Court, or through the establishment of a specialist Tikanga Court. The development of Te Ao Māori through its application in today's varied contexts is sorely needed. Her practical call to ensure that Indigenous law addresses real-world problems is a welcome addition to the literature. As she demonstrates by reference Māori over-representation in the justice system, innovative approaches are needed to tackle this pressing social issue. Reference to Māori law would not only benefit Indigenous peoples. As is the case with good law of any sort, Tikanga Māori holds the potential to aid and assist society as a whole.

Of course, Professor Toki understands the challenges involved in this undertaking. The arguments in this book anticipate those who might be supportive and/or critical of her claims. This book is a search for balance in understanding how people might live together in a more holistic manner when it comes to our legal commitments. Thus, Professor Toki discusses therapeutic justice while keeping her eye focused on the need to overcome domestic violence. She discusses the historic marginalisation of Tikanga Māori in New Zealand legal history while highlighting threads which can work towards the modern resurgence of Aotearoa's first laws. In showing how Indigenous law can be revitalised today Professor Toki recognises the importance of the country's constitutional structures. She calls for the use of legislative action alongside the application of the United Nations Declaration on the Rights of Indigenous peoples to make her thesis a reality. Drawing on comparative insights from other country's experiences of Indigenous law, Professor Toki outlines how such principles and processes can interact with national legal systems.

Ultimately, Professor Toki understands that the legal dimensions of this work can only be applied in a climate that nourishes the political will to address destructive colonial rules and conventions. As such, she argues that Aotearoa should not be constructed on constitutionally homogeneous foundations. She shows how law must not only draw on Anglo-settler values but must continue to extend its reach to apply insights from normative authorities which are

Indigenous to the country. At the same time, Professor Toki understands the needs to see Indigenous laws as flexible and adaptable to changing circumstances. This requires a focus on underlying principles and motivating philosophies rather than frozen understandings of Māori law lifted from prior eras when people lived very different lives. This recognition allows Professor Toki to call for an application of Tikanga Māori which is always practically attentive to the context in which it is applied.

The application of Indigenous peoples own law is not always pretty. Law does not only flow from the beauty of peoples' languages, cultures and traditions. Law is simultaneously forged through fierce disagreement, dissent, disparity and disputation. Any practical application of Tikanga Māori must recognise this fact. Law which is built on differences of opinion, even as it sifts through these opinions and makes judgments about their relative weight, is law which respects our capacities to participation in its formation. While law must ultimately address disagreements, it must do so in a context which enables our differences to be fully expressed. A law which does not apply Tikanga Māori in Aotearoa, would be a law which does not fully respect our humanity. In this book Professor Toki advances a view which embraces the complexity of the country's legal inheritance, while showing how this can be done in more respectful and humane ways. Her ideas not only have relevance for New Zealand, but for any country which struggles to improve relationships between Indigenous peoples and their neighbours. I am persuaded by her vision and I hope other readers likewise find insight and opportunity in what she has so ably presented in the following pages.

John Borrows
B.A., M.A., J.D., LL.M., Ph.D., LL.D. (Hons.), F.R.S.c.
Canada Research Chair in Indigenous Law
University of Victoria Law School

Introduction

"Only the law of the Pākehā custom is recognised [in New Zealand] ... The Māori who seeks justice and redress under Pākehā law must rely on the blunt instrument of that very same law which is embedded upon the mechanisms designed for his legal control"

Rev Maori Marsden[1]

Before the arrival of settlers, Māori adhered to their own form of 'law and order' and a world based on the collective. This changed dramatically with the imposition of a settler form of 'law and order' foreign to the Māori world. The control asserted by the settler government resulted in a break down of the collective and social order for Māori. This power and control was manifested in legislation that legitimised land alienations and the ability to incarcerate Māori for various offences. Subsequently Māori became landless and vulnerable to the whims of the settler government. Incarceration rates, for Māori, quickly rose and soon Māori were disproportionately represented within the criminal justice system. This has not changed and warrants an overdue, earnest and thoughtful study.

This book suggests that a more meaningful incorporation of concepts that underpin *tikanga* Māori, within the current criminal justice system, could potentially lead to a reduction in recidivism and offending rates for Māori. This book further suggests that the Marae could be the appropriate forum to implement these concepts. A review of comparative jurisdictions together with the discussion of therapeutic jurisprudence lends support for such an initiative. A proposed *marae* court or Indigenous court, underpinned by *tikanga* Māori concepts, operating within the current criminal justice system, provides an example of internal self-determination for Māori.

Statistics from the Justice Department and the Department of Corrections in New Zealand indicate Māori are proportionately over-represented as offenders within the criminal justice system and that these statistics have not changed in the

1 Māori Marsden "The Natural World and Natural Resources" in C Royal (ed) *The Woven Universe: Selected Writings of Rev Māori Marsden* (Estate of Rev. Māori Marsden, Masterton, 2003) at 101.

last 30 years.[2] This provides an undesirable groundswell and subsequent catalyst that drives this book to seek answers. For example, in 1999 the Justice Department in its publication *Responses to Crime: Annual Review* noted:[3]

> Both Māori and Pacific peoples of all age groups from 14 and older are over-represented as offenders. This is particularly so for offenders aged 14 to 16, then again for those aged 40 and over. Māori have particularly high rates of offending, with, for example, a rate of prosecutions for non-traffic offences 5.4 times higher than that of other New Zealanders excluding Pacific peoples. Māori and Pacific peoples are more likely to be victims of violent offences than are New Zealand Europeans, but less likely to be the victims of property offences.

Considering possible initiatives in response to these statistics, the Report notes that:[4]

> The relatively high rates of offending by Māori and Pacific peoples and the need for culturally appropriate responses point to the importance of both fostering diverse approaches to offending by these two groups and identifying those approaches that show most promise of reducing their over-participation in the criminal justice system as both offenders and victims.

This indicates that while Māori commit criminal offences at rates higher than those for any other ethnic group in New Zealand, there is a need to consider diverse approaches to reduce the over-representation of Māori in the criminal justice system both as offenders and victims.

In the report on the experience of Māori women in the criminal justice system,[5] the Law Commission concurred with this finding. The report observed that Māori are disproportionately represented in court proceedings, with higher

---

2   Department of Corrections *Trends in the Offender Population* (2013) <http://www.correc tions.govt.nz/__data/assets/pdf_file/0012/738939/Trends_in_the_Offender_Popula tion_2013_updated.pdf>, at 15 where the report notes 'The proportion of all prison sentenced offenders who are Māori increased from 44 per cent on December 31, 1983 to 50 percent on December 31, 2013'. See also Department of Corrections *Over-Representation of Māori in the Criminal Justice System: An Exploratory Report* (Department of Corrections, Wellington, 2007) <www.corrections.govt.nz>. See also <http://www. corrections.govt.nz/resources/research_and_statistics/quarterly_prison_statistics/PS_ March_2016.html#ethnicity> that indicates at March 2016, 51 per cent of the prison population identified as Māori.
3   Ministry of Justice *Responses to Crime: Annual Review* (Ministry of Justice, Wellington, 1999) at 7. Although this Report is from 1999, as the statistics have not altered between 1983 and 2013, for Māori, this remains relevant.
4   At 7.
5   Law Commission *Justice: The Experience of Māori Women* (New Zealand Law Commission, Wellington, 1999) R53 at para [326].

rates of criminal offending and incarceration than other ethnic groups when measured as a proportion of the total population.[6]

A report from the Department of Corrections also noted:[7]

> Relative to their numbers in the general population, Māori are over-represented at every stage of the criminal justice process. Though forming just 12.5% of the general population aged 15 and over, 42% of all criminal apprehensions involve a person identifying as Māori, as do 50% of all persons in prison. For Māori women, the picture is even more acute: they comprise around 60% of the female prison population.
>
> The true scale of Māori over-representation is greater than a superficial reading of such figures tend to convey. For example, with respect to the prison population, the rate of imprisonment for this country's non-Māori population is around 100 per 100,000. If that rate applied to Māori also, the number of Māori in prison at any onetime would be no more than 650. There are however currently 4000 Māori in prison – *six times* the number one might otherwise expect.

Dannette notes that:[8]

> The Department of Corrections has adopted a specific theory about the causes of criminal offending by Māori. A major assumption of this theory is that the contemporary overrepresentation of Māori in offending, incarceration, and recidivism rates is best understood as the outcome of Māori experiencing impairments to cultural identity resulting from colonisation. Central to this theory, therefore, is also the assumption that ethnicity is a reliable construct by which distinctions can be made between offenders regarding what factors precipitated their offending, as well as best practices for their rehabilitation.

In March 2013, the Ministry of Justice provided statistics noting the composition of the prison population disaggregated by sex, age and ethnicity of offenders.[9] At the time of this survey, Māori comprised 14 per cent of the population and yet 50 per cent of the male prison population identified as Māori and although women comprised 6 per cent of the total prison population (504 out of a total

---

6 At ch 5 in particular at para [341]. Also see Ministry of Justice *Responses to Crime*, above n 3, at 38.

7 Department of Corrections *Over-Representation of Māori in the Criminal Justice System*, above n 2, at 6; See also R Walter and T Bradley "Crime Statistics: 'Official' and 'Unofficial' Representations of Crime and Victimisation" in R Walter and T Bradley (eds) *Introduction of Criminological Thought* (Pearson Longman, Auckland, 2005) at 20–22.

8 Marie Dannette "Māori and Criminal Offending: A Critical Appraisal" (2010) 43 ANZ J of Criminology 2 at 283.

9 Ministry of Justice *Over representation of Māori in Prison* (2013) chapter 18 <www.justice. govt.nz>.

population of 8,611), Māori women made up 58 per cent of that female prisoner population (291 out of a total female prison population of 504).[10] More recently, in December 2016, the statistics indicate little change with 50.8 per cent of the prison population identifying as Māori whilst comprising 16 per cent of the population.[11] However for Māori women the statistics have risen to 63 per cent.[12]

Although concerning, Sumner notes that Western criminological theory has nothing to say about this genre of statistics and has little interest to contribute to their analysis.[13] Orthodox criminologists are reluctant to examine crimes and the colonial state as "you are returned to the criminal economic system underpinning your own state".[14] Nonetheless an examination of crime and justice can assist to understand the crimes committed by the powerful and the impact of human rights.

This position is similar to that of other Indigenous peoples in many post-colonial countries, including Australia and Canada.[15] Jim McLay, New Zealand's Permanent Representative to the United Nations, reported:[16]

10 Ministry of Justice *Over representation of Māori in Prison*, chapter 18, above. For a discussion on female offending see Paul Mazerolle 'The Poverty of a Gender Neutral Criminology: Introduction to the Special Issue on Current Approaches to Understanding Female Offending' (2008) 41(1) ANZ Journal of Criminology. In 2016, this statistic increased to 62 per cent of women serving custodial sentences and 57 per cent of women with community sentences identifying as Maori, see also Marianne Bevan and Nan Wehipeihana 'Women's Experiences of Reoffending and Rehabilitation' (November 2015) Department of Corrections <http://www.corrections.govt.nz/resources/research_and_statistics/womens_experiences_of_re-offending_and_reha bilitation.html> at 10.
11 http://www.corrections.govt.nz/.
12 Above.
13 C Sumner (ed) *Crime Justice and Underdevelopment* (Heinemann, London, 1982) as cited by Simone Bull "The Land of Murder, Cannibalism and all Kinds of Atrocious Crimes? Māori and Crime in New Zealand 1853–1919" (2004) 44 Brit J Criminol at 496.
14 Bull, above n 13, at 497.
15 See Chapter 6 'Initiatives in Comparative Jurisdictions' for statistics. Indigenous peoples is a term commonly used to describe any ethnic group who inhabit the geographic region with which they have the earliest historical connection. See also Caecilie Mikkelsen (ed) *The Indigenous World 2013* (Eks-Skolens Trykkeri IWGIA, Copenhagen, 2013).
16 Jim McLay "Statement to the Third Committee, 68th session of the United Nations General Assembly under Item 66: Rights of Indigenous Peoples" (United Nations General Assembly, New York, 21 October 2013) GA/SHC/4074 <https://www.un.org/press/en/2013/gashc4074.doc.htm>; also see <www.mfat.govt.nz>; also see United Nations Report from Committee Against Torture "Concluding observations on the sixth periodic report of New Zealand" where it was noted at [14] that the Committee is also concerned at information received that while making up 15 per cent of the State Party's population, Māori comprise 45 per cent of arrests and over 50 per cent of prison inmates, moreover more than 60 per cent of female inmates are Māori (arts 2, 11 and 16) <https://www.hrc.co.nz/files/2814/3192/5666/CAT_Rep ort_May_2015.pdf>

Despite many positive developments, we remain realistic about the challenges. We recognise that Māori are over-represented in the criminal justice system, that Māori women and children experience a greater prevalence of domestic violence and that Māori face a higher number of health problems. The New Zealand government is committed to addressing these issues by improving social and economic conditions for Māori.

Of note in the concluding observations of the sixth periodic report of New Zealand, the Committee against Torture recommended that:[17]

The State party should increase its efforts to address the overrepresentation of indigenous people in prisons and to reduce recidivism, in particular its underlying causes, by fully implementing the Turning of the Tide Prevention Strategy through the overall judicial system and by intensifying and strengthening community-based approaches with the involvement of all relevant stakeholders and increased participation of Māori civil society organizations.

Although it is difficult to ignore the disproportionate nature of these statistics, like many statistical surveys, they are limited by their disaggregation. To this end these statistics do not include whether the offenders are unemployed, uneducated, endure substandard housing and poverty. Offending rates are instead linked to population proportions and disaggregated by gender, ethnicity and age rather than these social development factors.[18] Simone Bull notes that "as far as our perceptions of Māori offending are concerned, reality has been overtaken by stereotypes and assorted misinformation much of which is generated by corporate media".[19] According to theorist Jean Baudrillard this "hyper-reality" has become a starting point for research as opposed to a sound evidence base.[20] In light of the absence of disaggregated data and empirical evidence, these assumptions form the basis for criminal justice intervention programmes that target Māori offenders.[21] Despite initiatives by the Justice System, these statistics have not altered significantly. In the last 30 years, the number of Māori starting a prison sentence almost doubled whereas the number of Pākehā decreased marginally.[22] Further, "proportionally, prisoners starting a prison sentence who are Māori increased

---

17 At [14].
18 John Braithwaite *Crime, Shame and Reintegration* (Cambridge, Cambridge University Press, 1989) as cited in Simone Bull *Changing the Broken Record: New Theory and Data on Māori Offending* <igps.victoria.ac.nz/events/downloads/2009/Simone%20Bull.doc>.
19 Bull, above n 13.
20 Jean Baudrillard *Simulacra and Simulation* (translated by Sheila Glaser, University of Michigan, Ann Arbor, 1995).
21 Dannette, above n 8, at 283.
22 Department of Corrections *Trends in the Offender Population*" , above n 2, at 8 <http://corrections.govt.nz>.

from 47 per cent to 56 per cent between 1983 and 2013".[23] The United Nations Working Group on Arbitrary Detention has urged the New Zealand government to investigate why Māori are continually over-represented in the nation's prisons.[24]

Statistics New Zealand has not signalled any steps to further disaggregate this data, referring instead to maintaining the status quo.[25] As this statistical disaggregation is unavailable, and not likely to be available, for Māori offending rates to be population 'proportionate' on the 2013 statistics, based on a prison population of 7,654 the number of Māori inmates would be 1,148 (15 per cent of 7,654) rather than the indicated 4,311.[26] Even if the social factors are taken into account and reflected in the statistics it is suggested that the imprisonment rate for Māori would still figure disproportionately.

It is also acknowledged that to be classified as Māori for the purposes of the statistics requires self-identification. Many Māori, for various reasons, chose not to be identified as Māori, distorting the statistics. Nonetheless, the importance of these social factors on offending is recognised and included in the drivers of crime policy.

The events of history and humanity, including instances of colonial annexation, reveal the need to control and protect.[27] For instance, the passing of legislation such as the New Zealand Settlements Act 1863,[28] the Suppression of Rebellion Act 1863 and the Disturbed Districts Act 1869 sanctioned land confiscations and criminalised actions taken by Māori to retain their land[29] thus controlling the

---

23 Above.
24 Australian Associated Press "A United Nations working group says it wants the New Zealand government to undertake a review of the degree of systemic bias against Māori in the justice system" (April 2014). United Working Group on Arbitrary Detention. <http://www.sbs.com.au/news/article/2014/04/08/un-wants-review-māori-nz-prisons>.
25 Statistics New Zealand *Review of Crime and Criminal Justice Statistics Report* (Statistics New Zealand, Wellington, 2009) 22 <www.statistics.govt.nz>.
26 Department of Corrections *Trends in the Offender Population*, above n 2, at 28 <http://corrections.govt.nz>.
27 Te Paparahi o te Raki Waitangi Tribunal Report (November 2014) Wai 1040 at 529 "Rather, in the explanations of the texts and in the verbal assurances given by Hobson and his agents, it sought the power to control British subjects and thereby to protect Māori." However, in ensuing years Māori lost control of their lands, territories and resources through imposed legislation; legislation, which in turn protected British subjects.
28 The New Zealand Settlements Act 1863 was "An Act to enable the Governor to establish settlements for colonisation in the North Island of New Zealand". The Act allowed for land confiscation without compensation to iwi who were deemed to be in rebellion against Her Majesty's authority. Subsequently the Government confiscated vast tracks of land from tribes such as Te Ati Awa, from the Taranaki district, who were passively protesting against the land policies of the government that resulted in the loss of Māori land.
29 Bull, above n 13, at 507. The imposition of policies and legislation to control and criminalise Māori, such as the Dog Tax, resulted in an increase in offending and charge rates for Māori in the 1890s.

actions of Māori through legislation and protecting colonial settlers by criminalising the actions of Māori, thereby making the land available for the colonial settlers.

Paul McHugh noted that the colonial legal system is one seeking to establish "a constitutionally homogenised population, one that reflected Anglo-settler values, rather than a pluralistic one with sources of political authority apart from the state."[30]

This desire is reflected in respective criminal justice systems, such as those in Australia[31] and North America,[32] where their accompanying ideologies have been imposed upon existing systems. Professor Robert Miller captures this by noting:[33]

> ... the European colonists pursued a mission to destroy the cultures, laws and governments of Indigenous peoples. A campaign to "civilize" these "others" by making illegal the practicing of their ways of knowing was sought through the means of law.

If a legal system did not conform to a Western jurist's perception of a legal system, premised on a constitutional framework, then it was not classified as a legal system.[34] The European claim was that "there is no law until there are courts".[35]

30 Paul McHugh *Aboriginal Societies and the Common Law: A History of Sovereignty, Status, and Self-Determination* (Oxford University Press, New York, 2004) at 49.
31 Australia Law Reform Commission *Recognition of Aboriginal Laws* (Australian Law Reform Commission, Sydney, June 1986) Report 31, chap 4 <http://www.alrc.gov.au/sites/default/files/pdfs/publications/ALRC31.pdf> where it is noted that "the decision to classify the 'new' country of Australia as a settled colony, rather than as conquered or ceded, meant that the new settlers brought with them the general body of English law, including the criminal law; see also *R v Jack Congo Murrell* (1836) 1 Legge 72 where the court held it had jurisdiction to try one aborigine for the murder of another confirming that the law of the colonists applied to the Indigenous aboriginal peoples. This has been reaffirmed in *Tuckiar v R* (1934) 52 CLR 335; *Milirrpum v Nabalco Pty Ltd* (1971) 17 FLR 141 at 261 per Blackburn J; *R v Wedge* [1976] 1 NSWLR 581. In the latter case Rath J concluded that "all the reasons of the court in *R v Murrell* are as valid today as they were when judgment in that case was given" at 587.
32 See Chris Cunneen "Colonial Processes, Indigenous Peoples and Criminal Justice Systems" in Sandra Bucerius and Michael Tonry (eds) *The Oxford Handbook of Ethnicity, Crime and Immigration* (OUP, New York, 2014) at 386–407.
33 Robert Miller and Jacinta Ruru "An Indigenous Lens into Comparative Law: The Doctrine of Discovery in the United States and New Zealand" (2009) 111 West Virginia L. Rev 849 at 914.
34 Moana Jackson *The Māori and the Criminal Justice System – He Whaipaanga Hou: A New Perspective: Part* 2 (Department of Justice, Wellington, 1988) at 37.
35 Sir Clinton Roper *Report of the Ministerial Committee of Inquiry into Violence* (March 1987) at 41. Also known as the Roper Report where it was urged that legislation be utilised to the fullest extent; see also Sue Carswell *Family Violence and the Pro-Arrest Policy: A Literature Review* (Ministry of Justice, December 2006) at ch 2.

Prior to colonisation Māori had effective legal, political and social systems in place.[36]

The "Crown government did not encounter a legal vacuum, unfilled until the exercise of the constituent power."[37] The Māori legal system was based on values rather than rules. Although such laws varied from iwi-to-iwi,[38] all Māori followed and adhered to the principles of *tikanga* Māori, particularly when a breach occurred.

Tikanga Māori is often viewed as Māori customary values and practices. Nonetheless, it is far more complex than a two dimensional definition. Hirini Moko Mead states that:[39]

> ... tikanga [Māori] is the set of beliefs associated with practices and proce-
> dures to be followed in conducting the affairs of a group or individual. These
> procedures are established by precedents through time, are held to be ritually
> correct, are validated by usually more than one generation and are always
> subject to what a group or individual is able to do ... tikanga are tools of
> thought and understanding. They are packages of ideas which help to orga-
> nize behavior and provide some predictability in how certain activities are
> carried out. They provide templates and frameworks to guide our actions ...
> they help us differentiate between rights and wrong ... there is a right and
> proper way to conduct one's self.

This position infers that in order to realise what is right and appropriate, there must be an element of flexibility and adaptability to *tikanga* Māori.[40] A balancing or weighing up would be required to determine the proper actions or responses.

Tikanga Māori is not only conceptual, representing beliefs and customs, but is also manifest in actions and practices.[41] The dynamic between the underlying concepts and customs, with actions and practices, assists to discern and maintain social understandings and balance within the community. This balance can change to reflect the mores of the community, but the essence of the concepts remain.[42] *Tikanga* Māori is a relational concept more akin to principles, which

---

36 Eddie T Durie "Will the Settlers Settle? Cultural Conciliation and Law" (1996) 8
    Otago L Rev 449 at 451; New Zealand Law Commission *Māori Custom and Values in
    New Zealand Law* (New Zealand Law Commission SP9, Wellington, 2001) at 17;
    Jackson, above n 34; Wai 1040, above n 27.

37 Paul McHugh *The Māori Magna Carta: New Zealand Law and the Treaty of Waitangi*
    (Oxford University Press, Oxford, 1991) at 83.

38 Hirini Mead *Tikanga Māori Living by Māori Values* (Huia, Wellington, 2003) at 8.

39 At 12.

40 NZ Law Commission above n 36, at [11] and [18].

41 Mead, above n 38, at 22.

42 For instance, in light of the health statistics, indicating that Māori have dispropor-
    tionate rates of diabetes, and are three times likely to contract diabetes as non-Māori,
    warranting kidney transplants, the *tikanga* attached to organ donation be reassessed.
    The general view is that, for Māori, the body is to return to Papatūānuku (mother

prescribed general actions, than rules that prescribed specific acts resulting in, for example, specific regulations and codes.[43] Upon colonisation most principles of *tikanga* Māori were neither encouraged nor recognised by the colonial authorities.[44]

The colonial values and ethics imported by the settlers were based on Victorian morals.[45] The introduced beliefs of the Church instilled a sense of religious morality demanding obedience to God and the will of the Church.[46] Central to these morals and values was the notion of the individual and individual rights to property that prevailed in the Victorian era.[47]

For philosophers such as Grotius and Hobbes, the defining institution of individual "property differentiated the savage state from the more advanced stages in society".[48] During this time of enlightenment, 'savages' or the 'uncivilized', such as Māori, were required to be transformed into a living model of humanity where a 'pleasanter way of life' was characterised by individual property rights.[49]

For Māori their cultural definitions and ontological assumptions that shaped notions of criminality and social order, were replaced by these values and morals

> earth) whole. However, as *tikanga* is flexible we are to perceive organ donation as one of *manaakitanga* (blessing) and *āwhina* (help) this would support the activity of organ donation. So, the primacy of the *tikanga* concepts may have changed but their essence remains the same, resulting in balance that is reflective of social mores.

43 Principles are commonly seen to apply from within to internally motivate and are fundamentally different to rules that are commonly seen to apply externally to compel action. For further discussion on the nature of rules see Joseph Raz "Legal Principles and the Limits of Law" (1972) 81 Yale LJ 838.

44 See also discussion in Nin Tomas "Indigenous Peoples and the Māori: The Right to Self-Determination in International Law – From Woe to Go" [2008] NZ Law Review at 645–647 where she notes that colonisation "resulted in the decimation of the social, political and legal organisation of indigenous societies and their marginalisation within new, imposed colonial regimes".

45 Victorian morals included sexual restraint, low tolerance of crime and a strict code of conduct; see also J M R Owens "Christianity and the Māori to 1840" (1968) NZJH at pps 18–40 <www.nzjh.auckland.ac.nz>; see also Wai 1040, above n 27, at 248.

46 See discussion in Michael King *The Penguin History of New Zealand* (Penguin, New Zealand, 2003) at 141; see also discussion in Leonie Pihema "Tihei Mauri Ora: Honouring Our Voices: Mana Wahine as a Kaupapa Māori Theoretical Framework" (PhD, University of Auckland, 2001) at ch 6 "Colonisation and the Importation of Ideologies, of Race, Gender and Class" <www.kaupapamāori.com>. Māori have now internalised these religious values e.g. Ratana Church.

47 Owens, above n 45; Wai 1040, above n 27, at 38.

48 Robert Williams Jr *Savage Anxieties: The Invention of Western Civilisation* (Palgrave, New York, 2012) at 204. Although the writings of these philosophers were based in Europe, Williams uses this to emphasise the wider effect this philosophy had on Indigenous peoples.

49 Williams Jr, above n 48, at 203–205. The alienation was premised on individual property rights doctrine. The Waitangi Tribunal was eventually established to ameliorate the alienation and confiscation of Māori land by the Crown; see Treaty of Waitangi Act 1975, s 4 which establishes the Waitangi Tribunal.

of the colonising power.[50] Although the applicability of this new social order and accompanying legal system was resisted, in reality, in many areas, English law was unknown, unenforced and unenforceable.[51] For a large number of communities, *tikanga* Māori was the only legal system in place;[52] nonetheless, this resulted in a changing world for Māori, compounded and exacerbated by events such as urbanisation.

To examine whether the application of Te Ao Māori philosophy is an appropriate way forward for Māori to ameliorate the disproportionate offending rates, Chapter One will set the scene with an overview of criminality and the relationship between Māori and the criminal justice system, including areas of criminal offending, parole and mental health. Chapter Two discusses who are Māori and what is *tikanga* Māori. The discussion of Māori ancestral conceptions of *tikanga* Māori and correct conduct establishes a potential framework for further consideration and is set against more commonly known theories of law: natural law and positivism. Two examples provide an insightful reflection of the implementation of English law on *tikanga* Māori: first, the changing significance of Māori women in society together with the related problem of domestic violence; and second, the issue of mental health and Māori.[53]

To provide further context and background, Chapter Three will examine the historical and contemporary criminal justice initiatives, including Māori juries, Māori wardens and Family Group Conferences. It could be that aspects of these initiatives, such as the role of the Māori warden, that have shown success could be employed within a proposed Indigenous court. A review of how Hauora Māori (Māori philosophy of health and well-being) adheres to the relational concept of *tikanga* Māori within the health system provides an interesting comparative analysis. Existing judicial initiatives to address the disproportionate representation of Māori in the criminal statistics will be investigated, including Te Kooti Rangatahi – a youth court held on a *marae*.

To examine the concerning question of the extent to which *tikanga* Māori has been marginalised, Chapter Four will provide an historical review of the introduction of English law and legal systems and the adverse impact this has had on *tikanga* Māori. An analysis of two key documents – the Treaty of Waitangi, in Chapter Four and the United Nations Declaration on the Rights of Indigenous

50 See comments by Ranginui Walker in *Ka Whawhai Tonu Mātou – Struggle without End* (Penguin, Auckland, 1990) at 10, where he notes that "the outcome of colonisation by the turn of the century was impoverishment of leaders and chiefly authority and a structural relationship of Pākehā dominance and Māori subjection. So in total was Pākehā dominance at a time when Māori population had fallen to its lowest point of 45,549, that the colonizer deluded himself into thinking that he had created a unified nation state of one people …".

51 McHugh, above n 30, at 180.

52 At 180.

53 The term '*English*' law refers to the law that was derived from the English Westminster system from the United Kingdom that was imported into New Zealand retrospectively clarified by the English Laws Act 1858.

Peoples in Chapter Five – will be undertaken to provide further context to this dialogue. Although the New Zealand government was reluctant to include Indigenous rights and the concept of *tikanga* Māori within a possible written constitution, an examination of comparative constitutions reveals that it is not unusual to entrench Indigenous rights. An evaluation of the pivotal right of self-determination, as set forth in the United Nations Declaration on the Rights of Indigenous Peoples, and the rights associated with tino rangatiratanga, in the Treaty of Waitangi provides a contextual right for the return to the philosophy of Te Ao Māori realised by an Indigenous legal system.

Chapter Six provides a review of initiatives from comparative jurisdictions, such as the Navajo Courts and the Koori Courts, which indicates State support for Indigenous people's right to culture and self-determination. This chapter will conclude that given the disproportionate representation of Indigenous peoples in areas of crime and mental health, drawing upon Indigenous concepts and doctrine may provide an answer.[54] An examination of the Navajo Courts lays the foundation for further discussion.

In light of the promising results from the doctrine of therapeutic jurisprudence Chapter Seven will examine this doctrine and suggest that because therapeutic jurisprudence already exists within the criminal justice system, it may provide a window to import *tikanga* Māori with a review of domestic violence courts and re-entry courts. Chapter Eight consolidates this research and tests the implications of a new framework. This includes an extension to the jurisdiction of the Māori Land Court,[55] or a specialised *Tikanga* Māori Court.[56]

54 *Indigenous law* relates to that system of law developed by, and relating to, Indigenous peoples. Terms such as Customary Law and Aboriginal Law can also be used. For Māori this system of law is '*tikanga*'; see also New Zealand Law Commission, above n 36 at chapter 3, for discussion on *tikanga* Māori and Māori custom law.

55 The jurisdiction of the Māori Land Court is currently to hear matters relating to successions, title improvements, Māori land sales and the administration of Māori Land Trusts and Incorporations. The jurisdiction also includes cases under the Māori Fisheries Act 2004 and Māori Commercial Aquaculture Claims Settlement Act 2004. An extension to the jurisdiction to capture criminal offending may be suggested. It is acknowledged that the Māori Land Court is based on the notion of individual property rights that is inconsistent with the Māori world and this presents a further challenge.

56 Although phrased as a 'new' Indigenous Court there are many such Courts already operating. In Canada the National Judicial Institute provides educational courses for the judiciary on Aboriginal Courts covering the reality, theory and future of these courts.

Chapter 1

Māori and criminality

A Criminality and causes of offending

Criminality

Schiller notes that the "behavioural definition of crime focuses on, criminality, a certain personality profile" that causes a crime.[1] The type of person likely to commit a crime is often "a style of strategic behavior characterised by self-centeredness and indifference to the suffering and needs of others".[2] More "impulsive individuals are more likely to find criminality an attractive style of behavior because it can provide immediate gratification through relatively easy or simple strategies".[3]

Some criminologists believe that the orthodox reasons for criminality that relate to sociological, psychological, biological or economic reasons do not explain criminal behaviour.[4] Rather, they state that the essential element of criminality is the lack or absence of self-control, so those with high self-control consider the consequences of their behaviour as opposed to those with low self-control who do not.[5] Further, once self-control is learned, it is highly resistant to change.

The Indigenous concept of criminality differs from a non-Indigenous concept of criminality. For Māori, a crime or *hara* was inextricably linked to, and explained by further concepts such as *tapu* and *mana* and the need to rebalance the harm that the *hara* has caused, rather than any associated behaviour of the offender.[6]

Nonetheless, it is acknowledged that the behaviour or criminality associated with a *hara*, such as trespass and taking of resources, could stem from conventional elements of criminality, such as self-centredness, indifference to the

---

1 Johann Schiller "Crime and Criminality" (University of California, Davis, California) Chap 16 at 285. <www.des.ucdavis.edu/faculty/>
2 See Michael R Gottfredson and Travis Hirschi *A General Theory of Crime* (Stanford University Press, Palo Alto, California, 1990).
3 Schiller, above n 1, at 285.
4 Gottfredson and Hirschi, above n 2.
5 Above.
6 See Chapter 2 'Māori and *Tikanga* for a full discussion.

suffering of others and possibly low self-control. However, the requirement to rebalance the harm caused is mandatory and takes precedence over behaviour that may be classified as criminal.

Causes of offending

Criminology, as a distinct field of study, is devoted to determining the causes of crime. It is no surprise that due to the dynamic and complex reasons why people offend, various theories, such as conflict and group theory, and various factors, such as social and economic factors, can be more heavily weighted than others when determining causes of offending.[7] Subsequently, sociological and economical theories often describe conditions in which crime frequently occurs, without explaining why it occurs and why some factors affect some people and not others.[8]

Further, it is difficult to avoid similarities and overlap in theories; for instance, the concept of conflict, as a reason to offend, is also labelled as critical or radical criminology.[9] To this end it is problematic to ascribe to one school of criminological thought when determining causes of offending. A closer examination of the different theories and how they may, or may not explain Māori causes of offending will be informative.

Theories that are based on scientific evidence, unfortunately, have provided little value when explaining causes of offending for Māori. The drive to provide a scientific explanation for criminality is a regular feature of the modern discourse on crime.[10] During the 2006 Conference of the International Congress of Human Genetics, it was claimed that the presence of a specific gene type, the monoamine oxidase gene, contributed significantly to explaining the criminality of Māori.[11] This finding was flawed and unnecessarily exacerbated the effect that a gene may have on Māori,[12] proving unhelpful in terms of seeking a cause of offending for Māori.

7   For a discussion on cultural factors see M O'Brien "What is Cultural about Cultural Criminology?" (2005) 45 British Journal of Criminology 599.
8   K D Harries *Crime and the Environment* (Charles C Thomas, Springfield, Illinois, 1980) 4–5.
9   See Werner J Einstader and Stuart Henry *Criminological Theory: An Analysis of its Underlying Assumptions* (2nd ed, Rowman & Littlefield, Maryland, 2006) 236, where it is stated that "the predominant cause of crime according to this perspective is societally generated conflict fuelled by a capitalist system of domination, inequality, alienation and injustice".
10 Ross Hogg "The Causes of Crime and the Boundaries of Criminal Justice" in Julia Tolmie and Warren Brookbanks (eds) *Criminal Justice in New Zealand* (LexisNexis, Wellington, 2007) at 87.
11 Hogg, above; See also G Raumati Hook "Warrior Genes and the Disease of Being Māori" (2009) 2 Mai Review, which refers to an Annual Meeting of the American Association of Physical Anthropologists in Tampa, Florida in 2004 where the 'warrior' gene, Monoamine oxidase (MAO) is also discussed.
12 See Rod Lea and Geoffrey Chambers "Monoamine Oxidase, Addiction, and the 'Warrior' Gene Hypothesis" (2007) 120 Jnl of the NZ Med Assoc at 1250; see also comments by Dr Sam Hancox "it is extremely unlikely that a single gene explains

The functionalist theory suggests that because crime exists in all societies it must have a function, and that function is to help to define what is normal, to make some behaviour more attractive and promote social cohesion.[13] Whereas the superiority theory suggests that humans are conditioned to strive for superiority, and therefore some people turn to crime as a means of achieving superiority.[14]

For Māori, applying a functionalist theory is problematic as *tikanga* determines what is normal, not the presence of crime. Similarly, the superiority theory suggests that Māori are conditioned to strive to be superior and turning to crime can achieve this. For Māori, committing a crime will not achieve superiority, rather the action of committing good deeds will result in an increase in *mana* and superiority, not committing a crime.

The strain theory suggests that people whose ambitions are severely frustrated will experience anger that will lead to rebellion against the real or perceived causes of those frustrations.[15] Ambition for Māori is linked to achieving the well-being or *ora* of the group. If this is not achieved the collective or group are responsible rather than the individuals at large.

Another theory holds that persons will be more likely to conform when they stand to benefit by conforming.[16] Evidence that violence begets violence is also perceived as a cause of offending.[17] It is difficult to assess the relevance of these theories for Māori without a suitable context. For instance, if an act in self defence was deemed violent, would that then be a cause of offending?

Theories related to culture and social factors are more relevant. For instance, the conflict theory suggests that when a person is influenced strongly by two conflicting cultures, the attachment to the rules of one is weakened and can

anything" in Jon Stokes "Māori 'warrior gene' claims appalling, says geneticist" *New Zealand Herald*, Thursday Aug 10, 2006 <www.nzherald.co.nz>.

13 Emile Durkheim "The Normal and the Pathological" (1938) and Robert A Dentler and Kai T Erikson "The Functions of Deviance in Groups" (1959) both in Stuart H Traub and B Craig (eds) *Little Theories of Deviance* (Itasca, FE Peacock Publishers, Illinois, 1975) as cited by Paul L A H Chartrand and Wendy Whitecloud (Commissioners) The Aboriginal Justice Implementation Commission *Report of the Aboriginal Justice Inquiry of Manitoba: The Justice System and Aboriginal Peoples* (2001) <www.ajic.mb.ca>.

14 Alfred Adler, referred to in John Braithwaite *Inequality, Crime and Public Policy* (Routledge, London, 1979) as cited by Chartrand, above n 13.

15 Theodore N Ferdinand "The Methods of Delinquency Theory" (1987) 25(4) Criminology at 849.

16 Michael Lynch and W Byron Groves *A Primer in Radical Criminology* (2nd ed, Harrow and Heston, Albany, New York, 1989). A related or overlapping theory is the differential association theory that provides that crime is learned by associating with others who have already rejected conduct norms and have committed themselves to deviance as a way to satisfy their desires, see Edwin H Sutherland "The Theory of Differential Association" (1947) in Traub and Craig, above n 13.

17 Jeffrey Fagan and Sandra Wexler "Family Origins of Violent Delinquents" (1887) 25 (3) Criminology at 643.

produce deviant behaviour.[18] For Māori who adhere to *tikanga* Māori this is usually to the detriment of the existing legal system, subsequently by not abiding by the rules of the existing legal system can result in behaviour classified as deviant or criminal. However, this theory fails to provide reasons why adhering to the other system cannot be accommodated, and thus the resulting actions are not classified as deviant.

For Pākehā, the imposition of legislation[19] dictated what a crime was. A crime was classified a crime without any consideration of what a crime meant for Māori, thereby marginalising their view. For Māori, a *hara* was not dependent on legislation for legitimation; a *hara* was identified as a 'crime' if the action or inaction breached a concept or concepts of *tikanga* Māori. The behaviour or criminality of the offender was secondary.

Historically justice was administered locally as there was no national centralised police system between 1853 and 1876.[20] Peaks in offending rates can be directly linked to historical events. Bull identifies four such episodes between 1853 and 1920, mid 1860s, 1881, 1897, and 1911. These periods are linked to gross violations of human rights and the criminalisation of Māori independence.[21]

The first peak corresponds to the anti liquor restrictions that were imposed.[22] According to classical criminology, "rational hedonism is the primary motivator of crime".[23] In this light Māori who took pleasure in supplying and consuming alcohol perceived this was a risk worth taking.[24] However, it is difficult to explain why "special restrictions were imposed on Māori as this is incompatible with the idea that everyone is driven by the same forces".[25] This is further compounded by the position of settlers who considered Māori as deviants, or members of a separate society, because they were different and criminalised them accordingly.[26]

The first peak during the 1860s also corresponds to war and the accompanying Suppression of Rebellion Act 1863, Disturbed Districts Act 1869 and the New Zealand Settlements Act 1863 legislation that criminalised Māori resistance to

18 Thorsten Sellin "Culture Conflict and Crime" (1938) in Traub and Craig, above n 13 at 49.
19 In New Zealand today, all crime is codified in statutes and therefore it is not possible to be charged with a criminal offence under common law. A breach of the legislation results in various forms of sentence ranging from community service to imprisonment. The Crimes Act 1961 (NZ), s 9 "Offences not to be punishable except under New Zealand Acts"; see also the Crimes Act 1961 (NZ), s 2 "For procedural purposes, there are four categories of offence"; see the Criminal Procedure Act 2011, s 6.
20 Simone Bull "The Land of Murder, Cannibalism and All Kinds of Atrocious Crimes? Māori and Crime in New Zealand 1853–1919" (2004) 44 Brit J Criminal, at 499.
21 Bull, above, at 496.
22 The Sale of Spirits to Natives Ordinance 1847, which prohibited the sale of spirits and limited the sale of other intoxicating liquors to Māori.
23 See for example Theories of Crime and Delinquency. <http://www.sheldensays.com/theories_of_crime1.htm.>
24 Bull, above n 20, at 502.
25 Bull, above n 20, at 502.
26 Pratt, as cited by Bull, above n 20, at 505.

settler encroachment on Māori land.[27] The Māori Prisoners' Trial Act and the West Coast Settlement Act 1880 also criminalised these actions. The third peak corresponds to the imposition of the Dog Tax that led to an increase in convictions, as did the Defence Act 1909, that coincides with the fourth peak.

The reasons for the imposition of the raft of legislation to control the liquor industry, to provide land for settlement, to raise revenue and for the desire of the New Zealand Government to establish its own armed forces, criminalised what were benign acts, such as owning a dog or passively protesting. Subsequently, Māori were criminalised for their actions, arrested and imprisoned as they came in conflict with legislation passed to promote the interests of the colonisers.

Criminologists seek to explain this through theories, including group conflict theory that states "crime is intimately related to conflict" and critical criminology that holds "unequal distribution of power is causally related to crime and this power needs to be specified".[28] While conflict occurred group conflict theory assumes a degree of political strength that, in reality, was minimal for Māori who had their own existing social, political and legal structures.[29] Notwithstanding, from 1911 onwards the dramatic increase in Māori offending rates and the decrease of non-Māori offending is "driven by renewed attention to law and order brought about by political strife".[30] Bull notes that:[31]

> Government harassment of Māori grows ever more subtle ... with a view to endorsing the illusion of state control, seemingly innocuous legislation is used to facilitate the over-policing of Māori. Before long, reported offending by Māori is seen as an issue of problem justifying the need for further official intervention and initiating a self-fulfilling prophecy that manifests itself today in the contemporary stereotype of the Māori criminal.

Although historically this may have been the situation for Māori, in contemporary times the orthodox reasons for criminality that relate to sociological, psychological, biological or economic reasons assist to explain the contemporary causes of offending for Māori. However, the examination of the effect of colonisation and the imposition of legislation is required to place causes of offending into context.

Related to the conflict theory is the social disorganisation theory that explains deviance as a side effect of rapidly changing society; for instance, industrialisation, urbanisation and rapid technological change.[32] Films and other forms of media,

27   Bull, above n 20, at 507.
28   G B Vold *Theoretical Criminology* (Oxford University Press, New York, 1958) as cited by Bull, above n 20, at 498.
29   Bull, above n 20, at 498.
30   Bull, above n 20, at 517; see Bull also for offending statistics.
31   At 517.
32   W Thomas and F Znaniecki "The Concept of Social Disorganization" (1920) and Robert E Park "Social Change and Social Disorganization" (1967) in Traub and Craig, above n 13.

an example of technological change, can also be sources of criminality.[33] The ecological theory that identifies conditions in which crime flourishes by focusing mostly on physical conditions as a result of urbanisation, such as high density population, poverty, transience (homeless people), dilapidation and overcrowding, could be an overlapping theory of the social disorganisation theory.[34]

Duncan concluded that higher rates of offending resulted from the effect of migration and the movement of Māori from rural areas to urban cities.[35] O'Malley focused "on culture conflict, recent urbanisation, low socio-economic status, high-risk mores, selective processing by control agencies as contextual factors leading to higher crime rates" for Māori.[36] This was supported through his examination of Magistrates' Court data revealing higher conviction rates for Māori compared to Pākehā.[37]

The effect of colonisation and urbanisation on Māori is closely tied to the theories of conflict and social disorganisation and assists to explain causes of offending for Māori by colouring these theories with the changing times and a changing society.

Many scholars have sought to understand why Māori are over-represented as offenders in New Zealand.[38] To determine a single cause of criminal behaviour is

33 See Y Jewkes "Theorising Media and Crime" at 10–37 <http://www.sagepub.com>; Richard Erickson "Mass Media, Crime, Law and Justice an Institutional Approach" (1991) 31(3) Br J Criminol at 219; see also Daniel Glaser "Criminality Theories and Behavioural Images" (1956) in Traub and Craig, above n 13.

34 Rodney Stark "Deviant Places: A Theory of the Ecology of Crime" (1987) 25(4) Criminology at 893.

35 L Duncan "Explanations for Polynesian Crime Rates in Auckland" (October, 1971) Recent law, as cited by Department of Corrections *Over-Representation of Māori in the Criminal Justice System: An Exploratory Report* (Department of Corrections, Wellington, 2007) <www.corrections.govt.nz> at 8.

36 P O'Malley "The Influence of Cultural Factors on Māori Crime Rates" in S D Webb and J Collette (eds) *New Zealand Society – Contemporary Perspectives* (John Wiley & Sons Australasia Pty Ltd, Sydney, 1973) as cited by Department of Corrections, above at 8.

37 At 8.

38 See Bull above n 20 at 496; J K Fifield and A A Donnell *Socioeconomic Status, Race, and Offending in New Zealand (Research Report No 6)* (Government Printer, Wellington, New Zealand, 1980); D M Ferguson, F Vitaro, L J Horwood and N Swain-Campbell "Ethnicity and Criminal Convictions: Results of a 21 Year Longitudinal Study" (2003) 36 Australian and New Zealand Journal of Criminology 354; Moana Jackson *The Māori and the Criminal Justice System – He Whaipaanga Hou: A New Perspective: Part 2* (Department of Justice, Wellington, 1988); K Maynard, B Coebergh, B Anstiss, L Bakkerand and T Huriwai "Ki te arotu: Toward a New Assessment: The Identification of Cultural Factors which may Predispose Māori to Crime" (1999) Social Policy Journal of New Zealand 13 at 43; Greg Newbold *The Problem of Prisons: Corrections Reform in New Zealand since 1840* (Dunmore Press, Wellington, New Zealand, 2007); John Pratt "Assimilation, equality, and sovereignty in New Zealand/Aotearoa" in Paul Havemann (ed) *Indigenous Rights in Australia, Canada and New Zealand* (Oxford University Press, Auckland, 1999); P Spier *Conviction and Sentencing of Offenders in New Zealand: 1991 to 2000* (Ministry of Justice, Wellington, 2001).

problematic as there are "as many causes as there are offenders and each offender's behaviour is in itself the result of several causes".[39]

In a study on the causes of youth offending,[40] various risk factors were identified, including family, school/work, association with peers and biological factors. The more risk factors present, the more likely it is that an offence will be committed. However, with just one factor present, the risk of offending is significantly less. Protective factors such as positive influences or role models can mitigate the risk of offending.[41] In noting the potential effect of the offender's background, Gendall J stated:[42]

> Equality before the law is fundamental to the administration of justice, but ... the penalty must reflect matters of mitigation arising from an offender's background and which recognises the structure and operation of the society within which he lives and in particular the degree to which the cultural or ethnic heritage predominates, in any problems of a cross-cultural nature.

Judge Becroft commented that:[43]

> It is very difficult to know which risks are actually causes, and of course, this may differ between individuals. It may be possible to look at a particular individual who has already committed an offence and determine the causes of his or her offending. But at a population level, the best information we can produce is a study of risk factors for offending, and an understanding that the more risk factors an individual possesses, the more likely they are to commit offences. *There is no single factor that can be specified as the 'cause' of anti-social or criminal behaviour* ... [emphasis added].

For Indigenous peoples "the causes of offending generally fail to explain crime satisfactorily, in part because there is so much confusion about correlations, causes and crime and when it comes to explaining disproportionate crime rates

---

39 Jackson, above n 38, at 57.
40 D M Fergusson and M T Lunskey "Adolescent Resiliency to Family Adversity" (1996) 37(3) Journal of Child Psychology and Psychiatry at 281.
41 Te Puni Kokiri *Addressing the Drivers of Crime for Māori* (Working Paper 014–2011, July 2011) identifies similar risks including social, economic and community factors. In attaining answers the focus is on the community who will also design, develop and deliver the initiatives, this is an example of self-determination and will be discussed in Chapter 5. <www.tpk.govt.nz>.
42 *Nishikata v Police* HC Wellington AP126/99, 22 July 1999, at [8].
43 Judge Becroft "What Causes Youth Crime and What Can We Do?" (paper presented to NZ Blue light Ventures Inc – Conference and AGM, Queenstown, 7 May 2009) <http://www.justice.govt.nz>; see also Judge Becroft presentation to the Healing Courts, Healing Plans, Healing People: International Indigenous Therapeutic Jurisprudence Conference October 9 and 10, University of British Columbia, Canada, 2014 where he states that poverty is a main factor that underpins offending.

there can be many different conclusions based on different interpretations of the same data".[44]

In order to elicit an improved understanding of the association between Māori ethnicity and offending, attempts have emerged from a number of different disciplines that provide a range of causal theories about criminal offending. What characterises this history, however, is the assumption that the problem is not only best construed and analysed as a population level phenomenon, but also that initiatives developed to address the problem should be targeted toward the population of Māori.

It has been proposed that socio-economic factors, such as unemployment, poverty, poor education, single parent families, and anti-social behaviour by Māori, are the cause of these disproportionately unfavourable outcomes in the criminal justice system. According to Moana Jackson:[45]

> These causes are offender specific and attempt to isolate the social and psychological factors that may predispose an individual to commit crime … they tend to define an offender by his social responses or his psychological makeup and ignore the interrelationships between the two and the role which culture plays in that interrelationship.

The existence of a multiplier or 'amplifier' effect between these stages of criminalisation suggests that, once apprehended, Māori are often subjected to harsher treatment than non-Māori.[46]

A government report noted that systemic factors exist at one or more of the stages in the process.[47] This serves to increase the likelihood that compared to other ethnic groups, Māori will progress further into the criminal justice system and will be dealt with more severely.[48] This report further noted, given that there is the potential for some degree of correlation between offender ethnicity and

---

44 Chartrand andWhitecloud (Commissioners) above n 13; see also Harries above n 8 at 4.

45 Jackson, above n 38, at 58.

46 See Department of Corrections above n 35, at 11 <www.corrections.govt.nz>; see also Gabrielle Maxwell "Impoverished Lives – Impoverished Childhoods: Research on Social and Economic Inequality and the Occurrence of Crime" (paper presented to the seminar "Does Inequality Matter? A Policy Forum, Wellington, November 2010) <igps.victoria. ac.nz>; see also Kim Workman "Māori Over-representation in the Criminal Justice System – Does Structural Discrimination Have Anything to Do with It?" (2007) Rethinking Crime and Punishment <http://www.rethinking.org.nz>.

47 For a comparative discussion on systemic discrimination within the criminal justice system for Indigenous peoples in North America see Chartrand and Whitecloud (Commissioners) above n 13.

48 See Department of Corrections, above n 35; see also Just Speak *Māori and the Criminal Justice System Position Paper* (2012) <www.rethinking.org.nz>; see also AAP "A UN working group says it wants the NZ government to undertake a review of the degree of systemic bias against Māori in the justice system" (April 2014) <http://www.sbs. com.au/news/article/2014/04/08/un-wants-review-māori-nz-prisons>.

these variables, reasonably sophisticated statistical analysis is required to understand the relative contributions to outcomes that may be made by diverse factors.[49] In the absence of such analysis, interpretations of apparent differences
must be made with great caution. However, it is clear that if Māori are to be
treated equally, some systemic transformations are required, not only at the time
of sentencing, but also from apprehension through to imprisonment and parole.

B Apprehension and prosecution

Although Māori comprise 15 per cent of the New Zealand population, they are
over three times more likely to be apprehended for a criminal offence than non-
Māori.[50] In 2006 Māori accounted for 43 per cent of all police apprehensions.[51]
From 1997 to 2006 Māori apprehensions increased by 10 per cent, whereas total
apprehensions only increased by 4 per cent.[52]

Although the number of apprehensions for violent offences increased overall
for Māori, the number of violent apprehensions increased by 40 per cent.[53] In
2006 nearly three times as many Māori were likely to be apprehended for robbery than were Pākehā; and more Māori were likely to be apprehended for
homicide, kidnapping and abduction, as well as grievous and serious assaults.[54] In
contrast, Pākehā[55] were more likely to be apprehended for minor assaults, inti-
midation and threats and the offence of unlawful group assemblies.[56]

Of all apprehensions 72 per cent of Māori apprehensions were resolved by
prosecution, compared with 66 per cent for Pākehā. Moreover, far fewer Māori
offenders were diverted, warned or cautioned.[57] Arguably, this manifests Moana

49 Just Speak, above.
50 Pat Doone *Hei Whakarurutanga Mo Te Ao* (Crime Prevention Unit, Wellington, 2000) at
    ch 4.
51 Kim Workman "Māori Over Representation in the Criminal Justice System" (2009)
    Rethinking Crime and Punishment <www.rethinking.org.nz>; see also Ministry of
    Justice "Māori over-representation in the Criminal Justice System" Strategic Policy
    Brief (Ministry of Justice, Wellington, March, 2009) <www.justice.govt.nz>.
52 Above.
53 Rethinking Crime, above n 51.
54 Above n 51.
55 The term Pākehā commonly relates to those of British or European descent.
56 Rethinking Crime, above n 51. Although, see section 16 of the New Zealand Bill of
    Rights Act 1990 which provides for 'Freedom of Peaceful Assembly'.
57 Rethinking Crime, above n 51; see also Gronfors (1973) study cited by Corrections
    Department, above n 35, that states "when controlled for socio-economic factors and
    seriousness of offending, he found that first offenders who were Māori were still sig-
    nificantly less likely than non-Māori first offenders to be discharged without convic-
    tion." Neill (1983) found no difference in sentencing according to ethnicity once type
    of remand, seriousness of offence, previous record, and age were accounted for.
    However, McDonald (1987), taking type of offence into account but not seriousness of
    offence and previous convictions, found that Māori offenders received more severe
    sentences. Lovell and Norris (1990), using a cohort of New Zealand males born in

Jackson's claim that the criminal justice system is institutionally racist toward Māori.[58]

The United Nations Working Group on Arbitrary Detention has recommended a review be undertaken of the degree of inconsistencies and systemic bias against Māori at all levels of the criminal justice system, and further:[59]

> The working group noted that Māori are over-represented in the prison population and warned that incarceration that is the outcome of bias "constitutes arbitrary detention in violation of international law".

Māori aged between 17 and 19 are nearly three times more likely to be prosecuted for a criminal offence than non-Māori in the same age bracket. Overall, Māori are over five times more likely to be prosecuted than non-Māori.[60] For all age groups, Māori are more likely to be convicted for a non-traffic criminal offence than non-Māori. Māori aged between 17 and 19 are more than three times more likely to be convicted than non-Māori of this age (excluding Pacific youth).[61] For those aged 40 and over, Māori are nearly seven times more likely to be convicted for a criminal offence than non-Māori.[62] Māori are nine times more likely than non-Māori to be remanded in custody awaiting trial.[63] In 2005, of all the criminal cases that resulted in conviction where the ethnic identity of the offender was known, 43 per cent were Māori.[64] Half of the prison population identify as Māori.[65]

1957, came up with a finding that, even controlling for nature of offence, age, and prior offending, Māori between the ages of 10 and 24 appearing in court were more likely than non-Māori to receive a custodial sentence. <http://www.justice.govt.nz/publications/global-publications/s/sentencing-policy-and-guidance-a-discussion-paper/10.-a-māori-view-of-sentencing>. This indicates that if the seriousness of the offence is known, type of remand, previous record and age are also known, it is less likely that Māori will receive more severe sentences; however, this is not assured.

58 Jackson, above n 38.

59 AAP "A UN working group says it wants the NZ government to undertake a review of the degree of systemic bias against Māori in the justice system" (April 2014) <http://www.sbs.com.au/news/article/2014/04/08/un-wants-review-māori-nz-prisons>. The final report was presented to the Human Rights Council in 2015.

60 Ministry of Justice *Responses to Offending by Māori and Pacific Peoples* (1999) <www.justice.govt.nz>.

61 Ministry of Justice, above.

62 Above.

63 Mark Burton, Minister of Justice "The Effective Interventions Initiatives and the High Number of Māori in the Criminal Justice System" (paper presented to Ngakia Kia Puawai, New Zealand Police Management Development Conference, November 2006).

64 Ministry of Justice *Conviction and Sentencing of Offenders in New Zealand 1996–2005: Executive Summary* (Ministry of Justice, Wellington, 2006) <www.justice.govt.nz>.

65 See <www.stats.govt.nz/browse_for_stats/snapshots-of-nz/yearbook/society/crime/corrections.aspx> that states at 30 June 2012, Māori comprised 51 per cent of the prison population; see also Bronwyn Morrison, Natalie Soboleva and Jin Chong

A review of the Statistics New Zealand data relating to prosecutions in 2011 revealed that Māori aged between 10 and 16 are significantly more likely to be prosecuted than Pākehā across a wide range of offences.[66] In the most extreme example, 46 per cent of Māori who were apprehended for dangerous or negligent acts were prosecuted, compared to 6 per cent of Pākehā offenders.[67]

These statistics indicate that Māori are more likely to be apprehended, prosecuted, convicted and imprisoned than non-Māori. At each stage of the criminal justice process from apprehension right through to prosecution, trial and sentencing, a significant degree of built-in discretion exists with respect to decision-making.[68]

Upon apprehension the police may exercise judgment about whether or not to detain an individual for questioning.[69] If an individual is apprehended, there is discretion about whether or not to arrest the person, and later, whether or not to proceed with prosecution. At the prosecution stage, the court may or may not convict the individual. Upon conviction, judges may remit the offender's sentence.

In 2006 over-representation patterns for Māori were evident within the court system. Furthermore, 13 per cent of Māori who were convicted of an offence received a custodial sentence compared with 8 per cent for Pākehā.[70]

Once sentenced, the offender, if applicable, has an opportunity to be released through an application for parole. Although the Annual NZPB Reports do not provide an ethnic breakdown of offenders, if Māori comprise 50 per cent of

Conviction and Sentencing in New Zealand: 1997–2008 (Ministry of Justice, Wellington, April 2008) at 118 <www.justice.govt.nz>; see also Michael Rich *Census of Prison Inmates 1999*(Department of Corrections, 2000) at 42 <www.corrections.govt.nz >.

66 See Lydia Nobbs "Just Speak exposes variation in youth prosecution rates" (April, 2013) <www.justspeak.org> where she cites Statistics NZ <www.statistics.govt.nz>; see also "Young Māori 'More Likely' to Be Prosecuted than Pākehā" *Radio New Zealand* (online, New Zealand, 10 April 2013) <www.radionz.co.nz >.

67 Above.

68 See also analysis by McDonald (1987), cited by Corrections Department above n 35, that states "of 1983 Justice statistics, taking type of offence into account but not seriousness of offence and previous convictions, found that Māori offenders received more severe sentences." <http://www.justice.govt.nz/publications/global-publications/s/sentencing-policy-and-guidance-a-discussion-paper/10.-a-māori-view-of-sentencing>.

69 Although you have the right not to be arrested, or detained, without good reason; see New Zealand Bill of Rights Act 1990, s 23 "Rights of Persons Arrested or Detained" which states that "Everyone who is arrested or who is detained under any enactment (a) shall be informed at the time of the arrest or detention of the reason for it".

70 Rethinking Crime, above n 51; see also Lovell and Norris (1990), study cited by Corrections Department, above n 35, which stated that "using a cohort of New Zealand males born in 1957, came up with a finding that, even controlling for nature of offence, age, and prior offending, Māori between the ages of ten and twenty-four appearing in court were more likely than non-Māori to receive a custodial sentence." <http://www.justice.govt.nz/publications/global-publications/s/sentencing-policy-and-guidance-a-discussion-paper/10-a-māori-view-of-sentencing>.

custodial sentences, then it is reasonable to assume that at least half of the offenders that come before the Parole Board will be Māori.[71] This taken together with the fact that more prisoners are serving the length of their sentence, or, alternatively more prisoners are not being granted parole, raises concerns for Māori. Despite these disproportionate statistics,[72] there is no clear policy direction on how the obligations of the Treaty of Waitangi impact on the decision-making processes of the NZPB. Similarly, there are no policy guidelines for cultural consideration. It is now timely to consider the process of parole.

C Parole

The New Zealand Parole Board (NZPB) can make a decision (now only for transitional cases) to release an offender in home detention cases as long as it is satisfied on reasonable grounds that the offender will not pose an undue risk to the safety of the community or any person or class of persons if he or she is detained on home detention rather than in a prison, or whether the prisoner should be granted an early release.[73] Parole reports and documents prepared by probation officers and psychologists can also be influential in such decision-making.[74]

As 50 per cent of the prison population identify as Māori,[75] it is previously assumed that at least half the offenders that come before the NZPB are Māori. Although there may be a moral incentive, the Parole Act is silent on any specific provision for gender balance and Indigenous representation on the NZPB.[76] Nonetheless, in light of the recent calls to encourage women, and those of an Indigenous background to apply for judicial positions,[77] it is presumed that this

71 The available statistics are not disaggregated to reflect the percentage of Māori that appear before the NZPB.
72 See Department of Corrections, above n 35 "from 2004 onwards, [the] proportion of sentence served has crept up and up, and is in fact still rising. Currently, around 30 per cent of prisoners who were eligible for parole are kept in until the entire sentence is served. Average across all parole-eligible prisoners is 75 per cent at present."
73 Section 33 (1) of the Parole Act 2002 provides that "The Board may impose on an offender the special conditions referred to in section 15 (3) (ab) (*residential restrictions*) if the residence in which it is proposed that the offender reside is in an area in which a residential restriction scheme is operated by the chief executive." From 1 October 2007 home detention was no longer an option for the Board, which now only considers "transitional" cases.
74 In light of the number of Māori offenders likely to come before the NZPB it is important that adequate and continual training of parole and probation officers within the area of culture and tīkanga issues is accomplished.
75 See Department of Corrections above n 35 "Māori have constituted 50 per cent of the prison muster since 1985, and it has hardly shifted at all – the rate of imprisonment for Māori is 660 per 100,000, and for New Zealand Europeans it is less than 95."
76 See Parole Act 2002, s 111.
77 See Rod Vaughan "Judicial makeover opens more doors to wannabe Judges" ADLSI 6 September 2013, <http://www.adls.org.nz/for-the-profession/news-and-opinion/2013/9/6/judicial-makeover-opens-more-doors-to-wannabe-judges/> See also

approach may eventually be entertained for positions on the NZPB. This would reflect gender and ethnic parity.

The role of the NZPB begins not upon incarceration, but when the offender applies for release. Although legislative amendments provide for the NZPB to monitor and, if necessary, recall the offender, hearings are before a panel, not a single judge. Despite the Parole Board's efforts to assess the same recalled parolee, there is no guarantee that the parolee will come before the same Judge and/ or the same panel. This reduces the benefits of a powerful 'one on one' relationship with the offender.[78]

Māori and parole

Statistics indicate that the current parole system is not working for Māori.[79] Under the Parole Act 2002, there is no clear direction within the policies of the NZPB as to how obligations relating to the Treaty of Waitangi[80] or cultural considerations might impact on the decision-making process. And there is nothing within the raft policy documents[81] to determine how this is to be achieved and, if it has not been achieved, whether any redress may be available. By default it is assumed that this obligation lies with the decision-maker. There is no specific allocation of Māori representation at the decision-making stage, despite the assumption that up to half of the offenders who appear before the NZPB are Māori. This raises procedural and substantive concerns for Māori about how they are treated in the decision-making processes of the NZPB. In comparison, other jurisdictions, such as Canada, have established a specialised Indigenous forum to act as an advisory group on cultural issues that come before the National Parole Board.

Popular disenchantment with the NZPB has led to calls for the overhaul of the New Zealand parole system.[82] The current framework policy of the NZPB acknowledges that the Treaty of Waitangi gives rise to certain rights and

District Court Judges – Expressions of Interest: The Attorney-General's Judicial Appointments Unit, where it is noted that "The Attorney-General is conscious of the value of increasing diversity on the District Court bench generally and therefore seeks to encourage expressions of interest from qualified women as well as those from under-represented ethnic groups." June 2013 <http://www.justice.govt.nz/courts/district-court-judges-expressions-of-interest>

78 For instance, the success of drug treatment courts has been attributed to this 'one on one' relationship.

79 See Bronwyn Morrison and others, above n 65 at 120.

80 See discussion in Mason Durie *Nga Tai Matatu – Tides of Māori Endurance* (Oxford University Press, Australia, 2005) at 146 for discussion on increasing government consciousness of Treaty of Waitangi obligations.

81 See NZPB policies available <http://www.paroleboard.govt.nz/nzpb-policies.html>.

82 "Justice groups urge government to tighten parole laws" Radio New Zealand (4 November 2010) <www.radionz.co.nz >.

obligations.[83] It indicates that the NZPB "will always operate in a way that is sensitive to *whānau, hapū, and iwi* as well as Māori communities".[84] The framework policy further states that the NZPB will ensure that Māori cultural concepts, values and practices are respected and safeguarded.[85]

The Parole Act 2002 requires the NZPB to develop policies on how it will discharge its functions.[86] To achieve this purpose, the NZPB regularly reviews its policies. As part of an effort to improve the decision-making process, the NZPB engaged Professor Jim Ogloff to develop a straightforward, comprehensive and user-friendly methodology for structured decision-making on New Zealand conditions and reflecting New Zealand concerns.[87] It is unclear whether or not this methodology will provide for cultural considerations on decision-making. It would be helpful if part of this review recognised the need to provide for Māori membership on the NZPB.[88]

Māori are not only disproportionately represented as offenders in the criminal justice system but are also disproportionately represented in the forensic mental health facilities. At least one in every two (50.6 per cent) Māori will suffer from a mental disorder during their lifetime.[89] Taken separately these are concerning facts. Taken together these issues provide disastrous results. It is timely to now consider criminality and mental health to discern whether the current system affords a meaningful recognition of *tikanga* Māori.

D Mental health

The Mental Health (Compulsory Assessment and Treatment) Act 1992 defines a *mental disorder*, in relation to any person, as:[90]

> ... an abnormal state of mind (whether of a continuous or an intermittent nature), characterised by delusions, or by disorders of mood or perception or volition or cognition, of such a degree that it –

83 NZPB "Framework Policy Covering the Development of the Board's Policies: Policy 1, Introduction" (2009) <www.paroleboard.govt.nz>.

84 Above.

85 Above.

86 Parole Act 2002, s 109.

87 Professor Jim Ogloff, Director, Centre for Forensic Behavioural Science, Monash University and Director of Psychological Services. This review was commissioned by Judge David Carruthers, the then Chair of the NZPB, in response to public concern on the release of high-risk offenders. Specifically Graeme Burton who murdered two people in two separate incidents. The second murder occurred 6 months after he was released on parole. See J Johnson and J Ogloff "Review of NZPB decision given on 28 June 2006 to release Graeme William Burton on Parole" (5 March 2007) <www.paroleboard.govt.nz>.

88 See Parole Act 2002, s 111 that provides for the Membership of the NZPB.

89 J Baxter *Māori Mental Health Needs Profile Summary. A Review of the Evidence.* (Te Rau Matatini, Palmerston North, 2008) at 22 <https://www.mentalhealth.org.nz/assets/ResourceFinder/Maori-Mental-Health-Need-Profile-full.pdf>

90 Mental Health (Compulsory Assessment and Treatment) Act 1992, s 2.

(a)   poses a serious danger to the health or safety of that person or of others; or
(b)   seriously diminishes the capacity of that person to take care of himself or herself ...

In New Zealand there are two legislative routes to address the psychological needs of offenders. The first is through "generic mental health legislation, permitting the compulsory detention of a person for assessment and treatment of a mental disorder that has manifested, or is at risk of manifesting dangerous behavior".[91] In such case the focus is on the protection of the individual.

The second route is through criminal justice legislation for people with a mental disorder who have been charged with a criminal offence.[92] For most mentally impaired offenders, the process is one of arrest and an initial court appearance in the District Court (criminal jurisdiction). Specialist services[93] are then triggered to assess the offenders' mental health status and, if required, make recommendations for treatment or diversion to either a mental health or a compulsory care facility. A well-integrated system of forensic psychiatric services is available to offenders entering the criminal justice system. Despite the availability of these services, offenders are often required to be processed through the criminal justice system before receiving any mental health assessment.[94] Accordingly, the stress of arrest, remand, the impending court appearance and possible sentencing can all lead to a further deterioration in their mental state.[95] There is no dedicated Indigenous forum to process Māori with mental disorders.

Although a defendant can be redirected from the criminal justice system through an insanity plea or unfitness to stand trial, the court will still determine whether insanity has been established (on the balance of probabilities) before any orders can be made.[96] A finding of unfitness to stand trial will result in diversion from the trial process. However, judges lack sentencing options to ensure that mentally impaired offenders will receive adequate services.[97]

---

91 Warren Brookbanks "Mentally Disordered Offenders" in Julia Tolmie & Warren Brookbanks (eds) *Criminal Justice in New Zealand* (LexisNexis, Wellington, 2007) at 419; Mental Health (Compulsory Assessment and Treatment) Act 1992.
92 Brookbanks above. Criminal Procedure (Mentally Impaired Persons) Act 2003.
93 See Brian McKenna and Kevin Seaton "Liaison Services to the Courts" in Warren Brookbanks and Sandy Simpson (eds) *Psychiatry and the Law* (LexisNexis, Wellington, 2005) at 447–463.
94 Above.
95 See Luke Birmingham "The Mental Health of Prisoners" (2003) 9(3) Advances in Psychiatric Treatment at 191.
96 Crimes Act 1961, s 23. See also s 20 of the Criminal Procedure (Mentally Impaired Persons) Act 2003, for the new procedure on determining insanity. This is the default for most insanity cases.
97 McKenna and Seaton, above n 93.

In New Zealand, the Family Court is responsible for the administration of the Mental Health (Compulsory Assessment and Treatment) Act 1992.[98] Although the Family Court has no criminal jurisdiction, it can oversee offenders who have entered the system of compulsory care through the Intellectual Disability (Compulsory Care and Rehabilitation) Act 2003.[99]

In New Zealand, Mental Health Tribunals review compulsory treatment orders as well as special and restricted patient orders issued by the Family Court. In certain circumstances these tribunals may discharge offenders who they no longer consider to be mentally ill.[100] These tribunals are subject to the procedural provisions under Schedule One of the Mental Health (Compulsory Assessment and Treatment) Act 1992.[101] Mental Health Tribunals can discharge civilly committed patients directly if they are no longer mentally disordered but only have the power to make non-binding recommendations in respect of special and restricted patients and their decisions are subject to judicial review.[102]

There is no specific reference to the Treaty within this raft of legislation, nor is there any recognition of *tikanga* Māori. In any event judicial deference is given to cultural identity, personal beliefs[103] and cultural assessment.[104]

The policy of de-institutionalisation in New Zealand has led to higher numbers of people with mental illness living in the community.[105] As one out of every two Māori will suffer from a mental disorder during their lifetime (50.6 per cent),[106] it

98 Section 17 of the Mental Health (Compulsory Assessment and Treatment) Act 1992 provides for "Applications to be heard and determined wherever practicable by Family Court Judge".

99 Section 74 of the Intellectual Disability (Compulsory Care and Rehabilitation) Act 2003 provides for "Review by Family Court" and section 76 provides that the "Family Court may make recommendations".

100 See *Re IM* [2002] NZFLR 846, where the Mental Health Review Tribunal reported on whether the applicant was fit to be released from care and considered the provisions under ss 4, 66, and 77 of the Mental Health (Compulsory Assessment and Treatment) Act 1992 and the Intellectual Disability (Compulsory Care) Bill.

101 This includes the power to call for reports, witnesses, evidence, examination of the patient, and attendance of the patient and other persons. The hearings are not open to the public.

102 *Waitemata Health v Attorney General & Ors* CA [2001] NZFLR 1122. The Court of Appeal reviewed a decision of the Tribunal under the Mental Health (Compulsory Assessment and Treatment) Act 1992 that the patient was no longer mentally disordered and was fit to be released from compulsory treatment.

103 See Section 5 of the Mental Health (Compulsory Assessment and Treatment) Act 1992, "Powers to be exercised with proper respect for cultural identity and personal beliefs".

104 See Section 23 of the Intellectual Disability (Compulsory Care and Rehabilitation) Act 2003; "Cultural assessment" provides that the coordinator must try to obtain the views of any suitable Māori person or Māori organisation concerned with, or interested in, the care of persons who have an intellectual disability.

105 McKenna and Seaton, above n 93.

106 Baxter, above n 89.

is no surprise that the policy of de-institutionalisation may have contributed to the fact that Māori are over-represented among the homeless.[107]

Many refuse to take their medication, and if left unchecked their mental illness can lead to inappropriate behaviour, such as petty theft or urinating in public.[108] The justice system treats such behaviour as 'criminal'. Social commentators have referred to this process of mentally ill offenders re-entering the criminal justice system post de-institutionalisation as "the criminalization of the mentally ill".[109]

The extreme stress of remand, court appearance and possible sentencing can lead to further deterioration among mentally ill offenders. Imprisonment will often be inappropriate for those individuals whose problems stem from their mental illness, as opposed to their criminality, unless the mental illness is treated whilst imprisoned.[110]

Psychiatric morbidity[111] within New Zealand prisons reveals a disproportionately high incidence of substance abuse and psychotic illness when compared with the community as a whole.[112] Such prisoners have a greater need for specialist forensic services. This high incidence of mental illness is not confined to the prison population, but as might be expected, extends to parolees and those serving non-custodial sentences.[113]

107　Steve Richards *Homeless in Aotearoa: Issues and Recommendations Report for Regional Public Health* (Ministry of Health, Wellington, 2009) <www. http://nzceh.org.nz/>.

108　Bruce Winick and David Wexler (eds) *Judging in a Therapeutic Key – Therapeutic Jurisprudence and the Courts* (Carolina Academic Press, Durham, North Carolina, 2003) at 59.

109　Robert Miller "The Continuum of Coercion: Constitutional and Clinical Considerations in the Treatment of Mentally Disordered Persons" (1997) 74(4) Denver University Law Review at 1169; Although see Eric B Elbogen and Sally C Johnson "The Intricate Link Between Violence and Mental Disorder Results From the National Epidemiologic Survey on Alcohol and Related Conditions" (2009) 66(2) JAMA Psychiatry at 152 where they state that recent "findings challenge perceptions that mental illness is a leading cause of violence in the general population. Still, people with mental illness did report violence more often, largely because they showed other factors associated with violence."

110　See Auditor General's report "Mental Health services for prisoners" (2008) that found that the most seriously mentally ill prisoners received adequate and prompt treatment. However, there was a risk that prisoners with mental health needs that are not picked up through initial screening or those who develop mental illness during imprisonment will not be identified and get access to treatment. Often for these people imprisonment is inappropriate <http://www.oag.govt.nz/>.

111　Psychiatric morbidity or psychiatric illness commonly refers to the occurrence of both physical and psychological deterioration resulting from a mental or psychological condition.

112　Alexander Simpson and others *The National Study of Psychiatric Morbidity in New Zealand Prisons: An Investigation of the Prevalence of Psychiatric Disorders among New Zealand Inmates* (Department of Corrections, Wellington, 1999) <http://www.corrections.govt.nz/__ data/assets/pdf_file/0007/671821/nationalstudy.pdf >.

113　Ministry of Health *Services for People with Mental Illness in the Justice System: Framework for Forensic Mental Health Services* (2001) at 6 <www.moh.govt.nz>.

The National Study indicated the need for a:[114]

> ... level of service provision that is quite beyond the capacity of current for-
> ensic psychiatric services ... *The high rates of common disorders argue for the use of*
> *screening techniques* [emphasis added].

This opens the door for the introduction of an alternative intervention approach,
such as a Mental Health Court. As Simpson has noted:[115]

> One way of limiting the entry of mentally ill into the prison system is to
> establish mental health courts [emphasis added], which link the offender with
> critically needed medical treatment, apply appropriate release conditions and
> use the threat of imprisonment as an incentive for compliance.

The onus is upon the criminal justice system and the mental health system to
investigate options that allow for the recognition of, and early intervention for the
mentally impaired prior to entering the criminal justice system. The lack of successful options of this kind has placed a burden on the criminal justice system,[116]
requiring innovative responses. According to Professor Warren Brookbanks:[117]

> It is clear ... that the New Zealand correctional system has a significant role in
> the management of offenders with varying degrees of mental impairment, and
> that this group makes heavy demands on the use of forensic patient services. The
> immediate challenge for New Zealand health and justice planners is to explore
> options which allow for the diversion of mentally impaired offenders from
> the correctional system. In my view, mental health courts offer one such option.

Māori and mental health

One out of every two Māori will suffer from a mental disorder during their lifetime (50.6 per cent).[118] For this reason Māori are disproportionately represented
within forensic mental health facilities. Within the health system,[119] recognition of

114 Simpson and others, above n 112, at 59.
115 Sandy Simpson "A Strategy that Works – Mental Health Courts" *Recap Newsletter: Re
     Thinking Crime and Punishment in New Zealand* (2008) Issue 35 at <www.rethinking.org.nz>.
116 McKenna and Seaton, above n 93.
117 Warren Brookbanks "Making the Case for a Mental Health Court in New Zealand"
     (Paper present to 3rd International Conference on Therapeutic Jurisprudence, 7–9
     June 2006, Perth, Western Australia).
118 Baxter, above n 89.
119 Section 4 of the New Zealand Public Health and Disability Act 2000 provides that
     "in order to recognise and respect the principles of the Treaty of Waitangi, and with
     a view to improving health outcomes for Māori, Part 3 provides for mechanisms to
     enable Māori to contribute to decision-making on, and to participate in the delivery
     of, health and disability services".

the Treaty is identified with allowing Māori to participate in decision-making and in the delivery of health services. In New Zealand District Health Boards must appoint two members who are Māori.[120] The Minister will appoint two Māori members if they have not been elected. Despite this provision, however, there is no clear direction within the policy documents as to how effective this contribution is, and if it has not been effectively achieved, whether any redress may be available.

There is much evidence to suggest that the current mental health framework is not delivering for Māori with mental disorders.[121] According to Dr R. Tapsell:[122]

> If some of the disparities currently apparent within our mental health system are to be reversed we must look for *alternative models* [emphasis added] that provide the highest quality of psychiatric care and rehabilitation, *yet reflect the Māori world view*... [emphasis added].

In order to facilitate improvements in Māori health, and especially in mental health, a number of principles have been identified. These include the principles of the Treaty.

It is clear that the New Zealand criminal justice system plays a significant role in the management of Māori offenders with a relatively high prevalence of mental illness. The onus is upon the criminal justice system and the health system to explore options that allow for the early recognition and intervention for the mentally impaired before they enter the criminal justice system. This has placed a burden on the criminal justice system requiring an innovative response.[123]

Māori are disproportionately represented in the criminal justice system. Māori are also disproportionately represented in the forensic mental health facilities. Separately, these are concerning facts, but together these issues provide disastrous results. Despite the incorporation of decision-making for Māori within health policies, these facts clearly indicate that another approach is required. Rees Tapsell stated in 2007:[124]

> ... the scientific evidence supporting the effectiveness of a specific model for forensic rehabilitation which reflects *the Māori World View does not yet exist* [emphasis added].

---

120 See New Zealand Public Health and Disability Act 2000, s 29(4)(b) which provides that "In making appointments to a board, the Minister must endeavour to ensure that ... (b) in any event, there are at least 2 Māori members of the board."

121 Rees Tapsell "The Treatment and Rehabilitation of Māori" in W Brookbanks and S Simpson (eds) *Psychiatry and the Law* (LexisNexis, Wellington, 2007) at 419.

122 At 419.

123 McKenna and Seaton, above n 93, at 448–499.

124 Tapsell, above n 121, at 419.

Further, Peter Jansen has commented:[125]

> In many ways, the essential aspects of such a model may have universal appeal ... as has been said many times before; *if we can get it right for Māori we will get it right for everyone* [emphasis added].

In his New Zealand Country Report, Professor James Anaya, the United Nations Special Rapporteur on the Rights of Indigenous Peoples, recommended:[126]

> In consultation with Māori leaders, the Government should redouble efforts to address the problem of high rates of incarceration among Māori. Specific attention should be given to the disproportionate negative impacts on Māori of any criminal justice initiatives that extend incarceration periods, reduce opportunities for probation or parole, use social status as an aggravating factor in sentencing, or otherwise increase the likelihood of incarceration.

These calls are also echoed by many commentators, including Kim Workman,[127] who has urged for the establishment of an independent research institute to examine the issues of Māori within the criminal justice system. Workman, of Ngāti Kahungunu and Rangitāne descent, has also highlighted the important role the *whānau* as a collective might play in reducing the disproportionate criminal offending rates for Māori. In an address, he noted:[128]

> Over many years, the government has introduced policies which have undermined and destroyed whānau as a social construct. It is only in recent times, that there has been official recognition that whānau continues to be a key cultural institution for Māori and is therefore a key (and potentially highly effective) site of intervention and/or development. The recent emphasis on whānau in social policy acknowledges that changes in the anti-social behaviour of individual Māori can be brought about by focusing on the collective of whānau. It is an area of research waiting to be fully explored.

125 Peter Jansen MD Pacific Region Indigenous Doctors Congress, Cairns, 2004, as cited by Rees Tapsell, above n 121.

126 James Anaya *Report of the Special Rapporteur on the Rights of Indigenous Peoples: The Situation of Māori People in New Zealand* (2011) (A/HRC/18/XX/Add.Y) at 83.

127 Kim Workman was the Head of Prison Services between 1989 and 1993, a retired public servant and currently a senior associate of the Institute of Policy Studies at the Victoria University, Wellington.

128 See Kim Workman "Redemption Denied: Aspects of Māori Over-Representation in the Criminal Justice System" (Paper presented to the Justice in the Round Conference, University of Waikato, Hamilton, 18–20 April 2011) at 14 <www.rethinking. org.nz >.

An announcement by the Minister for Māori Affairs calls for a review of the criminal justice system stating:[129]

> For most Māori, justice in New Zealand is not positive; it is a system that is unfair, biased and prejudiced ... the justice system, including the police, courts and corrections, systematically discriminates against Māori.

The current relationship between Māori and the criminal justice system is undeniably problematic on a number of different levels, resulting in and, confirming that Maori are disproportionately represented across all stages of the criminal justice system. The examination of two areas, parole and mental health highlight these issues. It is appropriate to now unpack the notion of *tikanga* Maori.

129 See Hansard Sitting (04 October 2011) 676 at 21637.

Chapter 2

Māori and *tikanga*

A Who are Māori?

Māori are the Indigenous peoples of Aotearoa, New Zealand.[1] The term Māori, as applied to people, was initially coined by Captain James Cook, an English navigator who sighted New Zealand on 6 October 1769. According to Dame Anne Salmond:[2]

> ... In 1910 ... Te Waaka Te Ranui of Ruaatoki wrote a letter to the editor of Te Pipwharauroa, a Māori language newspaper asking 'He aha tatou i kiia ai he Māori? Why are we called Māori?' In his letter, Te Waaka offered some answers ... when Captain Cook arrived at Tuuranga-nui in 1769, he was almost out of potatoes, so he asked the local people if they had any. They answered that they had a similar root, and when asked for its name they said it was 'Māori' (ordinary). Cook turned to his companions and said '*These people are Maori*' [emphasis added] ... according to Nikora the term Māori was a description for ancient things, ordinary things, things from inland and for local people.

Notwithstanding this unconventional beginning, Māori is now the commonplace term for the *tangata whenua*, or original peoples, of Aotearoa, New Zealand.

The legal definition of Māori has varied over time.[3] Prior to 1947 the legal term was usually 'native'. Early electoral provisions determined that to be 'Māori' and listed on the Māori roll that person must have more than 50 per cent Māori lineage or blood quantum.[4] If the person had exactly 50 per cent Māori blood

---

1 See Ian Hugh Kawharu *Waitangi: Māori and Pākehā Perspectives of the Treaty of Waitangi* (Oxford University Press, USA, 1989) for discussion; see also Manuka Henare *Nga Tikanga me nga Ritenga o te ao Māori: Standards and Foundations of Māori Society* (1988) 3(1) Royal Commission on Social Policy: Future Directions 3 at 36.

2 Anne Salmond *Between Worlds: Early Exchanges between Māori and Europeans, 1773–1815* (Penguin Books, Auckland, 1997) at 21.

3 For example, the term Māori includes Polynesians, Australasians and Melanesians under s 2 of the Juries Act 1908.

4 See Electoral Act 1893, s 148, Part V "'Māori' means an aboriginal inhabitant of New Zealand, and includes half-castes and their descendants by Natives."

quantum, then they could choose to enlist on the Māori or European roll. Prior to 1998 Statistics New Zealand provided the following definition:[5]

> A person is said to have Māori ancestry if they have any Māori ancestors, no matter how distant.

To be consistent with the 1993 Electoral Act and the 1974 Māori Affairs Act in 1998, Statistics New Zealand changed this definition to:[6]

> 'Māori' means a person of the Māori race of New Zealand; and includes any descendant of such a person.

Although this latest definition of Māori is more reflective of what it means to be Māori, for some Māori, identification by *iwi* was more appropriate. According to John Rangihau:[7]

> My being Māori is absolutely dependent on my history as a Tuhoe person as against being a Māori person … I have a faint suspicion that Māoritanga is a term coined by the Pākehā to bring the tribes together. Because if you cannot divide and rule, then for tribal people all you can do is unite them and rule.

It is acknowledged that in comparative Indigenous jurisdictions, such as First Nations in Canada,[8] blood quantum will dictate federal recognition as an Indigenous person and also membership in a tribal nation.[9] This will allow that person to access certain benefits and resources. Any inter-marriage with a non-Indigenous person or a person from a different tribe will reduce that blood quantum, effectively jeopardising the ability to access Indigenous or Indian status.[10]

In New Zealand blood quantum is not a contentious issue; it is within the purview of that person as to whether or not they identify as Māori.[11] For example, despite the

---

5   See Statistics New Zealand *Māori Descent* at <www.stats.govt.nz>.

6   See the Māori Affairs Amendment Act 1974 (No 73) which stated "that the present restriction in the legal application of the term 'Māori' to persons of more than a fixed degree of Māori blood should be relaxed"; see also the Electoral Act 1993 where the term 'Māori' is defined, in section 3, as a person of the Māori race of New Zealand; and includes any descendant of such a person.

7   John Rangihau "Being Māori" in Michael King (ed) *Te Ao Hurihuri Aspects of Māoritanga* (Reed Books, Auckland, 1992) at 190.

8   The term First Nations refers to various Indigenous groups in Canada that are neither Inuit nor Metis.

9   Paul Spuhan "Legal History of Blood Quantum in Federal Indian Law to 1935" (2006) 51 S D L Rev 1; see also Hilary Weaver "Indigenous Identity: What Is It and Who Really Has It?" (2001) 25(2) The American Indian Quarterly at 240.

10 Spuhan, above.

11 In the case of scholarship applications, however, there is usually a requirement to establish your connection with your culture e.g. *whakapapa* (family tree) and *marae*.

option for Māori to choose which roll (the Māori Electoral Roll or the General Electoral Roll) to be enrolled on, many Māori elect not to change from the General Electoral Roll.[12] Although factors such as voter apathy contribute to this, arguably this reflects the unwillingness of some Māori to self-identify as Māori and perhaps a reluctance to participate in an Indigenous court if such a court was established.

B What is *tikanga* Māori?

The Māori legal system is sourced from Te Ao Māori or the Māori World,[13] as opposed to the Māori Worldview, which can imply observing from a distance rather than a turning of the mind to the world in which Māori lived.[14] The Māori World is a complex three-dimensional philosophy that communicates concepts from the 'inside', whereas a view necessitates observations from outside.[15]

Cosmology and the creation accounts are intrinsic to Te Ao Māori. Cosmology establishes the relationships or *whakapapa* between people, the environment and the spiritual world.[16] The dynamic between these elements underpins a mechanism similar to that of a social constitution.[17]

Tikanga Māori is a contextual concept.[18] The commonly accepted meaning is "straight, direct, tied in with the moral notions connotations of justice and fairness including notions of correct and right".[19] This can, however, vary according to the people involved and in relation to particular circumstances.[20]

Further see an explanation of Harrison J's comments in *Mika v R* [2013] NZCA 648 where it was noted "Because he has some Māori blood – and we're not sure how much – he's somehow less blameworthy or culpable. That's an extraordinary proposition" in David Clarkson "Mob member wants short sentence for being Māori" Stuff.co.nz (online ed, Auckland, 20 November 2013); see also Tahu Kukutai "The Problem of Defining an Ethnic Group for Public Policy: Who is Māori and Why does it Matter?" (2004) Social Policy Journal 23.

12 Section 76 of the Electoral Act 1993 notes that "a Māori ... shall have the option of being registered either as an elector of a Māori electoral district or as an elector of a General electoral district".

13 Although Te Ao Māori is often referred to as the Māori worldview, Te Ao Māori more correctly is the Māori World.

14 See M Marsden "God, Man and Universe: A Māori view" in Michael King (ed) *Te Ao Hurihuri Aspects* of Māoritanga (Reed Books, Auckland, 1992) at 117.

15 Above.

16 See also Te Paparahi o te Raki Waitangi Tribunal Report (November 2014) Wai 1040, at 20.

17 At 22–25.

18 See New Zealand Law Commission *Māori Custom and Values in New Zealand Law* (NZLC SP9, Wellington, 2001); see also H W Williams *A Dictionary of the Māori Language* (7th ed, Government Printer, Wellington, 1971).

19 Richard Benton, Alex Frame and Paul Meredith (eds) *Te Mātāpunenga: A Compendium of References to the Concepts and Institutions of Māori Customary Law, compiled for Te Matahauariki Institute* (Victoria University Press, Wellington, 2013) at 429.

20 See also submission from Ngati Korokoro in Wai 1040, above n 16, at 495 that stated "...many hapu lived side by side practising different tikanga very successfully".

Correct practices that have been derived from the accounts of how the cosmos emerged are known as *ritenga*.[21] Whereas *tikanga* is a system prescribing what is considered normal and right, it is defined and influenced by contextual factors inferring flexibility; *ritenga* refers to those practices that are similar or equivalent to those followed by ancestors,[22] providing a 'standard' or 'precedent' in the same way as a legal precedent.[23] The use and implementation of this standard or 'precedent' gives effect to *kaupapa*, ground rules[24] or 'body of principles that create the law'.[25]

Ritenga, together with *kaupapa*, provides a framework by which further concepts such as *mana*, *tapu* and *mauri* are given effect. *Mana* is defined as:[26]

> A key philosophical concept combining notions of psychic and ritual force and vitality, recognised authority, influence and prestige, thus also power and the ability to control people and events.

However, within the Māori world, *mana* is simply effective power and authority sourced from the presence of ancestors in a person, *taonga*, event or place.[27]

Tapu is:[28]

> ... a key concept in Polynesian philosophy ... a term ... used to indicate states of restriction and prohibition whose violation will (unless mitigated by appropriate *karakia* and ceremonies) automatically result in retribution, often including the death of the violator and others involved, directly or indirectly. Its specific meanings include "sacred, under ritual restriction, prohibited".

But within the Māori world, *tapu* simply refers to the presence of ancestors, and the resulting restrictions that their presence places on people, places, *taonga* or events.[29]

---

21 Consistent with this view, section 9 of the Marine and Coastal Area (Takutai Moana) Act 2011 defines *tikanga* as "Māori customary values and practice". Satisfying the definition of *tikanga* is pivotal to the success of any claim of customary rights under the Marine and Coastal Area (Takutai Moana) Act 2011; see also Wai 1040, above n 16, at 25 and 47.

22 See also Wai 1040, above n 16, at 25 that notes "An example of ritenga, Aldridge said, was the requirement for people who went fishing to return the first fish to Tangaroa".

23 See Hirini Mead *Tikanga Māori Living by Māori Values* (Huia, Wellington, 2003), at 12.

24 *Kaupapa* derives from *kau'* which means to appear for the first time or be disclosed, while papa is a reference to the Earth or Papatuanuku, so together *kaupapa* means 'ground rules' or 'first principles'. See Maori Marsden "The Natural World and Natural Resources" in C Royal (ed) *The Woven Universe: Selected Writings of Rev Maori Marsden* (Estate of Rev. Maori Marsden, Masterton, 2003) at 173.

25 Wai 1040, above n 16, at 25.

26 Benton and others, above n 19 at 154. See also Marsden, above n 24 at 4.

27 Marsden, above n 14, at 118.

28 Benton and others, above n 19, at 404; see also Wai 1040, above n 16, at 22–24.

29 Marsden, above n 14, at 119.

Mauri is:[30]

> ... a central notion in Māori philosophy ... in its abstract sense [denotes] the essence which gives a thing its specific natural character ... The meaning of the word is difficult to grasp because it encapsulates two related but distinct ideas: the life principle or essential quality of a being or entity, and a physical object in which this essence has been located. Williams defines the abstract sense term first as 'life principle'... There is certainly no single English word to express this concept.

The principle of *whakapapa* is fundamental to Te Ao Māori. It is a complex network of reality linking animate and inanimate objects.[31] As a relational construct, it provides an explanation of how the universe emerged and how the convergence of complementary, or balancing pairs created new forms of life.[32]

Whakapapa has always been central to the identity of an individual. The individual forms part of the collective and, in turn, is linked to others by *whakapapa*. These flexible and dynamic collectives, or traditional organisational structures are *whānau, hapū* and *iwi*.

So through a 'legal' lens, *tikanga* is the 'legal' structure that gives effect to basic principles or ground rules.[33] And concepts such as *mana* and *tapu* assist in the regulation of the relationships or *whakapapa* between people, the environment and the spiritual world. The aim of *tikanga* Māori is to achieve balance.[34] The regulators – *tapu* and *mana* – assist in the restoring of any imbalance and are relevant for any dispute resolution process.

C *Tikanga* **Māori and disputes**

Tikanga is central to the Māori World, preserving balance (the aim of *tikanga*) and a positive dynamic. When conduct that is *hee* (a mistake or error) occurs, it destabilises the balance in the relational network constituting a *hara* that needs to be rectified.[35] This imbalance is the central issue in *tikanga* Māori.

Disputes between people are a manifestation of *hee*, resulting in, for example, an assault, rape or killing. All of these are a *hara*/crime or offence, breaching a personal *tapu*. This breach results in an imbalance in both the individual and in the community. Eloping, cheating on one's spouse and insults to one's reputation are insults to one's personal *mana* and a *hara*, also resulting in an imbalance.

---

30 Benton and others, above n 19, at 239.
31 In my grandfather's 'Hohaia Toki Pangari' writings, he traced this '*whakapapa*' of inanimate and animate objects from Te Kore to contemporary times; see also Wai 1040, above n 16, at 22–25.
32 Marsden, above n 14.
33 Above.
34 Wai 1040, above n 16, at 25.
35 See also Wai 1040, above n 16, at 31–34.

Disputes between groups are also a manifestation of *hee*; for example, when one tribe takes resources from another area without consent. This involves a breach of, and challenge to the collective *mana*. Historically, a trespass was an affront to the group's *mana whenua*.[36] These collective disputes may be criminally, politically or territorially based.

For Māori, through a *tikanga* lens, the intention to offend is not important. Rather, it is the action of breaching one's personal honour or authority that is considered relevant. It is this breach of personal or collective *mana* that forms the basis of disputes. Historically, the collective nature of disputes could result in inter-tribal fighting,[37] and matters would continue to deteriorate until a *rangatira/* leader intervened. The Wai 1040 Report notes that:[38]

> While hapū could cooperate, breaches of tapu and threats to mana (including challenges over territory or resources) could also lead them to conflict. Forceful responses were seen as legitimate and indeed essential means of restoring mana, reflecting universally accepted tikanga. Failure to respond would itself be degrading.

A major criticism of the Pākehā criminal justice system is that it does not recognise collective structures such as *iwi* or the relational construct that requires to be 'rebalanced'.[39] The Children, Young Persons, and their Families Act 1989 does, however, make a provision for a family group conference to acknowledge the *whānau* structure.[40]

The current criminal justice system, instead, provides a forum in which a series of individual rights become enforceable against other individuals, thereby making strangers of close relatives. To ameliorate this concern, it has been suggested that when Māori are both the offender and victim, a Family Group Conference be convened by Māori to provide more control to Māori, rather than by a coordinator who has no relationship or respect from the parties.[41] However, although Family Group Conferences facilitate the participation of Māori, their control is limited.

---

36 'Mana whenua' defined as trusteeship of land – a phrase that "links political responsibilities with land related authorities" – see Benton and others, above n 19, at 178.

37 From my history on Aotea (Great Barrier Island) – The taking of a pet pig from a *rangatira*'s daughter lead to an inter-*hapū* war.

38 Wai 1040, above n 16, at 33.

39 See Kim Workman, Director of Rethinking Crime and Punishment, New Zealand "Restorative Justice: Victims, Violators and Community- The Path to Acceptance" (International Conference and Workshop of Restorative Justice, Human Rights and Peace Education, Chang Jung Christian University, Taiwan, Taiwan, 6th March 2012) at 9 <www.restorativejustice.org>.

40 Children, Young Persons, and their Families Act 1989, ss 20, 21.

41 Gale Burford and Joe Hudson *Family Group Conferencing: New Directions in Community-Centered Child and Family Practice* (Transaction Publishers, New York, 2000).

Some Māori today, who are not familiar with *marae* justice, prefer to only use the Pākehā legal system and, for instance, will not opt for a hearing on a *marae* that the Youth Justice system offers.[42] The various reasons for this include anonymity, privacy and an unwillingness to take responsibility for their actions. In addition, the effects of colonisation[43] and urbanisation on past generations have effectively alienated many urban Māori from *tikanga*.[44]

It is acknowledged that issues of parental neglect, unemployment, poverty, homelessness, and drug and alcohol misuse and abuse are not confined to Indigenous people. Rather, these issues pervade all sectors of society. However, in light of the disproportionate social statistics, on these factors, experienced by Indigenous peoples generally, this book explores an Indigenous court as an appropriate vehicle to address these issues for Indigenous peoples. As an Indigenous court would be underpinned by Indigenous concepts, it is suggested that an Indigenous court, or similar adjudicative body could potentially be available to non-Indigenous people with a provision similar to the Rangatahi Courts.[45]

Facilitator

The facilitation of any type of dispute between Māori parties is usually conducted by a *rangatira*,[46] *kuia* or a *kaumātua* as an advocate.[47] For most disputes the responsibility lies with the group as a collective.[48] Most facilitators or *rangatira* have been born into the role[49] and are trained for this position from an early age.

42 For some urban Māori who do not desire to affiliate to an '*iwi*' group, it is generally not unusual that they find a *marae* forum alien and prefer to use the general court system.

43 For comments on the effect of colonisation see Ani Mikaere "Are We All New Zealanders Now? A Māori Response to the Pākehā Quest for Indigenity" (Bruce Jessop Lecture, 2004) <www.d.yimg.com>.

44 The onus is upon the individual to choose to learn their *tikanga* as opposed to *tikanga* being a part of everyday life. It is acknowledged that media, including Māori TV and Waatea Radio, and *kura kaupapa* assist to provide opportunities to reconnect with *tikanga*; however, it is not the norm but a conscious decision must be made to reconnect; for example, learning *te reo* is only successful if it is part of everyday life.

45 The Rangatahi Courts or Te Kooti Rangatahi are youth court proceedings that are held on a *marae*; see Chapter 5 'Māori and Current Criminal Justice Initiatives' for further discussion.

46 '*Rangatira*' is defined as chief (male or female), noble and a 'weaver of people'; see Benton and others, above n 19, at 325; and Wai 1040, above n 16, at 31.

47 It is acknowledged that s 62(1)(b) of the Te Ture Whenua Māori Land Act 1993 – "Additional members with knowledge and experience in *tikanga* Māori" provides an opportunity for "1 or 2 other members (not being Judges of the Māori Land Court) to be appointed by the Chief Judge"; see also Wai 1040, above n 24, at 30 that stated "Within hapū, political leadership was provided by rangatira ... They also mediated in disputes among their people, built consensus in group decision-making, and allocated land and other resources for people to live on within their rohe ..."

48 Responsibility for the *muru* and dispute.

49 It is acknowledged that instances can arise where a *rangatira* can be appointed by their people, for example, when a *hapū* loses a *rangatira*.

They have acted on behalf of their people in public forums and entered into binding agreements with other *hapū*. Although the leadership of some *rangatira* has gone unchallenged, those *rangatira* that are subjected to tests of character usually emerge with the support and respect of their *hapū*.[50]

The concept of *rangatiratanga* is complex and interconnected with related concepts, such as *awhina* (assistance, care, support). For instance, when Sir George Grey retold the story of Māui,[51] he stated that the virtue of *awhina* is upheld as the distinctive feature of *rangatiratanga*.[52]

In demonstrating *mana* and the need to strengthen the cohesiveness of the group, the *rangatira* demonstrated three principles of *whanaungatanga*/relatedness. The first was *aroha*/love, an emotional response instigated by kindness to others. The second was *atawhai*/foster, the obligation to protect the well being of their people. The third was *manaaki*/blessing, the ability to look after those temporarily in your care. A parallel exists here between the *rangatira* and a judge in a therapeutic jurisprudence forum.[53]

In the Pākehā criminal justice system, however, principles such as *aroha* and *atawhai* have been replaced by rules of statutory law. It is acknowledged that actors within the criminal justice system, including social workers and probation officers,[54] may exhibit *aroha* and *atawhai*. It is also acknowledged that a judge has a certain amount of discretion that could be couched in terms of *aroha* and *atawhai*. However, the judge's main task in a dispute is to supervise the proceedings and ensure that procedural fairness is adhered to,[55] rather than to provide *aroha* and *atawhai* for the parties.

The aim for the *rangatira* is to secure an outcome that is achieved by consensus and guided by principles of *tikanga* Māori.[56] In this way the well-being and balance of the group could be restored to enable the successful functioning of the community.[57]

---

50   This is commonplace particularly in view of Treaty settlements and the requirement for the rights of *iwi* members to be efficiently and effectively represented.

51   It is understood that in Governor Grey's collection of materials Te Rangikaheke of Te Arawa was the author and source.

52   Benton and others, above n 19, at 57 where noting, in the story, that the two oldest brothers persuaded the next two that they should not entertain the thought of killing Māui, the fifth and only recently re-discovered child, because of their jealousy of him.

53   See Chapter 7 '*Tikanga* Māori and Therapeutic Jurisprudence' for discussion on therapeutic jurisprudence.

54   Careers NZ indicates that, in 2012, there were 1050 probation officers and 6645 social workers see <www.careers.govt.nz>. The percentage of Māori is not indicated. However, based on Māori comprising 15 per cent of the total population, it is assumed 157 and 985 would be Māori. On this assumption, the numbers are too low to be effective in terms of administering *tikanga*. Moreover, these workers are required to adhere to the Department of Corrections Criminal Conviction policy.

55   Caslav Pejovic "Civil Law and Common Law Two Different Paths Leading to the Same Goal" (2001) 32 VUWLR at 817.

56   Wai 1040, above n 16, at 30.

57   This is analogous to the healing approach inherent in the doctrine of therapeutic jurisprudence; see Chapter 7 '*Tikanga* Māori and Therapeutic Jurisprudence'.

Forum and process

The importance of the *marae* as a forum for resolving disputes cannot be under-estimated.[58] It represents the body of ancestors and a world in balance. It is a place where *mana* could be restored and *wairua*/spirit healed. The *marae* protocol is similar to court protocol in the sense that there was an agreed framework.

The whole point of a *marae* encounter was to dispel *tapu* and bring people together, the notion of *pae here tangata*/binding together. Thus dispute resolutions and *marae* encounters dispel the *tapu* of visitors/disputants so that they may unite for a common purpose.

For Māori, the focus of the dispute resolution process is on the source of the problem, seeking the *take*/the reason for the offending – the cause and the effect. Any reoffending on a regular basis indicates an imbalance of the individual's *tinana*/body, *wairua* and *mauri*/life force. This results in the inability to establish a state of *ora*/well-being or balance, which, in turn, creates an imbalance within the community.

Inclusiveness, participation and accountability underpin the process of dispute resolution. All parties to a dispute must be represented and given the opportunity to be heard. These principles are similar to the natural justice requirements under administrative law: the duty to act in good faith and listen fairly to both sides, and the opportunity to be heard.

In contrast to the present criminal justice system, it is not essential that the individual is present. Rather, it is the collective that is the defendant and the plaintiff. In any event, an individual will suffer a loss of *mana* if they do not attend.

If a person alleges that another has, for example, taken his or her resources, then according to *tikanga*, they have. This is consistent with the notion of strict liability under the criminal law.[59] Taking responsibility, irrespective of fault, increases one's *mana*.[60] It is through the dispute resolution process that the matter is further discussed.

If the *hara* or wrong-doing is not admitted by the group or the offender, it is passed on to the living relations through the concept of *whanaungatanga*. This is because of the obligations between them; that is, an intergenerational relation-ship. The offender is encouraged to accept responsibility and, in doing so, re-establish *mana* amongst the group. The group will then decide what actions are required by the offender to establish *utu* with the victim and their community. The dispute process is one of *pono*/just and *tika*/right and proper. After the

58 In contemporary times, the '*marae*' refers to the traditional meeting house (*whare nui*) and the area in front. However, the orthodox definition of the *marae* refers to the courtyard or area in front of the *whare nui* only; see Wai 1040, above n 16, at 211 that describes the *marae* as a "centre for debate and discussion".

59 Strict Liability is a rule whereby a person is legally responsible for the damage or loss caused by his or her acts and omissions irrespective of fault.

60 See also Wai 1040, above n 16, at 31 that notes "... mana could [also] grow or diminish depending on exploits in warfare, diplomacy, hospitality, and in making their people more prosperous."

dispelling of *tapu* between people, visitors and the hosts, food is shared to show acceptance.

Traditionally, 'going through the process' was seen as therapeutic. For Māori, the process by which justice is achieved is just as important as the result. There was no distinction between the procedural or substantive justice. Māori place as much value on the process as on the outcome. Both have to be *tika* and restore a state of *ora*. The process is seen as an inherent good because it empowers the parties and the community to take responsibility for the future. Allowing time and resources for a proper airing of the grievance is, of itself, a large part of the healing process.[61] In practical contemporary terms, this is demonstrated within the Waitangi Tribunal Claims process,[62] where the therapeutic nature of 'airing the grievance' is an essential part of the process, thereby ensuring that healing can occur.[63]

Punishment

Within the criminal justice system, the concept of punishment is not always necessary. For instance, the court may impose a penalty, such as diversion[64] or a discharge without conviction.[65] Nonetheless, for Māori, a form of *utu* or reciprocity is always necessary to restore balance. Section 106 of the Sentencing Act 2002 provides:

(1)   If a person who is charged with an offence is found guilty or pleads guilty, the court may discharge the offender without conviction, unless by any enactment applicable to the offence the court is required to impose a minimum sentence.

(2)   A discharge under this section is deemed to be an acquittal.

A 's 106 discharge order' for domestic violence offences includes little by way of offender accountability. Discharges are frequently used in New Zealand family violence courts. For example, in the "Manukau Family Violence Court

---

61   See Benton and others, above n 19, at 63 where a traveller described a Ngapuhi gathering as "a time when parties joined together for a conversation and grievances were brought forward and rectified and resolutions were made"; see also Marsden, above n 14.

62   See Muriwhenua Waitangi Tribunal Claim Wai 45 particularly submissions given on 7 July 1993; see also Eddie Durie and Gordon Orr "The Role of the Waitangi Tribunal and the Development of a Bicultural Jurisprudence" (1990) 14 NZULR at 62.

63   This fundamental element is also a tenet central to therapeutic jurisprudence; see Chapter 7 '*Tikanga* Māori and Therapeutic Jurisprudence' for further discussion on therapeutic jurisprudence.

64   Diversion is a scheme that provides an opportunity for Police to deal with some offences and/or offenders without going through formal court prosecution.

65   See Section 106 of the Sentencing Act 2002 and Section 19 of the Criminal Justice Act 1985 (repealed).

15.9 per cent of offenders were given a Section 106 in comparison to just 1.5 per cent before the introduction of the court".[66] Further that "in the first three months of the Auckland court operation, 71 per cent of cases were given a recommendation that they complete a treatment programme with an indication that this will result in a Section 106 discharge without conviction".[67] This is inconsistent with *tikanga* Māori, mainly because reciprocity and balance are always required.

A civil case can also be taken by the victim to seek reparation. However, the offender is not normally in a financial position to pay damages. Although not usually part of a formal order, the court may order the offender to pay reparation to the victim in the case of a s 106 discharge order, a step towards achieving balance.[68] It is suggested that more use could be made of this provision to satisfy the *tikanga* requirements of reciprocity and balance.[69]

Both punishment and *utu* involve a deliberate response to an offence and aim to achieve retribution or to requite the wrong-doing. However, they differ in important aspects. Ethically speaking, punishment may be foregone, but *utu* cannot. Punishment should be unpleasant enough to deter further offending, but *utu* may be entirely friendly and welcoming. Punishment should be confined to offenders who have been proven guilty of intentional offences, but *utu* may be exacted from individuals, as members of a *whānau* or *hapū*, who have committed no wrong.[70] This alternative conceptual thinking cannot be accommodated within the existing criminal justice system.

Traditionally, *muru* was used to wipe or rub the *hara*. In doing so it absolved one of their wrong-doings. By extension *muru* included the act of ritual seizing to

66 A Mills, K Thom, C Meehan, and M Chetty *Family Violence Courts: A Review of the Literature* (Centre for Mental Health Research, Auckland, 2013) at 11 <www.la wfoundation.org.nz>

67 At 12.

68 Section 106(3) of the Sentencing Act 2002 provides:

A court discharging an offender under this section may –
(a) make an order for payment of costs or the restitution of any property; or
(b) make any order for the payment of any sum that the court thinks fair and reasonable to compensate any person who, through, or by means of, the offence, has suffered –

   (i)   loss of, or damage to, property; or
   (ii) emotional harm; or
   (iii) loss or damage consequential on any emotional or physical harm or loss of, or damage to, property:

(c) make any order that the court is required to make on conviction.

69 It is not uncommon for a discharge without conviction to be granted by the Court on the condition reparation is paid e,g. see *Latimer v R* [2013] NZCA 562 where the Court found that "s 106 should be considered, the burglary committed was reasonably serious but not premeditated, and a carpentry course had been completed by the defendant". Court ordered $2,500 in reparation and the conviction was quashed.

70 John Paterson *Exploring Māori Values* (Dunmore Press, Palmerston North, 1992) at 135.

address and correct the imbalance. An early example[71] noted that the action of a chief's wife remarrying created a *hee*, thereby destabilising the balance constituting a *hara* manifest in a breach of *mana*. To address this imbalance, a *muru*, or raiding party stripped the wife of what property she possessed. Unlike an act of war, a *muru* was accepted and well-planned. In assessing what *muru* was to be paid, factors such as precedents, the status of the parties, what could be afforded, and what was appropriate for the type of offending were often considered. This was not always the case, as in some instances, the appropriate *muru* could be death.[72]

The penalty agreed upon reflected a 'collective' concern. *Muru*, like *hara*, was inter-generational and receiving the penalty also increased the group's *mana*. It is acknowledged that non-Indigenous families will sometimes collectively meet the costs of a fine on behalf of the offender.[73] However, it is less likely that the collective would agree to meet the costs of an intergenerational debt.

The primary aim in the breach of *hara*, as in dispute resolution, is to restore the balance or *whakahoki mauri*. In other words, restore the *mauri* of the parties and the kin groups to which they belong, restore both the *mana* of the offender and the victim so that they can continue to be part of a functioning community and provide a healing approach. The group, as a collective, has an interest to maintain their *mauri*. Thus *utu* was an ongoing process of restoring the balance.[74]

Overall aim

The overall aim of dispute resolution remains the restoration of *mana* through *utu*; to achieve a balance in the relational networks and to achieve a consensus. Although the process can be inquisitorial, it is not usually an adversarial process. When a dispute has adversely impacted on one's spirit and *mauri*, the question is how to bring it back into balance. Regardless of societal level or the status of the parties involved, the same fundamental principle applies, namely, the principle of *whakahoki mauri* or, restoring the balance.[75]

---

71 Samuel Marsden in a journal entry, 1815, recounting the loss of the fowls given to a head chief as told by Elder 1932 as cited in Benton and others, above n 19, at 255.

72 See Wai 1040, above n 16, at 32 that stated "The ultimate physical sanction for transgression was to be killed and eaten – an action that resulted in the complete removal of the victim's tapu and its consequent transfer to the victor".

73 For instance, it is not uncommon for families of non-Indigenous university students who have traffic, library, or similar outstanding fines to meet these costs. However, if these fines remain unpaid it is less likely that the following generation will feel obliged to pay these.

74 Again, this holistic healing approach has similarities with therapeutic jurisprudence; see Chapter 7 '*Tikanga* Māori and Therapeutic Jurisprudence' for full discussion.

75 This system is often employed in smaller rural communities, such as at my *marae* in Motairehe, Aotea, for lesser offences such as burglary. For instance when a person had climbed through a neighbour's window and stolen some food the reparation was an apology and community work for two days; see also Stephanie Vieille "Māori

Two examples provide an insight into the traditional dispute resolution process. First, the changing significance of Māori women in society and the related problem of domestic violence provide compelling reasons to consider a return to a framework informed by *tikanga* Māori. The second example views the issue of mental health through a *tikanga* Māori lens.

D *Tikanga* Māori and women[76]

According to Ani Mikaere, the roles of men and women in traditional Māori society can be understood only in the context of Te Ao Māori, the Māori World, which acknowledged the interrelationship or *whanaungatanga* of all living things and the overarching principle of balance.[77] Both men and women were essential parts of the collective group. They formed part of the *whakapapa* that linked Māori people back to the beginning of the world, and women, in particular, played a key role in linking the past, present and the future.[78] The survival of the group as a whole was dependent on everyone; they were all part of the collective. In fact, it was a collective responsibility to see that their respective roles were valued and protected.

The gender neutral aspect of Māori language indicates the presence of gender balance, where men were given prominence in some roles and women in others.[79] The importance of women is also symbolised by language and concepts expressed through proverbs. Māori scholar Rose Pere has written on the association of positive concepts with females, highlighting the description of women as *whare tangata*/the house of humanity; the use of the word *whenua* to mean both land and afterbirth, and the use of the word *hapu* as meaning both pregnant and large kinship.[80]

Instances of abuse against women and children were regarded as *whānau* issues, and action could be taken against the perpetrator. Stephanie Milroy has noted:[81]

Customary Law: A Relational Approach to Justice" (2012) 3(1) The International Indigenous Policy Journal, Article 4.

76 As currently approximately 60 per cent of incarcerated women in New Zealand identify as Māori, the inclusion of this example assists to unpack this untenable position.

77 Ani Mikaere 'Collective Rights and Gender Issues: A Māori Women's Perspective' in Nin Tomas (ed) *Collective Human Rights of Pacific Peoples* (Indigenous Research Unit for Māori and Indigenous Education University of Auckland, Auckland, 2004) at 84; see also Ani Mikaere *Colonising Myths Māori Realities He Rukuruku Wahaaro* (Huia Publishers, Wellington, 2011).

78 Mikaere, *Colonising Myths* above.

79 Above.

80 Rose Pere "To Us the Dreams are Important" in S Cox (ed) *Public and Private Worlds* (Allen & Unwin, Wellington, 1987) at 53.

81 Stephanie Milroy "Domestic Violence: Legal Representation of Māori Women" unpublished paper 1994, at 12 as cited in Mikaere, "Collective Rights" above n 77, at 86.

In pre-colonial Māori society a man's house was not his castle. The community intervened to prevent and punish violence against one's partner in a very straight forward way.

Women could retain various roles. However, child rearing was a collective responsibility, with grandmothers, aunts and other females being responsible for all children in the *whānau*. By sharing the workload, mothers could still develop expertise in other areas and perform leadership roles.[82] Women had the role of keeping the affairs of the communal group in order and passing on the customs of the ancestors within the *whānau*.[83] This role of women conflicted with the colonialists' view that treated the man as head of the family.[84]

The role of high-ranking women as leaders was challenged by the Europeans' patriarchal views.[85] When a woman had a higher social status than her husband, it was common that the line of descent be traced through the woman, rather than through the male.[86]

Unlike Pākehā women Māori women maintained their rights over land and resources. Those rights were passed to her by either parent and remained her property upon marriage.[87] They were not the common property of the marriage or property of the woman's husband. She could then pass those rights on to any or all of her children. Prior to colonisation Māori women had both property and leadership rights. Pākehā women did not enjoy the same level of rights to property and leadership.

The colonisation of Aotearoa changed the order of affairs. The British settlers had culturally specific views on the role and status of women, which did not fit with *tikanga* Māori. After the arrival of the Pākehā, Māori women continued to play a significant role in Māori society.[88] Heni Pore of Te Arawa fought against the British in the 1860s in support of the Kingitanga movement, and also at the Battle of Gate Pa in 1864.[89] Māori women continued to be acknowledged as landowners as well as negotiators and religious leaders. However, the introduction of disease, a new economy, land grabbing and Christianity saw Māori women's role change.[90]

82   Mikaere, above.
83   See J Binney and G Chaplin *Ngā Mōrehu: The Survivors* (Oxford University Press, Auckland, 1986) at 24.
84   Law Commission *Justice: The Experience of Māori Women* (New Zealand Law Commission, Wellington, 1999) R53 at [38].
85   Mikaere, "Collective Rights" above n 77.
86   Law Commission above n 84, at [46]; see also discussion in Berys Heuer *Māori Women* (Reed Publications, Wellington, 1972) on the importance of leadership and Māori women leaders or wahine ariki.
87   Law Commission above n 84, at [51]; See also Michael King *The Penguin History of New Zealand* (Penguin, New Zealand, 2003) at 87.
88   Mikaere, *Colonising Myths* above n 77, at 191.
89   At 192.
90   For a comparative perspective see Sarah Carter "Categories and Terrains of Exclusion: Constructing the 'Indian Woman' in the Early Settlement Era in Western

With respect to landownership, the Native Land Court and accompanying raft of Native Land legislation progressively undermined land rights of Māori women.[91] By 1873 the legislation had been amended, with s 86 of the Native Land Act 1873 requiring husbands to be a party to any deed executed by Māori women. However, husbands could dispose of their wife's land interests without any requirement that the wife be party to that deed.[92] The move from communal land ownership into individual (usually male) ownership, as opposed to guardianship, further eroded the rights of Māori women.[93]

Pākehā officials insisted on the use of husbands' surnames for Māori women.[94] Pākehā writers rewrote many of the Māori stories and myths to marginalise the role played by women in them.[95] The practice of customary marriage was gradually eliminated in law.[96] The recognition of only legal marriage in accordance with English law contributed to the breakdown of the *whānau* and *hapū* unit.[97] The legal relationship of marriage places the husband and wife relationship above all others, including those that the woman has with her parents and siblings.[98]

The right to vote was extended to Māori men in 1867. In 1893 Meri Te Tai Mangakahia addressed the Māori Parliament to advocate for the right of Māori women to vote. Arguably, the rights of Māori women to property, together with their leadership roles, contributed to the 1893 Electoral Act, which gave all New Zealand women, including Māori, the right to vote.[99]

A Māori woman was viewed as equal and complementary to her Māori male counterpart. The Common Law notion of individual land ownership and property rights clashed with the relationship of women with the land, as well as the status of women.[100]

Tikanga *Māori* and domestic violence

As *tikanga* Māori is sourced from cosmology, issues such as domestic violence are premised on actions and resolutions from stories that underpin relational concepts found in the realm of the cosmos. For instance, domestic violence is an essential component of the story of Mataora and Niwareka where 'wife beating' was deemed unacceptable.[101] Violence against women was regarded as a *hee* that

Canada" in Mary-Ellen Kelm and Lorna Townsend (eds) *In the Days of our Grand-mothers* (University of Toronto Press, Toronto, Canada, 2006) at 146.
91 Law Commission, above n 84, at [74].
92 At [75].
93 At [76].
94 At [59].
95 Mikaere, *Colonising Myths* above n 77.
96 Law Commission, above n 84 at [66] and [79].
97 Mikaere, *Colonising Myths* above n 77; see also Law Commission above n 84 at [77].
98 Law Commission, above n 84 at [80].
99 See King, above n 87, at 203.
100 Law Commission, above n 84, at [38].
101 Mead, above n 23, at 243.

breached Niwareka's personal *mana*. This destabilised the balance for Niwareka and between her and her wider collective, as well as Mataora and his wider collective. This imbalance required reconciliation. It was only after a change in attitude from Mataora that the decision on whether he could return to his wife could be considered by her and her immediate family; the restoration of balance being pivotal.

Upon the introduction of British law and culture to Aotearoa, in particular the Marriage Act 1908, Māori women had no legal personality. They could not enter into contracts, be sued, or own property. Accordingly, the position of Māori women was rendered equivalent to their European counterparts.[102]

A woman's legitimate sphere of activity was now within the home. This private domain was beyond the reach of the law, where men were able to discipline their spouses and children. As a result of this paradigm shift, the laws of personal *tapu* and privacy fell apart. No longer was there a requirement to restore balance following a breach of personal *tapu*, such as wife beating. As such, the imbalance created is not addressed.

Apprehensions and convictions for domestic violence assisted.[103] The introduction of social services, such as the Labour Government's Domestic Purposes Benefit in 1973, provided financial assistance for solo parents. Despite some criticism that this benefit created a culture of dependence, it provided economic support for Māori women. Initiatives such as the Māori Women's Welfare League established a cultural reprieve.

However, the social and cultural imbalance has not been addressed.[104] In addition, many within Māori society have adopted discriminatory attitudes towards women as a result of colonial views and stereotypes, thereby compounding this imbalance. The detrimental effect of colonisation on Māori women is reflected in the disproportionate statistics, in which 60 per cent of incarcerated women identify themselves as Māori.[105] Arguably, the imposition of legislation[106] that

102 Law Commission, above n 84, at [60].

103 For a review of apprehensions and convictions see <http://www.corrections.govt. nz/__data/assets/pdf_file/0009/767646/TOPIC_SERIES_Family_violence.pdf> where they indicate "between 80,000 and 90,000 police investigations each year centering on family violence".

104 It is acknowledged that gender imbalance exists generally. However, barring equal pay, in theory, women have had equal rights for the last 100 years and yet imbalance remains. For instance, women are still paid less than men. For Māori women they face double discrimination; by gender and also by race.

105 See Department of Corrections *Over-representation of Māori in the Criminal Justice System – An Exploratory Report* (Policy, Strategy and Research Group, Department of Corrections, Wellington, September 2007) at 6. However, in 2012, 58 per cent of inmates identified as Māori and women; see <www.stats.govt.nz>.

106 For instance the Adoption Act 1955 provided that, "since the commencement of the Native Land Act 1909, no person shall have been capable of adopting a child in accordance with Māori custom and with certain exceptions, no adoption is of any force or effect" and Māori Affairs Act 1953, ss 8, 78 and 79 read together with the

deemed acts such as customary marriage and customary family arrangements as illegal, contributed as causes to these statistics.

E *Tikanga* Māori and mental health[107]

The overall aim of *tikanga* Māori remains the restoration of *mana* through *utu*. This involves a balance of all considerations, with the purpose of achieving a consensus or reconciliation.[108] Historically, this has included conflict or fighting as a means to restore balance. However, it is not necessarily an adversarial process as *tikanga* Māori is aligned with an inquisitorial model of dispute resolution, in which all parties seek a common goal.[109] When there has been a transgression of *tapu*, or a dispute that has affected one's *wairua*/immaterial element of a person and *mauri*/life force, the question is how to bring these back into balance. Regardless of the nature of the dispute or who is implicated, the same fundamental principle is involved: the principle of *whakahoki mauri* or restoring the life force.

With respect to mental illness, there is a difference between Māori and non-Māori concepts of health. For Māori, 'health' concerns are based on *mate Māori* or Māori sickness.[110]*Mate Māori* is a difficult term to define but may include a spiritual sickness brought about by transgression of *tapu*, perhaps even unwittingly, by the sufferer. It could also be the result of a *mākutu* or curse placed on the sufferer.[111] Due to the collective nature of responsibility, a breach of *tapu* may not even be brought about by the sufferer. Rather, it may come about as a result of the actions of his or her *tīpuna*/ancestors. Such sickness may be manifested in ways that non-Māori would identify as schizophrenia or other psychiatric disorders, although this is not necessarily the case.

When instances such as *mate Māori* arose often, a *tohunga* would be called upon to assist in healing. *Tohunga* were the traditional knowledge holders and were tasked with restoring balance in the community.[112] The introduction of the Tohunga Suppression Act 1907 provided that:[113]

Marriage Act 1955, resulted in no Māori customary marriage being considered valid for any purpose.

107 As half the prison population in New Zealand identify as Māori and half of all Māori are predicted to suffer from a mental illness this example assists to highlight this situation.

108 Paterson, above n 70 at 116.

109 Heath J "Problems in Applying Māori Custom Law in a Unitary State" Yearbook of NZ Jurisprudence (2010/2011) at 199.

110 See Mason Durie *Whaiora – Māori Health Development*(Oxford University Press, Auckland, 2006) at 66–78.

111 Mead, above n 23, at 55.

112 For comprehensive discussion on Tohunga see Samuel Timoti Robinson *Tohunga: The Revival Ancient Knowledge for the Modern Era* (Reed Publishing, Auckland, 2005).

113 Second clause of the Tohunga Suppression Act 1908.

Every person who gathers Māoris around him by practicing on their super-
stition or credulity, or who misleads or attempts to mislead any Māori by
professing or pretending to possess supernatural powers in the treatment or
cure of any disease, or in the foretelling of future events, or otherwise is liable
for prosecution.

The penalty included imprisonment. This effectively banned the use of *tikanga*
Māori by *tohunga* to address Māori health issues. The alienation of Māori from
their traditional healing methods and *tikanga* could provide one reason for their
appalling mental health statistics. In fact, it has been suggested that one in every
two Māori will suffer from a mental health disorder.

F *Tikanga* Māori in context

If *tikanga* Māori is to be considered as the appropriate doctrine to underscore a
proposed Indigenous court, it is now timely to consider how *tikanga*, as a discreet
system of law, compares with the more orthodox jurisprudential schools of
thought and legal sources, such as natural law, positivism and common law, that
our current justice system depends on.

Natural law

At a basic level, *tikanga* Māori is akin to theories of natural law and positivism.
Natural law theorists hold that law is properly understood as having been derived
from natural principles, such as divine will and the natural world.[114] The Māori
legal system originates from Te Ao Māori and embraces the creation stories that
determine our relationship to each other, the environment and the spiritual
world. In this sense it is comparable to natural law theory; that is, law is determined by nature and so is universal. Further, as with natural law, *tikanga* Māori
draws no distinction between law and morality.

Positivism

If one were to draw an analogy with Western concepts of jurisprudence, *tikanga*
would lie midway between natural law and positivism. There is a belief in the
nature of humankind and the way we should act. Laws reflect the ancestral
precedent from the *atua* or Gods

Positivism is based on the assumption that the law is properly understood as
the positive expression of those who make the law – the sovereign.[115] The

---

114 See Lon Fuller *The Morality of Law* (Yale University Press, New Have, Connecticut,
1969) for further discussion.
115 See H L A Hart *The Concept of Law* (2nd ed, Oxford University Press, New York,
1997) for further discussion.

leadership and decision-making structures in Māori society did not correspond with Austin's idea of law as the command of a sovereign,[116] as cited by Borrows:[117]

> At its origin, *a custom is a rule of conduct which the governed observe spontaneously, or not in the pursuance of a law set by a political superior* [emphasis added]. The custom is transmuted into positive law, when it is adopted by the courts of justice … but before it is adopted by the courts and clothed in legal sanction, it is merely a rule of positive morality: a rule generally observed by the citizens … but deriving the only force which it can be said to possess from the general disapprobation falling on those who transgress it.

However, not all law is deemed valid if created by a sovereign. The Māori social structure revolves around the *whānau* or extended family, and the *hapū* is the primary social and economic unit. *Tikanga*, as a discrete system of law, focused on communities, societies based around smaller social-political groupings, and local economies. The smaller size of the group anticipated consensual enforcement of laws, rather than law enforcement by objective courts and juries. If negotiations reached a stalemate, the *rangatira*, leaders with *mana*, would step in and exercise their influence to make a decision.

Tikanga Māori, a values-based doctrine, provides criteria against which other values are assessed. In this sense *tikanga* Māori could be aligned with Hart's "rule of recognition".[118] However, the flexibility of *tikanga* Māori to change and adapt to novel situations limits this alignment.[119] Nonetheless, according to Mamari Stephens:[120]

> … his [Hart's] rule of recognition also exists subjectively in the beliefs of officials that they are bound by it. For those who perceive the internal aspect of tikanga, fluidity presents no fatal uncertainty.

Hart's rule of change caters for the ability of a legal system to introduce a new primary rule, adapt rules already in use and powers to amend these rules.[121] *Tikanga* Māori provides the ability of the decision maker to adapt values, provided that *tikanga* was maintained.[122] These similarities between *tikanga* Māori and positivism, although somewhat tenuous, provide a degree of synergy.

---

116 John Austin is a well-known British jurist who wrote extensively on the philosophy of law and jurisprudence. He was a leader in the theory of legal positivism.
117 John Austin *The Province of Jurisprudence Determined* vol. 1, 2nd ed., ed. W Rumble (1832; reprint, Cambridge University Press, Cambridge, 1995), 176 as cited by John Borrows *Canada's Indigenous Constitution* (University of Toronto Press, Toronto, 2010) at 12.
118 Hart, above n 115.
119 Mamari Stephens "Māori Law and Hart: A Brief Analysis" (2001) 32 VUWLR at 861.
120 At 859.
121 Hart, above n 115.
122 Stephens, above n 119.

According to the Māori world, there is a belief in the nature of humankind and the way we should and do act. Laws derived from cosmology and Te Ao Māori established legal precedent, although they were also subject to change. If we are to assume, as previously stated, that *tikanga* lies between natural law and positivism, then perhaps examining facets of the middle ground can be helpful to assist the incorporation of *tikanga* concepts.

Common law

A function of *tikanga* is to enforce collective values so that communities can live in peace and attain stability.[123] This is also analogous to common law. Another similarity is the importance of precedent. The nature of *tikanga* depends on reference to traditional use and practice. For Māori, the tradition is oral, whereas the existing judicial system relies on a written tradition.[124]

Common law has been created by judges over the centuries. The landmark cases exhibit spirit and vision that society, once informed, accepts for that reason. For example, in *Oyekan v Adele*,[125] the Privy Council employed the judge-made concept of aboriginal title to convert Indigenous custom into property rights actionable under colonial law.

According to Justice Heath:[126]

> ... Māori custom law and the existing common law are not fundamentally different. While the values that inform it are different, their overriding function (as representing the practices of the community) is identical. Where Parliament permits (or does not prohibit) the development of common law, there is scope in theory for the development of substantive law which infuses European values and tikanga Māori.

Notwithstanding the ability of the common law to convert Indigenous rights into common law rights, this action still lies within the purview of a non-Indigenous decision-maker and a non-Indigenous paradigm.

Despite the relevance of common law to the rights of Māori, noted in *Ngāti Apa v Attorney-General*,[127] judges have not kept the common law up to date. This is seen

---

123 See for further discussion Robert Joseph "Re-creating Legal Space for the First Law of Aotearoa-New Zealand" (2009) 17 Waikato Law Review: Taumauri at 74; E W Thomas "The Treaty of Waitangi: E. W. Thomas Reviews Matthew Palmer's Book" [2009] NZLJ 277.

124 Heath J, above n 109, at 199.

125 *Adeyinka Oyekan v Musendika Adele* [1957] 1 WLR 876, [1957] 2 All ER 785; see also *Tijani v Secretary, Southern Nigeria* [1921] 2 AC 399.

126 Heath J, above n 109, at 199.

127 *Ngāti Apa v Attorney General* [2003] NZCA 117 which overruled the decision of *Re the 90 Mile Beach* [1963] NZLR 461 (CA). *Ngāti Apa v Attorney General* determined that the Māori Land Court had the jurisdiction to determine whether Māori held customary title to the foreshore area.

by some as the reason as to why Parliament has, all too often, decided to intervene.[128] The intersection between common law and *tikanga* was discussed by the court in *Takamore v Clark*. The issue in that case was whether the recognition of *tikanga* Māori prevailed over the common law right as to who decides the right to a deceased's body.[129]

Case law – Takamore

In 2007 Mr James Takamore died in Christchurch, where he had lived with his partner, Ms Clarke, and their children. James was from Whakatōhea and Tūhoe. In accordance with Tūhoe *tikanga*, Mr Takamore's family collected his body and buried him at Kutarere in the Bay of Plenty. Ms Clarke did not consent and, as the executor of James' will, she initiated proceedings to reclaim his body. In an action before the High Court, Fogarty J found that Mr Takamore's Tūhoe whānau had no right to take his body.

Ms Josephine Takamore, Mr Takamore's sister, appealed Fogarty J's decision to the Court of Appeal, which dismissed the case. In reaching their decision, all three of the justices noted a legal test, that in order to recognise Māori custom as part of the common law of New Zealand, the custom must:

1   Be long standing.
2   Have continued without interruption since its origin.
3   Be reasonable.
4   Be certain in its terms.
5   Not have been displaced by Parliament through clear statutory wording.

It was held that the custom or Tūhoe *tikanga* failed on the reasonableness criteria, in that the perceived use of force was contrary to the rule of law. The application of principles that are not sourced from *tikanga*, but from New Zealand common law does not provide for parity.

The justices also noted that this conclusion was also reinforced by the need to develop the common law, as far as possible with the Treaty of Waitangi, the importance of recognising the collective nature of Indigenous culture (as set forth in the United Nations Declaration on the Rights of Indigenous Peoples) and by international human rights covenants to which New Zealand is a party.

Leave was granted to Ms Takamore to appeal the decision of the Court of Appeal to the Supreme Court.[130] The central issue was whether the Court of

---

128 This occurs for instance when the common law rights applicable to women and minorities are not recognised by the courts, resulting in parliament seeking changes; see David Baragwanath "Good Faith Symposium" *New Zealand Māori Council v Attorney-General* [1987] 1 NZLR 687 A Perspective of Counsel "In Good Faith" (Symposium, University of Otago, Dunedin, 29 June 2007).
129 *Takamore v Clarke* [2011] NZCA 587.
130 *Takamore v Clarke* [2012] NZSC 116, [2012] 2 NZLR 733.

Appeal was correct to hold that New Zealand law entitled Ms Clarke, as executor of Mr Takamore's Will, to determine his place of burial and to take possession of his remains. The Supreme Court unanimously dismissed the appeal. Accordingly, Ms Clarke was entitled to collect James' body.

The Supreme Court had the difficult task of balancing the executor's (Ms Clarke) right over the deceased's body and the relevant *tikanga* protocols. Tipping, McGrath and Blanchard JJ stated:[131]

> The *common law is not displaced when* [emphasis added] the deceased is of Māori descent and *the whānau invokes the tikanga* [emphasis added] concerning customary burial practices ... *Rather, the common law of New Zealand requires reference to any tikanga* [emphasis added], along with other important cultural, spiritual and religious values, and all other circumstances of the case as matters that must form part of the evaluation. Personal representatives are required to consider these values if they form part of the deceased's heritage ...

Elias CJ concluded that Māori custom according to *tikanga* is a part of the 'values' of New Zealand's common law and is a matter to be weighed.[132] The exact meaning of 'value' is unclear, as are other 'values' that would need to be weighed or considered.

Despite the recognition tests set out by the Court of Appeal and whether *tikanga* can indeed satisfy these tests, it is clear that *tikanga* is now part of New Zealand's common law. This case sets a precedent for *tikanga* becoming a consideration or part of the 'values' that come to influence outcomes. Perhaps it may be that for a claim under existing legislation, such as the Marine and Coastal Area (Takutai Moana) Act 2011 or Te Ture Whenua Maori Act 1993, *tikanga* could be submitted as a 'value' to be weighed, rather than putting the onus on the claimants to establish *tikanga*.[133]

Legal scholar, Sir Edmund Thomas notes:[134]

> ... to vest tikanga Māori with legal status. *As tikanga are essentially principles rather than rules, and those principles are not static, tikanga Māori could readily be absorbed into the common law of this country* [emphasis added]. Again, there is no reason why the judges should not assimilate the principles of tikanga in the development of the law generally so as to *develop an endemic jurisprudence* [emphasis added], just as the judges in days gone by assimilated the customs of the times into the growing body of the common law of England.

131 At [164].
132 At [94] per Elias CJ.
133 It is acknowledged that section 51 of the Marine and Coastal Area (Takutai Moana) Act provides a test to establish a protected customary right. This comprises of three grounds to be satisfied of which *tikanga* relates to only one ground.
134 Thomas, above n 123.

Sir Edmund Thomas further noted:[135]

> The aim would be to *enrich the law by incorporating tikanga as and when appropriate* [emphasis added]. Māori principles regarding respect for the environment, for example, could have much to offer ...

This also suggests that *tikanga* should be a part of our common law and a value to be considered.

The nature of the Māori legal system is value-based, rather than rule-based. The advantage of a customary law system over a rules-based system that relies on written law and statutes is the flexibility of the former to disregard a custom when it becomes unpalatable, outdated or inconvenient.[136] It is acknowledged that some negative customs can be entrenched.[137] However, it could be easier to affect change in instances where there is no longer support for a particular custom.

Nevertheless, there is also an aspect of *tikanga* that is empirical; it is made and enforced having regard to practical observations in the world around us. This allows some flexibility in the application of laws emanating from principles rather than rules. For instance, where there is a need to be aware of particular circumstances, such as the appropriate time to harvest or impending warfare.

Indigenous traditions have been incorporated to further define the parameters of the common law.[138] It would follow that *tikanga* Māori could also be used to inform the common law by enforcing collective values in order to achieve balance and harmony. Alternatively, it could be used as a sword in checking the actions of the Crown if they are inconsistent with *tikanga* Māori.[139]

According to Gordon Christie:[140]

> Indigenous legal scholars ... have vital work to do in revealing ways in which *the dominant system has functioned to trap Indigenous aspirations within webs of theory*

---

135 Thomas above.
136 This aligns with Hart's concept of secondary rules allowing for change to laws.
137 For instance gender based customs in the Pacific. See Converging Currents Customs and Human Rights in the Pacific September 2006 *NZLC* Study Paper 17, at 94 where it is noted that "an introduced practice of 'bride-price' is now viewed by many men as a licence to treat their wives as property".
138 See Raymond Austin *Navajo Courts and the Navajo Common Law: A Tradition of Tribal Self Governance* (University of Minnesota Press, Minneapolis, 2009) at xii.
139 For instance this could be a cause of action taken by *iwi* groups who are challenging the decisions of the Crown to grant rights to another *iwi* in an area where they hold *mana whenua* i.e. overlapping claims when the Crown is failing to consider the *tikanga* concept of *mana whenua* and granting rights as a result of a Treaty claim to an *iwi* who does not hold *mana whenua* within that region.
140 Gordon Christie "Indigenous Legal Theory" in Benjamin Richardson, Shin Imai and Kent McNeil (eds) *Indigenous Peoples and the Law Comparative and Critical Perspectives* (Hart Publishing, Portland, 2009) at 231.

and principle [emphasis added] … and articulating how indigenous understandings and conceptualisations underpin the theoretical perspectives …

Exploring the questions of who are Maori and what is *tikanga* Maori are not only
insightful but consistent with the philosophy that underpins existing Indigenous
justice systems, such as the Navajo Court system.[141] Two examples, the changing
significance of Māori women in society and the related problem of domestic violence and the issue of mental health, provide compelling reasons to consider a
return to a framework informed by *tikanga* Māori. Contrasting *tikanga* Māori
against more traditional sources of law such as natural law and positivism assists
to illustrate the existing synergies.

It is appropriate to now consider the current legal provisions, practices and
policies that have been historically and currently implemented in the New Zealand
criminal justice system to alleviate the disproportionate statistics.

141 See Chapter 6 'Initiatives in Comparative Jurisdictions' for discussion.

Chapter 3

Māori and current criminal justice initiatives

Prior to the arrival of the British, Māori adhered to the realm of the Māori world. Colonisation impacted negatively on the realm of the Māori world, marginalising *tikanga* Māori.[1] Subsequent laws and policies were introduced, alienating Māori from their land and resources.[2] The failure to recognise *tikanga* Māori also resulted in the breakdown of existing familial structures and the legacy of violence in contemporary families is also attributed to colonisation.[3]

The Hunn Report recommended that New Zealand move beyond assimilation and towards integration where the two cultures would become one.[4] As Māori were the minority, the effect was the gradual erosion of *tikanga* Māori. This was reflected in the report's lack of provision to protect Māori identity and culture – *tikanga* Māori.[5] Ralph Piddington, a former Professor of Anthropology at the University of Auckland, stated that for most Pākehā, "Māori are envisaged as dark-skinned Pākehā, having no distinctive cultural characteristics of their own".[6]

The establishment of the Māori Education Foundation and New Zealand Māori Council provided positive vehicles for Māori to assert their rights.

1 See Iris Marion Young "Five Faces of Oppression" in Lisa Heldke and Peg O'Connor (eds) *Oppression, Privilege and Resistance* (McGraw Hill, Boston, 2004) for discussion on marginalisation.
2 See for example David Williams *Te Kooti Tango Whenua: The Native Land Court 1864–1909* (Huia Publishers, Wellington, 1999) for discussion on the alienating legislation. Williams coins the Native Land Court "the Engine of Destruction"; see also for example ss 102–103 Public Works Act 1928 where Māori land could be taken by an Order in Council without provision for any statutory notice or objection rights which were accorded to the owners of non-Māori.
3 See for example Te Puni Kokiri *Rangahau Tukino Whanau Māori Research Agenda on Family Violence* (2008) at 4 <www.tpk.govt.nz>. For general discussion see also Ranginui Walker in *Ka Whawhai Tonu Mātou – Struggle without End* (Penguin, Auckland, 1990).
4 See discussion in Richard Hill *Māori and the State Crown-Māori Relations in New Zealand/ Aotearoa 1950–2000* (Victoria University Press, Wellington, 2009) particularly the Hunn Report (1960).
5 See Walker , n 3; Jarod Gilbert *Patched: The History of Gangs in New Zealand* (AUP, Auckland, 2013) at 46 <www.press.auckland.ac>.
6 Gilbert, above at 46.

However, in 1965, 85 per cent of Māori children left school without any formal qualifications,[7] and the offending rates for Māori were still disproportionately high.[8] Not surprisingly the increase in Māori criminality, most noticeable in youth offending, continued unabated through the 1960s where Māori youth represented 1,269 or 23 per cent of the 'distinct cases' dealt with by the Children's Court.[9] By 1970 these figures had increased to 4,866 and 42 per cent respectively.

Ranginui Walker stated:[10]

> In 1970, there were 9,094 young Māori offenders before the Children's Court. The following year ... the offending rate of Māori boys under 16 years was 5.1 times the rate of Pākehā ... for Māori girls the rate was higher at 7.4.

Even though colonisation had a negative effect on Māori identity[11] and *tikanga* Māori, it also provided an impetus for Māori to protect and assert their identity.[12] This is reflected in historical events, including the Māori Land March and the establishment of groups such as Ngā Tamatoa to promote Māori rights.

Since colonisation the subsuming of *tikanga* Māori into the existing legal system has resulted in chequered policies seeking to oppress and also assist *tikanga* Māori, such as those included in the Hunn Report (1960). Notwithstanding these policies and contemporary social problems, such as unemployment and drug and alcohol addiction, the disproportionate offending rates of Māori remain.[13]

A Current legal provisions, practices and policies – New Zealand

The express and meaningful recognition of Indigenous law/*tikanga* Māori within the justice system varies from recognition of Māori customs and values[14] to rejecting claims based on lack of jurisdiction.[15] Within the criminal justice system,

---

7 At 47.
8 See NZDP 323 (1960) 1414; Antje Kampf *Mapping out Venereal Wilderness: Pubic Health and STD in New Zealand 1920–1980* (Transaction Publishers, London, 2007) at 184.
9 Gilbert, above n 5.
10 Walker, above n 3, at 208.
11 For example, Māori were punished by the colonists for speaking their language in schools thereby alienating Māori from their language. My father, Aterea Toki, recalls such events.
12 T Moeke Pickering *Māori Identity within the Whanau: A Review of Literature* (University of Waikato, Hamilton, 1996) <www.researchcommons.waikato.ac.nz>.
13 For a contemporary discussion, 1994–2009, of Māori rights see Margaret Mutu *The State of Māori Rights* (Huia Publishers, Wellington, 2011).
14 T Bennion "*Ngati Hokopu ki Hokowhitu v Whakatane District Council*" Māori Law Review July (2003) at 2.
15 *R v Toia* CRI 2005 005 000027 Williams J HC Whangarei 9 August 2006; *see also Hunt v R* [2011] 2 NZLR 499 at [82] and [85] for discussion on breach of *tikanga*, this claim was rejected by the Court.

this is further limited to incorporation into programmes by the Corrections Department,[16] and more recently inclusion in the Youth Court at sentencing. This book may suggest that, if Māori are to be fairly treated, some transformations are required not only at sentencing, but also from the time of apprehension through to imprisonment.

The term *tikanga* is incorporated into various statutes; however, only half of these provide a definition of *tikanga* and refer to concepts such as culture and custom. The inclusion of *tikanga* Māori can be found within a raft of Acts.[17] Within these Acts the inclusion of *tikanga* varies from *tikanga* being an express and relevant consideration in decision-making[18] to ensuring a knowledge base of *tikanga* exists on certain statutory boards[19] to where *tikanga* forms part of a policy directive.[20] These references are more descriptive than definitive.[21] This undermines the consistency and intention of the legislative provision.

As Māori are disproportionately represented in the prosecution process and in light of calls for a return to an all Māori jury, this would appear to support the proposition that the application of Te Ao Māori, realised by an Indigenous legal system, manifested by an Indigenous court, premised on fundamental Māori concepts and doctrine is the only way forward for Māori. A review of whether, or how the current legislative initiatives and programmes recognise Te Ao Māori and *tikanga* Māori will inform this analysis.

As offending is often linked to social and environmental factors, such as excessive alcohol or drug use, prevention of causative factors is of relevance to the rate of Māori offending and incarceration. Māori Committees established by the Māori Community Development Act 1962 provided a forum to address low level offending.[22] Māori wardens, also established by the Māori Community Development Act 1962, provided a voluntary service to the community to control disruptive social behaviour that may result from excessive alcohol and drug use by Māori. To this end, an examination of these two roles will be informative.

Māori wardens

Created by an Act of Parliament, the Māori Community Development Act 1962, the Māori warden programme attracts a voluntary status. Viewed as agents of social control, Māori wardens were perceived as continuing the policing role that

16 For example Te Whanau Awhina; see also domestic violence programmes at <http://www.justice.govt.nz.>
17 It is acknowledged that *tikanga* Māori also exists within the Māori prose of legislation, such as the Waikato Claims Settlement Act 1995 and the preamble to Te Ture Whenua Māori Act 1993.
18 For example Te Ture Whenua Māori Act 1993, ss 106, 107 and 114.
19 For example the Education Act 1989, s 61.
20 For example Historic Places Act 1993, s 42.
21 See Fiona Wright "Law, Religion and Tikanga Māori" (2007) 5 NZJPIL at 261.
22 An example of low level offending could be shoplifting.

had existed amongst various *iwi*, including the Ringatū and the King Con-federacy.[23] This legislative recognition was seen to consolidate the historical commitment to utilise *iwi* leaders to maintain public order.[24]

The provision of legislation allows Māori wardens to exercise control over other Māori and perform minor policing duties, such as the control of drunken behaviour and discouraging crime on the streets.[25] The role of the Māori warden is often applauded, with comments by Sir Douglas Graham to the inaugural meeting of Security New Zealand in 1996, entitled "The Role of the Private Sector in Law and Order" where he noted:[26]

> Here in New Zealand, Māori wardens are one of the most successful examples of the role of the private sector in law and order. They were established in 1945 by the Māori Social and Economic Advancement Act at a time when more than 80 per cent of Māori were living in rural areas. The wardens were well known to all members of the tribe by virtue of the fact that they had grown up within the community with a reputation established by ancestry and leadership qualities.
>
> Over the last 30 years there has been a spectacular movement of Māori people to the cities and the work of the wardens has become largely an urban function. Today they carry a heavier workload than their rural counterpart as they cope with some of the less savoury aspects of life in the city.
>
> Māori wardens were not introduced with the intention of usurping the duties of the Police, but rather they are an influence among the people in maintaining law and order.
>
> Their powers of arrest are only those of members of the public ... On many occasions I and the officials who accompanied me on this character-building exercise were extremely grateful for the presence of Māori wardens – backed up by kuia when the going got really tough ...
>
> The State observed Māori protocol and a potentially dangerous situation was diffused by skilful handling and a lot of wisdom and humour from kuia and Māori wardens.

Although the role of the Māori warden declined in the 1970s, it has enjoyed a resurgence, assisted in part by the announcement in 2008, by the then Minister of

---

23 Augie Fleras "Māori Wardens and the control of Liquor among the Māori of New Zealand" (1981) 90(4) Journal of the Polynesian Society at 495.
24 At 495; See also Richard Hill *Māori and the State Crown-Māori Relations in New Zealand/Aotearoa 1950–2000* (Victoria University Press, Wellington, 2009), at 128.
25 Sian Elias "Equality under Law" (2005) 13 Waikato Law Review 1 at 7. For a comparative perspective on the effectiveness of Indigenous community based policing groups – the presence of the Regional Coordinating Body of the Community Authorities/Community Police in Mexico has, due its presence, reported a 90 per cent decline in common crime.
26 As cited by Tom Bennion "Law and Order Māori and the Private Sector" (April 1996) Māori Law Review at 1.

Justice, Annette King, that NZ$2.3 million would be allocated to strengthen the capacity and capability of Māori wardens.[27]

However, the establishment of a Māori Warden's branch in Queensland, Australia, to promote safer communities, has been challenged by the broader community with allegations of racism and arrogance.[28] Nonetheless, the importance of their role is the subject of a review by Te Puni Kōkiri.[29]

Māori wardens contributed positively to the Māori Committee and Māori Courts' initiative. It is suggested that this role could be revived and accommodated within an Indigenous court as a lay advocate to support the offender between arrest and appearance before a judge or within a *marae* forum.[30]

Māori Courts

Historically Māori Committees, constituted under the Māori Community Development Act 1962, adjudicated on low level offending and were informally referred to as Māori Courts.[31] Chaired by at least three Māori Committee members, the intention was to prevent and deflect offenders from the criminal justice system. With the assistance and support of the community, the offender was reintegrated into the community. Māori wardens often contributed to the Māori Courts. However, the then Secretary for Māori Affairs, Jock McEwen, noted that the Māori Courts were struggling as the "traditional authority exercised by elders had been lost".[32] Despite the positive effect of the Māori Committees, a lack of funding and resources together with continual dislocation of Māori from their culture, and an unwillingness by some Māori to fall under the jurisdiction of the Māori Committee, led to its demise.[33] Notwithstanding this, it is suggested that a similar forum could be revisited.

Considering that the jury system, as a collective, provides a means to impart community norms and values into a judicial proceeding, a review and analysis of the historical involvement of Māori within this system is helpful.

27   Tom Bennion "Editorial" (May 2008) Māori Law Review at 6.
28   "Māori Wardens in Queensland under Fire" *Radio NZ News* (online, New Zealand, 18 July 2013) <www.radionz.co.nz >.
29   There are currently 883 warranted Māori wardens who are engaged on a voluntary basis; see Te Puni Kōkiri Māori Wardens Options for Change (2013) <www.tpk.govt.nz>. Current funding is $1,000,000 per annum to assist Māori Wardens deliver "community based services, improve organisational capacity and capability"; see <http://www.tpk.govt.nz/en/in-print/our-publications/publications/māori-wardens-project-funding-programme/page/1>
30   See Chapter 8 'A New Vision' on a proposed model.
31   Hill, above n 24 at 130.
32   At 131.
33   At 134.

Māori juries

Prior to 1844 Māori were unable to serve on ordinary juries. However, in 1844 the Native Exemption Ordinance was passed. This was one of a suite of exceptional laws; the others being the Unsworn Testimony Ordinance,[34] the Cattle Trespass Amendment Ordinance[35] and the Jury Amendment Ordinance. The Jury Amendment Ordinance authorised the Governor to exempt certain Māori from the property-ownership requirements and allow Māori to serve on mixed juries. Although no proclamation was ever made to authorise this, it was declared that any Māori whose capability was certified would qualify to serve on a mixed jury for the trial of any case in which the property or person of a Māori might be affected.[36]

Section 2 of the Juries Act 1908 provided a definition of Māori to include persons of the aboriginal race of New Zealand, including Polynesian, Melanesian and Australasian races as well as half castes, provided they lived with a Māori tribe or community.

According to Dr Ken Palmer:[37]

> The significance of the categorisation, is to allow for an all Māori jury in a criminal case involving Māori offending against another Māori, with like provision for civil cases. Where a civil case involves one Māori against a non-Māori, a mixed jury of races may be allowed but no equivalent provision applied to criminal charges involving non-Māori people.

A Māori accused of a crime against another Māori could claim trial before an all-Māori jury. However, no Māori could serve on a jury if either the accused or the victim was a non-Māori.[38]

In civil cases a Māori jury could be claimed if both parties were Māori, and a mixed jury if one party was Māori.[39] The law remained in this form for nearly a century. In 1962 legislation abolished separate Māori juries and placed Māori on an equal footing for jury service, including cases involving non-Māori.[40]

---

34   The Unsworn Testimony Ordinance enabled Māori who had no religious beliefs to provide sworn evidence.

35   The Cattle Trespass Amendment Ordinance required settlers to keep their cattle fenced in, rather than requiring Māori to fence them out of their cultivations.

36   Shaunnaugh Dorsett "*R v E Hipu Supreme Court Wellington* 1 December 1845" (2010) 41 (1) VUWLR 89 at 91.

37   Ken Palmer "Law Land and Māori Issues" (1988) 3 Canterbury Law Review at 323.

38   S Dunstan, J Paulin and K Atkinson *Trial by Peers? The Composition of New Zealand Juries* (Department of Justice, Wellington, 1995).

39   Dunstan, Paulin and Atkinson, above.

40   Mark Israel "Ethnic Bias in Jury Selection in Australia and New Zealand" (1998) 26 International Journal of the Sociology of Law at 35. The special provisions for Māori juries were abolished with effect from the end of 1964 by the Juries Amendment Act 1962.

Although regarded as equals, research has since confirmed that Māori are still under-represented on both panels of potential jurors as well as on trial juries.[41] This is a result of bias at both the out-of-court and the in-court selection stage.[42] The underlying reasons are many, including the nature of the boundaries of the jury districts, the exclusive use of the electoral roll as the source list and the criteria adopted for excluding people from the jury list.[43] However, a significant source of under-representation also derives from the use of challenges by prosecuting counsel.[44]

In 1988 a report written by Moana Jackson for the Department of Justice drew attention to fears that the continuing prevalence of monocultural juries might be denying Māori people a fair trial.[45] Jackson argued that an all-Māori jury should again provide for Māori defendants.

Children, Young Persons and Their Families Act and Family Group Conferences

A Family Group Conference (FGC) is a meeting where a young person who has offended, their family, victims and other people meet to discuss how to assist the young offender to take responsibility for their actions and implement practical ways to make amends.[46] The objective is to reach a group consensus on an outcome.

The preamble to the Children, Young Persons and Their Families Act 1989 Act (CYPF) states that the purpose of the Act is to:

> advance the well-being of families and the wellbeing of children as young persons as members of ... whānau, hapū, iwi ... make provisions for whānau, hapū, iwi ... and the matters to be resolved where possible by their own... whānau, hapū, iwi ...

Section 13 of the Act refers to principles and makes it clear that the primary role for caring and protecting the child or young person lies with the *whānau, hapū* or *iwi*. Various programmes, such as FGC,[47] are also provided for in the CYPF Act that acknowledge and support the participation of *whānau*.[48]

---

41 See Dunstan, Paulin and Atkinson, above n 38.
42 Israel, above n 40 at 35–54. See also, Dunstan, Paulin and Atkinson, above n 38, for empirical study.
43 Dunstan, Paulin and Atkinson, above n 38.
44 Above.
45 Moana Jackson *The Māori and the Criminal Justice System – He Whaipaanga Hou: A New Perspective: Part* 2 (Department of Justice, Wellington, 1988).
46 See also Ministry of Justice *The Family Group Conference in Youth Justice.* <www.justice. govt.nz>.
47 The immense contribution of Judge Mick Brown and Judge Fred McElrea to the area of Youth Offending and the Family Group Conference initiative has been invaluable. It was their pioneering approach that led to these reforms.
48 Specifically Part Two of the Act and ss 256 Procedure and 258 Functions.

Involving the victim in the process and encouraging mediation of concerns between the victim, the offender and their families is a means to achieve reconciliation, restitution and rehabilitation.[49] The FGC allows for the participation of *whānau* and *iwi*. There is also provision for the FGC to be held on a *marae*.

The success of the FGC and its adoption by other jurisdictions is to be applauded and adds weight to the case for an Indigenous court.[50] However, in practice, levels of restorativeness vary between FGCs as approximately half of FGCs do not have the victim or victims' representative present, thereby diminishing the effectiveness of the restorative initiative.[51]

Notwithstanding the inclusion of a *marae* setting, there is no impetus to connect the offender with their cultural identity. And although *tikanga* may be implicit, there is no explicit mention of '*tikanga*' within the CYPF Act 1989.

Restorative Justice[52]

Central to restorative justice is the objective for the victim and the offender to meet face-to-face and restore the relationship, focusing on redress for the harm done to the victim, while holding the offender accountable and repairing any damage to the community.[53] As a voluntary process, both the victim and the offender must agree and the offender must admit responsibility prior to the process. The outcome of a Restorative Justice Conference is taken into account by the judge at sentencing.

In recognition of the positive effect restorative justice can have, this process will soon be available in every court across New Zealand.[54] This is unsurprising given that benefits identified include:[55]

- 20 per cent reduction in reoffending by those who participated. The frequency of those who did reoffend dropped by nearly a quarter.

49 Youth Court of New Zealand *Family Group Conferences* <www.justice.govt.nz >.
50 FGC have been adopted in the United Kingdom and also United States where they are known as Family Guided Decision Making.
51 Yvette Tinsley and Elisabeth McDonald "Is There Any Other Way? Possible Alternatives to the Current Criminal Justice rocess" (2011) 17 Canterbury Law Review at 204.
52 It is acknowledged that Restorative Justice is similar to Therapeutic Jurisprudence. However, this book will be confined to Therapeutic Jurisprudence as it provides a 'broader umbrella' and more appropriate to consider for the purposes of this book.
53 Ministry of Justice *Restorative Justice* <www.justice.govt.nz>; see also discussion in Helen Bowen and Jim Consedine *Restorative Justice Contemporary Themes and Practice* (Ploughshare Publications, New Zealand, 1999); see also Gabrielle Maxwell and James Liu (eds) *Restorative Justice Practices in New Zealand: Towards a Restorative Society* (Institute of Policy Studies, Wellington, 2007) for discussion of New Zealand experiences and perspectives.
54 Frank Neill "Restorative Justice: Chance to Help Clients Turn Their Lives Around" *Law Talk* (New Zealand, November 2013) at 9: also noteworthy is the Government's funding of NZ$ 4.4 million investments in adult pre sentence Restorative Justice.
55 Neill, above, at 12.

- 77 per cent of victims were satisfied with their overall experience, before, during and after the conference.
- 74 per cent of victims said they felt better after attending the conference.
- 80 per cent of victims said they would be likely to recommend Restorative Justice to others in a similar situation.

More recently a follow up study by the Ministry of Justice confirmed the positive effect of a restorative justice process finding that:[56]

On average, offenders who participated in a Police or court-referred restorative justice conference committed 23 per cent fewer offences than comparable offenders over the following 12 month period; and had a 12 per cent lower rate of reoffending than comparable offenders over the following 12 month period.

Despite statistical threshold requirements the Report further noted:

The percentage difference in the frequency of reoffending remained stable over the four-year period of the study. Although the two to four-year results did not meet the threshold for statistical significance, nevertheless the findings suggest that restorative justice may continue to have a positive impact on the number of offences committed over time.

The study also suggested that conferenced offenders were 28 per cent less likely to be imprisoned for reoffending over the following 12 month period than comparable offenders. However, again that result was not statistically significant. It also needs to be viewed in light of the reoffending rates for high-level offending, which suggest restorative justice has no significant impact on the seriousness of reoffending.

Although restorative justice like *tikanga* may be implicit in legislation, such as the CYPF Act 1989, there is no explicit mention of restorative justice nor *tikanga* within the CYPF Act 1989.

Notwithstanding, the positive aspects of restorative justice and suggestion that *tikanga* Māori is consistent with restorative justice,[57] academics contend that through a *tikanga* Māori lens, the concept of restorative justice is incompatible with *tikanga* Māori.[58] Restorative justice infers that something has been broken

---

56 Ministry of Justice *Reoffending Analysis for Restorative Justice Cases 2008–2011* (Ministry of Justice, Wellington, April 2014) <www.justice.govt.nz>.

57 See David Carruthers "Restorative Justice: Lessons from the Past, Pointers for the Future" (2012) 20 Waikato Law Review: Taumauri at 1, who acknowledges that the principles underpinning restorative justice are consistent with those of *tikanga* Māori.

58 Tinsley and McDonald, above n 51, who state that there is limited research on whether restorative justice is compatible with Indigenous notions of justice.

and needs to be restored. For Māori, conduct that is *hee* unbalances the relational network. This conduct is not perceived as broken, but conduct that requires balance – the aim of *tikanga* Māori through the use of further *tikanga* concepts. Further, Juan Tauri contends that restorative justice was imposed upon Māori, is not community driven and is an adjunct rather than an alternative to conventional criminal justice.[59]

B Programmes

Before addressing how the criminal justice system has included *tikanga* within various programmes, the presence of *tikanga* values, such as *ora*, implemented by the Ministry of Health, Hauora, Māori Health Care Providers and Whānau Ora, as a firm policy directive, provides an interesting example.

Hauora – Māori Health

A survey revealed that over 80 per cent of New Zealanders reported good health.[60] For Māori, however, high smoking rates (two in five or 41 per cent of Māori adults are current smokers), obesity rates (44 per cent), mental health rates (Māori adults have higher rates of psychological distress than other adults, with one in ten Māori affected) indicate that Māori are disproportionately represented in adverse health statistics. This study confirms that Māori have the poorest health of any ethnic group in New Zealand.[61]

Māori health providers are contracted to deliver health services, predominantly to Māori under the Hauora scheme. According to Māori Marsden:[62]

> ... a synonym for mauri in certain contexts is hau (breath). 'Hau-ora' the breath of life is the agent or source by and from which mauri (life principle) is mediated to objects both animate and inanimate ... and hauora as applied to animate objects are synonymous ... mauri is applied to inanimate objects; whilst hau is applied only to animate life ... mauri was the force or energy mediated by hauora – the breath of the spirit life.

59 Juan Tauri "Family Group Conferencing: A Case Study of the Indigenistaion of New Zealand's Justice System" (1998) 10 CICJ 168 as cited by Tinsley and McDonald above n 51, at 206.
60 Ministry of Health *The Health of New Zealand Adults 2011/12 – Conclusions* at 130 <www.health.govt.nz >.
61 At 130.
62 Māori Marsden "The Natural World and Natural Resources" in C Royal (ed) *The Woven Universe: Selected Writings of Rev Māori Marsden* (Estate of Rev. Māori Marsden, Masterton, 2003) at 44.

Anne Salmond noted:[63]

> ... The hau, like the tapu and mana of the ancestors, was once dispersed
> throughout the kin group ... *gifts or insults to any part of the group thus affected the*
> *hau of the entire kin group* [emphasis added] ... in this way utu, *reciprocal exchange,*
> *required the return of hau* [emphasis added] whether by gifts or insults. Insults
> diminished the rangatira's hau and had to be requited. Gifts, by embodying
> mana and carrying the donor's hau created an obligation for return gift-
> ing ... *If gifts were not requited* this was hau whitia ... *in such a situation, the source*
> *of life was weakened, causing misfortune, even dying* [emphasis added].

In more recent times, the term *hauora* has been further developed into a model of
general well-being prescribing four dimensions: *Taha Tinana*/physical well-being –
health, *Taha Hinengaro*/mental and emotional well-being – self-confidence, *Taha*
Whānau/social well-being – self-esteem and *Taha Wairua*/spiritual well-being –
personal beliefs.[64] Should one component become damaged, a person or the
corresponding collective will become unbalanced and feel unwell, thus requiring a
re-balance.[65] This model recognises the importance of the relational dynamic and
ultimately the need for balance: the aim of *tikanga*.

The fundamental philosophy is consistent with *tikanga* values and programmes
such as He Korowai Oranga: Māori Health Strategy. This programme provides a
framework for the public sector to participate in supporting the health status of
Māori with an overall aim of *whānau ora*: Māori families achieving well-being.
Whānau ora is a strategic tool for the health and other government sectors to work
together with *iwi* Māori providers and Māori communities as well as *whānau* to
reduce the disproportionate health statistics for Māori. The Māori Action Plan
Whakatātaka Tuarua 2006–2011 further contributes by setting objectives.[66]

In response to Māori over-representation within the health system, the Ministry
of Health has implemented programmes and strategies that are underpinned by
tikanga values to reduce the disparity. The approach is relational, premised on the
interconnectivity of the four dimensions. Notwithstanding the similar rates of
disparity for Māori and offending rates, the Ministry of Justice does not provide
comparable programmes and plans.

The Department of Corrections has evaluated two programmes. The first, Te
Whare Ruruhau o Meri, is a dynamic programme that offers a Whānau Reconciliation Support Service. The programme recognises that many women want to

63 Anne Salmond *Between Worlds: Early Exchanges between Māori and Europeans* (Penguin,
    Auckland, 1997) at 176–177.
64 See Mason Durie *Te Whare Tapa Whā Māori Health Model Hauora Māori* (Ministry of
    Health, Wellington) available at <www.health.govt.nz/system/files/documents/pa
    ges/māori_health_model_tewhare.pdf>
65 Durie, above.
66 See Ministry of Health, *Whakatākata Tuarua: Māori Health Action Plan 2006–2011*
    (Ministry of Health, Wellington, 2006) <www.health.govt.nz > for full discussion.

return to their partners and the Service needs to support them to do so, while providing them with the best possible opportunity to be free from violence. The second programme, Tu Tama Wahine o Taranaki, provides a support network for Māori respondents.

An exciting initiative between Te Whare Whakaruruhau (Māori Women's Refuge in Hamilton) and prisoners within the Māori Focus Units has emerged. This initiative permits the members of the Māori Focus Units to perform work tasks, such as gardening and furniture removal, within the confines of Te Whare Whakaruruhau. Although still in its early days and under close scrutiny and monitoring, the 'relationship' between these two vehicles has provided a 'healing' process for the prisoners in the Māori Focus Units. Through this relationship the participants within the Māori Focus Units who provide this assistance become 'more aware' of the difficulties and trauma faced by the victims of domestic violence.

The Domestic Violence (Programmes) Regulations 1996 specify that Māori values and concepts are to be taken into account.[67] Three key principles evident in these programmes are the use of *te reo*/Māori language, the importance of *kaupapa*/Māori culture and the provision of healing for both the individual and the collective. This incorporation of *tikanga* has led to a favourable review.[68]

An evaluation of the Department of Correction's community-based *tikanga* Māori programmes shows that offenders with a heightened awareness of their Māori heritage are more likely to choose law abiding lifestyles.[69] By encouraging offenders to increase their cultural knowledge and reconnect with *whānau*, the report finds that *tikanga* Māori programmes are changing lives for the better. For Māori, the learning of *pepeha*/identify and *whakapapa*/family lineage is about reaffirming a connection with their tribes, ancestors and history.[70]

The Ministerial Review for Tikanga Māori Programmes (TMP) has confirmed that TMPs:[71]

a)   are motivational programmes incorporating principles that acknowledge Te Reo, Tikanga Māori solutions and whānau involvement;

b)   are programmes tailored to Māori offenders to motivate them to address the underlying causes of their offending behaviour;

---

67   The Domestic Violence (Programmes) Regulations 1996, r 27 and 28.

68   See Report by Fiona Cram and others *Evaluation of Programmes for Māori Adult Protected Persons under the Domestic Violence* Act 1995 (Ministry of Justice, Wellington, June 2002) <www.justice.govt.nz>.

69   See Department of Corrections *Underpinning the Department's Five-Year Strategic Business Plan is the Recognition that "To Succeed Overall We Must Succeed for Māori Offenders"* (Ministry of Justice, Wellington, 2010). <www.corrections.govt.nz>.

70   Department of Corrections, above.

71   Department of Corrections *Report on Tikanga Māori Programmes* (Department of Corrections, Wellington, 2010) <www.ssc.govt.nz>; "Tikanga based programmes share in a budget $100 million".

c)   have been operating nationally (male offenders) and locally (women) within the Public Prisons Service and the Community Probation Service;

d)   are well structured, and incorporated a range of active, passive and interactive teaching methods such as haka, waiata and kōrero to help increase responsivity; and

e)   are consistent with Corrections legislation.

One particular initiative which provides for assistance prior to release from prison is Whare Oranga Ake. This involves the establishment of *kaupapa* Māori centres to reintegrate Māori prisoners back into their communities. This initiative by Minister of Māori Affairs, Dr Peter Sharples, has attracted NZ$19.8 million to build and run two 16-bed units in Auckland and the Hawkes Bay.[72]

Integration has been identified as a problem with many prisoners not wanting to return to their dysfunctional families and peer groups.[73] During a recent visit to the Māori Focus Units the lack of support for offenders released into the community was identified as the major hurdle facing inmates. If there is no assistance for newly released offenders the slide back into an environment that fosters offending and recidivism is inevitable.[74] Although newly released offenders do not desire to reoffend if they are released into the same environment in which they offended, the probability of reoffending is high. On its own, initiatives such as Whare Oranga Ake are not enough. Whare Oranga Ake needs to be complemented with a wider education and support structure that will encompass the family, community and environment into which the offender is released.

It is acknowledged that initial problems with Whare Oranga Ake are inevitable. However, this should not stifle the enormous benefit this offers to prisoners re-integrating into society.

Youth Action Plan

Chester Borrows, the past Associate Justice Minister, released a Youth Action Plan to identify three strategies to influence how youth crime should be addressed. This initiative includes partnering with communities. In recognising the

72 Department of Corrections *Whare Oranga Ake* (Department of Corrections, Wellington, 2011) <www.corrections.govt.nz>.

73 Department of Corrections *Māori Focus Leads to Positive Gain* (Department of Corrections, Wellington, 2010) <www.corrections.govt.nz>; see also comments by Nigel Latta in Jimmy Ryan "Nigel Latta picks lock on prison system" <www.stuff.co.nz> where he noted that "to reduce offending, the issues driving criminal behavior have to be resolved... the need for a solid support structure that is there for inmates upon their release, which, if not present, can leave them between a lock and a hard place".

74 See Department of Corrections *Over-Representation of Māori in the Criminal Justice System: An Exploratory Report* (Department of Corrections, Wellington, 2007) www.corrections. govt.nz "the recidivism rates for Māori are higher than any other ethnicity in New Zealand and furthermore that within a 12 month period the impact on reoffending and prison rehabilitation falls between 0.0–3.3 for Māori Focus Units".

success of the youth justice system, Mr Borrows, as part of the Partnering with Communities strategy, announced a NZ$400,000 "innovation fund" to finance community-based youth justice initiatives. Further, Mr Borrows notes:[75]

> This plan brings together the gains we've made in youth justice recently, through initiatives like our Fresh Start reforms, Policing Excellence, and the Children's Action Plan, and looks at the gaps, challenges and opportunities that remain.

Statistics released with the plan indicate a decrease in criminal charge rates, down from 2007 (the highest proportion of 116 charged per 10,000 young people), and also down from 2011 (with 3,577 charged, representing 86 per 10,000) to 3,016 young people charged in court in 2012, which equated to a rate of 74 per 10,000 young people.

Whilst such initiatives and reports may be applauded, these programmes are the exception to what is generally available for Māori. Mainstream programmes offered by providers lack substance and often contribute to the disproportionate offending rates of Indigenous peoples, especially for women.[76] The Human Rights Commission has also suggested that many of these programmes that are focused on individual victims and offenders, rather than on broader relationships, are unlikely to satisfy the ambitions of those who seek the introduction or extension of programmes based on *tikanga* Māori and further that appropriate programmes should seek legislative backing.[77]

Further, Justice Joe Williams noted that despite the current legislative mechanisms in place, the judiciary is not being creative enough and is failing to make use of these provisions to encourage Māori participation and Māori self-governance.[78]

---

75 Chester Borrows "Action Plan the next step forward for youth justice" 31 October, 2013 <www.beehive.govt.nz>

76 Such as "Preventing Violence in the Home" programme. The Montgomery House violence prevention programme is a joint project between the New Zealand Department of Corrections and the New Zealand Prisoners' Aid and Rehabilitation. The programme is an 8-week group-based intervention established upon social learning and cognitive behavioural principles. Due to concerns the programme now includes a Te Whare Tapa Wha aspect that seeking to address *te taha tinana* (physical), *te taha hinengaro* (psychological), *te taha wairua* (spiritual), and *te taha whanau* (familial) needs of all residents. See The Montgomery House violence prevention programme <www.corrections.govt.nz>.

77 Human Rights Commission "Submission to the Justice and Electoral Select Committee on the Victims' Rights Bill, 6 March 2001" at [9] <www.hrc.co.nz>.

78 See Joseph Williams, Honourable Justice of the High Court of New Zealand "Lex Aotearoa: A Heroic Attempt at Mapping the Māori Dimension in Modern New Zealand Law" (Harkness Henry Lecture 2013, Te Piringa Faculty of Law, University of Waikato, 7 November 2013). Justice Williams was referring to provisions such as s 33 of the Resource Management Act 1991 that allows the transfer of powers to *iwi* from Local Council and ss 8(i) and 27 of the Sentencing Act 2002 that requires the Courts to take an offender's cultural background into account for rehabilitative

The inclusion of *tikanga* Māori within our justice system was recently considered by the High Court.[79]

Tikanga *Māori* in the criminal justice system

Māori have long advocated that *tikanga* Māori, the first law of Aotearoa New Zealand,[80] be meaningfully recognised within the New Zealand legal system. The case of *R v Mason* revisits the applicability of *tikanga* Māori within our current criminal justice system.[81] Referring to oral evidence provided by Moana Jackson, and writings of Māori academics, Dr Robert Joseph and Matiu Dickson, the case provides fertile ground for an invigorated and fresh judicial discussion of an area often traversed.

The case involved an application for a ruling to enable the accused charged with murder and attempted murder, to be dealt with in accordance with *tikanga* Māori.

The court considered that for the appellants to succeed, two distinct propositions would need to be met:[82]

a   that around the time He Whakaputanga o Nga Hapu o Niu Tireni (the Declaration of Independence of 1835) and Te Tiriti o Waitangi (the Treaty of Waitangi 1840), there was a developed Māori legal system (the customary system) that could investigate and impose sanctions for serious criminal conduct; and

b   the customary system continues in force today and represents a parallel system of criminal justice by which Māori charged with serious criminal offences may elect to be tried.

The second proposition can be split into two further subgroups:

a   whether Māori themselves practice *tikanga* Māori within a criminal
b   context; and
c   whether the law of New Zealand allows *tikanga* Māori to be practiced.

purposes, and allows the court to hear from any person on behalf of the offender thereby recognising that an offender's cultural background may contribute to offending, respectively.

79 *R v Mason* [2012] 2 NZLR 695.
80 Ani Mikaere "The Treaty of Waitangi and the Recognition of Tikanga Māori" in Michael Belgrave, Merata Kawharu and David Williams (eds) *Waitangi Revisited: Perspectives on the Treaty of Waitangi* (Oxford University Press, Australia, 2005), at 331–332. See also Ani Mikaere "Tikanga as the First Law of Aotearoa" 24 (2007) Yearbook of NZJ.
81 Past examples include the current Rangatahi Courts held on a *Marae*. This seeks to incorporate the *tikanga* of the *Marae* within the current criminal justice system see *R v Mason* [2012] 2 NZLR 695 at [41] also see V Toki "A Breath of Fresh, or Recycled Air – R v Mason" *NZLJ* (December 2012).
82 *R v Mason*, above, at [10].

Noting that there was a general acceptance that existing customary practices (*tikanga* Māori) had "the character and authority of law",[83] the court referred to a dispatch from Lord Russell, on behalf of the British Government, to instruct Governor Hobson to recognise the customs developed by Māori.[84] From this point on, the court also referred to the form of the 1873 judicial oath and the adoption of the term "usages", within that oath, as more likely to apply to Māori than the European settlers.[85] Section 71 of the Constitution Act 1852 and the cases of *Ngāti Apa v Attorney-General*[86] and *Takamore v Clark*[87] were also referred to as acknowledging the existence of laws, customs and usages of aboriginal or native inhabitants, and Māori customary title to land and customs associated with burial, respectively.[88]

The court found that there was:[89]

> no doubt that before the 1835 Declaration and the Treaty, Māori operated a customary system that could deal, for the social purposes of the time, with alleged breaches of societal norms of type now characterised as 'serious crime'.

However, the court notes that the combined effect of ss 5 and 9 of Crimes Act 1961 extinguished the customary system, so it was not possible to regard the customary system as an existing parallel system.[90] In doing so the court clearly negated the continuance of any customary system by which Māori charged with serious criminal offences may elect to be tried.

The court accepted that the first proposition was likely to be satisfied,[91] but found it more difficult to accept the second proposition, referring to the Crimes Act 1961 as extinguishing this ability.

In order to affirm the second proposition, regard must be paid to the first proposition together with the existence of any reliance between the two propositions.

The court accepted that at the time of the signing of the Treaty of Waitangi, Māori had a developed legal system. For Māori, reliance was placed on the imposed legal system to meaningfully recognise their own developed legal

---

83 At [13].
84 At [13].
85 At [14].
86 *Ngāti Apa v Attorney General* [2003] 3 NZLR 643 (CA).
87 *Takamore v Clarke* [2011] NZCA 587; [2012] 1 NZLR 573 (CA).
88 *R v Mason*, above n 81, at [14].
89 At [28].
90 At [31] and [37]; see also comments by Max Harris "More on Mason Cultural Factors in Sentencing" (February, 2013) Māori Law Review available also <māorilawreview.co.nz/2013/02/more-on-mason-cultural-factors-in-sentencing/>
91 Above n 81, at [28].

system – *tikanga* Māori. Notwithstanding this reliance, successive Court decisions and legislation have negatively impacted and effectively extinguished their legal system. If it was not for the Crown's reluctance to meaningfully accept the Māori's pre-existing system of law, it is highly likely that it would still exist, to the same degree, today.

It is acknowledged that Article III of the Treaty of Waitangi bestows on Māori the same rights and privileges of British subjects. However, the Māori text of the Treaty of Waitangi (Te Tiriti) guarantees to Māori *nga tikanga katoa rite tahi ki ana mea, ki nga tangata o Ingarangi/*the same customary rights as those given to the British. By implication, this bestowal could displace any existing system of law. However, when read together with Article I, where Māori arguably have not ceded sovereignty but governorship, this displacement is less clear.

If this "reliance" was meaningfully considered by the court, it would follow that the second proposition should be rephrased as:

> b) absent the incorrect legal findings[92], the customary system would have continued in force today, representing a parallel system of criminal justice by which Māori charged with serious criminal offences may elect to be tried.

The initial direction to acknowledge pre-existing Māori "customs and practices" originated from the British Government in 1840.[93] This direction was pitted against a backdrop of a need to secure land for European settlers. Consistent with this direction, early case law indicates the acceptance of existing native customs and practices and rights to land at a time when Māori still comprised the majority of the population.[94]

After the Constitution Act 1852, the judiciary evaded the obligation to continue the application of Māori customary usage and law.[95] The seminal case of *Wi Parata* in 1877 was decided against a very different backdrop when Māori were no longer the majority. Prendergast CJ found that Māori had no "body politic", reversing any prior acknowledgement of *tikanga* Māori. This finding was reinforced in *Rira Peti v Ngaraihi Te Paku,*[96] where Prendergast CJ denied any recognition of Māori custom law, despite s 10 of the New Zealand Government Act 1846.[97] His Honour stated:[98]

---

92 See *Wi Parata v Bishop of Wellington* where the existing political, social and legal systems by Māori were found not to exist.

93 *R v Mason*, above n 81, at [13]; Lord Russell was Home Secretary and then Leader of the Opposition.

94 *R v Symonds* (1847) NZPCC 387.

95 Robert Joseph *The Government of Themselves: Case Law, Policy and Section 71 of the New Zealand Constitution Act 1852* (Te Matahauariki Institute Monograph Series, University of Waikato, 2002) at 54.

96 *Rira Peti v Ngaraihi Te Paku* (1889) 7 NZLR 235 as cited in Joseph, above n 852.

97 Section 10 recognised the laws, customs and usages of Māori in native districts.

98 *Rira Peti v Ngaraihi Te Paku* (1889) 7 NZLR 235 at 238.

... The natives are British subjects; their relations to each other are governed by the laws of the land, and not by their usages.

This statement was a clear rejection of Māori custom. It was not until 1941 when *Te Heuheu Tukino v Aotea District Māori Land Board* was decided by the Privy Council, that recognition of *tikanga* Māori re-emerged.[99]

It would be inappropriate to cast aside the 70 years between *R v Symonds*,[100] and *Te Heuheu Tukino v Aotea District Māori Land Board*[101] without due consideration of the detrimental effect on *tikanga* Māori and Māori land rights. The raft of statutes,[102] consistent with Government's land acquisition policies, provided legitimate avenues for the Crown to continue the alienation process.[103] Redress for the wrongful acquisition of lands is addressed today through the Treaty Settlement process.

Had it not been for the imposition of a later incorrect legal finding – a finding "which can no longer be sustained"[104] – *tikanga* Māori would continue to be in force today and would represent a parallel system of criminal justice. It is acknowledged that *tikanga* Māori would have evolved considerably since 1840.

Tikanga Māori is not dependent on a statute for its existence. The failure of our current criminal justice system and legislative framework to recognise *tikanga* Māori does not minimise or detract from its existence. Developing case law observes that statutes, although addressing the general subject area, do not extinguish certain rights.[105] In this way the courts have confirmed this position, thus providing a small window to import the recognition of *tikanga* Māori.

In *R v Mason*, the court noted that:[106]

... [there is a need to] identify some problems that emerge from both the academic literature and the evidence of Mr Jackson. I identify them by reference to my own starting point: nothing should be done to move away from a core criminal justice system that is applicable to all New Zealanders.

Had the court turned its mind to the principles that underpin *tikanga* Māori that share similarities with the developing 'main stream' initiatives, such as therapeutic

---

99   *Te Heuheu Tukino v Aotea District Māori Land Board* [1941] AC 308.
100 *R v Symonds* (1847) NZPCC 387.
101 *Te Heuheu Tukino v Aotea District Māori Land Board* [1941] AC 308.
102 See for example Public Works Act 1928.
103 See discussion in David Williams *Te Kooti Tango Whenua* (Huia Publishing, Wellington, 1999)
104 *R v Mason*, above n 81, at [16].
105 See *Ngāti Apa v Attorney General* [2003] 3 NZLR 643 (CA) and *Paki and Ors v Attorney-General of New Zealand for and on behalf of the Crown* – [2012] NZSC 50 – Elias CJ, Blanchard, Tipping, McGrath and William Young JJ.
106 *R v Mason*, above n 81, at [46].

jurisprudence,[107] then perhaps the court might have adopted a different perspective. It is difficult to ignore the over-representation of Māori within all stages of the criminal justice system. This places a further obligation to meaningfully consider alternative discourses that have shown success in comparative jurisdictions.

With the promise of a fresh perspective on a well-worn request, the case delivered a recycled argument using different ingredients to reach the same conclusion.

C Specialist courts and the New Zealand judicial system

Courts are the guardians of the rule of law, providing a check and balance on the actions of the government and upholding the separation of powers. If the High Court were to be replaced by a specialised court, the High Court would become redundant and a constitutional conundrum would result.[108] This is perceived as an obstacle for the establishment of specialised courts.

The role of a specialist court is largely determined by substantive law and is usually to be found in areas where the rule of law is weak and the role of discretion and policy is strong.[109] The spread or implementation of specialised courts, such as Drug Courts, indicate that both practitioners and judges wish to expand the role of discretion and that the rule of law is weak.

It is acknowledged there are some compromises to the rule of law when specialised courts are implemented. However, if the benefits of specialised courts include the reduction of the offending and recidivism rates, then this must outweigh any compromise to the rule of law.

Family/Domestic Violence Courts

The repetitive nature of offending in a family violence context suggests that the conventional sentencing practices have been ineffective deterrents. Judge Mather noted that while recidivism is a feature of general criminal offending, it is particularly concerning when one victim (usually a partner or former partner) is the object of repeat offending against a number of victims/partners.[110] According to Judge Mather, it was these concerns, as well as the high failure rate for family violence prosecutions due to the refusal, or unwillingness of complainants to give evidence, that led to a new approach. This resulted in the

---

107 See Bruce Winick and David Wexler (eds) *Judging in a Therapeutic Key – Therapeutic Jurisprudence and the Courts* (Carolina Academic Press, Durham, North Carolina, 2003) for discussion.

108 See also Paul McHugh "Court Structure" (August, 2001) Editorial NZLJ at 261.

109 At 261.

110 Judge David Mather "The Waitakere Family Violence Court: A More Focused Approach" (Paper presented, 22 October 2005, District Court of New Zealand) <www.justice.govt.nz>.

establishment of a pilot Family Violence Court at Waitakere in 2001. These courts "specifically aim to respond quickly to cases of family violence, while ensuring the victims' safety and encouraging offenders to take responsibility for their actions in a coordinated way".[111]

The Family Violence Court and the Drug Court have no specific statutory recognition. An administrative action allows the judges to specialise procedures in anticipation of better outcomes. The continuation of these arrangements is not entrenched in legislation and reliant on the commitment by the judges, officials or community groups. It is suggested that should these specialised courts or a pro- posed Indigenous court prove successful then legislation be promulgated and adequate resourcing allocated.

In 2004 Judge Johnson called for a new, effective and workable model for processing family violence cases in the criminal court.[112] Basic certainty should be provided and the fear of unknown characteristics should be removed. According to Judge Johnson, any new system should provide immediacy of response, safety for victims, accountability for guilty defendants, consistency and co-ordination of information sharing, and community involvement. There should also be a ther- apeutic sentencing regime, properly balanced by traditional sentences, such as incarceration. In addition, the responses should be culturally workable.

Family Violence Courts have been established in Waitakere in 2001, Manukau in 2005 and Auckland in March 2007. Currently, the Family Violence Courts hear criminal cases in eight District Courts, with a dual focus on both the victim and offender.[113]

The attention paid to details, such as venue, rostering, and the communication and reflective processes between all the stakeholders (judges, defence bar, duty solicitors, family law, probation, victim advisors, Preventing Violence in the Home, prosecution, Legal Aid Services and court staff) contribute to the initial success of such a Court. As in Canada this continual sharing and communication between the stakeholders is viewed as key to the ongoing success.[114]

Whilst many aspects of the new Family Violence Courts are working well, there are fundamental problems that could seriously impede their long-term success.[115]

---

111   Elizabeth Richardson, Katey Thom and Brian McKenna "The Evolution of Problem-Solving Courts in New Zealand and Australia: A Trans-Tasman Comparative" in Richard Wiener and Eve Brank (eds) *Problem Solving Courts* (Springer, USA, 2013) at 193.
112   Catriona MacLennan "Judge Says Domestic Violence Court Process a 'Masquerade'" (2004) Auckland District Law Society Issue 18 <www.adls.org.nz>.
113   P Boshier "Investing in Life: Meeting the Cost of Family Violence" (2011) 39 NZ Lawyer Extra; see also Richardson, Thom and McKenna, above n 111, at 193.
114   Judge Lex de Jong "Family Violence Court Forum" (Paper presented to an Auckland District Law Seminar, Building, 9th April 2008, Auckland); see also A Mills and others, *Family Violence Courts: A Review of the Literature* (Centre for Mental Health Research, Auckland, 2013) at 7.
115   See T Knaggs, F Leahy and N Soboleva *The Manukau Family Violence Court: An Eva-luation of the Family Violence Court Process* (Ministry of Justice, Wellington, August 2008) where they note that the "Manukau Family Violence Court is providing an

One problem included the stopping violence programmes, as research has found that these do not guarantee success.[116] It is clear that most family violence occurs under the radar of the criminal justice system. The use of s 106 of the Sentencing Act 2002 (discharge without conviction) is of concern as it provides little in the way of offender accountability. In addition, s 106 orders do not leave an accurate record of offending which is required in order to make appropriate decisions about future offending.

Finally, there appears to be an emphasis and reliance on the role of the judge.[117] First, judges take proactive steps to monitor and encourage feedback from the stakeholders, thus ensuring the workability of the Family Violence Court. Secondly, judges consistently tell offenders that they must take responsibility for their abusive behaviour and that crimes of violence towards family members are unacceptable. Without firm sentencing directives or Family Violence Court policy guidelines, there is no guarantee that all judges who sit in the Family Violence Court will adopt the same practices.

According to Judge Lex de Jong, Family Violence Courts are here to stay and over the next few years the numbers of such courts will increase.[118] Co-operation between the stakeholder groups in monitoring the process and consistency from the judiciary are keys to the success of the Family Violence Courts. It is suggested that the shortcomings identified, such as offender accountability, reliance on stopping violence programmes and decisions relating to future offending, can be met through the implementation of a *tikanga*-based approach. Notwithstanding this success, attributed largely to the role of the judge, the ability to sustain this consistency can be problematic. It is suggested that the use of a traditional forum and *tikanga* practices can alleviate this concern.

Drug Courts

A New Zealand study indicated that 80 per cent of crime is driven by alcohol and other forms of drugs.[119] Alcohol and other forms of drugs feature in 33 per cent of all fatal road crashes and in 21 per cent of serious injury crashes with a social cost of $875 million, including costs for minor injuries.[120] The victims' costs are estimated at $400 million each year, and for alcohol and other forms of

alternative response to family violence and most key informants believed this court's approach was very positive because it attempted to respond to family violence holistically".
116 Deborah Mackenzie and Holly Carrington *Monitoring Report for the Auckland Family Violence Court The First Three Months 27 March 2007–30 June 2007* (Preventing Violence in the Home, Auckland, November 2007).
117 Like many specialist courts a factor of a Family Violence Court is one judge, one court and the use of treatment and education programmes.
118 Judge Lex de Jong, above n 114.
119 See Gerald Waters *The Case for Alcohol and Other Drug Treatment Courts in New Zealand* (2011) <www.drugcourts.co.nz >.
120 Above.

drugs, the overall cost to society is $6.88 billion.[121] In referring to recent statistics, a former Labour spokesman for the courts, Rick Barker noted:[122]

> The cost per year per prisoner is $91,000;[123] $44 million per year could be saved by reducing recidivism from its current rate of 68 per cent (74 per cent for Māori) to 20 per cent; and only 6.1 per cent of the Department of Corrections budget goes to 'reintegration', almost none of which is for low-level offenders.

Taken in context there are clear reasons for their introduction, according to Hon. Peggy Fulton Hora, Judge of the Superior Court of California (Ret.), we have 'Drug Courts' because:[124]

> Alcohol, other drugs and crime is [sic] too broad for any single agency to tackle alone, incarceration doesn't prevent crime for those with substance use disorders; and Drug courts bring judges, prosecutors, defense attorneys, court personnel, probation and treatment providers together to solve the problem.

In New Zealand there are two drug courts that operate within the youth justice system. One is based in Christchurch and focuses on enhancing the treatment of offenders who have a serious drug dependency that has contributed to their repeated offending.[125] The other is based in Auckland for 'at risk' youth with mental health and/or drug and alcohol issues, called the Intensive Monitoring Group.[126]

Appearances before these two courts are accepted following recommendations from FGCs. To be eligible the youth must be a repeat offender and exhibit a moderate to serious drug dependency. These courts, like other specialised courts, hold the offender accountable, whilst addressing the concerns and interests of the victims. The victim has opportunities to attend the initial FGC and together with the other stakeholders, including police, court staff and health agencies, will assist in the development of a treatment plan for the offender. After the successful

---

121 Above.
122 Rick Barker, cited in Waters, above n 119, at 14; see also New Zealand Labour Party "Barker Asks Committee to Hold Recidivism Inquiry" (Press release, 15 December 2010) <www.scoop.co.nz>; see also positive comments made by Rick Barker on Drug Courts in New Zealand Labour Party "A Pilot isn't a Policy" (Press release, 20 October 2011) <www.scoop.co.nz>.
123 See Department of Corrections *Men's Prison at Wiri: Facts and Factsheets* (Department of Corrections, Wellington, 2014) <www.corrections.govt.nz>.
124 Hon Peggy Fulton Hora Judge of the Superior Court of California (Ret.) "Adult Alcohol and Other Drug Treatment Courts: Will They Work in New Zealand?" (Seminar given at University of Auckland, School of Law, Auckland, 28 April 2011).
125 Richardson and others, above n at 190.
126 At 190.

completion of the treatment plan, balance or healing should be realised for the offender, victim and community.

A pilot Alcohol and Other Drug Treatment Court has been established in Waitakere. Again it is still early days, but it is suggested that, following international trends, some degree of success will be expected. A recent documentary on Māori Television of the pilot Alcohol and Other Drug Treatment Court suggests that the pilot is achieving success and if the offender successfully completes their treatment the probability of re-offending is low.[127]

Māori Land Court[128]

The Māori Land Court was established in 1865 as the Native Land Court of New Zealand with the primary purpose of changing title from Māori ancestrally owned land into individual titles to generate land availability for settlers. This purpose has now changed where the general objective of the Court is to retain Māori land and ensure its effective use.[129]

The jurisdiction of the Māori Land Court does not extend to criminality, but involves claims in law or equity related to the ownership of Māori freehold land, claims to recover damages for trespass to Māori freehold and to determine any proceedings founded on contract or tort where the damage relates to Māori freehold land.[130] Nonetheless, Te Ture Whenua Māori Act 1993 adheres to *tikanga* Māori values throughout. For instance, there is a provision for additional members to be called upon when the matter referred is one of *tikanga* Māori.[131] In light of the legislative inclusion of *tikanga* Māori within the Act, if the jurisdiction of the Court was expanded to initially include summary offences and available also to non-Māori, similar to the *marae*-based Courts, this potentially provides a basis for an Indigenous court.

Children, Young Persons and Their Families Act 1989 – Youth Court

The Youth Court is a division of the District Court[132] and hears most criminal cases involving young people between the ages of 14 and 16, including serious

127 "'Drug Court' Māori Television screened Monday 1 September, 2014". <https://www.māoritelevision.com/tv/shows/pakipumeka-aotearoa-new-zealand-documentaries/S01E001/drug-court>

128 See also Chapter 8 'A New System' for a discussion on a possible extension of the Māori Land Court jurisdiction to include criminal and civil cases.

129 Te Ture Whenua Māori Act 1993, s 17.

130 Section 17.

131 Section 32.

132 Children Young Persons and their Families Act 1989 s 329; see also recent presentation by Judge Becroft "Signed, Sealed (But Not Yet Fully) Delivered" at the Judges at the Healing Courts and Plans People, International Therapeutic Jurisprudence Conference October 9–10, First Nations Long House, Vancouver, British Columbia, Canada.

offences.[133] The public are generally excluded[134] as youth are seen as "less responsible than adults and may have offended as a result of disadvantage, or deficiencies in their background".[135] Further public access may impact negatively on rehabilitation for the offender.

Upon first appearance the young person is asked to plead 'denied' or 'not denied'. If not denied then the Judge will adjourn the case to allow a Family Group Conference (FGC) to be convened.[136] As long as the youth admits the offence, the FGC then has the task of agreeing on the appropriate actions and or sanctions that should result and subsequent recommendations are provided to the court.[137] A FGC can be ordered by the Judge at any stage of the proceedings if the Judge deems it warranted.[138]

If the charge is denied then a court date is set and the matter proceeds to a defended hearing. If the offence is proved, the Judge will adjourn the case and refer it to a FGC,[139] which will decide how the youth should be dealt with and provide recommendations to the court.[140] The Judge is not bound by these recommendations but must have regard for them.[141]

If the requirements of the FGC have been satisfied within the agreed time-frame, the case is usually discharged.[142] However, the Judge makes further orders where the FGC plan has not been completed successfully, such as imposing a fine, disqualification of driving or community work.[143]

Although there is no explicit mention of restorative justice in the CYPF Act, McElrea categorises three elements of the CYPF Act as restorative in nature. First, "the transfer of state power from the courts to the family and community; second, group consensus decision-making in the FGC; and third, the involvement of victims leading up to a healing process".[144]

Notwithstanding the positive effect and inclusion of FGC in the court process, the current legal system sidelines the essence of *tikanga* Māori in favour of a law devoid of, and not grounded in Indigenous values. Indigenous peoples, such as

---

133 See Institute of Judicial Studies *Youth Court Bench Book* (3rd ed, Institute of Judicial Studies, Wellington, 2008) for an example as cited by Tinsley and McDonald, above n 51 at 204.

134 Children Young Persons and Their Families Act 1989, s 258 (d).

135 New Zealand Law Commission *Seeking Solutions Options for Change to the New Zealand Court System* (New Zealand Law Commission, Wellington, December 2002) Preliminary Paper 52 at 149.

136 Children Young Persons and their Families Act 1989, s 258 (d) and 259 (1).

137 At s 258 (d).

138 At s 281B.

139 At s 247 (e).

140 At s 258 (d).

141 At s 279.

142 At s 282 or 283 (a).

143 At s 283 for full list.

144 F W M McElrea "A New Model of Justice" in F W M McElrea and B J Brown (eds) *The Youth Court in New Zealand: Four Papers* (Legal Research Foundation, Auckland, 1993) as cited by Tinsley and McDonald, above n 51 at 204.

Māori, are unduly susceptible to government interference. Those who first created and administered the law did not ensure that Indigenous people were granted the necessary structures to maintain and promote their identity against the assimilative pressures of the majority.[145]

The absence of provisions to protect Indigenous rights has resulted in an unacceptable socio-economic status for Indigenous peoples within a generally prosperous society.

Despite the statistics that indicate Indigenous people are disproportionately represented in the criminal justice system, unlike Australia, New Zealand has not yet developed or proposed an Indigenous court to address this issue. The recent initiative to establish a Drug Court in Auckland builds on the presence of the existing Drug Court in Christchurch. The drugs courts and *marae*-based courts, as alternatives to the Youth Court, are the only other specialised courts in New Zealand with respect to criminal offending.

The underlying philosophy of the Drug Court model is therapeutic jurisprudence. This approach recognises that the court processes, and in particular, the role of the judge can be used to facilitate treatment processes. Reports indicate that the rate of offending was lower for young people who attended the Youth Drug Court.[146] The key feature was the consistency of appearing before the same judge on a regular basis. The recent justice initiative of '*marae*-based courts' provides an interesting alternative.

Marae-*based courts* – Ngā Kooti Rangatahi[147]

The call for an alternative criminal justice system for Māori is not new. In 1988 Puao Te Ata Tu stated that:[148]

> Māori law observance depended on the maintenance of the mores of communal society. The Western Response ... was individuals distanced from their communities but later to be inflicted back on them ... It is not suggested that the old Māori ways should now be restored, but that ought not inhibit the search for a greater sense of family and community involvement and responsibility in the maintenance of law and order.

The *marae*-based courts originated from the Marae Youth Monitoring Court as a specialist Youth Court. The initiative to convene a specialised problem-solving

145 John Borrows *Drawing Out the Law* (University of Toronto Press, Toronto, 2010) at 21.
146 Ministry of Justice *Publications and Reports* (Ministry of Justice, Wellington, 2004) <www.justice.govt.nz>.
147 I am grateful to Judge Heemi Taumaunu for the opportunity to visit and attend the sitting of Te Kooti Rangatahi at Waipareira in December 2013.
148 The Report of the Ministerial Advisory Committee on a Māori perspective for the Department of Social Welfare (Department of Social Welfare, Wellington, 1988) at 74 <www.msd.govt.nz>.

Youth Court sitting at Poho-o-Rawiri Marae, Gisborne was piloted by Judge Heemi Taumaunu in 2008. There are now 12 operating in the North Island and the first South Island *marae*-based court was opened in Christchurch on 28 April 2014 with the first sitting. Former Minister Chester Borrows commented that:[149]

> ... the establishment of the latest court is a positive step for addressing youth offending in Christchurch. I want to congratulate Judge Taumanu and Principal Youth Court Judge Andrew Becroft, who have driven the successful expansion of the Rangatahi court programme, and thank them once for their commitment to helping our young people who have lost their way.

Marae-based courts are an initiative of the judiciary that builds on existing programmes for offenders[150] and are informed by the Koori Courts in Australia.[151]

This is the first time that a New Zealand Court has conducted criminal cases on a *marae* within the jurisdiction of the Youth Court. Most offenders referred to the programme are Māori and the process incorporates Māori *tikanga*/customs and protocols.

The judges of Ngā Kooti Rangatahi consider that "*rangatahi*/youth offending is related to lack of self-esteem, a confused sense of self identity and a strong sense of resentment which in turn leads to anger and ultimately leads to offending".[152] Judge Bidois noted:[153]

> Most offending is feelings based. Resentment, anger, greed, and hate are common feelings that motivate offending. To change an offender one therefore needs to change how they feel. The best way to encourage this change is to place the offender in a community of people who understand and recognise his or her feelings, but who also have the power and respect to alter those feelings. With understanding comes a commitment to accept the burden of punishment and with support comes the commitment to accept the burden of rehabilitation. There needs to be inclusion rather than exclusion to effect change. This process can be achieved on a marae.

The ability to reconnect the offender with their identity and *whānau* is seen to contribute positively to the success of the process. The ultimate outcome for the

---

149   See New Zealand Law Society "First South Island Rangatahi Court for Christchurch" (24 March 2014) <www.my.lawsociety.org.nz>.
150   For example Te Whānau Āwhina programme, a restorative justice programme that involves the voluntary participation of the victim of the crime and the offender and *whānau* in discussions, usually within a *marae* setting, to 'restore' the relationship, fix the damage that has been done and prevent further crimes from occurring.
151   *Evaluation of the Early Outcomes of Ngā Kooti Rangatahi*. Submitted to the Ministry of Justice 17 December 2012 at 8.
152   At 8.
153   At 25.

judge is "for the *rangatahi* to be empowered to achieve their potential".[154] Challenges including adequate resourcing and continuing support by the *whānau* and wider community, however, will influence the outcome.[155] According to Judge Clark:[156]

> Of course Te Kooti Rangatahi cannot 'just' happen. We rely heavily on the support of a number of people and organisations. Kirikiriroa Marae and marae whānau, the kuia, the kaumatua and the trustees have been all embracing of this initiative. The Courts, Ministry of Justice, Child Youth and Family, Police Youth Services, Iwi Liaison Officers, Iwi Social Services, Programme Providers, Youth Advocates and our Lay Advocate are all critical to this initiative happening to give our rangatahi and their whānau the opportunity to have cases heard in arguably a more appropriate way and with the opportunity for greater rangatahi whānau and community engagement and involvement.

Process

The *marae* process is open to all, providing a possibility that non-Māori may also seek to be heard in this process.[157] Although Ngā Kooti Rangatahi are designed specifically to support *tikanga* Māori, they are available to any young person, regardless of their ethnicity or identity. There is no mandatory requirement for young people to be dealt with on the *marae*. If this option is not sought, the normal Youth Court process applies.

Before the consideration of a *marae* as a venue, the process adheres to the normal Youth Court procedures. Upon appearance at the Youth Court, the *rangatahi* is assigned an advocate and the case is remanded.

The charges are usually for lower level offending; for instance, burglary, unlawful interference with motor vehicles, traffic offences, shoplifting, theft and willful damage. However, more serious charges, including aggravated robbery and cases of serious offending by 12 and 13 year olds, may also be heard.

The charge is usually not denied or admitted in the normal manner in the Youth Court. If the charge is admitted, a lay advocate is still appointed.

A Family Group Conference (FGC) is convened and held in the normal manner where the young person who has offended and their family, victim,

---

154 At 9.
155 See also Study by the Expert Mechanism on the Rights of Indigenous Peoples *Access to justice in the promotion of indigenous peoples, restorative justice, indigenous juridical systems and access to justice for indigenous women, children and youth, and persons with disabilities* A/HRC/27/65 August 2014 that notes "An additional crucial hurdle is the financing of indigenous juridical systems. Without sufficient resources, these systems are not sustainable and their contribution to ensuring access to justice is compromised."
156 At 74.
157 Judge Heemi Taumaunu "Te Kooti Rangatahi o Hoani Waititi Ka pu te ruha, ka hao te rangatahi!" (2010) unpublished.

agencies, social worker and advocate discuss and approve a FGC plan. The aim of the plan is to encourage the young person to accept responsibility for their actions, find practical ways to rectify the situation, ascertain why they have offended and how amends can be made.[158] The *marae* hearings are designed to monitor the young person's performance of the FGC plan and also to sentence the young person on completion of the FGC plan. If the victim disagrees with the referral to Ngā Kooti Rangatahi, the *rangatahi* will not be referred. The presiding judge, after considering the FGC plan, will make the final decision on the eligibility of the *rangatahi* to have their case monitored by Ngā Kooti Rangatahi. If the referral is accepted, the *rangatahi* is remanded until the next sitting date. Whilst on remand the *rangatahi* is encouraged to learn their *whakapapa*/family tree and *pepeha*/sayings to inform the judge when they appear before him or her.[159] Unlike the Koori Courts in Australia, the presiding judge does not meet with the Elder and Respected Persons (ERP) to discuss the list commencing each morning.

Similar to the Koori Courts and in accordance with Māori protocol, the *marae* hearings begin with a *pōwhiri*/a formal Māori welcome that is initiated on the morning of the court hearing. A *kuia*/respected female elder stands outside the *whare nui*/traditional meeting house and calls the judge, court staff, lawyers, social workers, lay advocates, respected elders, as well as young people appearing and their families onto the *marae*. The *pōwhiri* is supported by the *tangata whenua*/local people.

A *kuia* from the visitor group will respond to the call of welcome. All those present then move inside the *whare nui* where formal speeches are conducted. Once the formalities are completed, everyone proceeds to the dining hall for a cup of tea.

The court then convenes and the proceedings commence inside the *whare nui*. The *kaumatua*/respected elder, who also assists in the *Marae* Court process, then recites a *karakia*/a prayer. When each case is called, the *kaumātua*, who sits next to the judge, will give a specific speech of welcome to the young person and their family.

The young person is encouraged to respond to the welcome by saying a *mihi*/a Māori speech. This is aimed at re-establishing the young person in their identity as Māori.

The young person and his or her family are invited to participate fully in the hearing, as are all of the professionals. Together with the *whānau*/families, *hapū*/sub-tribes and *iwi*/tribes, solutions are actively sought with the co-operation of agencies.

Additional applicable principles include holding the young person accountable for their actions, ensuring the victim's issues and interests are recognised and

---

158 See Ministry of Justice *Rangatahi Court: Evaluation of the Early Outcomes of Te Kooti Rangatahi* (Ministry of Justice, Wellington, 17 December, 2012) at 21.
159 At 21.

addressing the underlying causes of the offending behaviour. The ultimate goal is to keep communities safer by reducing recidivism.

The judge will then sum up the proceeding by noting the next date for appearance of the *rangatahi*. At the completion of the hearing, *whānau* members are invited to address the *rangatahi*.

The hearing concludes with the *kaumātua* and judge participating in a *hongi*/a pressing of noses symbolising the meeting of *mauri*, with the young person and their families, and finally a *karakia*. This is in accordance with Māori protocol.

Holding the process in the *whare nui* on the *marae* is a positive step. It provides an environment that seeks to reconnect the offender with their culture and community. The implementation of the Māori language, *tikanga* Māori/Māori practices and protocols, into the court process further consolidates this reconnection. Encouraging the offender to be accountable and addressing the underlying reasons for offending also contribute to the positive nature of *marae*-based courts. The environment of the *marae* has engendered the ability for *rangatahi* to engage, with one *rangatahi* noting:[160]

> It's easier to stand up in court cause [sic] you feel like everyone is your family. You're able to let it out. Go hard – let it out. Youth Court is a cold court. The judges and lawyers – everyone is more subdued and long faced. We all share kai here. It makes a huge difference to how you feel. A far better process. When we hongi we are connecting our mana to one another. It's less tense. Obviously we are willing to speak a bit freer, more comfortable. (Male *rangatahi*)

The criminal justice system should be applauded for seeking a creative path to assist Māori youth offending. However, *tikanga* Māori and the realm of Te Ao Māori are far more complex than expressed in the current *marae*-based court process.[161]

The *marae*-based procedure is time consuming and lengthy thus restricting the ability to effectively reduce the long hearing lists. This would need to be factored in and economically weighed against the costs of incarceration if a *marae*-based Indigenous court was to be established.

Case study[162]

A 14-year-old who has admitted a charge of graffiti crime stands before Judge Heemi Taumaunu.

---

160 At 36.
161 Matiu Dickson "The Rangatahi Court" [2011] 19 Waikato Law Review at 86.
162 Marty Sharp *"Rangatahi Courts: A Quiet Revolution in Teen Justice" Newswire* (online, New Zealand, October 2011) <www.newswirenz.wordpress.com>.

"Have you got your mihi ready to go today?" the judge asks.

"*No.*"

"I'm sure we can help your maunga"

"*My what?*"

"Your maunga."

"*Not too sure.*"

"You knew it last time. Have you forgotten it?" the judge says, referring to the boy's previous appearance on the same charge in May.

"*Yep.*"

"What's the name of your marae?"

"*I dunno.*"

"Have you ever been to it?"

"*Nah.*"

Kaumatua Denis Hansen, who sits alongside the judge, stands and recites the entire *mihi*, naming the boy's mountain, river, *marae*, *iwi* and *hapū*.

Then he tells the boy: "Lunch is at one o'clock. Don't go away after that. You're going to have a bit of whakapapa education."

"Matua will teach you your *mihi*," the judge says. "After that you can go away. We're going to see a lot of improvement next time. We expect that from you. I expect you to be able to say the *mihi* the *kaumatua* just said to you," the judge says.

He says that the boy, who is Ngati Kahu, needs more monitoring.

The boy's advocate, Steve Trent, says he has improved attendance of his alternative education course, turning up 80 per cent of the time.

What was ... [a] zero attendance a few months ago, the judge [now] ... expects 100 per cent attendance and [enquires] ... why this is not happening. The boy says he has lost his bus pass.

When the boy first appeared, he was sentenced to 80 hours community work, and was ordered to attend courses on life skills as well as alternative education. He was also put under a 24-hour curfew.

It transpired that he had not been completing his community work.

After a brief conversation involving elders, a social worker and the judge, a *kaumatua* volunteers to collect the boy from his home each weekend to bring him to the *marae* where he can carry out his community work. The *kaumatua* says this will also provide an opportunity for him to teach the boy his *mihi*.

Judge Taumaunu is pleased with that and adds that it has been three months since the boy last offended. He remands him on bail to reappear on October 6.

Evaluation

Offences before the *marae*-based court system are confined to those perpetrated by youth.

While the Rangatahi Court process is focused on Māori youth, both Māori and non-Māori are eligible. This is an attempt to overcome the perception that separate procedures or special treatment have been instituted. It is suggested that this should also apply to any Indigenous court that is established.

The key findings of the Rangatahi Court Evaluation Report noted:[163]

> Rangatahi reported experiencing positive outcomes as a result of their engagement with Ngā Kooti Rangatahi. The outcomes reported by rangatahi were consistent with the views of youth justice professionals and the observations of the evaluation team.

The significant factors of success included the *marae* as a venue, the positive impact of *kaumatua* on the *rangatahi*, the impact of the lay advocates, and the collective commitment of the participants.[164] A fuller explanation of the actual outcomes noted that:[165]

> the levels of attendance by rangatahi and whanau were high and rangatahi felt welcome and respected. Rangatahi experienced a sense of pride and achievement as a result of delivering their pepeha and felt better connected to their culture. Rangatahi understood the court process showing improved behavior and positive attitude, taking responsibility for their offending and its impact. When nearing the end of the FGC monitoring process rangatahi showed improved communication skills.

Notwithstanding the recognition of *tikanga*, the underlying principle that applies to this approach is not based on *tikanga*, but on the law; that is, to honour and apply the objects and principles in the Children, Young Persons and their Families Act 1989. Although this project represents an attempt to incorporate Māori *tikanga* within the law, it is not designed to abandon the law and start a *tikanga*-based court. That is beyond the jurisdiction of the Rangatahi Court.

When *tikanga* is placed under the auspices of legislation, the robust nature of any *tikanga*-based outcome will become compromised.[166] Further, if the *kawa/* protocol or *tikanga* is not one to which they adhere, this may undermine the

---

163 Ministry of Justice, above n 158, at 9.
164 Ministry of Justice, above n 158, at 60 as cited in *NZ Lawyer Magazine* Issue 200 (25 Jan 2013) <www.nzlawyermagazine.co.nz>.
165 Ministry of Justice, above n 158, at 10.
166 Primarily because the decision maker inevitably will be non-Māori and also when concepts are translated the meaning can be lost; see N Tomas "Māori Concepts of Rangatiratanga, Kaitiakitanga the Environment and Property Rights" in David Grinlinton and Prue Taylor *Legal Aspects of Sustainable Development Property Rights and Sustainability The Evolution of Property Rights to meet Ecological Challenges* (Martinus Nijhoff Publishers, Netherlands, 2011) at 219.

respect that any offender or *whānau* will have for an outcome based on a hybrid process. At this stage it is not clear whether such concerns have been addressed.

It is difficult to overlay two different worldviews; that of Te Ao Pākehā over Te Ao Māori.[167] There are questions about how to handle urban Māori who do not identify with *tikanga* or the notion of the collective, and where they fit in a *marae* court process.[168] One might also ask, which *kawa*/protocol is to be adopted during the *marae* court process? The local *marae* protocol, that of a court, or a protocol with elements of both? What if the *kawa* of the offender does not align with the *kawa* of the marae court process? If the process is to be a *marae* process, then this implies that a *kaumatua*, rather than a judge, should lead the process. In such a situation, if a person who does not affiliate with the *marae* or the offender leads the process, this is a slight and a trampling on the *mana*/ancestral power of the *kaumatua* and the *whānau*.

Ideally, the *kaumatua* should be connected to the offender through *whakapapa* as it is the *kaumatua* who holds the responsibility for the offender. It is difficult to understand how, in a *marae* court, the judge can have the same status as a *kaumatua*, when there is no *whakapapa* connection or kin-based sense of responsibility.[169]

In smaller communities, such as the *hapū*/sub tribe of Ngati Rehua on Aotea/ Great Barrier Island, this is even more pronounced. Primarily because in these small communities, *kuia* and *kaumatua* are often intimately linked to the offender and a judge is effectively viewed as an outsider, attracting a lesser standing. In this instance it is difficult for the offender to respect the judge, as the offender often perceives their *kuia* or *kaumatua* as having the *mana*/prestige not the judge. And further, the *marae* is his *tūrangawaewae*/place to stand and not that of the judge.

According to Matiu Dickson:[170]

> … Judges are doing the kaumatua's job and thus taking away the last bastion of Māori ownership of the process.
>
> On a marae, he says, all decisions are made by people who are affiliated to the marae, but the final decision rests with the kaumatua who hold the mana of the pā … the marae community should have the right to decide how low-risk young offenders are dealt with.

---

167   Above.
168   See discussion Juan Tauri "Reforming Justice the Potential of Māori Processes" in Eugene McLaughlin and others (eds) *Restorative Justice Critical Issues* (Sage Publications, London, 2003).
169   See also discussion in New Zealand Law Commission *Converging Currents* (NZLC SP 17, Wellington, 2006) at 207 where it notes that "Although expatriate judges are cultural outsiders which may make this task more challenging, some national judges may be cultural outsiders too. In countries with a multiplicity of different customs it is just as difficult for a local judge from a different part of the country to rule on matters of custom as it is for an expatriate judge."
170   "Judges Doing Kaumatua's Job in Youth Courts" *Radio NZ* (online, New Zealand, 13 October 2011) <www.radionz.co.nz>.

Although anecdotal evidence and the Rangatahi Court Evaluation Report indicate some level of success for *marae*-based courts, and this initiative should be applauded, concerns still exist. Dickson stipulates two conditions that should be satisfied prior to the establishment of a *marae*-based court: that the court should "retain *mana* and authority for decisions made concerning the young offender", and that "the young offender should be connected by *whakapapa* to the *marae*".[171] The use of the *marae* as a forum will attract respective *kawa* of the relevant *iwi* group. However, there are concerns when court protocol can supercede the *kawa* of the *marae*.[172]

Marae courts build on the precedent of the Koori Courts in Australia, but do not tackle the root problems of Indigenous offending, such as the legacy of government oppression and the effects of colonisation.[173] This is a view shared by Marchetti and Daly, who state:[174]

> … any effort to address the over-representation of Indigenous people in the criminal justice system must also confront a legacy of government policies and practices over the past two centuries, which systematically disadvantaged and oppressed Indigenous people.

Also, these courts may place further strain on Indigenous communities who are already affected by economic marginalisation and have few social services/resources. Often *kuia* and *kaumatua* voluntarily contribute their time and efforts to this process, thus compounding the economic strain on small Indigenous communities. Unlike the Koori Courts where ERPs are statutorily appointed and are paid a sitting fee, the *kuia* and *kaumatua* from the *marae*-based courts are not.

Having regard to the growing success of these courts and the subsequent increase in numbers of both offenders accessing this court and courts themselves, the economic impact this will have on small regional communities will only be exacerbated. It is notable that the Rangatahi Court Evaluation Report provides positive outcomes for the participants. Although hard statistical data on recidivism rates is notably absent, the former Minister of Justice, Judith Collins, announced that the government's Drivers of Crime progress report indicated that the offending rates for Māori youth between 2008 and 2012 had decreased by 32 per cent.[175]

171 Dickson, above n 161.
172 Judge Stephanie Milroy "Nga Tikanga Māori and the Courts" (2007) Yearbook of NZJ at 18 where she notes can one feel comfortable telling a *kaumatua* (elder) to sit down as it is not his turn to speak?
173 See discussion in Juan Tauri and R Webb "A Critical Appraisal of Responses to Māori Offending" (2012) 3(4) The International Indigenous Policy Journal.
174 Elena Marchetti and Kate Daly "Indigenous Sentencing Courts: Towards a Theoretical and Jurisprudential Model" (2007) 29(3) Sydney Law Review at 443.
175 Judith Collins and Pita Sharples "Youth Māori Offending Down 32 per cent" (press release, 20 August 2013) <www.beehive.govt.nz>; see also Drivers of Crime Progress Report December 2012 Cabinet Social Policy Committee.

Notwithstanding the critique, if a *marae*-based court led by a *kaumatua* who was linked by *whakapapa* to the offender can reduce the offending and recidivism rates for Māori, this would contribute to confronting the legacy of government policies and practices that have systemically disadvantaged Indigenous people. This would result in Māori administering *tikanga* values, imbuing a sense of identity for the offender with the aim of achieving balance in the individual and within the community. Further, if successful, these courts should be adequately resourced to, at the minimum, alleviate the strain on the *marae* and accompanying support people who currently provide these services voluntarily.

Judge Andrew Becroft noted that:[176]

> ... his [Rangatahi Court] is a significant step and there is much overseas interest. That said, I am concerned that in this evolutionary development of Rangatahi Courts the community understands more clearly what Rangatahi Courts are and what they aren't. *They are not a fully-fledged separate youth justice system, and neither are they a sentencing Court* [emphasis added]. None of those involved in Rangatahi Courts (Judges included) are 'imposing a sentence' as is the process in an adult Court. *Those Rangatahi who come to a marae have already undergone a family group conference and it is that conference that has set in place a comprehensive plan to ensure the young person is held to account and that the causes of his/her offending are addressed* [emphasis added]. In the youth justice system (unlike the adult system) the quality of the response to a young person's offending will usually stand or fall on the quality and appropriateness of the family group conference plan. In most cases, it is FGC plan which is accepted by the Youth Court as constituting the complete and the appropriate intervention. The Youth Court imposes no 'sentence' as such other than approving the FGC plan. In a few cases where there can be no agreement as to the components of the plan or the offending is too serious the Court will need to impose a formal Youth Court order which can include a conviction and transfer of the young person to the District Court. But *the Rangatahi Court process is reserved for those young people who admit their offending and who have an appropriate family group conference plan in place* [emphasis added]. The Rangatahi Court aims to ensure that this plan is completed and the young person and their family are supported during their journey to fulfil every aspect of the plan. In this sense, *the Rangatahi Court is not a sentencing Court, but it is a Court that helps empower and galvanise a community based response to the young person's offending* [emphasis added]; it supports and monitors all the components of the family group conference plan formulated in response to the young person's offending.

We have much to learn. We will doubtless make many mistakes as we continue to develop and adjust the Rangatahi Court role and process. But we have begun a journey that we cannot retreat from. To change metaphors, we

---

176 The Rangatahi Newsletter "Special Edition: Rangatahi Courts Hui" at 2 <www.jus tice.govt.nz>.

are all on something of a wave that is now bigger than any of us. We are now riding that wave to its conclusion, and landfall can only be when the disproportionate rates between Māori and non-Māori in the youth justice process are eliminated.

It may be the case that these courts will achieve a transformation of the law in a way that reduces the disproportionately negative outcomes for Māori. Only time will tell.

Matariki Courts

In Kaikohe an initiative led by the former Chief Judge of the District Court, the late Judge Johnson, was the establishment of a Matariki Court. This specialist court, which opened in February 2012, deals with cases involving adult Māori offenders, both prior to sentencing and in potential sentencing options, by focusing on ss 27 and 25 of the Sentencing Act 2002. Of interest is the ability of this court to consider sentencing when the offender has committed a serious violent offence.[177]

Importantly, this court has the support and involvement of the local *iwi*, Nga Puhi and Te Mana o Ngāpuhi Kowhao Rau (TMONK), who work with the offender to address the underlying issues during the sentencing phase. By December 2012 four hearings had been held.

Section 27 stipulates:[178]

> If an offender appears before a court for sentencing, the offender may request the court to hear any person or persons called by the offender to speak on –
>
> (a) the personal, family, whānau, community, and cultural background of the offender:

177 The Crimes Act 1961 section 2 defines a *serious violent offence* as any offence –

(a) that is punishable by a period of imprisonment for a term of 7 years or more; and

(b) where the conduct constituting the offence involves –

    (i) loss of a person's life or serious risk of loss of a person's life; or

    (ii) serious injury to a person or serious risk of serious injury to a person; or

    (iii) serious damage to property in circumstances endangering the physical safety of any person; or

    (iv) perverting the course of justice, where the purpose of the conduct is to prevent, seriously hinder, or seriously obstruct the detection, investigation, or prosecution of any offence –

178 Judge David Carruthers "Community Involvement in Treatment of Offenders Prior to Sentencing: The New Zealand Experience" (paper presented to UNAFEI 147th International Training Conference, Japan, 13 January–10 February 2010) <www.una fei.or.jp/english>.

(b)   the way in which that background may have related to the commission of the offence:

(c)   any processes that have been tried to resolve or that are available to resolve, issues relating to the offence, involving the offender and his or her family, whānau, or community and the victim or victims of the offence:

(d)   how support from the family, whānau, or community may be available to help prevent further offending by the offender:

(e)   how the offender's background, or family, whānau, or community support may be relevant in respect of possible sentences.

This provides a chance for the offender's *whānau, hapū* and *iwi* to address the court. Section 25 stipulates:

Power of adjournment for inquiries as to suitable punishment

(1)   A court may adjourn the proceedings in respect of any offence after the offender has been found guilty or has pleaded guilty and before the offender has been sentenced or otherwise dealt with for any 1 or more of the following purposes:

(a)   to enable inquiries to be made or to determine the most suitable method of dealing with the case:

(b)   to enable a restorative justice process to occur:

(c)   to enable a restorative justice agreement to be fulfilled:(d) to enable a rehabilitation programme or course of action to be undertaken:

(da)   to determine whether to impose an instrument forfeiture order and, if so, the terms of that order:

(e)   to enable the court to take account of the offender's response to any process, agreement, programme, or course of action referred to in paragraph (b), (c), or (d).

The programme offers four options for the offender, ranging from no involvement with sentencing proceeding to full involvement with both the victim and offender participating and completing participation prior to sentence. The four options are:[179]

Option 1 – the defendant declines a section 27 hearing then the sentencing process would proceed in the usual way.

Option 2 – the defendant chooses a section 27 hearing, they may have a member of their whānau to speak on their behalf. If the speaker is there then the sentencing is likely to go ahead on that day. Alternatively, counsel may ask for an adjournment so that the support person can attend. There

179 Hauauru Takiwa *Te Kooti o Matariki* (Report No 1210, 16 October 2012) <www.haua uru.org>.

are no referrals; however, the defendant may offer restorative justice if the victim is willing.

Option 3 – the defendant chooses a section 27 hearing. An initial assessment is made by the court Kairuruku (co-ordinator), who talks to the defendant about what section 27 offers as well as what community services and other agencies are available to help or support the defendant. The Kairuruku then connects the defendant with these services as required, which could include restorative justice. Either the Kairuruku or defence counsel will then stand up and suggest to the Judge that option 3 is the pathway for that particular offender. The sentencing is then adjourned to give the defendant time to complete any programmes that may be deemed to be helpful.

Option 4 – the defendant chooses a section 27 hearing. This is a much more intensive option and requires a commitment from both the defendant and their whānau. This is where Te Mana o Ngāpuhi Kowhao Rau (TMONK) get involved. They are very clear with the defendant that this opportunity is not a "get out of jail free card" and that they will commit to the process as long as the defendant and their whānau commit to the work. This then involves the sentencing being adjourned to an interim date. This is to give TMONK time to start working with the defendant and their whānau and to complete a report which includes a plan that will help the defendant to address any underlying courses [sic] to their offending. If this report and plan is accepted by the Judge then the sentencing is adjourned again so that the plan can be completed. An important part of this process is that the work is completed before the sentencing, this gives the defendant the opportunity to prove their commitment, to the victim, their whānau and the court.

This provides an opportunity for the offender to access available community services in order to address their social needs and the underlying causes of offending. By addressing the cause of offending together with the support of the *whānau*, it is suggested that this will help reduce the recidivism and disproportionate offending rates for Māori.

By increasing the involvement of *whānau*, including the use of *te reo*,[180] and assisting the offender with available services, this Court seeks to empower the community. As such, it is unsurprising that early results have been positive. However, unlike the Rangatahi Courts where the victim's consent is required, in the Matariki Court, the victim's consent is not required for the offender to fall within the jurisdiction of the court.

Institutions such as courts and correctional facilities often perform roles of local communities in identifying and dealing with their own problems, particularly for

---

180 See s 3 of the Māori Language Act 1987 that provides for the Māori Language to be an official language of New Zealand; and s 4 of the Māori Language Act 1987 provides for the right to speak Māori in legal proceedings.

less serious offences.[181] The challenge, according to Judge Carruthers, is returning that power and responsibility back to the communities from which these
offenders originate.[182] It is acknowledged that many players within the criminal
justice system, including judges, probation officers and officials, support and
include the involvement of the community and Māori. The Matariki Courts are an
example of this. It is unfortunate that in these early stages accurate statistics are not
available.[183]

In light of the paucity of statistics, reflecting on how this court would
operate, a suggestion on how existing cases may be processed by a Matariki
Court may prove helpful. In this regard the following section analyses two
cases *Tutakangahau v R*[184] and *R v Wawatai*[185] against the Sentencing Act and
Bail Act respectively.

Sentencing Act 2002

R v Wawatai

The offender, Mr Wawatai,[186] has been charged with manslaughter, arson and
male assaults female.[187] After considering the offending, the impact of the
offending and personal circumstances the court begins to determine the appropriate sentence with reference to previous case law, elements of premeditation,
violence and vulnerability. A sentence of 13 years imprisonment is passed after no
mitigating factors could be found.

Had this case been determined by a Matariki Court, in light of the seriousness
of the offending, it would be recommended that Option 4, a much more intense
option, be taken. Any sentencing would be deferred until a later date to allow an
organisation, such as TMONK, to work with the offender and *whānau* to address
underlying issues. From the facts it appears that the offender has the support of
his family.[188] It may be that an anger management or a male against violence
course is planned for the offender. As alcohol was identified as linked with the
offending[189] an appropriate Drug and Alcohol rehabilitation course should also

181 Carruthers, above n 57.
182 Above.
183 The Ministry of Justice acknowledges the difficulty in recording the data from the
Matariki Courts and therefore cannot provide accurate statistics of utilisation or
results but are endeavouring to find methods to do so. At the time of writing these
were not available http://www.justice.govt.nz/.
184 *Tutakangahau v R* [2014] NZCA 279.
185 *R v Wawatai* [2014] NZHC 2374 [3 October 2014].
186 Although not explicit it is understood that the offender is of Māori descent.
187 Respective penalties are provided for in the Crimes Act 1961, s 177(1); Maximum
penalty is life imprisonment, s 267(1). Maximum penalty is 14 years' imprisonment s
194. Maximum penalty is two years' imprisonment *R v Wawatai* at [1].
188 At [13] and [17].
189 At [18].

be undertaken.[190] It may also be that some form of *muru* is paid to the victim's family; this may assist to overcome the ill feelings held by the victim's family.[191] *Muru* could be a form of financial payment, together with work related assistance for the family and regular group or community meetings. This plan and report from TMONK would then be submitted to the Judge who, if accepted, will adjourn the sentencing so the plan can be completed.

Alternatively, if the offender chose Option 1, the provisions of the Sentencing Act 2002 would apply. The Sentencing Act provides a raft of sentencing options,[192] including imprisonment, home detention, home detention or community based sentences that includes community work, supervision, intensive supervision or community detention,[193] a fine[194] and or a combination of these options.[195] If the offender presents with, for instance, a mental illness, the judge can intervene and commit the offender to a programme, such as Odyssey House, and impose judicial monitoring.[196] If successfully completed this may provide grounds for variation or cancellation of their sentence.[197]

Mr Wawatai has been charged with an offence punishable by imprisonment, so it is highly unlikely that any option other than prison would be considered by the court. However, if he was to apply for supervision,[198] this could be granted if the court was satisfied that a sentence of supervision would reduce the likelihood of his reoffending through rehabilitation and reintegration of the offender.[199] As Mr Wawatai is charged with more than one offence, the offences would be served concurrently.[200] If supervision was granted, the sentence would be not less than six months but not more than one year, substantially less than 13 years sentence imposed by the court. The standard reporting conditions would be required to be followed, including reporting and residential address notification.[201]

It would be assumed that in light of the nature of the offender and the offence committed, special conditions are imposed,[202] including counselling[203] and

---

190 The nature of offending is serious and unlikely that a deferral to the existing AODT Court would be an option, nonetheless the programmes utilised by the Court may be instructive for cases such as this.
191 *R v Wawatai* at [14].
192 Section 10A (2) lists the hierarchy of sentences.
193 Section 44 (a), (b), (c), (d).
194 Section 39 as a monetary penalty.
195 Although it is noted that a prison sentence can not be combined with any option except some form of reparation and fine only if authorised by an Act specifying the offence. Also home detention cannot be combined with supervision, intensive supervision or community detention.
196 Subpart 2B Sentencing Act 2002.
197 Section 80ZM.
198 Section 45 (1) (a).
199 Section 46.
200 Section 47.
201 Section 49.
202 Section 50.
203 Section 51 (a).

placement within a *marae* environment to take advantage of any existing programmes, such as Te Whānau Āwhina.[204] If the offender was unable to fulfil these requirements the supervision sentence can be cancelled and the original sentence of 13 years imprisonment reinstated.[205]

If a supervision sentence was not granted due to the seriousness of Mr Wawatai's offending, he could apply for a sentence of intensive supervision.[206] The requirements and access to programmes are similar to that of supervision,[207] but the time period is longer and the reporting obligations more rigorous. In light of Mr Wawatai's alcohol problem, the judge could impose a special condition that Mr Wawatai be subject to judicial monitoring. Nonetheless, again due to the seriousness of his offence and the purpose of the Act, balancing public safety, deterrence and rehabilitation,[208] it is unlikely that a sentence other than prison is imposed. It is more probable that a supervised sentence would apply to *Tutakangahau v R* (below), as the offence is less serious.

The provisions of the Sentencing Act 2002 support the use of programmes that are centred around the *marae* and *iwi* and *hapū* groups. The ability to address any psychiatric or addiction issue is also available, as is judicial monitoring. These attributes would underpin a proposed Indigenous court. It could be that if such a Court was established, reliance could be placed on these provisions of the Sentencing Act 2002.

Nonetheless, although the Act contains provisions for *marae* programmes and *iwi* and *hapu*, these are very, very seldom used, indicative of an unwillingness of the judge to commit to these alternatives.[209] Although there is provision for judicial monitoring, unlike a specialist court that is underpinned by therapeutic jurisprudence, there is no requirement or obligation on the judge to entertain a relationship with the offender or with community members in a *marae* setting. On the occasion a *marae*-based sentence is imposed, there are often challenges from other players within the justice system.[210]

It is suggested that a more inclusive approach, such as that of the Matariki, Te Kooti Rangatahi and AODT Court, be adopted. This would require a change in behaviours.

Although these programmes could contain a requirement to provide reparation services to the victim, it is not explicit.[211] Reparation, as *muru*, may be necessary to fulfil any reciprocity obligations. Further, there is a lacuna between arrest and

204 Section 51 (c) (ii).
205 Section 54.
206 Section 54B.
207 Sections 54B–54L.
208 Section 7 and 8.
209 This is based on a raft of personal court observations and also academic discussions with counsel attending court.
210 See "Police unhappy at marae sentence" NZH Nov 27, 1999. Judge Unwin granted a *marae*-based sentence and a 15-month suspended prison sentence for two years.
211 Although available within a sentence of community work, see Section 55.

sentencing where there is no express provision for *iwi* involvement or support that an Indigenous court could potentially oversee.

Tutakangahau v R

The offender, an 18-year-old Māori youth, was convicted of two counts of burglary, pleaded guilty, was sentenced to 11 months imprisonment and now appeals this sentence to the Court of Appeal.[212] In reviewing the previous lower court's decision, the Court of Appeal found that there has been no recognition of the fact that one of the reasons identified for a discount for youth was the greater capacity for rehabilitation.[213] Further, that it was not clear that any uplift for that offending would cancel outright the discount for youth.[214] In conclusion, the Court found that a lesser sentence of imprisonment should have been imposed.

Had this case been determined by a Matariki Court, Option 3 would be suggested. After an initial assessment is made by the *Kairukuruku* they will then advise the offender of the provisions in section 27 as well as the community services and agencies that can support the offender.

Although the Matariki Court focuses on section 27 of the Sentencing Act, it is not mandatory for the sentencing officer to offer a section 27 process to the offender nor draw attention to that process.[215] If the Matariki Court shows signs of success, it is anticipated that this finding could be revisited.

The process of restorative justice between the offender and victim should be, in my opinion, mandatory. Upon the court hearing, the defence counsel will then suggest to the sentencing Judge that Option 3 is the pathway for the offender. Subsequently the sentencing Judge will adjourn to allow the defendant time to complete any programmes or community service that may be helpful.

It is noted that in this case bail was refused. Before proceeding to consider comparative jurisdictions a review and contextual analysis of the bail proceedings is helpful.

Bail

The Children, Young Persons and their Families Act 1989 requires, where possible, that all policies and services provided have particular regard for the values, culture and beliefs of the Māori people and support the role of *whānau, hapū* and *iwi*.[216] The Sentencing Act 2002 also contains provision where culture can be considered by the court.[217]

---

212 *Tutakangahau v R* at [2].
213 At [45].
214 At [45].
215 *RS v R* [2014] NZCA 484.
216 Children Young Persons and Their Families Act 1989, ss 7 (c) (ii) and (iii).
217 Sentencing Act 2002 in particular s 27 (a) and (e).

In New Zealand the Bail Act 2000 was introduced in order to reduce rates of offending by persons released on bail by raising the threshold for release on bail.[218]

However, it contains no provision for the decision maker to take into account cultural factors when determining a bail application.[219] Unlike comparative jurisdictions there remains a paucity of case law to support the consideration of cultural factors during a bail application.[220]

It is acknowledged that even if granted bail, often, the offender is bailed to the existing environment in which they offended, increasing the likelihood of re-offending whilst on bail. Dr Johnston has noted that:[221]

> 92% of people charged with criminal offences are granted bail and do not spend time in custody remand; of these however, around a fifth commit new offences while on bail; of this offending, approximately 15% of this offending is violent in nature.

These statistics are not disaggregated for Māori; however, in light of the disproportionate rates of offending for Māori, an intervention during the bail application could include that the offender is bailed to a local *marae*, such as Waipereira, as a condition of bail. This is similar to when an at-risk offender is bailed to Odyssey House and subject to judicial monitoring under the Sentencing Act 2002. When the offender reappears before the Judge, any programme they may have undertaken during a supervised bail term can be taken into account. It is suggested that there could be a provision within the Bail Act where culture can be a factor in considering a bail application and thereby support an application to a local *marae* as a bailable option.

Had this provision been available in the case of *Tutakangahau v R*, it is suggested that the offender could have been bailed into a *marae* programme and when he reappeared for sentencing there would have been an opportunity for counsel to submit that in view of the community work and/or programmes undertaken, including a restorative approach, this should mitigate any sentence. Arguably a *marae* programme would offer more opportunity for rehabilitation than a short

218 See Department of Corrections *Over-Representation of Māori in the Criminal Justice System: An Exploratory Report* (Department of Corrections, Wellington, 2007) <www.correc tions.govt.nz>.

219 However see s 7 (5) Rules as to granting bail, which states "a defendant who is charged with an offence and is not bailable as of right must be released by a court on reasonable terms and conditions unless the court is satisfied that there is just cause for continued detention." In view of *R v Sim* it could be argued that culture may account as a reason for not continuing detention.

220 *R v Sim* [2005] OJ No 4432 (Ont CA).

221 Dr Peter Johnston "The NZ Department of Corrections Role and Purpose in the Criminal Justice Pipeline" presentation to the Auckland Law Faculty, University of Auckland, Part 2 Criminal Law students October 2014; see also Department of Corrections, above n 218.

prison term. Further, a *marae* programme is consistent with *tikanga* and its aim of balance. The intervention of a culturally appropriate model such as this is not novel. The evaluation of the Australian Murri Courts noted:[222]

> While the program was initially conceived as a more culturally-appropriate alternative to mainstream court processes for sentencing Indigenous offenders, stakeholders involved in the Murri Court program identified *a trend towards an expanded intervention model involving the use of bail programs* [emphasis added], case management plans and pre- and post-sentence *support provided by Elders, CJG members and community based organisations* [emphasis added].

An examination of the current initiatives within the criminal justice system, reveal some exciting and promising developments. It is now timely to consider the constitutional setting to ascertain whether potential support for such an initiative is possible.

---

222 Anthony Morgan and Erin Louis *Evaluation of the Queensland Murri Court: Final Report* (2010) Australian Institute of Criminology, Australian Government, Reports and Technical Background Paper 39, Key issues at xii.

Chapter 4

Constitutional frameworks – the Treaty of Waitangi

A Introduction of European law

The British sought to establish their own form of legal system upon the colonisation of territories including New Zealand, Australia and Canada.[1] As in the case for Australia, New Zealand[2] was regarded by the British as a settled territory[3] and vacant upon discovery. This is the view maintained by scholars and also by the courts.[4] Scholars, such as Austin, have tended to belittle this approach because societies, such as First Nations peoples and Māori, have been inappropriately labelled as inferior or even savage.[5] According to First Nations legal scholar, Borrows:[6]

1 See Te Paparahi o te Raki Waitangi Tribunal Report (November 2014) Wai 1040, at 38 that stated "these victories made Britain the world's pre-eminent imperial and naval power … provided protection for core elite values such as … rule of law, sanctity of private property rights and the spread of Christ's Protestant gospel."

2 See *Wi Parata v Bishop of Wellington* (1877) 3 NZ Jur (NS) (SC) 72; see also discussion in David Williams "Wi Parata is Dead, Long Live Wi Parata" in Andrew Erueti and Claire Charters (eds) *Māori Property Rights and the Foreshore and Seabed: The Last Frontier* (Victoria University Press, Wellington, 2007).

3 Despite the Treaty travelling around the country and receiving further signatories, Captain William Hobson, the first Governor of New Zealand, on 21 May 1840 declared the sovereign rights of Britain in two proclamations. One proclaimed sovereignty over the North Island by virtue of cession under the Treaty of Waitangi and the other over the South Island on the ground of discovery. The British Government acknowledged this where the proclamation was published in the *London Gazette* on 2 October 1840.

4 See J E Cote "Reception of English Law" (1977) 25 Alberta Law Review 29 at 38; see also, for example, Norman Arthur Foden *New Zealand Legal History (1642 to 1842)* (Sweet & Maxwell, Wellington, 1965) at 24 and 179; Alan Ward *A Show of Justice: Racial "Amalgamation" in Nineteenth Century New Zealand* (Auckland University Press, Auckland, 1995); Peter Adams *Fatal Necessity: British Intervention in New Zealand, 1830–1847* (Auckland University Press, Auckland, 1977) at chap 7.

5 John Borrows *Canada's Indigenous Constitution* (University of Toronto Press, Toronto, 2010), at 12.

6 At 13.

While Indigenous peoples lived in the territory prior to its colonization it has been said that *"their laws and customs were either too unfamiliar or too primitive to justify compelling British subjects to obey them* [emphasis added]".

Williams, an Indigenous (Lumbee) law professor, noted that, in respect of the Indigenous Cheyenne peoples:[7]

Cheyenne ... demonstrated the 'juristic beauty' ... underlying assumption that the *Cheyenne were not stereotypical lawless savages but sophisticated legal thinkers and actors showed that the evolution and practice of law among the so called primitive peoples of the United States was far more advanced and nuanced than had been generally supposed* [emphasis added].

This is not the line of reasoning expressed in early New Zealand case law. Richmond J and Prendergast CJ in the 1877 Supreme Court decision of *Wi Parata v Bishop of Wellington*,[8] Professor David Williams noted:[9]

In the judgment of Prendergast C.J. and Richmond J., delivered by the Chief Justice, the 1841 Ordinance was said to 'express the well-known legal incidents of a settlement planted by a civilised Power in the midst of *uncivilised tribes*' [emphasis added]. The Treaty of Waitangi was dismissed 'as a simple nullity. *No body politic existed capable of making a cession of sovereignty, nor could the thing itself exist*' [emphasis added].

And further Williams noted:

Prendergast CJ and Richmond J had opined in 1877, that 'the supreme executive Government *must acquit itself as best it may, of its obligation to respect native proprietary rights,* and of necessity must be the sole arbiter of its own justice [emphasis added]'.

---

7 Robert Williams "Foreword" in Raymond Austin *Navajo Courts and the Navajo Common Law: A Tradition of Tribal Self-Governance* (University of Minnesota Press, Minneapolis, 2009) at ix.
8 *Wi Parata v Bishop of Wellington* (1877) 3 NZ Jur (NS) (SC) 72.
9 Williams, above n 2. This perspective is consistent with that of Sir Edward Coke's report of the Calvin case where Coke asserted that the "laws of a conquered Christian nation survived, but the laws of an infidel nation were abrogated" see Calvin's Case (1608) 7 Co Rep 1a, 77 ER 377 (Comm Pleas). However, Paul McHugh *The Māori Magna Carta: New Zealand Law and the Treaty of Waitangi* (Oxford University Press, Oxford, 1991), at 89 where he notes that Lord Mansfield did not follow this line of reasoning by Coke and Lord Mansfield clarified that Indigenous laws enjoyed the same presumption of continuity as found in The Case of Tanistry (1608) Davies 28, 80 ER 516 (KB).

However, Borrows commented that:[10]

> *Indigenous legal traditions will not receive the respect they deserve if* [emphasis added] governments, courts, lawyers, *political scientists and law professors fail to more fully articulate their place in our country* [emphasis added].

Upon the Crown's acquisition of sovereignty, the status of *tikanga* Māori was initially contingent on the common law. The doctrine of continuity recognised that "British sovereignty ... of itself did not make legal order from chaos, but rather, extended some legal recognition to the pre-existing tribal system of government and law".[11]

Although as Paul McHugh asserts, continuity is "a deep-seated trait of human nature",[12] *tikanga* Māori was nonetheless marginalised. To understand why, an historical review of the introduction of British legal systems provides a background to discussing the almost fatal impact British law had on *tikanga* Māori.

To provide some context for the question of how any domestic and international instruments impacted upon or may recognise 'culture' or '*tikanga* Māori' within the New Zealand justice system, a review of three broad timeframes will assist in 'setting the scene'. This will also trace the presumed cession of Māori sovereignty and the imposition of a new legal order for New Zealand. The first timeframe covers the pre-Treaty era. The second timeframe ranges from the signing of the Treaty to the year 1900. The third and final period ranges from 1900 to the present day.

Law is generally defined as a system of rules that relate to a community, regulating and determining the actions of its members and enforcing these rules through the imposition of penalties. In contrast, *tikanga* Māori is a contextual concept derived from a completely different source, with the imposition and consideration of measures to achieve balance. Although there may be some abstract similarities, *tikanga* Māori and British Law were influenced by different historical and philosophical doctrines.[13] Notwithstanding these differences, it is only through a Westminster or British lens that *tikanga* Māori can be claimed to be the first 'law' of Aotearoa.[14]

New Zealand's present constitutional framework derives from the British Westminster system of government, which advocates parliamentary sovereignty and the rule of law.[15] While the judiciary scrutinise the actions of Parliament to

---

10 Borrows, above n 5, at 180.

11 McHugh *Māori Magna Carta*, above n 9, at 83; see also Wai 1040, above n 1, at 44 "Crown sovereignty whilst also recognizing the continuity of the indigenous polity and the exemption of indigenous peoples from English law ...".

12 McHugh, above at 84.

13 For further discussion see Wai 1040, above n 1, chapter 2 'Two Peoples, Two Worlds', at 19.

14 Ani Mikaere "The Treaty of Waitangi and the Recognition of Tikanga Māori" in Michael Belgrave, Merata Kawharu and David Williams (eds) *Waitangi Revisited: Perspectives on the Treaty of Waitangi* (Oxford University Press, Australia, 2005) at 334.

15 See Philip Joseph *Constitutional and Administrative Law in New Zealand* (4th edition, Thomson Brookers, Wellington, 2014) at 515.

ensure they are consistent with New Zealand's constitutional framework (using tools of statutory interpretation and alternative formulations of the rule of law),[16] the courts inevitably respect parliamentary sovereignty in all its forms – the supreme power of Parliament.

As a British colony and a member of the Commonwealth, New Zealand inherited many of its laws from England at various stages in time.[17] English laws were deemed to have been in force in New Zealand from 14 January 1840, at least "so far as applicable to the circumstances of the ... colony".[18] In addition to its many laws, New Zealand inherited an unwritten constitution that is untidy, inaccessible, sullied by colonisation and not reflective of the community.[19] New Zealand's unwritten constitution is comprised of a collection of statutes, the Treaty of Waitangi, decisions of the courts and certain unwritten constitutional conventions.[20] This distinctive feature must be contended with when determining the place of Māori and *tikanga* Māori within it.[21] Further, as the Treaty is only one of many constitutional components, the exact role and constitutional influence the Treaty may hold is unclear.

Pre-Treaty of Waitangi

While Abel Tasman arrived in 1642, it was Captain Cook who was ultimately credited with the 'discovery' of New Zealand.[22] In the early phases of European settlement, Māori significantly outnumbered the British settlers and Britain's policy towards New Zealand was one of non-intervention.[23] This approach is supported by obiter dicta statements in *R v Symonds*; that is, until 1840, New Zealand was "not within His Majesty's dominions".[24] Further, Justice Chapman upheld the notion of native title and observed:[25]

16 Sections 4, 5 and 6 were intentionally inserted into the New Zealand Bill of Rights Act 1990 to protect the sovereignty of Parliament from such a situation. This being said, the courts will strive to uphold the rights contained therein given the nature and content of the Act; see *Shaw v Commissioner of Inland Revenue* [1999] 3 NZLR 154 (CA) for further information.

17 For general discussion see Peter Spiller (ed) *A New Zealand Legal History* (2nd ed, Brookers, Wellington, 2001).

18 English Laws Act 1858, s 1.

19 Bruce Harris "The Treaty of Waitangi and the Constitutional Future of New Zealand" [2005] 2 NZLR 189 at 212; see also D Williams "The Foundation of Colonial Rule in New Zealand" (1988) 13 NZULR.

20 Only two other states have unwritten constitutions: the United Kingdom and Israel.

21 Harris, above n 19, at 212.

22 To provide full context to the time period prior see Anne Salmond *The Trial of the Cannibal Dog: Captain Cook in the South Seas* (Pengiun Books, Auckland, 2004); Wai 1040, above n 1, at 57–58.

23 Wai 1040, above n 1, at 156, 193, 231 and 268.

24 *R v Symonds* (1847) NZPCC 387 at 395; see also D Williams "*Queen v Symonds* Reconsidered" (1989) 1(9) Victoria U Wellington Law Review at 385.

25 *R v Symonds*, above, at 232.

Whatever may be the opinion of jurists as to the strength or weakness of the *Native title*, whatsoever may have been the past vague notions of the Natives of their country, whatever may be their present clearer and still growing conception of their dominion over land, it cannot be too solemnly asserted that it *is entitled to be respected, that it cannot be extinguished (at least in times of peace) otherwise than by the free consent of the native occupiers* [emphasis added].

On the matter of the Treaty itself, Justice Chapman declared that it was simply a declaration of the law the court had applied in making its judgment on this matter:[26]

It follows ... that in solemnly guaranteeing the Native title, and in securing what is called the Queen's pre-emptive right, the Treaty of Waitangi, confirmed by the charter of the Colony, does not assert either in doctrine or in practice anything new and unsettled.

The interventions of the Imperial Statutes of 1817, 1823 and 1828 collectively, founded a paradox: they disclaimed New Zealand as part of the British Empire and not within His Majesty's domains, yet they extended the jurisdiction of the New South Wales' Courts to punish crimes committed by British subjects in New Zealand.[27]

To some extent the only other British intervention was the Declaration of Independence of 1835, He Whakaputanga o te Rangatira o Nui Tireni ('the Declaration of Independence'). Signed by 34 Māori Chiefs and James Busby, the official British Resident, on 28 October 1835, the Declaration declared independence of the country, confirmed that all sovereign power rested in the hereditary chiefs, agreed to meet regularly in Congress and thanked the King for acknowledging the independence flag of 1834.[28]

Thus the Declaration of Independence was a clear articulation binding the Crown and proclaiming the sovereign independence of the signatories (mainly Northern *rangatira*), and affirming their independence from all other sovereign powers.

The proclamation was recognised by King William IV and perceived as a response to concern over lawless British subjects in New Zealand coupled by fears that France would declare sovereignty over the territory.[29] The Declaration of Independence signalled a step towards a formal constitutional relationship with the Crown and affirmation of Māori sovereignty. The Wai 1040 report stated:[30]

---

26 At 390.
27 See Claudia Orange *Treaty of Waitangi* (Bridget Williams Books, Wellington, 2010) at 3; see also Wai 1040, above n 1, at 326, 504 and 108.
28 See also Wai 1040, above n 1, at 153–155.
29 Wai 1040, above n 1, at 157, 330–331.
30 At 501.

There can be no doubt that he Whakaputanga was a resounding declaration of the mana and rangatiratanga of those who signed it on behalf of their hapū. Nor can there be any doubt that it amounted to a declaration of sovereignty and independence of those hapū.

Although the recent Waitangi Tribunal Report has addressed the debate as to whether the Declaration of Independence secured sovereign rights for Māori,[31] for some legal commentators, the Treaty received a greater and wider range of signatories, usurping the status of the Declaration of Independence.[32] Some question its validity on the grounds that it is not representative of all Māori. In this way the Declaration of Independence is viewed as a mere step towards the signing of the Treaty of Waitangi.

Nonetheless, the Declaration of Independence provides a clear purpose of the signatories' intention: to declare independence, thereby reinforcing the claim that the Northern chiefs did not cede sovereignty to the Crown when signing the Treaty. The Waitangi Report, Wai 1040 stated:[33]

> To those rangatira who signed, none of this – including the agreement to meet annually – would have implied any loss of authority on the part of either themselves or their hapū, or any transfer of authority to a collective decision making body. Rather, he Whakaputanga was an unambiguous declaration that hapū and rangatira authority continued in force – as, on the ground, it undoubtedly did – and that Britain had a role in making sure that state of affairs continued as Māori contact with foreigners increased.

Historian Paul Moon has argued that the Declaration of Independence represented "regional goodwill".[34] This is consistent with Britain's immediate response to the Declaration that indicated it did not see itself as being bound by the Declaration of Independence.[35] The Waitangi Report, Wai 1040 noted that:[36]

> The official response to the declaration in 1836 by the Secretary of State for War and Colonies, Lord Glenelg, did not take those commitments any further, and rather signalled only a very conditional willingness to protect Māori independence.

---

31 Margaret Mutu "Constitutional Intentions: The Treaty of Waitangi Texts" in Malcolm Mulholland and Veronica Tawhai (eds) *Weeping Waters The Treaty of Waitangi and Constitutional Change* (Huia Publishers, Wellington, 2010); see also Wai 1040, above n 1.

32 Above.

33 Wai 1040, above n 1, at 502.

34 See NZ History "Taming the Frontier" <https://nzhistory.govt.nz/culture/declaration-of-independence-taming-the-frontier>

35 Wai 1040, above n 1, at 502.

36 At 502.

Michael King maintained that the Declaration of Independence had no substance "since there was in fact no national Indigenous power structure within New Zealand".[37] King also noted that some of the United Tribes were at war with one another within a year of signing the document.[38]

Notwithstanding these views many historians, including Tom Brooking, assert that the Colonial Office accepted that the Confederation of United Tribes, the Māori signatories, retained "title to the soil and sovereignty of New Zealand".[39] Māori have relied on this affirmation of sovereignty in the Declaration of Independence in contemporary legal proceedings.[40] For example, although unsuccessful, Ngāti Whātua argued before the High Court that they remained an independent sovereign state under the Declaration of Independence (1835), which preceded the Crown annexation of New Zealand in 1840.[41] In light of the Wai 1040 Report,[42] although only recommendations, if this case taken by Ngāti Whātua was heard today, the findings from the High Court may have been different.

The Declaration of Independence is a source of Indigenous rights. In view of the recent findings from the Waitangi Tribunal[43] on its examination of the intersection of the powers successively reserved to Māori in the Declaration of Independence, an examination of the Treaty will be important.

1840–1900

With the signing of the Treaty of Waitangi in 1840, the Crown claimed, contentiously, that Māori ceded sovereignty and the New Zealand Parliament was subsequently established. The current Waitangi Tribunal Claim, Te Paparahi o te Raki, Wai 1040, questions whether the Māori signatories of the Treaty did cede sovereignty. Stage one of the Wai 1040 report, released on 14 November, 2014, found that the chiefs who signed the Treaty did not cede sovereignty to the British Crown, but agreed "to share power and authority with Britain".[44] The report further stated that "the detail of how this relationship would work in practice, especially where the Māori and European populations intermingled, remained to be negotiated over time on a case-by-case basis".[45] The report is silent on how and when the Crown acquired sovereignty. However, Paul McHugh, in the report, states that "the Crown acquired sovereignty not through

---

37 Michael King *The Penguin History of New Zealand* (Penguin, New Zealand, 2003).
38 Above. See also Wai 1040, above n 1, at 157.
39 Tom Brooking *Māori and Pākehā Relations: 1800–1860* (Ministry of Education, Wellington, 1991).
40 See *Morunga v Police* 16/3/04HC Auckland, CRI-2004-404-8.
41 *Re Manukau* HC Auckland M 1380/92, 10 June 1993.
42 Wai 1040, above n 1.
43 Wai 1040 above n 1.
44 At 529.
45 At 529.

the Treaty but a series of jurisdictional steps" so the signature gathering was no longer necessary after securing the following jurisdictional steps and proclamations.[46] Wai 1040 notes:

> Entering into a Treaty with Māori would meet Britain's self-imposed condition prior to asserting sovereignty, but the assertion of sovereignty itself would be an entirely independent step.

In the six months preceding the signing, New Zealand transformed from an independent Māori nation into an appendage of New South Wales before becoming an infant colony of Great Britain. During this time several proclamations were issued in anticipation of New Zealand becoming a British possession.[47]

On 15 June 1839 Letters Patent were issued under the Great Seal, altering the boundaries of New South Wales. Pursuant to the Letters Patent, New Zealand became a British possession as an appendage of the Australian Colony of New South Wales.[48] On 19 January 1840 the Governor of New South Wales, Sir George Gipps, issued three proclamations, which he retrospectively dated to 14 January 1840.[49] The first extended the boundaries of New South Wales to include:[50]

> ... any territory which is or may be acquired in sovereignty by Her Majesty... within that group of Islands ... commonly called New Zealand.

The second and third proclamations announced that he had administered oaths of office to Hobson,[51] as Lieutenant Governor "in and over the same", and that the Queen would not recognise any title to land purchased directly from Māori after 14 January 1840.[52]

On 6 February 1840 the Treaty of Waitangi received its first signatories. Despite the Treaty travelling around the country and receiving further signatories, on 21 May 1840 Hobson declared the sovereign rights of Britain in two proclamations.[53] One proclaimed sovereignty over the North Island by virtue of

46 At 329 and 474. In a brief statement responding to the report, Attorney-General and Treaty of Waitangi Negotiations Minister Chris Finlayson said: *"There is no question that the Crown has sovereignty in New Zealand. This report doesn't change that fact"* in Kate Kenny "Māori did not give up sovereignty: Waitangi Tribunal" 14 November 2014 <http://www.stuff.co.nz/national/politics/63196127/Māori-did-not-give-up-sovereignty-Waitangi-Tribunal>.

47 Foden, above n 4 at 12.

48 Joseph, above n 15, at 45; Wai 1040, above n 1.

49 Above.

50 Wai 1040, above n 1, at 314 and 340.

51 William Hobson was the first Governor of New Zealand and assisted in the drafting of the Treaty.

52 Foden, above n 4.

53 At 17–20

cession under the Treaty of Waitangi, and the other over the South Island on the grounds of discovery. The British Government acknowledged Hobson's proclamations, which were subsequently published in the *London Gazette* on 2 October 1840.

On 16 June 1840 the Legislative Council of New South Wales passed an Act extending the laws of New South Wales to "Her Majesty's Dominions in the Islands of New Zealand".[54] New Zealand was now part of New South Wales.[55] On 7 August 1840 the New South Wales Continuance Act of 1840 provided that New Zealand was a separate colony from New South Wales, and now a British Colony.[56]

Hobson was appointed as Governor of the new colony, pursuant to Letters Patent issued on 24 November 1840, and officially in existence on 3 May 1841.[57] This signalled the beginning of New Zealand as an infant colony.

Constitutional beginnings

Between 1840 and 1860 New Zealand's constitutional and legal structures provided Parliament the power to pass laws in New Zealand under the English Laws Act of 1858 (UK).[58] Section 1 of this Act ensured the adoption of the common law in New Zealand.[59] The English Laws Act of 1854, the English Laws Act of 1858 and the English Laws Act of 1908 were recognised as part of New Zealand municipal law as of 14 January 1840.[60]

It was not until the 1852 Constitution Act (UK) ("1852 Act") that New Zealand's constitutional beginnings were formalised.[61] The 1852 Act was the third 'constitutional' Act in New Zealand.[62] The first, the Charter of New Zealand 1840, came into force in 1841 when New Zealand was separated from New South Wales and constituted a separate colony. The second constitution passed by the Imperial Parliament (Westminster) was the New Zealand Constitution Act of 1846.[63]

---

54 Joseph, above n 15, at 46.
55 New Zealand Charter 1840 was the first constitutional document, the second was the Constitution Act 1847 (UK) which Governor Grey did not apply, the New Zealand Constitution Act 1852 (UK).
56 Joseph, above n 15, at 46.
57 Above.
58 Joseph, above n 15, at 26.
59 See *Attorney General v Ngāti Apa* [2003] 3 NZLR 643 at [17–19]; see also *Fuller v MacLeod* [1981] 1 NZLR 390 where the Court established that subject to statutory limitations there is a common law right, in this instance, for the owner of land fronting a road to have access.
60 Joseph, above n 15, at 26. *R v Symonds* (1847) NZPCC 387.
61 See also Phillip A Joseph and Gorden R Walker "A Theory of Constitutional Change" (1987) 7 Oxford J Legal Stud 155 at 157. See also Joseph, above n 15 at 511.
62 Joseph, above n 15 at 25–28.
63 Governor Grey refused to administer the 1846 Act.

Inclusion of tikanga Māori

The implementation of this constitution did not consider the inclusion of *tikanga* Māori or the requirement of the "right ways of acting and being", subsequently marginalising these values. For Māori, if the action did not result in a breach of personal or collective *tapu*, it was not regarded as a crime. This perception did not always equate with the provisions of the British law that had been imposed upon Māori. Collective responsibility for individual transgressions, in accordance with *tikanga* Māori, had no place in British law.[64]

The Native Exemption Ordinance No. 18 came into effect on 16 July 1844 to assist the "aboriginal native population to yield a ready obedience to the laws and customs of England" as this "may be more speedily attained by gradual rather than immediate enforcement of the law so that in the course of time the native population may willingly submit".[65] Under this Ordinance, if the victim and offender were both Māori, the proceedings could be instigated by two chiefs from the tribe to which the offender belongs.[66] This "positioned Māori outside the jurisdictional boundaries"[67] and was more consistent with how Māori *rangatira* perceived their exception rather than subjection to the colonial law.[68]

If the victim was non-Māori, then any action taken was not to disturb the peace of the community.[69] The chiefs were remunerated for their time and effort.[70] Consistent with the notion of reciprocity and *utu*, and in lieu of imprisonment, this Ordinance enabled the payment of a fine for a debt incurred.[71] In the case of *R v E Hipu*,[72] the court records show that:

> E Hipu, a native, was tried and found guilty of having stolen a piece of print from Mr. Lyon's store about twelve months since, and sentenced (under the Native Exemption Ordinance) to pay eight pounds, or four times the value of the goods stolen. The fine was paid for the prisoner. The prisoner had escaped from custody and was recaptured only a fortnight before trial.

---

64 See Wai 1040, above n 1, at 33 that stated "Consistent with the principle of whanaungatanga, utu would be taken against the group, rather than solely against the offending individual if there was one."

65 Preamble Native Exemption Ordinance (No. 18).

66 Native Ordinance, s 1: Mode of procedure in cases of crime committed by the natives inter se.

67 Nan Seuffert *Jurisprudence of National Identity: Kaleidoscopes of Imperialism and Globalisation from Aotearoa New Zealand* (Ashgate, Aldershot, 2006) at 32.

68 Paul McHugh *Aboriginal Societies and the Common Law: A History of Sovereignty, Status, and Self-Determination* (Oxford University Press, New York, 2004), at 170.

69 Section 2: By Natives against others.

70 Section 4: Allowance for Chiefs for causing apprehension of offenders.

71 Section 12: Aborigines not to be imprisoned for debt.

72 *R v E Hipu* 1 December 1845 Supreme Court, Wellington, Chapman J as cited at <www.victoria.ac.nz/law>.

A later Ordinance extended this to include assault.[73]

In recognition by Governor Fitzroy of the negative effect imprisonment had on Māori, he insightfully noted:[74]

> The Natives [do] not regard imprisonment as we [do], deprivation of personal liberty often ended in the death of the savage; and regarding them in a transitional state, he thought *imprisonment would tend to retard their improvement* [emphasis added].

Today the disproportionate criminal justice statistics for Māori confirm this comment by Governor Fitzroy. Notwithstanding the potential for this Ordinance to assist in achieving balance, it was not popular amongst the settler population.[75]

This Ordinance was replaced by Governor Grey with the Resident Magistrates Court Ordinance 1846. Perceived as a successful initiative, the 1846 Ordinance sought to incorporate Māori decision-making and *tikanga* into legislation. The 1846 Ordinance provided that, for disputes involving only Māori, a Resident Magistrate was to sit with two Māori *rangatira* (chiefs) appointed as Native Assessors. As a non-Māori system, each case was determined according to the principles of equity and good conscience, without being constrained by strictly legal evidence.[76] In accordance with s 22, the decision was to be made by consensus. *Rangatira* were responsible for their own people, delivering to the magistrate those individuals who were guilty of serious offences against settlers, and reporting regularly on the state of their districts.[77]

The ability to incorporate concepts of *tikanga* Māori, including the notion of consensus together with strong leadership and the involvement of the Resident Magistrates system with Māori Assessors, all contributed to the success of this Ordinance.

Through seeking to recognise *tikanga* Māori in *R v Rangitapiripiri*,[78] Chapman J noted that:[79]

73 Fines for Assault Ordinance 1845.
74 Legislative Council Minutes, Tuesday 9 July, printed in the *Daily Southern Cross*, 13 July 1844 at 3 <www.victoria.ac.nz>; see also comments from Paul Butler "… less punitive crime policy is in our collective self interest" as cited by J Forman in "Why Care about Mass Incarceration?" (2010) 108 Michigan Law Review at 1009.
75 *New Zealand Spectator and Cooks Strait Guardian* (15 February 1845) at 2 <www.victoria. ac.nz/law/nzlostcases>.
76 As per ss 7, 10, 13, 19 and 20; see Robert Joseph "Re-Creating Legal Space for the First Law of Aotearoa, New Zealand" (2009) 17 Waikato Law Review at 74.
77 At 74.
78 1 December 1847 Supreme Court, Wellington, Chapman J heard together with *R v Native*.
79 For further information, see Shaunnagh Dorsett "Sworn on the Dirt of Graves: Sovereignty, Jurisdiction and the Judicial Abrogation of 'Barbarous' Customs in New Zealand in the 1840s" (2009) 30 The Journal of Legal History at 175; Damen Ward, "A Means and Measure of Civilisation: Colonial Authorities and Indigenous Law in Australasia" (2003) 1 History Compass AU 049 at 001.

as far as the law to be applied in the new colony, this only indicated that as between the settlers, or the settlers and Māori that English law should be applied.

For matters between Māori, Chapman J stated that "Māori laws and customs remained in place unless specifically abrogated on the basis that they were against the law of humanity".[80] This reasoning supports the notion of a parallel justice system or the application of Te Ao Māori, realised by an Indigenous legal system, manifested by an Indigenous court, and premised on fundamental Māori concepts and doctrine, is the appropriate way forward for Māori.

The two constitutions, the Charter of New Zealand 1840 and the New Zealand Constitution Act of 1846,[81] remained in force until the Constitution Act of 1852 was passed in 1853. The Constitution Act of 1852 established the organs of government. Section 32 of the Constitution Act of 1852 (UK) established a General Assembly consisting of the Governor, the House of Representatives and the Legislative Council. Section 53 granted the General Assembly the power to make laws for New Zealand. Section 71 provided the Governor with the power to set apart 'Māori districts', where Māori laws and customs would prevail, stating:[82]

And whereas it may be expedient that the laws, customs, and usages of the Aboriginal or native inhabitants of New Zealand, so far as they are not repugnant to the general principles of humanity, *should for the present be maintained for the government of themselves* [emphasis added], in all their relations to and dealings with each other, and that particular districts should be set apart within which such laws, customs, or usages should be so observed:

It shall be lawful for her Majesty, by any Letters Patent to be issued under the Great Seal of the United Kingdom, from time to time to make provision for the purposes aforesaid, any repugnancy of any such native laws, customs, or usages to the law of England, or to any law, statute, or usage in force in New Zealand, or in any part thereof, in anywise notwithstanding.

This carried the potential to create domestic dependent Māori nations, analogous to those in the United States.[83] The provisions for 'Māori/Native Districts' implied that Māori customary law could prevail over national laws.[84]

It is suggested that had this statutory intention been realised, Māori would be on par with their Native American counterparts. It is also plausible that a tribal

---

80 Dorsett, above; Ward, above.
81 Governor Grey refused to administer the 1846 Act.
82 *Constitutions of Nations Volume II France to New Zealand* (Brill Archive) at 798.
83 See Chapter 6 'Initiatives in Comparative Jurisdictions' for further discussion on the Navajo Courts.
84 McHugh, above n 68, at 200; see also Jim Cameron "Plural Justice, Equality and Sovereignty in New Zealand" (unpublished paper for the Law Commission, 22 October 1997) at 48.

system of governance, such as the Navajo Tribal Court System[85]which recognises and implements Navajo customary law, could have been accomplished.[86] Although many Native Americans still experience disproportionate social statistics, a *tikanga*-based court system may have alleviated the current disproportionate social statistics for Māori.

However, s 71 was never invoked.[87] No districts were 'set apart' in terms of the Act, despite the efforts of various Māori groups, including the Kīngitanga movements, to have the provisions of s 71 implemented.[88]

The Kīngitanga movement attempted to use s 71 in their claims for self-governance. However, that section is no longer available as it was eventually repealed by the Constitution Act of 1986. No analogous section, allowing the legal recognition of customary governance, was included in the 1986 Act.

Despite the fact that s 71 was never implemented, Ngāi Tūhoe has always sought *tino rangatiratanga* within Aotearoa. The Urewera District Native Reserve Act 1896 (Urewera Act) provided for the "ownership and local government of the native lands in the Te Urewera district".[89] In recognition of the existing *tikanga* of Ngāi Tūhoe, the preamble noted:

> It is desirable in the interests of the Native race that the Native ownership of the Native lands constituting the Urewera District should be ascertained in such manner, not inconsistent with Native customs and usages, as will meet the views of the Native owners generally and the equities of each particular case, and also that provisions be made for the local government of the said district.

This clear statutory recognition of traditional customary structures within the traditional area or 'te Rohe Pōtae'[90] of Ngāi Tūhoe, provided internal self-governance through local government, protecting the Ngāi Tūhoe from external

85   See Chapter 6 'Initiatives in Comparative Jurisdictions' for further discussion.
86   See Nicola Roughan "Conceptions of Custom in International Law" <www.ssrn.com> for further discussion including a greater role for 'custom'.
87   For a current comparative example where laws established by the State recognising Indigenous rights have not been utilised see the law On Territories of Traditional Nature Use of Indigenous, Small Numbered Peoples of the North, Siberia and the Far East of the Russian Federation (7 May 2001, No 49-FZ) adopted by Russia in 2001 provided for the creation of Territories of Traditional Natural Use. This law guaranteed land use rights to Indigenous peoples; however, more than a decade after adoption no territory has been established.
88   See New Zealand Law Commission *Māori Custom and Values in New Zealand Law* (New Zealand Law Commission SP9, Wellington, 2001) at [92]. For a discussion on the development of, and attempts to implement, s 71 of the Constitution Act 1852 see Robert Joseph "Historical Bicultural Developments: The Recognition and Denial of Māori Custom in the Colonial Legal System of Aotearoa/New Zealand" (LIANZ: Te Matahauriki Research Unit, Hamilton, 1998).
89   Urewera District Native Reserve Act 1896.
90   Te Rohe Pōtae is the name given to describe the boundaries of the Tūhoe territory.

alienation. However, "the Act was designed not to guarantee autonomy to Ngāi Tūhoe, but to open up Te Urewera to the Europeans".[91]

> Government policy, however, was firmly focused on the purchase of Urewera land, not on the promotion of Māori development of land and agricultural enterprise (in spite of Tūhoe efforts at Ruatoki). This came in spite of Ngata's assurances in Parliament that section 8 of the Urewera Amendment Act 1909 was 'for the purpose of promoting settlement on their lands by Natives themselves'. From this point onward, Tūhoe non-sellers were placed in a position of reacting to and protesting against aggressive Government purchase policy in the Urewera.

During the reading of the Bill, the then Leader of the Opposition, Captain Russell, focused on the illusion that Tūhoe would be given self-governance and states the Bill:[92]

> ... pretends to confer upon the Native people the complete isolation and control of a portion of the country about 665,000 acres in extent, but I am happy to say it will do no such thing ... To give effect to this Bill we have to make a district with which the land-law of the Native people shall be *absolutely different* [emphasis added] from that in any other part of the colony.

Tūhoe were granted something far less than self-government. The aspirational beginnings of the Urewera Act resulted in legislation with the purpose of gaining land ownership.[93]

Unfortunately, the overlaying of non-Indigenous values, such as individualism, has led to conflict and the marginalisation of fundamental Māori values, such as reciprocity, relatedness and balance. To meaningfully recognise these fundamental values, concepts based on state and private ownership would need to be abandoned in favour of concepts underpinned by a relational worldview – one that is closely aligned with the Indigenous worldview and the Māori world.

Despite this positive intention, it did not translate into meaningful Māori governance structures.[94] What did eventuate were four Māori seats under the Māori Representation Act 1867. The 1852 Act disenfranchised Māori from political participation. It stipulated that eligible land ownership was a requirement of the Māori Representation Act 1867.

---

91 Danny Keenan "Autonomy as Fiction: The Urewera Native District Reserve Act 1896" in Danny Keenan (ed) *Terror in our Midst* (Huia Publishers, Wellington, 2008) at 91.

92 Judith Binney *Encircled Lands: Te Urewera* (Bridget Williams Books, Wellington, 2010).

93 See Robert Joseph "Colonial Biculturalism? The Recognition & Denial of Māori Custom in the Colonial & Post-Colonial Legal System of Aotearoa/New Zealand" (paper prepared for Te Mātāhauariki Research Institute, University of Waikato FRST Project, 1998), at 74 for full discussion.

94 Above, at 2 (abstract).

After the 1852 Act, the judiciary evaded the obligation to continue the application of Māori customary law and usage until customary title was extinguished. In *Re The Lundon and Whitaker Claims Act 1871*, the Court of Appeal reasserted:[95]

> The Crown is bound, both by the common law of England and by its own solemn engagements, *to a full recognition of native proprietary rights* [emphasis added]. Whatever the extent of that right by established native custom appears to be, the Crown is bound to respect it. But the fullest measure of respect is consistent with the assertion of the technical doctrine, that all title to land must be derived from the Crown; this of necessity importing that the fee-simple of the whole territory of New Zealand vested and resides in the Crown, until it be parted with by grant from the Crown.

This judicial recognition of Māori aboriginal or customary title was unfortunately short lived. During the following time frame, Māori customary law was gradually displaced and alienated by a raft of statutes.

1900 – present day

The beginning of the 20th century marked a period during which New Zealand seceded from the United Kingdom and developed into an independent country. The Constitution Act 1852 gave the New Zealand Parliament the power to pass its own legislation. However, as a dominion of the United Kingdom, Parliament could not pass laws repugnant to the United Kingdom, nor amend the Constitution Act 1852, thus limiting its law making power.

The Imperial Parliament enacted the Statute of Westminster in 1931 to give Great Britain's dominions greater legislative autonomy.[96] This statute purported to allow laws to be valid even where they were repugnant to the laws of Great Britain.[97] However, s 8 of the Statute of Westminster 1931 provided an important qualification to the broadening of local law-making powers.[98] It did this by articulating that the New Zealand Constitution Act 1852 was only to be altered or repealed in accordance with the law as it existed before the commencement of the 1931 Act.[99] This left the then General Assembly without the power to amend or repeal the remaining entrenched provisions of the 1852 Act that limited the law making powers for New Zealand. The passing of the New Zealand Constitution (Amendment) Act 1947 (UK) provided such a power.[100]

---

95 In *Re The Lundon and Whitaker Claims Act 1871* (1872) 2 NZCA 41 at 49.
96 See Bruce V Harris "Law-making Powers of the New Zealand General Assembly: Time to Think about Change" (1984) 5 Otago LR 565 at 565–571. See also Joseph and Walker, above n 61, at 157.
97 See section 4 of 1931 Act; Harris, above.
98 Harris, above.
99 Harris, above.
100 Above.

The New Zealand Constitution (Amendment) Act 1947 (UK) gave Parliament full powers of constitutional amendment, thereby allowing New Zealand to pass laws repugnant to the Constitution Act 1852. While the 1947 Act was considered a breakthrough, it added to the growing number of complex and fragmented sources of New Zealand's constitution.

The Constitution Act 1986 ("1986 Act") provided some clarification by amalgamating the constitution process into a single Act, replacing the 1852 Act, the Statute of Westminster Act 1947 and the New Zealand Constitution (Request and Consent) Act 1947. The 1986 Act removed the power of the United Kingdom to pass laws for New Zealand and consolidated the constitutional sources within a single Act, representing our current constitutional arrangements.[101]

Although the Ordinances provided for the recognition of *tikanga* Māori, the 1986 Act does not include any reference to the Treaty. The lack of Māori involvement has been an implicit feature throughout New Zealand's constitutional history. However, during the 1980s there was a period of Māori Renaissance, which led to the establishment of the Waitangi Tribunal, among other innovations.[102] In light of this historical context, it is surprising the Treaty was not expressly included in New Zealand's constitutional arrangements.

This very concern was raised with the passing of the Bill of Rights Act in 1990. The Labour Government, led by Prime Minister David Lange, tabled a White Paper to include the Treaty of Waitangi within the Bill of Rights.[103] Under the Bill the Treaty would strike down other Acts that "unreasonably encroached" upon the Treaty.[104] However, many Māori did not agree with inserting the Treaty into a rights charter. Some Māori believed that the Treaty had the status as the founding document rather than a mere right.[105] No mention of the Treaty was made in this Act, nor has one been made in our current Constitution Act 1986.

Had the 1986 Act and the New Zealand Bill of Rights Act 1990 included a reference to the Treaty of Waitangi, the 1986 Act would have provided effective tools for promoting Indigenous rights. A resulting re-focus upon the right of self-determination as the cornerstone for Indigenous peoples and Māori rights, supported by international Indigenous jurisprudence, may have offered a degree of protection for Māori.

The 1986 Act repealed s 71 of the 1852 Act, which provided for customary Māori governance and the establishment of native districts where the first law – *tikanga*

---

101 Joseph above n 15, at 5.
102 See Ken A Palmer "Law, Land and Māori Issues" (1988) 3 Canterbury Law Review 322; see also McHugh *The Māori Magna Carta*, above n 9; see also discussion in Richard Hill *Māori and the State Crown–Māori Relations in New Zealand/Aotearoa 1950–2000* (Victoria University Press, Wellington, 2009) on the aspirations of Māori for *rangatiratanga* with the establishment of, for instance, Māori Womens Welfare League and Māori Committees.
103 See discussion under Entrenchment of the Treaty.
104 Joseph, above n 15, at 83–85.
105 See discussion under Entrenchment of the Treaty.

Māori – would prevail. The repeal of s 71 halted any contemporary devolution of power to uphold customary Māori governance.

The next feature within this period concerns the abolition of the Privy Council as our final appellate court. The Supreme Court Act 2003 established the New Zealand Supreme Court as our final appellate court.[106] It was enacted by the Labour Government and ignited a debate in New Zealand society around our constitutional directions. The establishment of the Supreme Court indicated that New Zealand was becoming more independent.[107] The New Zealand court structure is now governed by the Judicature Act 1908 (High Court and Court of Appeal), the District Courts Act 1947 and the Supreme Court Act 2003.

Despite the above issues and recent developments, there remains the thorny obstacle of where the Treaty of Waitangi and *tikanga* Māori will sit within the unwritten Constitution.[108] The recent recommendations by the Constitutional Advisory Panel highlighted this issue by noting there is no broad support for a supreme constitution. However, it also noted that there is support for entrenching elements, although this does not include the Treaty of Waitangi or *tikanga* Māori.[109] On the matter regarding the role of the Treaty of Waitangi, the Constitutional Review Panel put forward the following recommendations:[110]

- continues to affirm the importance of the Treaty as a foundational document;
- ensures a Treaty education strategy is developed that includes the current role and status of the Treaty and the Treaty settlement process so people can inform themselves about the rights and obligations under the Treaty;
- supports the continued development of the role and status of the Treaty under the current arrangements as has occurred over the past decades;
- sets up a process to develop a range of options for the future role of Treaty, including options within existing constitutional arrangements and arrangements in which the Treaty is the foundation; and
- invites and supports the people of Aotearoa New Zealand to continue the conversation about the place of the Treaty in our constitution.

B Treaty of Waitangi

In 1840 the Crown and Māori signed the Treaty of Waitangi (the Treaty). This action subsumed the existing social, political, legal and economic rights for Māori

---

106 Joseph, above n 15 at 5.
107 A major reason was the geographical proximity of Privy Council to New Zealand. The Law Lords could not appreciate New Zealand's context.
108 For further discussion see <www.beehive.govt.nz>.
109 Ministry of Justice *Constitutional Advisory Panel New Zealand's Constitution: A Report on a Conversation* (He Kōtuinga Kōrero Mōte Kaupapa Ture o Aotearoa, Wellington, November 2013) at 16.
110 Ministry of Justice, above.

into a non-Māori paradigm. According to David Williams, the Treaty of Waitangi may be seen as:[111]

> ... the starting point and the foundation stone for the legitimacy of an auto-chthonous constitution that springs from all peoples of this nation.

Text

There were several different texts of the Treaty in English and in Māori. Although it is the English text that is always referred to, for the purposes of the developing jurisprudence, it is the Māori that should be preferred.[112]

Signed in 1840, Article 1 of the English text stated:[113]

> The Chiefs of the Confederation of the United Tribes of New Zealand ... cede to Her Majesty the Queen of England absolutely and without reservation all the rights and powers of Sovereignty which the said Confederation ... respectively exercise or possess ...

In Article 2 the Crown, in exchange, confirmed and guaranteed:

> Her Majesty the Queen of England confirms and guarantees to the Chiefs and Tribes of New Zealand ... the full exclusive and undisturbed possession of their Lands and Estates, Forests, Fisheries and other properties which they may collectively or individually possess ...

In Article 3, the Crown also extended:

> [...] Her Majesty the Queen of England extends to the Natives of New Zealand Her royal protection and imparts to them all the Rights and Privileges of British Subjects.

Te Tiriti text stated:[114]

> Ko Wikitoria te Kuini o Ingarani i tana mahara atawai ki nga Rangatira me nga Hapu o Nu Tirani i tana hiahia hoki kia tohungia ki a ratou o ratou

---

111 David Williams "Indigenous Customary Rights and the Constitution of Aotearoa New Zealand" (2006) 14 Waikato Law Review 106 at 132.

112 This is consistent with the contractual doctrine 'contra proferentum' which "holds that the words of a document are construed more strongly against the party who drafted the document or in whose benefit it is intended to operate" Peter Spiller *New Zealand Law Dictionary* (LexisNexis, Wellington, 2005) at 63.

113 Ian Hugh Kawharu "The Treaty of Waitangi (the text in English) by I Hugh Kawharu" in M Belgrave, M Kawharu and D Williams (eds) *Waitangi Revisited: Perspectives on the Treaty of Waitangi* (Oxford University Press, Australia, 2005) at 389.

114 Professor Dame Anne Salmond's "Brief of Evidence for the Waitangi Tribunal Wai 1040" dated 17 April 2010 at 4.

rangatiratanga me to ratou wenua, a kia mau tonu hoki te Rongo ki a ratou me te Atanoho hoki kua wakaro ia he mea tika kia tukua mai tetahi Rangatira – hei kai wakarite ki nga Tangata māori o NuTirani – kia wakaaetia e nga Rangatira māori te Kawanatanga o te Kuini ki nga wahikatoa o te Wenua nei me nga Motu – na te mea hoki he tokomaha ke nga tangata o tona Iwi Kua noho ki tenei wenua, a e haere mai nei.

Na ko te Kuini e hiahia ana kia wakaritea te Kawanatanga kia kaua ai nga kino e puta mai ki te tangata māori ki te Pakeha e noho ture kore ana. Na kua pai te Kuini kia tukua a hau a Wiremu Hopihona he Kapitana i te Roiara Nawi hei Kawana mo nga wahi katoa o Nu Tirani e tukua aianei, amua atu ki te Kuini, e mea atu ana ia ki nga Rangatira o te wakaminenga o nga hapu o Nu Tirani me era Rangatira atua enei ture ka korerotia nei.

Ko te tuatahi

Ko nga Rangatira o te wakaminenga me nga Rangatira katoa hoke ki hai i uru ki taua wakaminenga ka tuku rawa atu ki te Kuini o Ingarani ake tonu atu – te Kawanatanga katoa o o ratou wenua.

Ko te tuarua

Ko te Kuini o Ingarani ka wakarite ka wakaae ki nga Rangatira ki nga hapu – ki nga tangata katoa o Nu Tirani te tino rangatiratanga o o ratou wenua o ratou kainga me o ratou taonga katoa. Otiia ko nga Rangatira o te wakaminenga me nga Rangatira katoa atu ka tuku ki te Kuini te hokonga o era wahi wenua e pai ai te tangata nona te wenua – ki te ritenga o te utu e wakaritea ai e ratou ko te kai hoko e meatia nei e te Kuini hei kai hoko mona.

Ko te tuatoru

Hei wakaritenga mai hoki tenei mo te wakaeetanga ki te Kawanatanga o te Kuini – Ka tiakina e te Kuini o Ingarani nga tangata māori katoa o Nu Tirani ka tukua ki a ratou nga tikanga katoa rite tahi ki ana mea ki nga tangata o Ingarani.

[signed] W. Hobson Consul & Lieutenant Governor

Na ko matou ko nga Rangatira o te Wakaminenga o nga hapu o Nu Tirani ka huihui nei ki Waitangi ko matou hoki ko nga Rangatira o Nu Tirani ka kite nei i te ritenga o enei kupu, ka tangohia ka wakaaetia katoatia e matou, koia ka tohungia ai o matou ingoa o matou tohu.

Ka meatia tenei ki Waitangi i te ono o nga ra o Pepueri i te tau kotahi mano, e waru raue wa te kau o to tatou Ariki.

Although not widely acknowledged, a fourth article was added to the Māori text. This stated:

E mea ana te Kawana ko nga whakapono katoa o Ingarani, o nga Weteriana, o Roma, me te ritenga Māori hoki e tiakina ngatahitia e ia,

This has been translated as:[115]

The Governor says that the several faiths (beliefs) of England, of the Wesleyans, of Rome and also of Māori custom shall alike be protected by him.

Thus Article 4 of the Treaty confirms the support for religious freedom and the ability for Māori to retain their own customs and culture. Notwithstanding this support, it is the first three articles that are referred to by the Crown.

There are several different translations of the Māori text into English. The reconstruction of the Māori text by Sir Ian H. Kāwharu is widely recognised and accepted. The reconstruction states:[116]

In Article 1:

The Chiefs of the Confederation ... give absolutely to the Queen of England forever the complete government over their land.

Kāwharu noted that Māori signatories had no understanding of 'government' in the sense of sovereignty when signing the Treaty. There was no equivalent translation of *kāwanatanga*.

In Article 2:

The Queen of England agrees to protect the chiefs ... in the unqualified exercise of their chieftainship over their lands, villages and all their treasures ...

In Article 3:

[...] the Queen of England will protect all the ordinary people of New Zealand and will give them the same rights and duties of citizenship as the people of England.

The exact meaning of the Treaty is often debated.[117] However, it is commonly accepted that Article 2 confirms and guarantees to Māori the full, exclusive and

115 Salmond above.
116 Ian Hugh Kawharu "A Reconstruction of Māori Text" in Michael Belgrave, Merata Kāwharu and David Williams (eds) *Waitangi Revisited: Perspectives on the Treaty of Waitangi* (Oxford University Press, Australia, 2005) at 389.
117 See, for example, discussion in Maui Solomon "The Wai 262 Claim" in Michael Belgrave, Merata Kawharu and David Williams (eds) *Waitangi Revisited: Perspectives on the Treaty of Waitangi* (Oxford University Press, Australia, 2005) at 216.

undisturbed possession of their lands, estates, forests, fisheries and other treasures. The use of *taonga*, or treasures, implies a connection between the Treaty and Māori social and economic development. Thus, although Article 2 may seem to be restricted to forests and fisheries, the 1988 Royal Commission on Social Policy broadened the application of Article 2 to conclude that the Treaty also has implications for health and social policies.[118]

Article 3 of the Treaty states that the "Queen of England will protect all Māori of New Zealand and will give them the same rights as those of the people of England." This not only includes protection and equality, but also, arguably, extends to include the provision of health.[119] According to Te Kani Kingi:[120]

> It is little wonder, therefore, that Māori have come to view the Treaty as an ideal framework for Māori health development … [;] it is clear that above all else it [the Treaty] is concerned with equity and the promise that Māori can enjoy, at the very least, the same health and well-being as non-Māori.

However, a more accurate translation is provided by Merimeri Penfold and Professor Anne Salmond:[121]

> Victoria the Queen of England in her caring concern [mahara atawai] for the rangatira and the hapū of New Zealand, and in her desire that their chieftainship [rangatiratanga] and their land should be preserved to them, and that lasting peace and also tranquil living [te Rongo … me te Atanoho hoki] should be theirs has thought it right that a Rangatira should be sent – as a mediator [kai wakarite] to the māori people [tangata māori pl.] of New Zealand – that the māori rangatira might agree to the Governorship [Kāwanatanga] of the Queen over all parts of the land and the islands, since many of her people have settled in this land, and others are yet to come.
>
> Now the Queen wishes that the Governorship should be established, so that evil may not come to the māori people and the pākehā who are living without law [ture].
>
> Now the Queen has been pleased that I, William Hobson, a Captain in the Royal Navy, should be sent [tuku] as Governor for all those parts of New Zealand which are now or shall be released [tukua] to the Queen, and declares to the rangatira of the Confederation [whakaminenga] of the tribes [hapū] of New Zealand the laws [ture] that are spoken here:

118 Royal Commission on Social Policy, *The April Report: Volume II Future Directions* (Government Printer, Wellington, 1988) 27 at 80.
119 Te Kani Kingi "The Treaty of Waitangi and Māori Health" Te Mata o Te Tau Lecture Series, Massey University, New Zealand (2 March 2006). More recently see also Waitangi Tribunal (Wai 2358, 2012) *The Interim Report on the National Freshwater and Geothermal Resources Claim* "Treaty conferred a development right" at 106.
120 Te Kani Kingi, above.
121 Salmond, above n 114, at 11.

The first

The rangatira of the confederation and all of the rangatira who have not joined that confederation give completely [tuku rawa atu] to the Queen of England forever – all the Governorship [Kāwanatanga] of their lands.

The second

The Queen ratifies [whakarite] and agrees to the unfettered chiefly powers [tino rangatiratanga] of the rangatira, the tribes and all the people of New Zealand over their lands, their dwelling-places and all of their valuables [taonga]. Also, the rangatira of the Confederation and all the other rangatira release [tuku] to the Queen the trading [hokonga] of those areas of land whose owners are agreeable, according to the return [utu] agreed between them and the person appointed by the Queen as her trading agent [kai hoko].

The third

In recognition of this agreement to the Governorship of the Queen – the Queen will care for [tiaki] all the māori people [nga tāngata māori pl. katoa] of New Zealand and give [tukua] to them all and exactly the same customary rights [tikanga rite tahi] as those she gives to her subjects, the people of England.

[Signed] W. Hobson Consul and Lieutenant Governor

Now we the Rangatira of the Confederation of the hapū of New Zealand assembled here at Waitangi, and also we the Rangatira of New Zealand see the likeness of these words. We accept and agree to all of this, and so we sign our names and marks.

This is done at Waitangi on the sixth day of February in the year one thousand, eight hundred and forty of our Lord [Ariki].

The discrepancies between the English and Māori texts and translations of the Treaty/te Tiriti are to be noted and have caused much debate and misunderstanding.[122] One of the functions of the Waitangi Tribunal is to have regard to the two texts and the Tribunal has exclusive authority to determine the meaning and effect of the Treaty, as embodied in both texts and to decide issues raised by the differences between them.[123]

122 For discussion, see Claudia Orange *The Treaty of Waitangi* (Allen & Unwin, Wellington, 1997) at 32 and also *He Tirohanga o Kawa ki te Tiriti o Waitangi* (Te Puni Kokiri, Wellington, 2001) at 37 www.tpk.govt.nz; see also Wai 1040 above n 1, at 348.
123 Treaty of Waitangi Act 1975, s 5(2). Section 6 (1) also provides that the jurisdiction of the Tribunal is for actions inconsistent with the "principles of the Treaty" as opposed to the "text".

According to Professor Salmond, this is due to the fact that the Treaty of Waitangi and Te Tiriti are:[124]

> ... two very different documents, with divergent textual histories and political implications; and for that reason, it is a mistake to bracket them together. I have observed that this error has led to a confused and confusing historiography of the Treaty, which should not be perpetuated.

From a legal perspective, the most important discrepancy lies within the translation of *kāwanatanga* to mean governorship, and not sovereignty.

According to Professor Salmond:[125]

> In summary, one must conclude that in 1840, kāwanatanga was not an accurate or even a plausible translation equivalent for sovereignty – supreme, irresistible, absolute, uncontrolled authority. Rev. Richard Davis's back translation of Te Tiriti, which translated rangatiratanga (which was guaranteed to the chiefs) as entire supremacy indicates that the missionaries were aware that what was proposed in Te Tiriti was a balance of powers, with the rangatira in the ascendant within their own domains.
>
> The fact that so many subsequent commentators have claimed that at Waitangi and elsewhere, the rangatira ceded the sovereignty of New Zealand to Queen Victoria, tells us more about the political interests involved, the rhetorical dominance of the English draft of the Treaty and perhaps unexamined assumptions about those hands in which goodness, wisdom and power are most likely to be found (to quote Blackstone) than it does about the weight of the evidence ...

And further:[126]

> I do not believe, however, that in signing Te Tiriti, the rangatira ceded sovereignty to the British Crown.

If Māori did not, in fact, cede sovereignty as the Waitangi Report, Wai 1040, has found, then the Crown's subsequent actions to acquire sovereignty require close scrutiny and review, otherwise these actions can be perceived as illegitimate. For that reason alone, the implementation of an Indigenous legal system should be supported.

Entrenchment of the Treaty

In 1985 a government White Paper proposed a Bill of Rights for New Zealand that would control the powers and actions of the legislature as well the

124 Salmond, above n 114, at 84.
125 Salmond, above n 114 at 26.
126 Salmond, above n 114 at 87.

executive.[127] The White Paper's authors dealt with the Treaty of Waitangi in the same way that s 35 of the Constitution Act 1982 (Canada) dealt with the rights of native Canadian peoples and proposed that the Treaty be included within a Bill of Rights. Once enacted, the Bill of Rights would be "supreme law".[128] Irrespective of which text should be entrenched, the added debate on the place of the Treaty in New Zealand's constitutional framework contributes to this confusion.

The majority of submitters to the Justice and Law Reform Committee on the White Paper did not favour this approach. The principal reason was the power the White Paper would have given to the judiciary. Including the Treaty in the Bill of Rights also proved unpopular for some Māori. The lack of enthusiasm among some Māori was enough to thwart its enactment as supreme law, the Government having indicated that success of the White Paper proposal would require the support of Māori.[129]

The long title and preamble of the 1985 Bill read:

Whereas

(1) New Zealand is a democratic society based on the rule of law and on principles of freedom, equality and the dignity and worth of the human person;

(2) New Zealand in 1978 ratified the International Covenant on Civil and Political Rights;

(3) *The Māori people, as tangata whenua o Aotearoa, and the Crown entered in 1840 into a solemn compact known as te Tiriti o Waitangi, and it is desirable to recognise and affirm the Treaty as part of the supreme law of New Zealand* [emphasis added];

(4) It is desirable to affirm the human rights and fundamental freedoms of all people of New Zealand without discrimination and to ensure their recognition and observance as part of the supreme law of New Zealand by the Parliament and Government of New Zealand.

Part 2 of the Bill was entitled "The Treaty of Waitangi" and consisted of a single article as follows:

---

127 Geoffrey Palmer "A Bill of Rights for New Zealand: A White Paper" (1985) 1 AJHR A6; Andrew Butler and Petra Butler *The New Zealand Bill of Rights Act: A Commentary* (LexisNexis, Wellington, 2005) at 27.

128 Paul Rishworth "The New Zealand Bill of Rights" in Paul Rishworth, Grant Huscroft, Scott Optician and Richard Mahoney (eds) *The New Zealand Bill of Rights* (Oxford University Press, Auckland, 2003); Paul Rishworth "Human Rights" [2003] NZLR 261 at 276; Ripeka Evans "Is the Treaty of Waitangi a Bill of Rights?" in *A Bill of Rights for New Zealand* (Legal Research Foundation Seminar, Auckland, 1985) at 195; Shane Jones "The Bill of Rights and Te Tiriti o Waitangi" in *A Bill of Rights for New Zealand* (Legal Research Foundation Seminar, Auckland, 1985) at 207.

129 Rishworth, above "Human Rights", at 18.

4 The Treaty of Waitangi

(1) *The rights of the Māori people under the Treaty of Waitangi are hereby recognised
     and affirmed* [emphasis added].
(2) The Treaty of Waitangi shall be regarded as always speaking and shall
     be applied to circumstances as they arise so that effect may be given to
     its spirit and true intent.
(3) The Treaty of Waitangi means the Treaty as set out in English and
     Māori in the Schedule to this Bill of Rights.

The original Bill recognised both texts of the Treaty, but clause 26 provided that
in the event of any inconsistency between an enactment and the Treaty, application could be made to the Waitangi Tribunal.[130] This avenue would have avoided restrictive judicial interpretations of s 5 of the New Zealand Bill of Rights
Act, and the concept of 'reasonable limits' that are demonstrably justified in a free
and democratic society. However, Māori were unhappy with including the Treaty
in a legal system, where it might be subjected to restrictive judicial interpretations, even as supreme law.[131] Many Māori considered that the matter should be
dealt with separately and not subordinated in any way to other constitutional
measures.[132]

Bearing in mind the unique place that the Treaty holds for Māori, Geoffrey
Palmer, who was the Prime Minister at the time, considered that a Bill of Rights
that ignored the Treaty would, at best, be an incomplete document.[133] By
declaring that certain rights were the supreme law of New Zealand and saying
nothing about the Treaty, a Bill of Rights could be seen as relegating the Treaty
and the rights of Māori to second class citizens.[134] This would also be consistent
with relegating human rights for Māori to an Indigenous or minority right.
Palmer described the effect of affirming and recognising the Treaty as part of the
supreme law of New Zealand:[135]

> Governments, Courts and Parliament will no longer be able to claim that
> these rights are only moral rights and have no substance in law, or that they
> can be overridden, expressly or impliedly, by the ordinary process of
> legislation.

---

130 See also Second Reading of the NZ Bill of Rights Bill 14 August 1985 <www.justice.
     govt.nz>.
131 Jones, above n 128 at 195 and 207; Claire Charters "Māori, Beware the Bill of
     Rights Act!" [2003] NZLJ 401; Claire Charters "BORA and Māori: The Funda-
     mental Issues" [2003] NZLJ 459.
132 Butler and Butler, above n 127 at 27.
133 At 27.
134 At 30.
135 At 30.

Although judicial decisions have limited the application of the Treaty,[136] there has been legislative recognition of the principles of the Treaty in public and private acts. Although it could be assumed that, if the 1985 proposal was reintroduced today, it would find more support from Māori. The recent report from the Constitutional Advisory Panel indicates this as unlikely, but the discussion should continue.[137]

The rights indicated in s 4 (1) of the 1985 draft suggest legislative recognition of the Treaty obligations with respect to human rights for Māori. However, if enacted, the principles of the Treaty would need to be applied compatibly with New Zealand's international obligations. It is assumed that the human rights standards contained in the International Covenants, to which New Zealand is a party, together with the general principles of international law that form part of municipal law, without the express words of a statute, provide techniques for balancing interests.[138]

The Treaty is the main vehicle through which Māori continue to express their desire to survive as distinct peoples. In this regard the Treaty stands on its own,[139] as a source of rights and obligations between Māori and the Crown.[140]

It is clear that the Māori text enables ongoing *rangatiratanga* of Māori tribes over their possessions and *taonga* (including intangibles such as language and culture) and that the Crown should protect that *rangatiratanga*. This also includes the right to self-determination and the right of development. The Crown would receive the right to govern a delegated power, subject to continuing Māori authority.[141]

Rights and duties created by the Treaty

The Treaty has significant moral, spiritual and legal force. It is seen as "the founding document of New Zealand" and has been referred to variously as "a constitutional document".[142] The late Lord Cooke of Thorndon even referred to the Treaty as "simply the most important document in New Zealand's history".[143] It has also been referred to in case law as "essential to the foundation

---

136 See for example *New Zealand Māori Council v Attorney-General* [2008] 1 NZLR 318; [2007] NZAR 569 (CA).
137 Ministry of Justice, above n 109 at 16.
138 Ian Brownlie *Treaties and Indigenous Peoples* (Oxford University Press, New York, 1992) at 93.
139 See, however, further discussion in point "Legal Status of the Treaty" and *Te Heuheu Tukino v Aotea District Māori Land Board* [1941] NZLR 590.
140 Alison Quentin-Baxter "The International and Constitutional Law Contexts" in Alison Quentin-Baxter (ed) *Recognising the Rights of Indigenous Peoples* (Institute of Policy Studies, Victoria University of Wellington, New Zealand 1998) at 32.
141 Salmond above 114, at 25.
142 Geoffrey Palmer *Constitutional Conversations* (Victoria University Press, Wellington, 2002) at 22.
143 Sir Robin Cooke "Introduction" (1990) 14 NZULR 1 at 1.

of New Zealand", "part of the fabric of New Zealand society"[144] and "of the
greatest constitutional importance to New Zealand".[145]

Baragwanath J states:[146]

> It is time to recognize that the Treaty did not contemplate a society divided
> on race lines between two groups of ordinary citizens – Māori and non-
> Māori – set against one another in opposing camps.

Baragwanath J further states:[147]

> Because the Treaty itself picked up the need to apply British justice in New
> Zealand it follows that any construction of the RMA that will work injustice
> to non-Māori is likely to infringe the principles of the Treaty as injustice to
> Māori.

The Treaty is designed to ensure unity within the state, while recognising Māori
as *tangata whenua*. It has been proposed as a vehicle that may offer *tino rangatiranga/*
self-governance for Māori, from which Māori could negotiate the ongoing development of New Zealand, and prescribe a relationship in the form of human
rights, social policy, economic policy and Indigenous peoples' rights.[148] Or perhaps even an Indigenous court underpinned by *tikanga* Māori.

Although that option may exist, the realisation and manifestation of *tino rangatiratanga* is more problematic.[149]

There are some issues of general principle to consider. Notwithstanding s 7 of
the New Zealand Bill of Rights Act 1990 (NZBORA),[150] and the now repealed

---

144 Chilwell J in *Huakina Development Trust v Waikato Valley Authority & Bowater* [1987] 2
 NZLR 188; (1987) 12 NZTPA 129 (HC) especially at [206] and [210]. See, however,
 also the obiter reservations of Casey and Hardie Boys JJ in *Attorney-General v New
 Zealand Māori Council (No 2)* [1991] 2 NZLR 147 (CA) at [149].
145 *New Zealand Māori Council v Attorney-General* [1994] 1 NZLR 513 (PC) at 516.
146 *Ngāti Maru ki Hauraki Inc v Kruithof* [2005] NZRMA 1 at [48].
147 At [52].
148 Mason Durie "Tino Rangatiratanga" in Michael Belgrave, Merata Kawharu and
 David Williams (eds) *Waitangi Revisited: Perspectives on the Treaty of Waitangi* (Oxford
 University Press, Australia, 2005) at 3–18.
149 For example even though the Urewera District Native Reserve Act 1896 provided for
 the "ownership and local government of the native lands in the Te Urewera district"
 and allow *tino rangatiratanga* for the Tuhoe people this was eventually to result in the
 opening up of traditional lands to settlers. Compare Tuhoe Claims Settlement Act
 2014; Te Urewera Act 2014, ss 17 and 18 (management of Te Urewera).
150 Section 7 provides: Attorney-General to report to Parliament where Bill appears to
 be inconsistent with Bill of Rights –

 Where any Bill is introduced into the House of Representatives, the Attorney-General
 shall, –

 (a) In the case of a Government Bill, on the introduction of that Bill; or

Foreshore and Seabed Act 2004,[151] it is possible to apply to the High Court to seek a declaration that certain legislation is discriminatory based on the Crown's Treaty obligations.

In examining the relationship between the principles of the Treaty and the International Human Rights Covenants, it would not be impossible to determine whether analysing the principles of the Treaty against international human rights standards would result in the enhancement or subversion of the economic and social rights of Māori.[152] Nevertheless, there is no domestic legislative direction to uphold to Māori the guarantees of *tino rangatiratanga*. Māori are reliant on the Treaty principles of partnership, including utmost good faith and reasonableness, active protection and the honour of the Crown.[153]

C Status in law

Initially viewed as a simple nullity,[154] the orthodox view on the legal status of the Treaty is that unless it has been adopted or implemented by statute, it is not part of domestic law and creates no rights enforceable in Court. In *Te Heuheu Tukino v Aotea District Māori Land Board,* the Privy Council ruled that:[155]

> ... it is well settled that any rights purported to be conferred by such a Treaty of cession cannot be enforced by the Courts, except so far as they have been incorporated in municipal law.

Viscount Simon LC then quoted the passage from Lord Dunedin's judgment in *Vajesingji Joravarsingji v Secretary of State for India,*[156] and continued:

> So far as the appellant invokes the assistance of the Court, it is clear that he cannot rest his claim on the Treaty of Waitangi, and that he must refer the Court to some statutory recognition of the right claimed by him.

(b) In any other case, as soon as practicable after the introduction of the Bill, – bring to the attention of the House of Representatives any provision in the Bill that appears to be inconsistent with any of the rights and freedoms contained in this Bill of Rights.

151 Marine and Coastal Area (Takutai Moana) Act 2011 replaced the Foreshore and Seabed Act 2004.
152 Brownlie, above n 138, at 24.
153 See Mason Durie *Te Mana, Te Kāwanatanga The Politics of Māori Self Determination* (Oxford University Press, Melbourne, 1998); see also discussion in Kelly Russ "Modern Human Rights: The Aboriginal Challenge" (LLM unpublished thesis, The University of British Columbia, April 2006) at ch 2.
154 *Wi Parata v Bishop of Wellington* (1877) 3 NZJur (NS) 72 at 78 per Prendergast CJ. However, see also *R v Symonds* (1847) NZPCC(SC), per Chapman J at 390 for earlier recognition of native title at common law and consideration of the Treaty.
155 *Te Heu Heu Tukino v Aotea District Māori Land Board* [1941] 2 All E.R. 93 at 98; [1941] NZLR 590.
156 *Vajesingji Joravarsingji v Secretary of State for India* (1924) LR 51 Ind App 357.

This view was consistent with the constitutional principle that treaties are not part of the law in New Zealand, and if rights and duties are to be altered, legislation is required.[157] This was also the view in *Ashby v Minister of Immigration,* where Cooke J commented:[158]

> ... a treaty that Parliament had not incorporated into New Zealand law could not possibly override the broad discretion conferred by Parliament on the Minister.

Sir Kenneth Keith noted that:[159]

> ... the Court of Appeal has yet to consider fully the proposition stated by the High Court of Australia that the ratification of a treaty gives rise to a legitimate expectation, in the absence of any legislation or executive indication to the contrary, that the executive would act in accordance with the treaty.

It is now generally accepted that the Treaty has constitutional importance and is part of New Zealand's constitutional arrangements.[160] There is, however, major disagreement on its precise role and the nature and extent of the importance of the Treaty.[161]

In 1986 the Royal Commission on Electoral Law recommended that:[162]

> Parliament and Government should enter into consultation and discussion with a wide range of representatives of the Māori people about the definition and protection of rights of the Māori people and the recognition of their constitutional position under the Treaty of Waitangi.

---

157   See Morag McDowell and Duncan Webb *The New Zealand Legal System* (4th ed, LexisNexis, Wellington, 2006) at 181.

158   *Ashby v Minister of Immigration* [1981] 1 NZLR 222 (CA) at 224; see also comments by Michael Taggart "Rugby, the Anti-apartheid Movement and Administrative Law" in Rick Bigwood (ed) *Public Interest Litigation* (LexisNexis, New Zealand, 2006) at 81 where the conferral of a broad discretionary power does not of itself exclude or displace the interpretive principle.

159   Sir Kenneth Keith "Roles of the Courts in New Zealand in Giving Effect to International Human Rights – With Some History" (1999) 29 VUWLR 27; see also *Minister of Immigration and Ethnic Affairs v Teoh* (1995) 128 ALR 353 (HCA) and *New Zealand Māori Council v Attorney-General* [1996] 3 NZLR 140 (CA) at 184.

160   See comments by Palmer, above n 142 at 22 and comments by Lord Woolf in *New Zealand Māori Council v Attorney-General* [1994] 1 NZLR 513; [1994] 1 AC 466 (PC) at 516; 469.

161   See notes on the presentation by Sir Geoffrey Palmer "The Treaty of Waitangi – Where to From Here? Looking Back to Move Forward" (Presented to Te Papa Treaty of Waitangi Debate Series, 2 February 2006) at [25].

162   *Royal Commission on the Electoral System: Towards a Better Democracy* (1986) at [3.111].

In 2005 the Constitutional Arrangements Committee recommended that:[163]

> ... there should be some specific process for facilitating discussion within Māori communities on constitutional issues.

Notwithstanding this recognition, it is the "Principles of the Treaty"[164] that are referred to in legislation,[165] and policy documents,[166] rather than the text of the Treaty itself.

Principles of the Treaty

Legislation and policy require decision-makers to take into account, when appropriate, the principles of the Treaty.[167] For instance, when assessing an application for resource consent, the decision-maker is required by the Resource Management Act 1991 to take into consideration the principles of the Treaty.[168]

The Ministry of Health strategy *Moving Forward: the National Mental Health Plan for More and Better Services*, identified the Treaty of Waitangi as its fourth principle to satisfy.[169] Both of the Ministry of Health Strategies, *Moving Forward* and *An Approach for Action*, describe the principles of the Treaty as relevant to mental health programmes. Nonetheless, the Treaty reference is general, rather than specific.[170] Although this is positive for Māori, it is a strategic, as opposed to a legislative recognition.

A breach of Treaty obligations by the Crown, such as failing to provide for the health and well-being of Māori, can be heard by the Waitangi Tribunal. The Tribunal then recommends to the Crown the appropriate form of redress.[171] This could include negotiations to address health inequalities and the inclusion of Māori within the decision-making process.[172] It would follow that the consideration of the principles of the Treaty is vital when providing adequate care for Māori mental health.

---

163 See *Inquiry to Review New Zealand's Existing Constitutional Arrangements* (2005).
164 See decision of Cooke P in *New Zealand Māori Council v Attorney General* [1987] 1 NZLR 641.
165 For example Conservation Act, s 4; State Owned Enterprises Act, s 9.
166 For example see the policy for the Office for Disability Issues where the Treaty underpins the development of their Strategy and is consistent with the relevant principles of the Treaty at <www.odi.govt.nz>.
167 *New Zealand Māori Council v Attorney-General* [1987] 1 NZLR 641 (CA).
168 Resource Management Act 1991, s 8; for general discussion see Mason Durie *Nga Tai Matatu – Tides of Māori Endurance* (Oxford University Press, Australia, 2005).
169 Mason Durie *Mauri Ora: The Dynamics of Māori Health* (Oxford University Press, 2005) at 258.
170 At 259.
171 See Waitangi Tribunal, Contemporary Aspects of the Napier Hospital and Health Services Report (Wai 692). The claim concerned the Crown's treaty obligation to Māori in respect of health services.
172 Waitangi Tribunal, above.

Although the courts have rejected the argument that s 5(2) of the Treaty of Waitangi Act 1975 requires the Waitangi Tribunal to apply the principles of the Treaty or consider them a mandatory relevant consideration,[173] Baragwanath J, in considering s 6(6) of the Act, found that it does not actually remove the jurisdiction of the Tribunal to consider a claim at a time when a Bill to settle a claim or a related one is before Parliament, confirming the right of legal access.[174]

Partnership reflects the purpose of the Treaty, where Māori and the Crown have equal roles with "responsibilities analogous to fiduciaries".[175] The principle of partnership is arguably the most important principle. In *New Zealand Māori Council v Attorney-General*, the Court of Appeal unanimously held that:[176]

> The Treaty signified a partnership between races … the issue becomes what steps should have been taken by the Crown, as a partner acting towards the Māori partner with the utmost good faith which is the characteristic obligation of partnership …

The principle of partnership acknowledges both parties and requires that the Crown and Māori act towards each other reasonably and with the utmost good faith. Justice Casey noted that the partnership principle required the Crown to recognise and actively protect Māori interests. In his Honour's view, to assert this was "to do no more than assert the maintenance of 'the honour of the Crown' underlying all its treaty relationships".[177] Justice Richardson also agreed, stating that the concept of the honour of the Crown:[178]

> … *[C]aptures the crucial point that the Treaty is a positive force in the life of the nation and so in the government of the country* [emphasis added]. What it does not perhaps adequately reflect is the core concept of the reciprocal obligations of the Treaty partners. *In the domestic constitutional field … there is every reason for attributing to both partners that obligation to deal with each other and with their treaty obligations in good faith* [emphasis added]. That must follow both from the nature of the compact and its continuing application in the life of New Zealand and from its provisions.

Referring to Richardson J's comments, Gendall J stated:[179]

> The Lands case recognises that the Treaty created a continuing relationship of a fiduciary nature, akin to a partnership, and that there is a positive duty

173 *Attorney General v Mair* [2009] NZCA 625 per Chambers and O'Regan JJ.
174 See also Natalie Baird "Administrative Law" [2010] NZLJ.
175 *New Zealand Māori Council v Attorney-General* [1987] 1 NZLR at 664 per Cooke P (CA).
176 At 641 per Cooke P (CA).
177 At 703 per Casey J (CA).
178 At 682 per Richardson J (CA).
179 *New Zealand Māori Council v Attorney-General* HC Wellington CIV-2007-485-95, 4 May 2007 at [62].

to each party to act in good faith, fairly, reasonably and honourably towards the other.

Māori are reliant on the Treaty principles of partnership, such as utmost good faith and reasonableness, active protection and the honour of the Crown.[180] The strict application of partnership, half the representation in Parliament, would be difficult to justify. The intention of this principle is to promote greater protection and participation by Māori.

Sir Robin Cooke (as he was at the time) also noted that the Treaty must be viewed as a living document capable of adapting to new circumstances. As a living document, it is proposed that the new circumstance of Māori as a minority should neither diminish their status as *tangata whenua* and Treaty partner, nor the rights of partnership. This would necessarily include Māori's rights to participation and representation within the rule-making and decision-making bodies.

Although partnership is given a range of legislative expressions, the reality is that political power is not shared equally as partners.[181] The Treaty partnership is also subject to the constitutional norm of parliamentary sovereignty,[182] which gives little status to *rangatiratanga*/Māori self-determination. The former New Zealand Deputy Solicitor-General, Matthew Palmer, has summarised the position at the constitutional level:[183]

> Because of the political nature of the New Zealand constitution, I conclude that Māori political representation is the most significant manifestation of the Treaty of Waitangi in New Zealand's constitution in reality. This accords with representative democracy and parliamentary sovereignty being fundamental norms of New Zealand's constitution. Māori political representation relies on representative democracy to access influence over the exercise of parliamentary sovereignty. Māori have managed to convert a pragmatic Pākehā initiative, the Māori seats, into a symbolic representation of their own identity and political relationship with the State. MMP has broadened that representation and given it real political power. This ensures that Māori have a voice in the constitutional dialogue in New Zealand – in the branch of government that speaks the loudest, Parliament.

---

180 See Durie, above n 153 at 183; see also discussion in Russ, above n 153 at ch 2.
181 See Matthew Palmer *The Treaty of Waitangi in New Zealand's Law and Constitution* (Victoria University Press, Wellington, 2008) at 85–152 for an overview of this material.
182 See Constitution Act 1986, s 15(1) which states "the Parliament of New Zealand continues to have full power to make laws".
183 See Palmer, above n 181, at 291.

Palmer does, however, sound a note of caution:[184]

> However loudly Māori voices are heard within Parliament, that institution is ultimately ruled by the majority and Māori do not now constitute a majority in New Zealand. A group of people that consistently forms the majority [i.e Pākehā] has few incentives not to exploit, or ignore a group of people that consistently forms a minority.

As a minority in Parliament, Māori concerns are at the whim of Parliament and dependent on the political mood, and Māori may suffer in consequence. High Court Justice, David Baragwanath, echoed this point, commenting that:[185]

> The Treaty should like any other treaty be a mandatory consideration when it is relevant to decision-making, including adjudication ... it is an expression of the rule of law: a statement that Western norms do not exhaust the values of society: that even in the absence of entrenched rights we cannot tolerate any tyranny of the majority.

However, Williams observes that "it appears that the Treaty is a mandatory relevant consideration, unless the context otherwise requires but it will not sustain a separate cause of action".[186]

Māori are reliant on the principles of the Treaty, but as Professor James Anaya, United Nations Special Rapporteur on the Situation of Human Rights and Fundamental Freedoms of Indigenous People, noted:[187]

> From what I have observed, the Treaty's principles appear to be vulnerable to political discretion, resulting in their perpetual insecurity and instability.

The principle of partnership and the guarantee of *rangatiratanga* from the Treaty have established limited mechanisms that facilitate a distinct Māori voice in both central and local government decision-making to achieve the implementation of *tikanga*. However, there is no special constitutional protection for the Treaty.

---

184   See Palmer above n 181, at 292; see also comments by Philip Joseph "The Māori Seats in Parliament: A Study of Māori Economic and Social Progress" (Working Paper 2, New Zealand Business Roundtable, 2008) where he advances the proposition that separate seats are unnecessary to secure effective Māori representation <www.nzinitiative.org.nz>.

185   Hon Justice David Baragwanath "The Evolution of Treaty Jurisprudence" (2007) 15 Waikato Law Review 1 at 10.

186   Joseph Williams "Māori in New Zealand Law at the End of the Cooke Era – Where Have We Got To?" in P Rishworth (ed) *The Struggle for Simplicity in Law: Essays for Lord Cooke of Thorndon* (Butterworths, Wellington, 1997) at 168.

187   Statement of the United Nations Special Rapporteur on the Situation of the Human rights and Fundamental Freedoms of Indigenous Peoples, Professor James Anaya, upon conclusion of his visit to New Zealand, 22 July 2010 at 9.

There is, on occasion, a lack of support and political will to implement measures to ensure effective participation.[188] And a simple Act of Parliament can revoke the protection for Māori measures in government.[189] Nevertheless, this does not detract from the fundamental right of Māori to engage in the implementation of *tikanga* Māori – their legal system. Yet there are hurdles and challenges in the road ahead.

Treaty – summary

The Treaty has a significant moral, spiritual and legal force, encapsulating many rights for Māori that complement Indigenous peoples' rights.[190] It is viewed as "the founding document of New Zealand",[191] "a constitutional document",[192] "simply the most important document in New Zealand's history",[193] "essential to the foundation of New Zealand", "part of the fabric of New Zealand society"[194] and "of the greatest constitutional importance to New Zealand".[195] The Treaty is now a vehicle for Māori to negotiate the ongoing development of New Zealand, prescribing a relationship in the form of human rights, social policy, economic policy and Indigenous peoples' rights.[196] It also provides a platform for the right to implement *tikanga* Māori within an Indigenous court.

The Māori text of the Treaty provided for the continuing *rangatiratanga* of Māori tribes over their possessions and *taonga* and that the Crown would protect that *rangatiratanga*. The Crown received the right to govern – a delegated power – subject to continuing Māori authority.[197]

The Waitangi Tribunal found that Māori did not cede sovereignty.[198] Subsequently the ensuing actions by the Crown to secure sovereignty require close examination, otherwise all actions by the Crown may be considered illegitimate.

188 See Hon Peter Salmon, Dame Margaret Bazley and David Shand *Royal Commission Report on Auckland Governance* (March 2009) that recommended three Māori seats on the new Auckland Council. Nonetheless lack of political will to support this recommendation resulted in no Māori seats allocated. In its stead a Māori Advisory Board was established.

189 For instance the ongoing dialogue to remove the dedicated Māori seats in Parliament as noted in speech from National Party Leader Don Brash, Orewa Rotary Club, Auckland 7.30pm January 27, 2004; see also the Foreshore Seabed Act 2004 which although now repealed vested ownership of the foreshore into the Crown (s 13).

190 For further discussion see "Status in Law".

191 Palmer, above n 181.

192 Palmer, above n 142 at 22.

193 Cooke, above n 143 at 1.

194 See *Huakina Development Trust v Waikato Valley Authority and Bowater* [1987] 2 NZLR 188, especially at 206, and 210; but see also the obiter reservations of Casey and Hardie Boys JJ in *Attorney General v New Zealand Māori Council (No 2)* [1991] 2 NZLR 147 at 149.

195 *New Zealand Māori Council v Attorney General* [1994] 1 NZLR 513, 516 (PC).

196 Durie, above n 148.

197 Salmond, above n 114, at 25.

198 Wai 1040, above n 1.

However, it is the English text that is preferred and the principles of the Treaty that are included in domestic legislation, not the text itself, further diluting the rights guaranteed to Māori. The Treaty stands on its own as a source of rights and obligations between Māori and the Crown,[199] including the principle of partnership and participation. The Crown's duty to Māori is analogous to a fiduciary duty that informs the key characteristics arising from the relationship between Māori and the Crown, including that of reasonableness and consultation.[200]

Claims before the Waitangi Tribunal,[201] with respect to resources and rights guaranteed by the Treaty, have had mixed results.[202] Despite the provision enabling the Waitangi Tribunal to pass binding recommendations for claimants, case law highlights the reluctance of the Waitangi Tribunal to do so.[203]

Irrespective of the positive social, economic and cultural obligations provided for in the Treaty, these obligations and rights for Māori are not always realised through a Treaty claim. Māori social, economic and cultural rights are often marginalised to that of a minority group.[204] Māori are not a minority group, but first and foremost *tangata whenua* – the Indigenous peoples of Aotearoa.[205] For this reason Māori should be accorded these rights that may support an Indigenous court structure. Although Indigenous rights for Māori are marginalised within our domestic legislation, comparative jurisdictions in the seven regions, recognised by the United Nations, have acknowledged Indigenous rights within their respective constitutions.[206]

199 See *Te Heu Heu Tukino v Aotea District Māori Land Board* [1941] NZLR 590 for further discussion.

200 *New Zealand Māori Council v Attorney General* [2008] NZLR 318 (CA) at [81] per O'Reagan J; see also *Greenpeace v Minister of Energy* CIV-2011-485-1897 [22 June 2012] HC Wellington where Gendall J describes active protection as akin to a fiduciary duty. More recently *Wakatu v Attorney-General* [2017] NZSC 17, confirms that the Crown can owe Maori a fiduciary duty when certain circumstances arise, at [1], [379], [495] and [588].

201 Waitangi Tribunal was established in 1975 pursuant to the Treaty of Waitangi Act 1975 to hear breaches of the Treaty; see Fisheries Claim and see also Taranaki Petroleum claim.

202 The "Sealord" or Fisheries claim was perceived by most Māori as a successful outcome for *iwi* Māori. For discussion of claim see M Robinson "The Sealord Fishing Settlement an International Perspective" (1992) AULR at 559. However, the Taranaki Treaty claim to petroleum was unsuccessful; see Waitangi Tribunal, *The Petroleum Report* (Legislation Direct, Wellington 2003) at 44.

203 *Haronga v Waitangi Tribunal and Others* (SC54/2010) [2011] NZSC 53.

204 Don Brash, National Party Leader (Orewa Rotary Club, Auckland, 7.30pm January 27, 2004) where he noted that the Treaty should not create any greater right for Māori than any other New Zealander – in doing so relegating Māori to a minority group.

205 Mikaere above n 14, at 330–345.

206 See report written for the United Nations Permanent Forum on Indigenous Issues by Professor Megan Davis, Simon William M'Viboudoulou, Valmaine Toki, Paul Kanyinke Sena, Edward John, Álvaro Esteban Pop and Raja Devasish Roy "Study on National Constitutions and the United Nations Declaration on the Rights of Indigenous Peoples" (2013) E/C.19/2013/18.

Chapter 5

Constitutional frameworks – the United Nations Declaration on the Rights of Indigenous Peoples

While there is no separate treaty to provide for Indigenous rights, there is the United Nations Declaration on the Rights of Indigenous Peoples 2007 (Declaration).[1] As a Declaration the orthodox view is that it will not be legally binding upon the States.[2] However, the Declaration provides a benchmark against which Indigenous peoples can measure state action as well as a means of appeal in the international arena.[3] It may also represent binding international law.[4]

A Background

The Declaration on the Rights of Indigenous Peoples was the initiative of the Working Group on Indigenous Populations (WGIP). Established in 1982, the mandate of the WGIP was to develop international standards concerning Indigenous peoples' rights. The Declaration was a manifestation of this mandate and a clear articulation of international standards on the rights of Indigenous peoples. It was not until 25 years later, in September 2007, that the final text was adopted by the United Nations General Assembly, with a majority of 143 states in favour. Eleven states abstained,[5] while four states opposed the Declaration altogether: Australia, Canada, the United States of America (the United States) and New Zealand.

---

1 United Nations General Assembly Resolution 61/295 of 13 September 2007: the full text is available at <www.un.org/esa/socdev/unpfii/en/drip.html>.
2 Megan Davis "To Bind or not to Bind: The United Nations Declaration on the Rights of Indigenous Peoples Five Years On" (2012) 19 Austl Int'l L J 17 at 36.
3 See generally Megan Davis "United Nations Reform and Indigenous Peoples" (2005) 6(14) Indigenous Law Bulletin at 12.
4 S James Anaya *International Human Rights and Indigenous Peoples* (Aspen Publishers, New York, 2009) at 80; see also Kiri Toki "What a Difference a Drip Makes: The Implications of Officially Endorsing the United Nations Declaration on the Rights of Indigenous Peoples" (2010) 16 Auckland UL Rev at 243; see also Paul McHugh *The Māori Magna Carta: New Zealand Law and the Treaty of Waitangi* (Oxford University Press, Oxford, 1991), for a general discussion on the development of Indigenous rights through international instruments, at 203.
5 Azerbaijan, Bangladesh, Bhutan, Burundi, Colombia, Georgia, Kenya, Nigeria, Russian Federation, Samoa and Ukraine.

This position has now changed with Australia,[6] New Zealand,[7] Canada[8] and the United States[9] all signalling their support for the Declaration. While perceived as a major moral victory, a closer analysis of the wording for support of the Declaration provides concern about intentions to meaningfully recognise the Indigenous rights articulated in the Declaration.

To ascertain whether these rights can support the implementation of culture and *tikanga* Māori, after providing a background to the genesis of the Declaration and highlighting the key provisions, including that of self-determination and participation, this section will analyse the wording of the support that has been offered by Australia, New Zealand, Canada and the United States. The legal effect of the Declaration will be examined and some thoughts will be provided as to a creative way to realise the Indigenous rights articulated in the Declaration, including the provision that will support the application of the philosophy of Te Ao Māori.

B Indigenous peoples – Indigenous rights

The Declaration provides no definition of Indigenous peoples. Sha Zukang offers the following definition:[10]

> Indigenous communities, peoples and nations are those which, having a historical continuity with pre-invasion and pre-colonial societies that developed on their territories, consider themselves distinct from other sectors of the societies now prevailing on those territories, or parts of them. They form at present non-dominant sectors of society and are determined to preserve, develop and transmit to future generations their ancestral territories and their ethnic identity as the basis of their continued existence as peoples, in accordance with their own cultural patterns, social institutions and legal systems.

A Background Paper noted that:[11]

> In the thirty-year history of indigenous issues at the United Nations, considerable thinking and debate have been devoted to the question of definition

---

6 Jenny Macklin "Statement on the United Nations Declaration on the Rights of Indigenous Peoples" (2009) at <www.jennymacklin.fahcsia.gov.au>.
7 "Announcement of New Zealand's Support for the Declaration on the Rights of Indigenous Peoples" at <www.converge.org.nz>.
8 "Canada's Statement of Support on the United Nations Declaration on the Rights of Indigenous Peoples" (2010) at <www.ainc-inac.gc.ca>.
9 Susan E Rice "Announcement of U.S. Support for the United Nations Declaration on the Rights of Indigenous Peoples" (2010) at <usun.state.gov>.
10 Sha Zukang "State of the World's Indigenous Peoples" ST/ESA/328 (Department of Economic and Social Affairs, Division for Social Policy and Development, United Nations, New York, 2009) at v.
11 See PFII/2004/WS.1/3 – (New York, 19–21 January 2004).

of 'indigenous peoples', but no such definition has ever been adopted by any UN-system body.

One of the most cited descriptions of the concept of the term Indigenous was given by Jose R. Martinez Cobo, the Special Rapporteur of the Sub-Commission on Prevention of Discrimination and Protection of Minorities, in his *Study on the Problem of Discrimination against Indigenous Populations*.

Significant discussions on the subject were held during the drafting of the Declaration. After consideration of the issues involved, the Special Rapporteur offered a working definition of "indigenous communities, peoples and nations". In doing so, he expressed a number of basic ideas to provide the intellectual framework for this effort, which included the rights of Indigenous peoples themselves to define what and who is Indigenous. The working definition of "indigenous communities, peoples and nations" read:[12]

> Indigenous communities, peoples and nations are those which, having a historical continuity with pre-invasion and pre-colonial societies that developed on their territories, consider themselves distinct from other sectors of the societies now prevailing on those territories, or parts of them. They form at present non-dominant sectors of society and are determined to preserve, develop and transmit to future generations their ancestral territories, and their ethnic identity, as the basis of their continued existence as peoples, in accordance with their own cultural patterns, social institutions and legal system.
>
> This historical continuity may consist of the continuation, for an extended period reaching into the present of one or more of the following factors:
>
> a   Occupation of ancestral lands, or at least of part of them;
> b   Common ancestry with the original occupants of these lands;
> c   Culture in general, or in specific manifestations (such as religion, living under a tribal system, membership of an indigenous community, dress, means of livelihood, lifestyle, etc.);
> d   Language (whether used as the only language, as mother-tongue, as the habitual means of communication at home or in the family, or as the main, preferred, habitual, general or normal language);
> e   Residence on certain parts of the country, or in certain regions of the world;
> f   Other relevant factors.
>
> On an individual basis, an indigenous person is one who belongs to these indigenous populations through self-identification as indigenous (group

12 See Special Rapporteur, Mr. José Martínez Cobo *Study of the Problem of Discrimination Against Indigenous Populations*. Final report submitted by the Introduction 30 July 1981E/CN.4/Sub.2/476, 10 August 1982E/CN.4/Sub.2/1982/2, 5 August 1983E/CN.4/Sub.2/1983/21.

consciousness) and is recognized and accepted by these populations as one of its members (acceptance by the group). This preserves for these communities the sovereign right and power to decide who belongs to them, without external interference.

During the period leading up to the formulation of the Declaration, many Indigenous organisations rejected the idea of a formal definition of Indigenous peoples that would be adopted by States. Similarly, government delegations expressed the view that it was neither desirable nor necessary to elaborate a universal definition of Indigenous peoples.

Finally, at its fifteenth session in 1997, the Working Group concluded that a definition of Indigenous peoples at the global level was not possible at that time, and certainly not necessary for the adoption of the Draft Declaration on the Rights of Indigenous Peoples. Article 8 of the Draft Declaration, stated that:

> Indigenous peoples have a collective and individual right to maintain and develop their distinct identities and characteristics, including the right to identify themselves as indigenous and to be recognized as such.

International Labour Organisation (ILO) Convention No. 169 – a legally binding instrument that articulates the rights of Indigenous and tribal peoples – provides a statement of coverage rather than a definition. Article 1 states that the Convention applies to:[13]

> a)   tribal peoples in independent countries whose social, cultural and economic conditions distinguish them from other sections of the national community and whose status is regulated wholly or partially by their own customs or traditions or by special laws or regulations;
>
> b)   peoples in independent countries who are regarded as indigenous on account of their descent from the populations which inhabited the country, or a geographical region to which the country belongs, at the time of conquest or colonization or the establishment of present state boundaries and who irrespective of their legal status, retain some or all of their own social, economic, cultural and political institutions.

Article 1 also indicates that self-identification as Indigenous or tribal shall be regarded as a fundamental criterion for determining the groups to which the provisions of the Convention apply. The terms 'Indigenous peoples' and 'tribal peoples' are used by the ILO as there are tribal peoples who are not 'Indigenous'

---

13 International Labour Organization Indigenous and Tribunal Peoples Convention No. 169 (opened for signature 27 June 1989, entered into force 5 September 1991), art 1.

in the literal sense, but who nevertheless live in a similar situation. An example would be Afro-descended Saramaka Peoples (Suriname); or tribal peoples in Africa such as the San (Botswana) or Maasai (Kenya and Tanzania) who may not have occupied the region they currently inhabit longer than other population groups. Cultural difference is a criterion required by the ILO Convention to determine an Indigenous or tribal people as opposed to a group of people who have occupied an area since time immemorial.

Nevertheless, many of these peoples refer to themselves as 'Indigenous' in order to fall under discussions taking place at the United Nations.[14]

For practical purposes, the terms 'Indigenous' and 'tribal' are used as synonyms in the UN system when the peoples concerned identify themselves as Indigenous. The lack of formal definition of 'peoples' or 'minorities' has not been crucial to the organisation's successes or failures in those domains, nor to the promotion, protection or monitoring of the rights recognised for these groups. With regard to the concept of 'Indigenous peoples', the prevailing view today is that no formal universal definition is necessary. For practical purposes the common under-standing of the term is the one provided in the Martinez Cobo study mentioned above.

The rights of Indigenous peoples that have been recognised are essentially those associated with and intrinsic to their custom and culture, such as control over their lands and resources.[15] For the Sami peoples (Norway, Sweden, Finland and Russia), it was the watershed *Alta* case that provided the catalyst for recognition of their Indigenous rights to natural resources.[16] In Australia the Aboriginal peoples have sought recognition of title to their traditional lands in a series of cases illustrated by *Mabo*,[17] and in Canada, recognition was sought through the *Calder* case.[18] In New Zealand, the *Attorney General v Ngati Apa* case[19] also centred on determining land and resource rights as well as the rights of due process.[20]

---

14 Andrew Erueti "The Demarcation Of Indigenous Peoples' Traditional Lands: Com-paring Domestic Principles Of Demarcation With Emerging Principles Of Interna-tional Law" (Fall, 2006) 23(3) Arizona Journal of International and Comparative Law 3 at 543.

15 The realisation of these rights is recognised as a form of self-determination.

16 Henry Minde "The Challenge of Indigenism: The Struggle for Sami Land Rights and Self-Government in Norway 1960–1990" in Svein Jentoft, Henry Minde and Ragnar Nilsen (eds) *Indigenous Peoples, Resource Management and Global Rights* (Eburon, Nether-lands, 2003) at 75.

17 *Mabo v Queensland* (No 2) (1992) 175 CLR; *Wiks Peoples v Queensland* (1996) 121 ALR 129.

18 *Calder v Attorney General of British Columbia* [1973] SCR 313.

19 *Attorney General v Ngati Apa* [2003] NZCA 117.

20 These instances of progress have sometimes been reversed; for example, the ensuing Foreshore and Seabed Act 2004 vested ownership of the foreshore in the Crown, limiting any customary claim. Although this Act has now been repealed, with the Takutai Moana Act, customary claims are still limited.

UN Declaration on the Rights of Indigenous Peoples

Perceived as a major triumph, the Declaration[21] is the only international instrument that views Indigenous rights through an Indigenous lens.[22] As a Declaration the orthodox view is that it will not be legally binding upon the States.[23] However, it provides a benchmark as an international standard, against which Indigenous peoples can measure State action, and a means of appeal in the international arena.[24] Parts of the Declaration may also represent binding international law. According to Professor James Anaya:[25]

> ... *the Declaration may be understood to embody or reflect, to some extent, customary international law* [emphasis added]. A norm of customary international law emerges – or crystallizes – when a preponderance of states ... converge on a common understanding of the norm's content and *expect future behaviour to conform to the norm* ... [emphasis added]

The Declaration opens with general statements. Articles 4 and 5 then provide fundamental additions from the perspective of Indigenous people's rights:

Article 4
Indigenous peoples, in exercising their right to self-determination, have the right to autonomy or self-government in matters relating to their internal and local affairs, as well as ways and means for financing their autonomous functions.

Article 5
Indigenous peoples have the right to maintain and strengthen their distinct political, legal, economic, social and cultural institutions, while retaining their right to participate fully, if they so choose, in the political, economic, social and cultural life of the State.

Other articles build upon these basic provisions, including the rights against assimilation or destruction of Indigenous culture and effective redress for past breaches of this right (Art 8), the right to practice and revitalise the cultural

---

21 "United Nations Declaration on the Rights of Indigenous Peoples: Adopted by the General Assembly 13 September 2007" (2007) <www.un.org>.
22 It is acknowledged that ILO Conventions 107 and 169 also recognise Indigenous rights. However, unlike ILO Conventions 107 and 169, the Declaration has been adopted and/or endorsed by the majority of States.
23 Davis, above n 2 at 36.
24 Toki, above n 4 at 245.
25 Anaya, above n 4 at 80; Toki, above n 4, Claire Charters "Developments in Indigenous Peoples' Rights under International Law and Their Implications" (December 2005) 21 NZULR at 519.

traditions and customs of Indigenous peoples is also accompanied by redress for past removal of cultural property (Art 11),[26] and the right to establish their own media (Art 16). It is clear that cultural rights are central to the Declaration. In relation to other economic, social and cultural rights, Art 21 provides that:

1. Indigenous peoples have the right, without discrimination, to the improvement of their economic and social conditions, including, inter alia, in the areas of education, employment, vocational training and retraining, housing, sanitation, health and social security.
2. States shall take effective measures and, where appropriate, special measures to ensure continuing improvement of their economic and social conditions. Particular attention shall be paid to the rights and special needs of indigenous elders, women, youth, children and persons with disabilities.

This is supplemented by other specific rights, including rights to presently occupied lands as well as rights to lands that were traditionally, but no longer occupied by the Indigenous peoples concerned (see Arts 26–28).

The Declaration clarifies and places Indigenous peoples within a human rights framework.[27] In doing so it recognises Māori, the Indigenous peoples of New Zealand, as a collective, not just as individuals.

The Declaration contains more than 20 provisions affirming Indigenous peoples' collective right to participate in decision making. It emphasises Indigenous peoples' right to participate as a core principle of international human rights law. In particular, Article 18 provides:

Indigenous peoples have the right to participate in decision-making in matters which would affect their rights, through representatives chosen by themselves in accordance with their own procedures, as well as to maintain and develop their own indigenous decision-making institutions.

Further provisions supporting Indigenous peoples' right to participation include Articles 19 and 20 of the Declaration. Article 19 states:

States shall consult and cooperate in good faith with the indigenous peoples concerned through their own representative institutions in order to obtain

26 See also art 13, relating to the protection of the histories, languages, philosophies, and art 14, relating to educational systems; art 31 provides for the protection of traditional knowledge, including sciences and technologies.
27 Rainforest Foundation US "Promoting Indigenous Rights Worldwide: S. James Anaya" (7 July 2009) Blogging the Rainforest <www.rainforestfoundationus.wordpress.com>.

their free, prior and informed consent before adopting and implementing legislative or administrative measures that may affect them.

The more significant right is contained in Article 20. This provides:

1. Indigenous peoples have the right to maintain and develop their political, economic and social systems or institutions, to be secure in the enjoyment of their own means of subsistence and development, and to engage freely in all their traditional and other economic activities.
2. Indigenous peoples deprived of their means of subsistence and development are entitled to just and fair redress.

The lynchpin of the Declaration, however, is contained in Article 3, which provides:

Indigenous peoples have the right of self-determination. By virtue of that right they freely determine their political status and freely pursue their economic, social and cultural development.

The principle of participation in decision-making has a clear relationship with Indigenous peoples' right to self-determination, which includes, the right to autonomy or self-government (Arts 4 and 5), and the State's obligation to consult Indigenous peoples in matters that may affect them based on the principle of free, prior and informed consent (Art 19). These legal concepts are integral to the right of Indigenous peoples to participate in decision-making.

It is acknowledged that the Declaration provides no explicit text to establish a judicial system for criminal or civil matters beyond or outside the existing respective judicial or legal system. Nonetheless Article 5 (right for Indigenous peoples to maintain their own distinct legal institutions, such as *tikanga* Māori), when read together with Article 20 (right to develop this legal institution) and Article 3 (right to freely pursue their culture), provides support for the implementation of an Indigenous court underpinned by *tikanga* Māori within our current legal system.[28]

---

28 It is acknowledged that the right of Indigenous peoples to use their own systems of law is also recognised by the International Labour Organization Convention No. 169. Articles 8 and 9 of ILO C169 outline the right of Indigenous peoples to preserve and apply their legal system. However, this right is not absolute, as its exercise must not be incompatible with fundamental national and international human rights. Art. 8(1) "In applying national laws and regulations to the peoples concerned, due regard shall be had to their customs or customary laws." Art. 8(2) "These peoples shall have the right to retain their own customs and institutions, where these are not incompatible with fundamental rights defined by the national legal system and with internationally recognised human rights."

Legal effect of the Declaration

The orthodox view is that the Declaration is soft law[29] and will not be legally binding upon the State unless it is incorporated into domestic legislation.[30] The doctrine of state sovereignty provides a restriction on international instruments, such as the Declaration, to regulate matters within the realm of the state.[31]

Incorporation

In Bolivia the recently promulgated Constitution has fully incorporated the collective rights of Indigenous peoples, including those rights contained in the Declaration.[32] Bolivia's Electoral Transition Law created seven special Indigenous electoral districts. For the first time, the Indigenous peoples of Bolivia have direct representation in the Legislative Assembly. Nonetheless, Indigenous leaders believe that the current number of electoral districts does not give Indigenous peoples enough voice in the Assembly. The intention is that the new electoral law will propose a fairer representation system.[33] Ecuador has also incorporated the Declaration into its Constitution, the Constitution of the Republic of Ecuador 2008.

If New Zealand followed this approach and incorporated the Declaration into domestic legislation, the onus would be on the New Zealand government to provide Māori the ability to fully participate in decision-making matters that may affect them socially, politically and economically. This could be achieved through the meaningful application of Te Ao Māori. As in Latin American countries, discrete legislation could be enacted to ensure meaningful Indigenous representation in government.[34]

29 The term "soft law" refers to quasi-legal instruments that do not have any legally binding force. The term is traditionally associated with international law including most resolutions and declarations of the United Nations General Assembly.

30 Davis, above n 2 at 36. It is acknowledged that in June 2006 the International Law Association Executive Council approved the establishment of a Committee on the Rights of Indigenous Peoples. At the first meeting of the Committee (Pretoria, 2007), it was decided that the Committee would focus on the actual legal meaning of the UN Declaration on the Rights of Indigenous Peoples (UNDRIP), adopted by the UN General Assembly in September 2007. This work is currently in progress focusing on relevant cases that may reviewed and evaluated against the UNDRIP.

31 S James Anaya "The Rights of Indigenous People to Self-determination in the Post-Declaration Era" in Claire Charters and Rodolfo Stavenhagen (eds) *Making the Declaration Work: The United Nations Declaration on the Rights of Indigenous Peoples* (International Working Group for Indigenous Affairs, Copenhagen, 2009) at 194; see also International Law Association *The Hague Conference (2010): Rights of Indigenous Peoples*, Interim report (2010) <www.ila-hq.org>.

32 United Nations High Commissioner for Human Rights "Report of the United Nations High Commissioner for Human Rights on the Activities of Her office in the Plurinational State of Bolivia" (2010) United Nations Human Rights Council A/HRC/13/26/Add.2 18 at [4] <http://daccess-dds-ny.un.org>.

33 At [16].

34 See discussion by Bartolome Clavero "Cultural Supremacy, Domestic Constitutions and the Declaration on the Rights of Indigenous Peoples" in Charters and

Legal reception[35]

How the Declaration is received depends, in part, on the respective jurisdictions of the area.[36] For instance, notwithstanding the current status of the Declaration as soft law, Chief Justice Conteh in the Supreme Court of Belize found that:[37]

> Given the Government's support of the *Declaration on the Rights of Indigenous Peoples* [emphasis added] … which embodies the general principles of international law relating to Indigenous peoples … *the Government will not disregard the Declaration* [emphasis added].

Belize is a common law jurisdiction. Should reliance be placed on the Declaration, this decision could provide a persuasive authority for extending the ability for Māori to fully participate in decision-making affairs, as one example.

Furthermore, Bolivia and Ecuador have incorporated the Declaration into domestic law,[38] with Ecuador also incorporating the Declaration into its legislative framework.[39] In 2010 Professor James Anaya, the Special Rapporteur, visited New Zealand and commented that:[40]

> Stavenhagen above 31 at 344–350. It is encouraging that the UN Secretary-General has requested that a system wide action plan be developed to ensure a coherent approach to achieving the ends of the United Nations Declaration on the Rights of Indigenous Peoples be implemented (A/RES/69/2, paragraph 31).

35 It is acknowledged that a growing body of case law from all jurisdictions is currently being collated in the form of a database; see UNDRIP Online Public Database <http://www.ilc.unsw.edu.au/research/undrip-online-public-database>

36 See Patricia Borraz and Loreta Ferrer (ed) *Indigenous Peoples' Human Rights in Domestic Courts* (Human Rights Office of the Spanish Ministry of Foreign Affairs and Cooperation 2013) where it is noted that "in Latin America, although variable between regions, there is a body of developing jurisprudence on the recognition of Indigenous peoples' rights and those incorporated in UNDRIP. For instance, under the guidance of its Constitutional Court, in Colombia reference to the UNDRIP and to the Inter American jurisprudence is common. In the recent Tres Islas case in Peru, the Constitutional Court interprets the provisions of the Constitution in the light of the Inter American jurisprudence, but also on Articles 3 and 4 of UNDRIP. Undoubtedly, the progressive interpretation of the Inter American human rights system has been instrumental for these developments, as well as the constitutional and legal recognition in the countries of the region. Nevertheless, reference to the UNDRIP, in domestic courts reasoning is non-existent in many of the countries in the region"; see also Davis, above n 2 at 31.

37 *Cal & Ors v the Attorney General of Belize & Anor* (2007) Claim Nos 171 and 172 of 2007, Conteh CJ (Belize Sup Ct) at [132].

38 New Political Constitution of the State Act 2009 (Bol), s 1(1), art 2.

39 For example Article 57 of Ecuador's Constitution recognises the right to "Free, Prior and Informed *Consultation*", however, this does not always translate into the right of Indigenous peoples to oppose projects that will adversely impact on their traditional lands. See also Chapter 6 'Initiatives in Comparative Jurisdictions'.

40 Statement of the United Nations Special Rapporteur on the Situation of the Human Rights and Fundamental Freedoms of Indigenous Peoples, Professor James Anaya, upon conclusion of his visit to New Zealand 22 July 2010 at [4]. <www.ohchr.org>.

It should be noted that certain initiatives underway in New Zealand represent important steps towards advancing the purpose and objectives of the United Nations Declaration on the Rights of Indigenous Peoples. This Declaration, far from affirming rights that place indigenous peoples in a privileged position, aims at repairing the ongoing consequences of the historical denial of the right to self-determination and other basic human rights. I am, of course, very pleased to note that New Zealand recently declared its endorsement of the Declaration, thus joining the overwhelming majority of States that have expressed their support for this historic instrument.

In New Zealand the utilisation of the Declaration in a judicial forum is not novel.[41] The Waitangi Tribunal has positively referred to the then Draft Declaration in respect to claims relating to *tino rangatiratanga*.[42] The High Court decision of *Ngai Tahu Māori Trust Board v Director General of Conservation* also referred to the Draft Declaration.[43] More recently the Supreme Court, in referring to the Declaration, noted that:[44]

> ... whether Ms. Clarke's decision as executor as to the burial of Mr. Takamore was one to which she was entitled to come, in application of common law principles as developed in conformity with human rights norms, the Treaty of Waitangi, and the Declaration of the Rights of Indigenous Peoples (which recognises the interest of many indigenous peoples in the repatriation of human remains and which emphasises the collective nature of the rights of indigenous peoples).

If Māori engaged in a judicial challenge to realise their right to participate fully in the decision-making process, reliance could be placed on Conteh CJ's comments in *Cal & Ors v the Attorney General of Belize & Anor*.[45] Māori could argue that, as New Zealand has endorsed the Declaration, the government should not disregard the general principles contained therein.

In the absence of direct incorporation by statute, there are different methods of recognising international human rights instruments, including recourse through administrative law. First, the (outdated) concept of legitimate expectation in Australia[46] and mandatory relevant consideration in New Zealand[47] have been

---

41 See also reference to the Declaration in *Takamore v Clarke* SC 131/2011 [2012] NZSC 116, [2012] 2 NZLR 733 at [12] and [35].
42 "The Taranaki Report: Kaupapa Tuatahi" (Waitangi Tribunal, Wellington, 1996) Wai 143 <www.waitangi-tribunal.govt.nz.>
43 *Ngai Tahu Māori Trust Board v Director General of Conservation* [1995] 3 NZLR 553.
44 *Takamore v Clarke* [2012] NZSC 116 at [35] per Wild J and Glazebrook J.
45 *Cal & Ors v the Attorney General of Belize & Anor* (2007) Claim Nos 171 and 172 of 2007, Conteh CJ (Belize Sup Ct) at [132].
46 *Minister for Immigration and Ethnic Affairs v Teoh* (1995) 183 CLR 273 (HCA).
47 *Tavita v Minister of Immigration* [1994] 2 NZLR 257; (1993) 11 FRNZ 508; (1993) 1 HRNZ 30 (CA).

utilised to treat unincorporated international obligations as considerations for the decision maker. Also the presumption of consistency, a common law principle of statutory interpretation, recognises that Parliament is presumed not to legislate intentionally in breach of its obligations.[48] In *Zaoui v Attorney-General*, the Supreme Court applied this presumption using New Zealand's international law obligations.[49]

Notwithstanding the successful application of administrative law to recognise international obligations in *Zaoui*, Gieringer expresses some concern with the application of the principle of mandatory relevant considerations.[50] Based on this analysis, recourse to the principle of mandatory relevant consideration to recognise the Declaration's provisions could provide a useful option for Māori. Through this, the New Zealand Courts could uphold Māori rights to full participation in decision-making, as per Article 20 of the Declaration.

C Can the principles of the Treaty be used as an aid to clarify and import the rights contained in the UN Declaration on the Rights of Indigenous Peoples?

Wilton Littlechild proposes that the application of Treaty principles, such as partnership, can assist to bridge the gap between the recognition of an Indigenous right and the relevant article in the Declaration.[51] Is this a viable perspective for Māori?

Treaty of Waitangi

Viewed as a simple nullity,[52] unless the Treaty has been implemented by statute, it creates no enforceable rights.[53] It is the "Principles of the Treaty"[54] that are

48 See Philip Joseph *Constitutional and Administrative Law in New Zealand* (4th edition, Thomson Brookers, Wellington, 2014) at 563; Treasa Dunworth "Public International Law" [2000] NZLR 217 at 225, states this area is shrouded in much uncertainty; see, for example, *Brind v Secretary of State for the Home Department* [1991] 1 All ER 720 (UK).

49 *Zaoui v Attorney-General* [2004] 2 NZLR 339; see also Claudia Gieringer "International Law through the Lens of Zaoui: Where is New Zealand At?" (2006) 17 PLR 318.

50 Although Gieringer above still considers *Tavita* to be good law.

51 Oral statement provided to the pre-sessional meeting of the UNPFII, Ottawa, Canada, March 2011. Wilton Littlechild is a past member of the United Nations Permanent Forum for Indigenous Issues and past Chair of the United Nations Expert Mechanism on the Rights for Indigenous Peoples, a well-respected Indigenous leader.

52 *Wi Parata v Bishop of Wellington* (1877) 3 NZJur (NS) 72 at 78 per Prendergast CJ. However, see also *R v Symonds* (1847) NZPCC (SC), per Chapman J at 390 for earlier recognition of native title at common law and consideration of the Treaty.

53 *Te Heuheu Tukino v Aotea District Māori Land Board* [1941] 2 All E.R. 93 at 98; also [1941] NZLR 590 per Viscount Simon LC.

54 See decision of Cooke P in *New Zealand Māori Council v Attorney General* [1987] 1 NZLR 641.

referred to in legislation[55] and policy documents,[56] rather than the text of the Treaty itself. Professor James Anaya, United Nations Special Rapporteur on the Situation of Human Rights and Fundamental Freedoms of Indigenous People noted:[57]

> From what I have observed, the Treaty's principles appear to be vulnerable to political discretion, resulting in their perpetual insecurity and instability.

Nevertheless, this does not detract from the ability of the Treaty principles to provide clarity on the rights articulated in the Declaration. In the case of *Huakina v Waikato Valley Authority*, Chillwell J noted that:[58]

> The Treaty is a part of the fabric of New Zealand society and can provide judicial aid in *interpreting statutes* 'when it is proper, in accordance with the principles of statutory interpretation, to have *resort to extrinsic material*' [emphasis added].

Similarly, during a United States Senate Committee meeting, Professor James Anaya noted:[59]

> [T]he courts should take account of the Declaration in appropriate cases concerning indigenous peoples, just as federal courts, including the Supreme Court, have referred to other *international sources to interpret statutes* [emphasis added], constitutional norms, and legal doctrines in a number of cases.

If the principles of the Treaty could be imported to act as a bridge between the recognition of Māori rights and the relevant Articles of the Declaration, it would then follow that the principles of the Treaty could also, where appropriate, be used as an aid to provide support for the rights articulated in the Declaration.[60]

---

55 For example, Section 4 Conservation Act 1987; Section 9 State Owned Enterprises Act 1986.
56 For example, Office for Disability Issues "New Zealand Disability Strategy Discussion Document: Incorporating the Treaty of Waitangi" at <www.odi.govt.nz>.
57 James Anaya "New Zealand: More to be Done to Improve Indigenous Peoples' Rights Says UN Expert" (2010) Office of the High Commissioner for Human Rights <www.ohchr.org>.
58 *Huakina v Waikato Valley Authority* [1987] 2 NZLR 188 at 210.
59 "US Senate Committee Holds Controversial Hearing on UN Indigenous Declaration" (10 June 2011) <www.bsnorrell.blogspot.com>.
60 Despite the requirement for domestic legislative recognition, the Waitangi Tribunal established under the Treaty of Waitangi Act 1975 can hear and make recommendations as to claims relating to acts or omission of the Crown that breach the promises made in the Treaty; see also article 37 of the United Nations Declaration on the Rights of Indigenous Peoples that recognises Indigenous peoples' treaty rights.

For example, if the New Zealand government were to grant rights over matters that affected Māori without their participation and if the legislation directed that the principles of the Treaty of Waitangi have to be taken into account, then Māori could place reliance on Article 18 to contextualise these rights. Article 18 of the UNDRIP recognises the right for Indigenous peoples to participate in decision-making in matters which would affect their rights.[61]

Status quo

The Declaration does not create any new rights,[62] but it is the only international instrument that views Indigenous rights through an Indigenous lens:[63]

> The Declaration ... will go a long way in consolidating gains made by indigenous peoples in the international arena toward rolling back inequities and oppression. It builds upon numerous decisions and other standard setting measures over recent decades by a wide range of international institutions that are favourable to indigenous peoples' demands ...
>
> There should not have been a Declaration on the Rights of Indigenous Peoples, because it should not be needed. But it is needed. The history of oppression cannot be erased, but the dark shadow that history has continued to cast can and should be lightened.

The Declaration simply affirms rights derived from generic human rights principles, such as equality and self-determination.[64] The Declaration seeks to recognise Indigenous peoples' rights and contextualises those rights in light of their particular characteristics and circumstances, and promotes measures to remedy the rights' historical and systemic violation.[65]

The significance of the Declaration lies in its normative effect. The Declaration provides a benchmark, as an international standard, against which Indigenous peoples may measure State action. State breach of this standard provides Indigenous peoples with a means of appeal in the international arena.[66]

61 See also Valmaine Toki "Indigenous Rights – Hollow Rights?" [2011] 19 Waikato Law Review 29 for a further example.
62 The rights affirmed are those derived from human rights principles that are deemed of universal application, such as those contained in the Universal Declaration on Human Rights.
63 Anaya, above n 4 at 63. See also S James Anaya "Why There Should not have to be a Declaration on the Rights of Indigenous Peoples" 52nd International Congress of Americanists Sevilla, Summer 2006.
64 Although see also Karen Engle "On Fragile Architecture: The UN Declaration on the Rights of Indigenous Peoples in the Context of Human Rights" (2011) 22(1) EJIL 141 where she examines the limitations of the Declaration and that notes it "temporarily mediates multiple tensions" but there may still be some potential.
65 Anaya, above n 4 at 63.
66 Three United Nations Indigenous mechanisms that can be petitioned to when breaches occur include the United Nations Permanent Forum on Indigenous Rights, the

Recognised and supported by United Nations member states,[67] the Declaration contains norms that are already binding in international law. Thus the Declaration provides an additional international instrument for Indigenous peoples when their rights, such as the right to participate fully in decision-making, have been breached. Indigenous peoples can now argue that not only have international treaties been broken, but a breach of a right in the Declaration has occurred. The available remedy is uncertain; nonetheless, it would be reasonable to conclude that this would provide an avenue to engender effective dialogue between the State and Indigenous peoples.[68] In any event the Declaration provides Indigenous peoples with an international opportunity to shame or embarrass a government.[69] More recently the Secretary-General, requested that the Inter-Agency Support Group on Indigenous Peoples' Issues and Member States in consultation and cooperation with Indigenous peoples, begin developing a system-wide action plan to ensure a coherent approach to achieving the ends of the Declaration. Any progress was to be reported to the General Assembly at its seventieth session.[70] This marks an important development.

Summary

The recent support of the Declaration by Australia, New Zealand, Canada and the United States is significant. Their actions contribute a moral air of robustness to the Indigenous rights articulated in the Declaration.

The orthodox position on the Declaration is that it will not be legally binding upon the State,[71] unless it is incorporated into domestic legislation. Notwithstanding this position, principles of administrative law provide a window to import the rights contained in the Declaration. Adopting the perspective of Wilton Littlechild, the principles of the Treaty can be employed to provide clarity and act as a bridge to the rights articulated in the Declaration.

United Nations Expert Mechanism on the Rights of Indigenous People and the United Nations Special Rapporteur on the Rights of Indigenous Peoples.

67 148 member states have adopted/supported the Declaration. Colombia and Samoa have reversed their abstention leaving nine states still abstaining; see <www.un.org>.

68 The recent support of the World Conference Outcome Document/High Level Plenary Meeting Document by the General Assembly of States in September 2014 signals a further recognition by States of these fundamental rights.

69 As happened on 11 March 2005, when the United Nations Committee on Elimination of Racial Discrimination concluded, in its 66th session, that New Zealand's Foreshore and Seabed Act 2004 contained discriminatory aspects against Māori; see "Committee on the Elimination of Racial Discrimination: Decision on Foreshore and Seabed Act 2004" Sixty Sixth session Decision 1 (66): New Zealand CERD/C/DEC/NZL/1. <www.converge.org.nz>.

70 Sixty-ninth session Item 66 of the provisional agenda Rights of Indigenous Peoples. A/69/L.1, 15 September 2014. Draft resolution submitted by the President of the General Assembly Outcome document of the high-level plenary meeting of the General Assembly known as the World Conference on Indigenous Peoples, [31].

71 Davis, above n 2 at 36.

According to Sir Taihākurei (Eddie) Durie:[72]

> We have completed the trilogy. The 1835 Declaration acknowledged indigenous self-determination. The 1840 Treaty upheld it within the structures of a State. This Declaration now confirms it and says how it should be applied. As rights go, that's a big step. It fills the gaps in the Treaty of Waitangi. It is something to, famously, applaud.
>
> Already it has had practical effect. Last week it was the basis for submissions before the Waitangi Tribunal in North Auckland, to support a more principled approach to managing Treaty settlements, and before the Māori Affairs Select Committee in Wellington, to support a greater Māori role in Māori policy development.

Irrespective of the concerns surrounding the wording of support given to the Declaration, and the legal effect of the Declaration itself, it is without a doubt the most significant document on the rights of Indigenous peoples. The current perspective of States and United Nations Agencies[73] is one of support and willingness to engage and implement the rights contained in the Declaration. The challenge ahead will be the practical manifestation of these rights for Indigenous peoples and, in particular, whether applying the philosophy of Te Ao Māori, realised by an Indigenous legal system, manifested by an Indigenous court and premised on fundamental Māori concepts and doctrine is the most promising way forward for Māori to ameliorate the disproportionate offending rates.

Self-determination has been identified as a key provision in the Declaration. *Tino rangatiratanga* is a key provision in the Treaty of Waitangi. A closer analysis of the synergy between these two concepts may assist to inform this discourse.

D Self-determination

The right of self-determination is provided for in Article 3 of the Declaration:

> Indigenous peoples have the right to self-determination. By virtue of that right they freely determine their political status and freely pursue their economic, social and cultural development.

72 Eddie Taihakurei Durie "Address on the Declaration" (Statement given May 2010 Parliament Buildings).
73 For example, a recommendation from the 10th session of the United Nations Permanent Forum on Indigenous Issues noted "The Permanent Forum welcomes the World Intellectual Property Organization facilitating a process, in accordance with the Declaration, to engage with Indigenous peoples on matters including Intellectual Property, Genetic Resources, Traditional Knowledge and Folklore".

According to Professor James Anaya:[74]

> Understood as a human right the essential idea of self-determination is that human beings, individually and as groups, are equally entitled to be in control of their own destinies and to live within governing institutional orders that are devised accordingly.

The term self-determination is synonymous with terms such as equality and freedom.[75] There is no definition of self-determination within the Declaration. However, there are different schools of thought as to its meaning, namely 'external' self-determination, or the right to secede, and 'internal' self-determination. As an alternative, Professor Anaya articulates 'substantive' versus 'remedial' self-determination.

The underlying rationale for 'substantive' versus 'remedial' self-determination derives from "the substance of the right of self-determination, as opposed to any remedies that may have resulted from violations of the right of all peoples to control their own destinies under conditions of equality".[76] The process of decolonisation reversed the process of colonialism and the associated implementation of foreign rule. This was a process that did not, on its own, address the substantive right of self-determination. Rather, it was a remedy to address the violation of rights that existed prior to colonisation. Anaya argues that rather than self-determination requiring that each group form its own state or enjoy external self-determination, self-determination provides the right for people to be entitled to participate freely and equally in the constitution and governing institutional order of the State. However, those peoples who have suffered extreme violations of their right to self-determination would be entitled to a regime separate from the existing regime as would those peoples who have been denied effective remedies within the existing regime. Anaya appears to be insinuating that the more serious the violations of basic human rights, the more likely the group would be entitled to external self-determination. Conversely, those groups who have not suffered from similar human rights violations would be entitled to exercise self-determination within the existing regime.

For Māori, the latter form of self-determination would apply, thereby allowing them to exercise self-determination within the existing regime.[77] Extensions to the

74 Anaya, above n 31 at 187.
75 See also discussion by Federico Lenzerini "The Trail of Broken Dreams, the Status of Indigenous Peoples in International Law" in Federico Lenzerini (ed) *Reparation for Indigenous Peoples International and Comparative Perspectives* (Oxford University Press, Oxford, 2008) at 98–102.
76 Anaya, above n 31 at 189.
77 This is consistent with comments by Jeremy Waldron "The Cosmopolitan Alternative" in Will Kymlicka *The Rights of Minority Cultures* (OUP, New York, 1995) at 103 where he notes that "indigenous communities make claims for special provision and for the autonomous direction of their own affairs ... and must accept some responsibility to participate in ... [the] wider life".

jurisdiction of the Māori Land Court or the creation of a Tikanga Court provide two such examples of this form of self-determination. That is, a form of self-determination captured in the United Nations Declaration on the Rights of Indigenous People.

Self-determination and tino rangatiratanga

According to Article 2 of the Treaty of Waitangi (Māori text), Māori retain their *tino rangatiratanga*. In contrast, the English version only guarantees to Māori possession over their lands and estates.

Tino rangatiratanga and self-determination are both rights that have not yet been incorporated by the State into domestic legislation. To this end, both are aspirational rights, representing ideals as opposed to fixed standards.[78] Both advocate for legal pluralism, thereby enabling *iwi* to practice internal self-government and manage their own affairs.[79] However, they differ slightly.

It is suggested that *tino rangatiratanga* provides the stronger claim for Māori.[80] The Waitangi Tribunal has acknowledged that sovereignty was acquired subject to *tino rangatiratanga* and more recently that Māori did not cede sovereignty to the Crown.[81] This implies that *tino rangatiratanga* can exist independently to State sovereignty.

In contrast, the right of self-determination derives from, and exists under sovereignty.[82] Furthermore, self-determination has clear boundaries; it can either prevail or fall when in conflict with other human rights. In the context of *tino rangatiratanga*, it is uncertain whether such boundaries exist.[83] Finally, *tino rangatiratanga* expresses the unique Māori concept of *rangatiratanga* that relates to concepts such as leadership and governance. Self-determination, however, is a creation of a Western paradigm.[84]

While self-determination acts and strives for similar goals, it is philosophically distinct from *tino rangatiratanga*. Nonetheless, the right of self-determination will support and complement Māori claims to *tino rangatiratanga*. Mason Durie regards the Treaty Settlements as the perfect union between *tino rangatiratanga* and

78 Toki, above n 4 at 256.
79 The Waitangi Tribunal has defined *tino rangatiratanga* as "self-determination"; see Waitangi Tribunal *Taranaki Kaupapa Tuatahi Report* (Wai 143, 1996) at 307; see also Toki, above at 210.
80 Toki, above n 4, at 256.
81 See the Waitangi Tribunal *Report of the Waitangi Tribunal on the Orakei Claim* (Wai 9, 1987) and Te Paparahi o te Raki Waitangi Tribunal Report (November 2014) Wai 1040.
82 Toki, above n 4.
83 The Waitangi Tribunal views the Crown's right to govern may only override *rangatiratanga* as a last resort Waitangi Tribunal *The Whanganui River Report* – Wai 167 (1999) at 330. The Tribunal saw the "national interest in conservation [was] not a reason for negating Māori rights of property".
84 Toki, above n 4.

self-determination.[85] They provide for *tino rangatiratanga* in the sense that they recognise the *mana* of the Māori people and often provide an economic basis for their development.

Thus Treaty Settlements could provide an opportunity for *iwi* to financially support an initiative, such as an Indigenous court, either as a pan *iwi* Court or an *iwi* jurisdictional Court. However, the settlements themselves require legislation and delegated authority. In this way the two concepts support each other.

This analysis shows that *tino rangatiratanga* is the stronger right for Māori, unlike self-determination. Self-determination does not fundamentally change the nature of existing Indigenous Māori rights. Rather, it supports and complements *tino rangatiratanga*.

A right to secede

Many Māori commentators, such as Andrea Tunks,[86] have argued that Māori do not seek secession, but rather *tino rangatiratanga*. According to Moana Jackson, *tino rangatiratanga* is more akin to sovereignty.[87] Such an approach would facilitate the implementation of *tikanga* Māori.

Brookfield acknowledges that, prior to the Declaration, a right of self-determination and the right to secession for Indigenous peoples was uncertain.[88] Nonetheless, in light of its development, some states considered that the Declaration would provide Indigenous peoples with a similar right to secede from the encapsulating State.[89] This would impact on concepts such as state sovereignty and political unity.

The right to secession is limited by existing international law norms and is confined to particular peoples such as those who are subject to 'alien domination'.[90]

According to Anaya, secession is available when it is remedial in nature,[91] and distinguishes this from a substantive form, in which self-determination is a human right. When this substantive form of self-determination is denied, a breach occurs, requiring a remedy. This remedial form of self-determination is proportionate to the nature of the breach or violation.[92] Following this reasoning, secession would only be invoked when the nature of the violation was so great that secession, or external self-determination, is the only remedy.

85 Mason Durie, *Te Mana Te Kāwanatanga* (Oxford University Press, Auckland, 1998).
86 Andrea Tunks "Pushing the Sovereign Boundaries in Aotearoa" (1999) 4(23) Indigenous Law Bulletin 15 at 69.
87 Moana Jackson "Where Does Sovereignty Lie?" in Colin James (ed) *Building the Constitution* (Institute of Policy Studies, Wellington, 2000) at 196.
88 F M (Jock) Brookfield *Waitangi & Indigenous Rights* (updated ed, Auckland University Press, Auckland, 2006) at 77.
89 Brookfield, above.
90 Claire Charters "The Rights of Indigenous Peoples" October (2006) NZLJ 335 at 336.
91 Anaya, above n 31 at 59, 190–194.
92 Above.

In order for Māori to claim secession, the violations and actions, or inactions, by the Crown would need to be viewed as so harmful that secession or external self-determination is justified. Although it is uncertain when this would apply, alternatives such as self-government, legal pluralism or internal self-determination may be appropriate. An Indigenous court, premised on fundamental Māori concepts and doctrine through an extension to the jurisdiction of the Māori Land Court or a Tikanga Court, could be an example of such a situation.

The key distinction between internal and external self-determination is that internal self-determination operates within the existing legal framework.[93] 'Internal self-determination' or self-government is viewed as the right for a people to freely choose their own political and economic regime.[94] Internal self-determination is consistent with Article 46 of the UN Declaration on the Rights of Indigenous Peoples:

> Nothing in this Declaration may be interpreted as implying for any State, people, group or person any right to engage in any activity or to perform any act contrary to the Charter of the United Nations or construed as authorizing or encouraging any action which would dismember or impair totally or in part, the territorial integrity or political unity of sovereign and independent States.

And, also Article 4:

> Indigenous peoples, in exercising their right to self-determination, have the right to autonomy or self-government in matters relating to their internal and local affairs, as well as ways and means for financing their autonomous functions.

It would appear that the Declaration provides for two schools of self-determination. An external form of self-determination may be more difficult to achieve, nonetheless an internal form of self-determination is also available.

Thus Article 4 bestows the ability for Indigenous peoples to realise their right of autonomy or self-government over their internal and local affairs. Read together with Articles 5, 18 and 19, the Declaration provides for Indigenous people the right to participate fully, if they so choose, in the political, economic, social and cultural life of the State, and to participate in all decisions affecting them or their rights. Although the orthodox concept of self-determination was important in mobilising the international Indigenous movement, it does not capture or reflect the diversity within national systems.[95] This provides fertile grounds for the

93 Toki, above n 4.
94 See A Cassese *Self Determination of Peoples* (Cambridge University Press, Cambridge, 1995) at 101.
95 Malgosia Fitzmaurice "The Question of Indigenous Peoples Rights: A Time for Reappraisal?" in Duncan French (ed) *Statehood and Self-Determination* (Cambridge University Press, Cambridge, 2013) at 350.

ability of Māori to apply their philosophy of Te Ao Māori, realised by an Indigenous legal system, manifested by an Indigenous court, premised on fundamental Māori concepts and doctrine at the same time as their right to participate in external decision making processes and the political order of the State.

The thrust of self-determination is to enable Indigenous peoples to be in control of their destinies and to create their own political and legal organisation of their territories.[96] This does not necessarily amount to separate statehood, although that possibility remains.[97] Erica Irene Dias argues that Indigenous peoples have a mutual duty to share power with the existing state and perceives Article 3 as grounds for an argument for external self-determination.[98] Further, Professor James Anaya argues, that although secession often is not the intention of Indigenous peoples, it has, nevertheless, held a symbolic rhetoric.[99]

Self-determination: a human right

Despite the text of the articles in the Declaration, the Declaration couches the right of self-determination as a fundamental human right for Indigenous peoples. To this end attributes of statehood or sovereignty are, at the most, instrumental to the realisation of these values. But according to Professor James Anaya, they are not the essence of self-determination for Indigenous peoples:[100]

> And for most peoples, especially in light of cross cultural diverse identities, full self-determination, in a real sense, does not justify a separate state and may even be impeded by a separate state. It is a rare case in the post-colonial world in which self-determination, understood from a human rights perspective, will require secession or the dismemberment of states.

The objective of this section is to ascertain whether the Treaty of Waitangi and the United Nations Declaration on the Rights of Indigenous Peoples could support the implementation of an Indigenous court, premised on fundamental Māori concepts and doctrine. Intrinsic to this review is the right of self-determination provided in international documents. In this regard the internationally recognised right to self-determination is fundamental to recognising and realising the rights of Indigenous

---

96 See discussion by Iris Marion Young "Together in Difference: Transforming the Logic of Group Political Conflict" in Will Kymlikca *The Rights of Minority Cultures* (OUP, New York, 1995) at 155 where she notes that "what a bicultural society means... for Māori ... has not ended" highlighting the importance for Indigenous peoples to be in control of their destinies.

97 See also discussion by James Tully "Indigenous Peoples and Freedom" in J Tully (ed) *Public Philosophy in a New Key* (Cambridge University Press, New York, 2008) at 285.

98 As cited in Fitzmaurice, above n 95; see also Anaya, above n 31.

99 Anaya, above n 4, Anaya, above n 31 at 190–194.

100 S James Anaya *Indigenous Peoples in International Law* (Oxford University Press, New York, 1996) at 8.

peoples, including that of culture, *tikanga* Māori. Achieving self-determination would allow Māori to freely choose and determine their own political and legal systems. The synergy with *tino rangatiratanga* provided for in the Treaty of Waitangi further supports this dialogue.

New Zealand's legal system ascribes to parliamentary sovereignty[101] and the rule of law as articulated in the Constitution Act 1986, which stipulates that the Parliament continues to have full power to make laws.[102] The duties and obligations contained in the Treaty recognise the human rights responsibilities between the Crown and Māori. It is suggested that to alleviate the disproportionate social and economic statistics of Māori, the entrenchment of fundamental Indigenous rights, including that of self-determination, is required. In the absence of entrenchment, it is foreseeable that applying the text of the Treaty consistently with the United Nations Declaration on the Rights of Indigenous People could provide an avenue for Māori to attain self-determination.[103]

The Declaration on the Rights of Indigenous Peoples simply affirms rights derived from human rights principles such as equality and self-determination. These basic rights have been denied to Indigenous peoples and the Declaration on the Rights of Indigenous Peoples seeks to recognise such rights and contextualises them in light of their particular characteristics and circumstances.[104] Moreover, the Declaration promotes measures to remedy the historical and systemic denial of Indigenous people's rights.[105]

The Declaration on the Rights of Indigenous Peoples is the only United Nations document dedicated to Indigenous human rights and addresses Indigenous-specific concerns. The Declaration does not create any new rights; however, it is the only international instrument that views Indigenous rights through an Indigenous lens.[106]

Professor James Anaya stated:[107]

> I have observed several positive aspects of New Zealand's legal and policy landscape, as well as ongoing challenges, in relation to Māori issues. A unique feature of New Zealand is the Treaty of Waitangi of 1840, which is understood to be one of the country's founding instruments. The principles

101 Supreme Court Act 2003, s 3(2).
102 Constitution Act 1986, s 15(1).
103 With the support of the provisions in the ICCPR and ICESCR. However, the ICESCR and ICCPR contain general human rights and, on their own, do not meet the cultural and political concerns of Indigenous people. However, considered in light of favourable general comments and creative legal interpretations of treaty monitoring-body decisions can, advance indirectly Indigenous rights.
104 Anaya, above n 4 at 63. See Anaya, above n 31.
105 Anaya, above n 4.
106 Anaya above.
107 Statement of the United Nations Special Rapporteur on the Situation of the Human Rights and Fundamental Freedoms of Indigenous Peoples, Professor James Anaya, upon conclusion of his visit to New Zealand, 22 July 2010.

of the Treaty provide a foundation for Māori self-determination based on a real partnership between Māori and the New Zealand State, within a framework of respect for cross cultural understanding and the human rights of all citizens. I have learned of steps being taken within this framework, which can be described as constituting a good practice in the making, and I hope that concerted efforts will continue to be made in this regard.

If the right, for Māori, of self-determination was realised through a Treaty partnership, this would result in a pluralistic society. It is now timely to consider the concept of pluralism.

Pluralism

Sally Engle Merry describes legal pluralism as "a situation in which two or more legal systems coexist in the same social field".[108] However, Anne Griffiths notes that "legal pluralism has been invoked to uphold notions of authority and legitimacy, to favour or promote one set of legal claims over another, or to validate and acknowledge the existence of alternative or coexisting forms of legal ordering within a particular domain".[109] This raises questions regarding the power to make law and who is to benefit. As the formulation of law is underscored by differing epistemologies if claims are made that are inconsistent with the dominant legal order, they will be ignored.[110] Anne Griffiths further contends that "with the rise of the nation-state a particular paradigm of law became predominant, one in which state law acquired jurisdiction and took precedence over other forms".[111]

With the use of case studies from Australia and Canada, Kristen Anker provides convincing dialogue on ways to make space for Indigenous legal traditions within a sovereign nation.[112] Anker states:[113]

> that an approach to law known as 'legal pluralism' provides a more apt language for treating 'the justice question' of the place of Indigenous law than orthodox legal theory because, in the way I conceive it, a legal pluralist

---

108 Sally Engle Merry "Legal Pluralism" (1988) 22 Law and Society Rev 869 at 870; see also Nicole Roughan "Conceptions of Custom International Law" <http://ssrn.com/abstract=1072965>, for an interesting discussion on compound custom and community 84.

109 Anne Griffiths presentation to Human Rights and Legal Pluralism in Theory and Practice Conference 5th to 6th December 2014, Norwegian Centre for Human Rights (NCHR) in co-operation with the Rights, Individuals, Culture and Society Research Centre (RICS) at the Faculty of Law, University of Oslo, Norway.

110 Above.

111 Above.

112 Kirsten Anker *Declarations of Interdependence A Legal Pluralist Approach to Indigenous Rights* (Ashgate Publishing, UK, 2014).

113 Above.

recognition is an engagement about the nature of law and not about a formal relationship between two fixed entities.

She 'looks out' to other laws and the second 'looks in' towards the nature of state law.[114] Whilst this may be logically sound, on a practical note, within a legal system that fiercely adheres to the principle of Parliamentary Sovereignty underpinned by legal positivism, entertaining the notion of legal pluralism in New Zealand to accommodate *tikanga* Māori appears unworkable.[115]

Equally, in order to adopt legal pluralism, Māori would be required to accept a legal system that was responsible for land alienation and displacement of their customs. Although Eddie Durie contends that "the Treaty of Waitangi is not just a Bill of Rights for Māori but also for Pākehā too"[116] and to this end if the Treaty of Waitangi was entrenched constitutionally it could realise a legal pluralism within New Zealand society,[117] Ani Mikaere and Moana Jackson are sceptical of any benefits in legal pluralism for Māori and depict it as "inherently assimilative and racist".[118] Moana Jackson further contends that under "a guise of sensitivity and good faith the colonial certainty of overt dismissal [*tikanga* Māori] has been replaced by a new-age legalism".[119] Further Jackson has stated that:[120]

The redefinition and incorporation of basic Māori legal and philosophical concepts into the law is part of the continuing story of colonization. Its implementation by government, its acceptance by judicial institutions, and its presentation as an enlightened recognition of Māori rights are merely further blows in that dreadful attack to which colonization subjects the indigenous soul.

Despite the international jurisprudence and constitutional examples articulating the recognition of Indigenous rights,[121] including that of self-determination, the

114 Above.
115 Also Nicole Roughan "The Association of State and Indigenous Law: A Case Study in 'Legal Association'" (2009) 59 UTLJ 135 at 143.
116 *The Treaty of Waitangi: The Symbol of our Life Together as a Nation* (Wellington: NZ 1990 Commission, 1989) 14.
117 R Stavenhagen "Mission to New Zealand" in United Nations Economic and Social Council, Commission on Human Rights, Indigenous Issues (62nd session, item 15) 13 March 2006 at [85].
118 Moana Jackson "Changing Realities: Unchanging Truths" in Commission on Folk Law and Legal Pluralism (ed) *Papers Presented to the Congress at Victoria University of Wellington, August 1992: Volume II* (Law Faculty, Victoria University of Wellington, Wellington, 1992) at 444.
119 Jackson, above.
120 Moana Jackson "Justice and Political Power: Reasserting Māori Legal Processes" in Kayleen Hazlehurst (ed) *Legal Pluralism and the Colonial Legacy: Indigenous Experiences of Justice in Canada, Australia and New Zealand* (Avebury, Aldershot, 1995) at 254.
121 See Chapter 7 '*Tikanga* Māori and Therapeutic Jurisprudence' for further discussion.

right to implement the philosophy of Te Ao Māori within the criminal justice system in New Zealand is still unclear.

In the next section, a review of comparative jurisdictions of the constitutional recognition for the right to implement Indigenous courts will assist to contextualise the potential development of an Indigenous court.

Chapter 6

Initiatives in comparative jurisdictions[1]

A Constitutional recognition of Indigenous rights

It is clear that some settler nations are taking steps to recognise Indigenous rights within their respective constitutions. Some constitutions, such as in Ecuador, are explicit, providing constitutional recognition of an Indigenous legal system. Moreover, the interim Constitution of Nepal makes provision for Indigenous courts.[2]

Whilst some countries have incorporated the rights articulated in the Declaration on Rights of Indigenous Peoples, such as Congo;[3] others, such as Chile and Bangladesh, are not so progressive in including these rights. Although Indigenous peoples within jurisdictions, such as the United States, already enjoy a level of self governance and have established tribal courts, incorporation of Indigenous rights within domestic constitutions would support any initiative to establish an Indigenous court. It is suggested that States that do not currently recognise Indigenous peoples or Indigenous rights in their constitutions should move towards a constitutional reform process in consultation with Indigenous peoples.[4]

---

1 See report written for the United Nations Permanent Forum on Indigenous Issues by Professor Megan Davis, Simon William M'Viboudoulou, Valmaine Toki, Paul Kanyinke Sena, Edward John, Álvaro Esteban Pop Ac and Raja Devasish Roy (2013) *Study on National Constitutions and the United Nations Declaration on the Rights of Indigenous Peoples* E/C.19/2013/18. I would also like to acknowledge the academic conversations with Professor Brad Morse and the provision of the research material that has been reproduced, in particular the Technical Report "Indigenous Provisions in Constitutions around the World".

2 Although not explicit, some constitutional provisions, such as in the Norwegian Constitution, when read together with other articles, provide tentative opportunities for the implementation of an Indigenous court.

3 Congo-Brazzaville as opposed to Democratic Republic of Congo.

4 It is noted that New Zealand and Australia undertook a review of their 'constitutional' position. For New Zealand this included questioning the place of the Treaty of Waitangi within a constitution. One of the recommendations from the UNPFII Report above n 1 was that Indigenous Peoples should be recognised in national constitutions and States that do not currently recognise Indigenous rights in their constitutions should move towards a constitutional reform process, in consultation

Countries including Canada, Australia and the United States have moved towards implementing an Indigenous court.[5] In parts of Malaysia, native courts have been established primarily to deal with breaches of native law and customs.[6] In addition, a number of Indigenous courts have emerged across the African continent, dealing exclusively with Indigenous law.[7] In terms of their success, the anecdotal evidence is positive. Like the Rangatahi Courts in New Zealand however, most are relatively new initiatives and reliable statistical information is lacking.

Constitutional recognition of an Indigenous right to culture and a right of self-determination provides fertile ground for the meaningful implementation of cultural concepts to address the over-representation of Indigenous peoples within the criminal justice system. Two progressive jurisdictions are Ecuador and Bolivia. Some states in the Pacific, such as Vanuatu, have also recognised a right to culture in their constitution.[8]

Ecuador

The common denominator in the Ecuadorian Constitution is the idea of increased inclusion of people and nature in a participatory democratic project.[9]

with Indigenous People, and entrench the Declaration in national constitutions. See also Patricia Borraz and Loreta Ferrer (ed) *Indigenous Peoples' Human Rights in Domestic Courts* (Human Rights Office of the Spanish Ministry of Foreign Affairs and Cooperation, 2013) that reviews the incorporation of the international standards for the protection of Indigenous rights in the decisions of domestic courts.

5 See discussion on Koori Courts, Gladue and Cree Courts.

6 In Sarawak and Sabah, the Native Courts were set up primarily to deal with breaches of native law and customs; see Ramy Bulan Associate Professor Director, Centre for Malaysian Indigenous Studies "Indigenous Peoples and the Right to Participate in Decision Making in Malaysia" Discussion paper prepared for International Expert Seminar on Indigenous Peoples and The Right to Participate in Decision Making, Chiang Mai, Thailand, 20–22 January 2010; see also presentation given to the International Expert Seminar on Access to Justice including Truth and Reconciliation Processes (University of Columbia, New York, 27 February–1 March 2013).

7 However, the Traditional Courts Bill has caused controversy. See Sipho Khumalo "Activists Berate Traditional Courts Bill" *The Mercury* (online ed, South Africa, 12 April 2012). It is also acknowledged that the jurisprudence recognising Indigenous peoples' rights is just emerging and beyond well known cases in South Africa or Botswana it is difficult to find any single decision in domestic courts which takes UNDRIP into account. The lack of a legal framework which recognises the existence and rights of Indigenous peoples is an important obstacle in this context. However, the Endorois decision, will have an impact.

8 See Vanuatu constitution, Part II Section 7 Fundamental Duties – "Every person has fundamental duties to … support and assist … culture and custom of the people of Vanuatu" and Chapter 5 Section 30 Functions of Council "… may make recommendations for the preservation and promotion of ni-Vanuatu culture and languages".

9 This is an ongoing project. Rafael Correa: "I maintain that Ecuador and Latin America have elections but have yet to arrive at what is democracy. In truth, I don't believe that there is democracy in a country where there is so much injustice, so much

Drawing on the commonality of a global culture, the Constitution aims to construct an ecological citizenship, recognising the interconnectedness of all peoples to nature.

Two Indigenous terms, *pacha mama* and *sumak kawsay*, are included in the preamble of the Ecuadorian Constitution. The preamble "celebrates nature, the *pacha mama*/Mother Earth of which we are a part and which is vital to our existence". Further, the preamble builds on "a new form of public coexistence, in diversity and in harmony with nature to achieve the good way of living the *sumak kawsay*".

Pacha Mama broadly translates as 'Mother Earth' and in this sense is analogous with *Papatūānuku*/earth mother for Māori. Although often translated as 'good life' or 'living well', the term *sumak kawsay* is from the Kichwa language relating to an ancestral Andean term that highlights the importance of harmony with nature and communities. Together with the further "recognition of our age-old roots" within the preamble, this concept confirms the relatedness between humans and nature. In this sense, it is closely aligned with *whakapapa* and *whanaungatanga* for Māori.

The concept of *sumak kawsay*, which is referred to five times in the Constitution (once in the preamble and in four articles), encapsulates and reflects an Indigenous worldview. Although the right to a healthy environment is codified in other constitutions, the Ecuadorian constitution is unique in that it connects the environment to cultural/spiritual principles in the realisation of the *sumak kawsay*.

'Living well' is ecocentric and holistic in nature and is based on an ontological assumption of 'relationality', that "all beings exist always in relation and never as 'objects' or 'individuals'".[10] This relational understanding is also at the core of nature as Pachamama.[11] Arturo Escobar suggests that a relational worldview must lead to a 'politics of responsibility' that is "a sequitur of the fact that space, place, and identities are relationally constructed".[12] A relational awareness such as this implicates us in acting responsibly towards all other living beings, both human and non-human.[13]

inequality." Justin Delacour (trans), "Interview with Ecuadorian President Rafael Correa" (North American Council on Latin America, June 18 2009) <www.ecua dor-rising.blogspot.com>. For discussion on reaching legal pluralism in Ecuador see Marc Simon Thomas "Legal Pluralism and the Continuing Quest for Legal Certainty in Ecuador: A Case Study from the Andean Highlands", (2012) 7 Onati Socio-Legal Series 57.

10 Arturo Escobar "Latin America at a Crossroads: Alternative Modernizations, Post-Liberalism, or Post-Development?" (Revised version of paper prepared for the Wayne Morse Center for Law and Politics and presented at the Conference "Violence and Reconciliation in Latin America: Human Rights, Memory, and Democracy" (University of Oregon, Eugene, January 31–February 2 2008)) at 38.

11 A close analogy can be drawn between Pachamama and Papatūānuku of Māori cosmology. Similarly, a relational responsibility of *kaitiakitanga* as care for Papatūānuku is analogous to the *sumak kawsay* or *suma quemaña* care for Pachamama.

12 Escobar, above n 10, at 41.

13 See Chapter 2 'Māori and *tikanga*' on What is *tikanga*? which notes the interrelatedness of animate and inanimate objects, the concept of *whanaungatanga* and *whakapapa*.

Article 14 notes:

> The *right of* [emphasis added] the population *to live in a healthy and ecologically balanced environment that guarantees sustainability and the good way of living (sumak kawsay)* [emphasis added], is recognized.
>
> Environmental conservation, the protection of ecosystems, biodiversity and the integrity of the country's genetic assets, the prevention of environmental damage, and the recovery of degraded natural spaces are declared matters of public interest.

Article 250 provides:

> The territory of the Amazon provinces is *part of an ecosystem that is necessary for the planet's environmental balance of the planet* [emphasis added] [sic]. This territory shall constitute a special territorial district, for which there will be integrated planning embodied in a law including social, economic, environmental and cultural aspects, with land use development and planning *that ensures the conservation and protection of its ecosystems and the principle of sumak kawsay* [emphasis added] (the good way of living).

Section VII, "The Good Way of Living System", of the Constitution is an example of framing otherwise ephemeral principles in the language of human rights. This serves two purposes.

First, it makes the rights justiciable. Although the *sumak kawsay* will be interpreted and practised in ways unique to the Amerindian peoples living relatively autonomously in the Amazon and remote Andean regions, it will also increasingly be brought for determination in the courts.[14] Second, it brings the system of rights into line with the international regime of rights as expressed in the International Labour Organisation Convention 169, the Universal Declaration of Human Rights,[15] the International Covenant on Economic, Social and Cultural Rights, and the United Nations Declaration on the Rights of Indigenous Peoples.[16]

Remarkably, in the section on development, *sumak kawsay* is cited as a primary consideration to guide decision makers.

Article 275 notes:

> The *development structure is the organized, sustainable* [emphasis added] and dynamic group of economic, political, socio-cultural and environmental

14 Particularly the newly created Environmental Court.

15 For instance, second and third generation rights.

16 For a summary of the insistence of the Latin American countries on the inclusion of these rights during the negotiation of the terms of the Universal Declaration of Human Rights, see Geoffrey Robinson *Crimes Against Humanity* (3rd ed, Penguin, Melbourne, 2008) at 37.

systems which *underpin the achievement of the good way of living (sumak kawsay)* [emphasis added].

The State shall plan the development of the country to assure the exercise of rights, the achievement of the objectives of the development structure and the principles enshrined in the Constitution. Planning shall aspire to social and territorial equity, promote cooperation, and be participatory, decentralized, deconcentrated and transparent.

The good way of living shall require persons, communities, peoples and nationalities to effectively exercise their rights and fulfill their responsibilities within the framework of interculturalism, respect for their diversity, and harmonious coexistence with nature [emphasis added].

One of the main concerns with the statement of a general principle that is not amenable to clear and easy interpretation in the context of an existing, property-focused legal system is that it is left to be defined, interpreted and implemented in a non-specific time frame and manner. Alternatively, this flexibility may be a significant advantage, allowing the concept to be adapted to novel situations and emerging social perspectives without the concepts being 'frozen' in time.[17]

The *sumak kawsay* is not to be rooted solely in 'ancient' or 'traditional' practices. Article 387 renders it the responsibility of the State to promote and generate knowledge in terms of the 'good life' through science and technology and provides:

The following shall be *responsibilities of the State* [emphasis added]:

1. To facilitate and promote incorporation into the knowledge society to achieve the objectives of the development system.
2. *To promote the generation and production of knowledge* [emphasis added], to foster scientific and technological research, and *to upgrade ancestral wisdom to thus contribute to the achievement of the good way of living (sumak kawsay)*... [emphasis added].

The Ecuadorian Constitution also enables Indigenous groups to practise their own traditional justice in their territories and their decisions and punishments are to be respected by State bodies, except where they substantially clash with other provisions of the Constitution. Article 57(10) provides that:

Indigenous communes, communities, peoples and nations are recognized and guaranteed, in conformity with the Constitution and human rights agreements, conventions, declarations and other international instruments, the following collective rights ...

17 For the New Zealand interpretations addressing this concern see, Ministry for the Environment *Case Law on Tangata Whenua Consultation* (Ministry for the Environment, Wellington, 1999).

To create, develop, apply and practice their own legal system or common law, which cannot infringe constitutional rights, especially those of women, children and adolescents.

The constitutional right to nature provided by the Ecuadorian Constitution, driven by a right that recognises their Indigenous legal system, provides an opportunity to import Indigenous concepts, such as reciprocity, harmony and balance, so as to attain environmental sustainability.

Concepts such as balance, harmony and healing are intrinsic to the philosophy of all Indigenous peoples. For jurisdictions like Ecuador, appealing to environmental values and a right to nature provides an innate conduit for the recognition of Indigenous values within a constitution. The embrace of these articles would lead to a re-imagining and re-founding of the State by abandoning conventional development narratives based on State and private ownership. Instead, a collective and relational worldview would be cultivated, focusing on the aims of solidarity, complementarity, co-operation and in particular, self-determination.[18]

Notwithstanding the environment falling outside the jurisdiction of the criminal justice system,[19] this example provides a clear and tangible analogy and application of *tikanga* Māori concepts. Furthermore, there is an extensive decentralisation of power to localities with the freedom to choose representative, direct, communal or Indigenous versions of democracy for governance of local affairs.[20] Indigenous groups are able to practise their own traditional justice in their territories and their decisions and punishments are to be respected by representative bodies, except where they substantially clash with other provisions of the constitution.

Notwithstanding the right of self-determination to implement constitutional Indigenous rights, comparative jurisdictions, including those of Bolivia, engage concepts of plurination[21] and culture within their constitution to achieve the same.[22] This is not dissimilar to the notion of legal dialogue in the courtroom to legitimise state practices and judicial authority as a means to embed legal practices.

18 See also Chapter 2 'Māori and *tikanga*' on What is *tikanga* Māori? and the discussion of the Māori world.
19 However see *Auckland Regional Council v Holmes Logging Limited* HC Auckland CRI-2009-404-3 where failure to comply with the legislation and/or breaches of the Resource Management Act 1991 can lead to criminal charges.
20 Title IV, Part One 'Participatory Democracy', Articles 95–117 generally.
21 Plurination is the coexistence of two or more national groups within a community.
22 Although see comments in Will Kymlicka *Liberalism, Community and Culture* (Oxford University Press, New York, 1989) where he defends the idea of minority rights with a discussion of the example of "the special status of First Nations Peoples as opposed to the segregation of blacks"; see also Will Kymlicka *Minority Rights* (Oxford University Press, New York, 1995) particularly Part III discussion on Forms of Cultural Pluralism and Legal Pluralism at 123–155.

Bolivia

The 2001 census indicated that 62 per cent of the Bolivian population is of Indigenous origin.[23] The Constitution of Bolivia provides:[24]

> Cultural diversity is an essential foundation of the Plurinational State Community. Interculturality is the instrument for cohesion and harmony and balance between all peoples and nations. Interculturality will take place with respect to differences and equal footing.

The 1994 constitutional reform recognised Bolivia as an alternative to the nation-state; that is, a plurinational state.[25] This model offers the coherence of the State, but also allows for difference by way of Indigenous 'nations' in a way that the assimilationist tendency of nationalism does not. It is recognition of the ethno-ecological identity of the Indigenous peoples of the plurination.[26] A concept originally developed by Confederation of Indigenous Nationalities of Ecuador (CONAIE),[27] plurinationality is defined as:[28]

> The recognition of a multicultural society in the insoluble political unity of the state that recognises and promotes unity … equality and solidarity among all existing peoples and nationalities … regardless of their historical, political and cultural differences.

---

23 See Cæcilie Mikkelsen (ed) *The Indigenous World* (International Work Group for Indigenous Affairs, Copenhagen, 2013) at 150; see also <http://www.ine.gov.bo/>

24 Article 99 (I); The terms are used 24 times in the Bolivian constitution, primarily in the sections on education: Articles 77–98.

25 Article 1 of the 2009 Constitution reads: "Bolivia, free, independent, sovereign, multi-ethnic and pluricultural, embodied in a single republic, adopts representative democracy as its form of government, based on the union and solidarity of all Bolivians"; see also Giselle Corradi "The Right to a Fair Trial in Legally Plural Jurisdictions: The Case of Bolivia" presentation at *Human Rights and Legal Pluralism in Theory and Practice Conference 5th to 6th December 2014*, Norwegian Centre for Human Rights (NCHR) in co-operation with the Rights, Individuals, Culture and Society Research Centre (RICS) at the Faculty of Law, University of Oslo.

26 New Zealand can (contentiously) be considered a 'plurination'. The Māori electoral option to register to vote within a Māori list is an unusual measure among the world's democracies; see also Catherine Walsh "The Plurinational and Intercultural State: De-Colonisation and State Re-Founding in Ecuador" (2009) 6 Kult 65 at 71–73 where Walsh suggests that Belgium, Finland (The Saami Parliament), Switzerland and Canada may also be considered to be plurinational to a greater or lesser degree.

27 The Spanish initials for the Confederation of Indigenous Nationalities of Ecuador, the country's largest Indigenous federation.

28 Confederation of Indigenous Nationalities of Ecuador (CONAIE) *Politicas para el Plan de Gobierno Nacional. El Mandato del CONAIE*, January 2003 at 2. Quoted from Walsh, above n 26, at 78.

The concept of an Indigenous 'nation' existing within the 'nation-state' is affirmed in Article 9 of the Declaration on the Rights of Indigenous People. It provides:

> Indigenous peoples and individuals have the right to belong to an indigenous community or nation, in accordance with the traditions and customs of the community or nation concerned. No discrimination of any kind shall arise from the exercise of such a right.

The ability of Indigenous peoples who claim membership of an Indigenous nation is not to be impaired in their right to hold citizenship of the State in which they live.[29]

The Bolivian Constitution cements many of the rights outlined in the Declaration on the Rights of Indigenous Peoples,[30] thus supporting the notion of Indigenous self-government and self-determination. Importantly, the Constitution affords Indigenous people organised in an autonomous territory the right to compose their own statutes, provided these do not violate any laws or the Constitution.

The Bolivian Constitution includes not only an Indigenous right to culture, but also in Article 30(II) a right to exercise their political, legal and economic system. When read together with the right to self-determination (Article 30(II)), it establishes a clear right for the Indigenous peoples of Bolivia to an Indigenous legal system and an Indigenous court. It would be appropriate to realise an Indigenous court within an autonomous area, for instance in Awas Tingi, established pursuant to the Constitution in Nicaragua.[31]

By embedding many of the articles from the Declaration on the Rights of Indigenous Peoples within its constitution, Bolivia has substantiated a clear acceptance and support of the fundamental rights and freedoms of Indigenous peoples, including that of respect and promotion of traditional knowledge.

Pacific

Historically states such as Fiji have implemented Fijian Magistrates and Fijian Courts. After the Native Affairs Department was established in 1874, the primary purpose was to "impress upon the 'Natives and High Chiefs of Fiji' the need to have a separate institution so that the interests and welfare of the native population could be protected and to reduce colonial government interference in

---

29 UNDRIP, Arts 6 and 33(1); Constitution of Bolivia Art 30(II)(3).
30 *United Nations Declaration on the Rights of Indigenous Peoples*, GA Res 295 UN GAOR, 61st sess, 107th plen mtg, UN Doc A/Res/295 (2007).
31 In 2001, the Inter-American Court of Human Rights ("IACHR") delivered a landmark judgment in *Mayagna (sumo) Awas Tingni Community v The Republic of Nicaragua* ("*Awas-Tingni*") Inter-American Court of Human Rights No 79 (31 August 2001). The IACHR extended the universal human right of property consistently with emerging Indigenous rights, to include an Indigenous right to property. Subsequently an autonomous zone was created for the Indigenous peoples.

matters affecting native rights".[32] The office of the Fijian Magistrate was created in 1876, and subject to some limitations, Fijian Magistrates were given the same powers as European Magistrates.[33]

The Native Courts Regulations 1927 outlined the powers of the Native Magistrates and the practice and procedure of the Native Court. These included the power to try persons charged with an offence such as assault and disorderly conduct. This Regulation also enabled the Court to take into account Fijian custom. For instance, in lieu of a punishment, the Court could direct the person to supply turtles or make mats.[34] Tikina Courts were a place where a Fijian Magistrate sat alone[35] and Provincial Courts with three Fijian Magistrates were also established.[36] It was not until independence that the Fijian Courts ceased to function. Consequently, Fijians are now served by the police and the central justice system.[37]

Unlike New Zealand, an important characteristic of the legal systems of the Pacific and Melanesian culture is the continued use and support of customary law systems within a Westminster structure.[38] Furthermore, various constitutions in the Pacific, including those of Vanuatu, the Solomon Islands, Tonga and Papua New Guinea, recognise customary law systems or kastom,[39] particularly in relation to areas of conflict.[40]

Several authors note that "the struggle is not to persuade a coloniser state to provide space for the recognition of Indigenous interests but to adjust the state to fit the needs of the Indigenous community".[41] This is perhaps reflective of some States enjoying post-colonial independence and reverting to older, familiar justice systems after independence.[42]

It is not a novel idea that the recognition of culture and tikanga Māori through the right of self determination be realised to allow Māori to address the disproportionate social statistics.[43] The implementation of the philosophy of Te Ao

---

32 Guy Powles and Mere Pulea (ed) *Pacific Courts and Legal System* (Institute of Pacific Studies USP, Suva, 1988) at 78.

33 At 79.

34 At 80.

35 Jurisdiction included lower level offending.

36 Jurisdiction included more serious offending and could be heard by two Magistrates and a District Court Officer.

37 Powles and Pulea, above n 32.

38 See New Zealand Law Commission *Converging Currents* (NZLC SP 17, Wellington, 2006).

39 Sinclair Dinnen "Restorative Justice in the Pacific Islands" in Sinclair Dinnen, Anita Jowitt and Tess Newton Cain (eds) *A Kind of Meaning: Restorative Justice in the Pacific Islands* (Pandanus Books, Canberra, 2003) at 14.

40 See Tui Efi and others (eds) *Pacific Indigenous Dialogue on Faith, Peace, Reconciliation and Good Governance* (USP, Samoa, 2007); see also New Zealand Law Commission *Converging Currents* (NZLC SP 17, Wellington, 2006) for further discussion.

41 Dinnen, above n 39, at 44.

42 At 14.

43 See Nin Tomas "Indigenous Peoples and the Māori: The Right to Self-Determination in International Law – From Woe to Go" (2008) NZLR 639.

Māori, realised by an Indigenous legal system and manifested by an Indigenous court for Māori, should be pursued and supported within the domestic legal framework of New Zealand's justice system. A review of existing judicial initiatives in comparative jurisdictions to address the over-representation of Indigenous peoples within respective criminal justice systems in the areas of criminal offending, women and parole provides a helpful indication for the validity of the research question.

B Criminality statistics

Indigenous offending

The over-representation of Indigenous peoples in prisons is endemic.[44] In Fiji approximately 54 per cent are native Fijians and Indo-Fijians comprise 38 per cent. Out of a total prison population of 1,279, Indigenous Fijians made up 984 prisoners of all prisoners (nearly 80 per cent), while only 222 were Indians (17 per cent).[45] A cross sectoral programme formed in 2003, and working with the formal institutions of the Government of Fiji, identified the need to establish policies to reduce the over-representation of Indigenous Fijians in conflict with the criminal justice system.[46]

In other jurisdictions the statistics for the imprisonment of Indigenous women are even more alarming. It is well established in international literature that the offending and imprisonment rates for Indigenous peoples far surpass those for non-Indigenous peoples.[47] Furthermore, in a number of 'nation-states', statistics indicate that for Indigenous women, the rates of apprehension, prosecution and recidivism surpass those not only for non-Indigenous women, but also for Indigenous men.

In Australia, for instance, where the Indigenous population comprises a mere 2.5 per cent of the population,[48] the imprisonment rate for Indigenous or

---

44 'Indigenous peoples' is a term commonly used to describe any ethnic group who inhabit the geographic region with which they have the earliest historical connection.

45 Ratu Filimone Ralogaivau "Problem Solving Courts of the Fiji Islands: Blending Traditional Approaches to Dispute Resolution in Fiji with Rule of Law – The Best of Both Worlds" (July 2007) at 5. <www.aija.org.au>.

46 At 4. Law and Justice Sectoral Objectives – No 11. Formulated in consultation with the law and justice agencies across the Fiji Islands in conjunction with the Australia Fiji Law and Justice Sector Program.

47 See for example William Tyler "Aboriginal Criminology and the Postmodern Condition: From Anomie to Anomaly" (1999) 32(2) Australian & New Zealand Journal of Criminology at 209 where he notes that the "very high rates of Aboriginal over-representation in the criminal justice systems of the white 'settler' societies are conventionally explained in terms of pervasive effects of cultural dispossession and social and economic disadvantage and dislocation".

48 Human Rights and Equal Opportunity Commission *Face the Facts* (2005) <http://www.hreoc.gov.au>.

Aboriginal adults is approximately 15 times higher than that for non-Indigenous Australian adults.[49] Of the prison population in Australia, 24 per cent identify as aboriginal.[50] In 1989 Aboriginal women represented 16.3 per cent of the female prison population, while Aboriginal men comprised 14.1 per cent of the total male prison population. This indicates that the situation for Aboriginal women is much worse than that for Aboriginal men.[51]

In Canada and the United States of America where Indigenous people comprise 3.6 and 1.7 per cent of the population respectively,[52] their over-representation in prisons and jails is well documented.[53] The following statistics indicate that the over-representation of Indigenous people in the Canadian prison system is growing at a faster rate for women than for men. In the provincial system in 2005, for instance, 30 per cent of female prisoners were Aboriginal,[54] while in the federal system in 2006, 25 per cent of female inmates identified as Aboriginal. Among federally sentenced women prisoners in Canada (those serving two years or more), over 30 per cent are Aboriginal women,[55] whereas 21 per cent of the male prisoner population identified as Indigenous.[56] American Indians and Alaska Natives are 2.5 times more likely to be a victim of violent crimes than other ethnic groups.[57]

As at February 2013 Aboriginal women represented 33.6 per cent of all federally sentenced women in Canada. According to Statistics Canada, "the disproportionate number of Aboriginal people in custody [is] consistent across all provinces and territories and particularly true among female offenders".[58]

In New Zealand the situation is similar. Apprehension rates for Māori women far surpass those for non-Māori women. While Māori women comprise just 15 per cent of the female population,[59] in 1996, they constituted 44.4 per cent of female apprehensions, and 45.83 per cent in 2005. In the same year, 50.52 per cent of Māori women apprehended were prosecuted, compared to 40.1 per cent of non-Māori women. Of custodial sentences 58 per cent were given to Māori

---

49 See Chris Cuneen *Conflict, Politics and Crime: Aboriginal Communities and the Police* (Allen and Unwin, Sydney, 2001) available at SSRN: <http://ssrn.com/abstract=2196235>
50 Law and Justice *Fact Sheet* (2010) <www.reconciliaction.org.au>.
51 S Payne *Aboriginal Women and the Law* (Law and Justice Section Aboriginal and Torres Strait Islander Commission, Canberra, 1993) at 66 <www.aic.gov.au>.
52 Mikkelsen (ed), above n 23, at 54 and 44.
53 Carol La Prairie "The Impact of Aboriginal Justice Research on Policy: A Marginal Past and an Uncertain Future" (1999) 41(2) Canadian Journal of Criminology at 252.
54 Statistics Canada (2010) <http://www.vcn.bc>.
55 The Elizabeth Fry Society of Manitoba, Canada "A Canadian Perspective on Addressing the Overrepresentation of Indigenous Women and Girls in the Canadian Criminal Justice System" (2009) at 7 <www.aija.org.au>.
56 Statistics Canada (2010) <www.vcn.bc.ca>.
57 L Greenfeld and S Smith *American Indians and Crime NCJ 173386* (Bureau of Justice Statistics, Department of Justice, Washington, DC, 1999) <www:bjs.ojp.usdoj.gov>.
58 Office of the Correctional Investigator "Backgrounder: Aboriginal Offenders a Critical Situation" (2012) <www.oci-bec.gc.ca>.
59 Department of Statistics "Ethnic Diversity of Women" (2010) <www.stats.govt.nz>.

women and only 36 per cent to non-Māori women.[60] In 2005 58 per cent of the 329 female inmates in the New Zealand prison system identified as Māori.[61]

These statistics indicate that Indigenous women are more likely to be apprehended, prosecuted and imprisoned than non-Indigenous women. As such, earnest consideration of gender and cultural issues should be given and reflected in the formulation of the relevant policies and legislation.

Criminality and Indigenous women – international response

In October 2005 the United Nations Human Rights Committee noted its concern that, in Canada, Aboriginal women were far more likely to experience a violent death than other non-Aboriginal women.[62] The Committee recommended that accurate statistical data be collected and that the root of this problem be fully addressed; namely the economic and social marginalisation of Aboriginal women, and the need for effective access to justice. The Committee also expressed concern about the situation of Aboriginal women in prisons, and recommended independent adjudication for decisions related to involuntary segregation or alternative models.[63]

The Committee on the Elimination of Racial Discrimination (CERD)[64] noted that:[65]

> ... the Committee remains concerned about serious acts of violence against Aboriginal women, who constitute a disproportionate number of victims of violent death, rape and domestic violence. Furthermore, the Committee is concerned that services for victims of gender-based violence are not always readily available or accessible, particularly in remote areas.

The United Nations Declaration on the Rights of Indigenous People provides three instances where Indigenous women are specifically mentioned:[66]

Article 21(2) calls upon States to pay "particular attention" to the "rights and special needs of Indigenous elders, women, youth, children and persons with

---

60 N Soboleva, N Kazakova and J Chong *Conviction and Sentencing of Offenders in New Zealand: 1996 to 2005* (Ministry of Justice, Wellington 2006) at 116.

61 These statistics have not significantly changed. See Ministry of Justice *Over Representation of Māori in Prison* (2013) "as at 31 March 2013 Māori women made up 58 per cent of that female prisoner population (291 out of a total female prison population of 504)".

62 Office of the High Commission of Human Rights *UN Human Rights Committee: Concluding Observations, Canada (CCPR/C/CAN/CO/5)* (2006) at [23] <www.pch.gc.ca>.

63 At [18].

64 At [12].

65 CERD Report CERD/C/CO/18 25 May 2007 Seventieth Session 19 February–9 March 2007 at Point 20 <www.unhcr.org>.

66 *Declaration on the Rights of Indigenous Peoples*, GA Res 61/295, UN GAOR, 61st sess, UN Doc A/RES/47/1 (2007).

disabilities in the context of special measures to improve economic and social conditions".

Article 22(1) indicates that particular attention should be paid to the rights and special needs of Indigenous elders, women, youth, children and persons with disabilities in the implementation of the Declaration; while Article 22(2) provides that States should take measures, in conjunction with Indigenous peoples, to ensure that Indigenous women and children enjoy the full protection and guarantees against all forms of violence and discrimination.

Read together, Articles 21(2) and 22(1) emphasise the 'rights and special needs' of Indigenous women.[67] The inclusion of "full" and "all forms" in Article 22(2) further supports the State to provide particular protection to Indigenous women.[68]

Article 22(2) also derives from an extensive body of international human rights law relating to the protection from, and the elimination of, all forms of violence and discrimination.[69] This includes general prohibitions against violence and discrimination contained in the Universal Declaration on Human Rights,[70] as well as the two International Covenants.

Article 22(2) is also supported by general international law pertaining to women-specific rights and protections against violence and discrimination,[71] as well as children-specific rights and protections.[72] This body of law includes the Declaration on the Elimination of Violence Against Women, the Convention on the Elimination of All Forms of Discrimination Against Women, (CEDAW) and extensive treaty body comments including General Recommendation 19: Violence Against Women of the Committee on the Elimination of All Forms of Discrimination Against Women.[73]

Despite these provisions to protect Indigenous women against violence and discrimination, Indigenous women are disproportionately represented in the criminal justice system.

---

67 See Eva Biaudet and others *Study on the Extent of Violence against Indigenous Women and Girls in Terms of Article 22 (2) of the UNDRIP* (2013) (UNPFII Report, E/C.19/2013/9) in particular paras [7], [8] and [9].
68 Above.
69 Above.
70 UNDRIP, Articles 2, 3, 5 and 7.
71 General women's rights and protections are included in Article 3 International Covenant on Civil and Political Rights; Art 3 International Covenant on Economic and Social Rights; Human Rights Committee, General Comment 28: Equality of Rights Between Men and Women (Article 3), 68th sess, UN Doc CCPR/C/21/Rev.1/Add.10 (2000); and the Convention on the Elimination of All Forms of Discrimination Against Women, as cited in the report by Biaudet and others, above n 67.
72 Biaudet and others, above n 67, at 9.
73 11th sess (1992), UN Doc A/47/38 at 1 (1993) as cited in report Biaudet and others, above.

C Canada

Background on Indigenous offending

The Canadian Centre for Justice Statistics indicates that Indigenous peoples constitute only 3 per cent of the total population, but comprise 19 per cent of federal prisoners. Between 1997 and 2000 Indigenous peoples were ten times more likely to be accused of homicide than non-Indigenous peoples. The rate of Indigenous peoples in Canadian prisons climbed 22 per cent between 1996 and 2004, while the general prison population dropped 12 per cent.[74] As at February 2013, this figure had risen slightly, with 23.2 per cent of the federal inmate population identifying as Indigenous.[75]

Statistics Canada indicates that the overall rate of domestic violence between 1999 and 2004 remains unchanged.[76] Aboriginal women continue to be victims of domestic violence.[77] In her work with native women, Gorelick illustrates this problem by noting that:[78]

> ... the vast majority of incarcerated aboriginal women, who make up a staggering 30 per cent of female prisoners in Canada, are locked up for addiction-related crimes or for self-defense in a situation of domestic violence.

More recently Professor James Anaya noted:[79]

> Canada's relationship with the indigenous peoples within its borders is governed by a well-developed legal framework a number of policy initiatives that in many respects are protective of indigenous peoples' rights. But despite positive steps, daunting challenges remain ... The well-being gap between aboriginal and non-aboriginal people in Canada has not narrowed over the last several years, treaty and aboriginals claims remain persistently unresolved, indigenous women and girls remain vulnerable to abuse, and overall there appear to be high levels of distrust among indigenous peoples toward government at both the federal and provincial levels.

In light of this, and in recognition of the failure of traditional criminal and civil justice proceedings to appropriately address domestic violence matters, it

74 Melissa Gorelick *Discrimination of Aboriginals on Native Lands in Canada: A Comprehensive Crisis* UN Chronicle (2007) <www.un.org>.
75 Office of the Correctional Investigator, above n 58.
76 See "Domestic Violence Rate Unchanged Statistics: Canada Report" *CBC News* (online, Canada, 14 July 2005) <www.cbc.ca>.
77 Phil Lane, Judie Bopp and Michael Bopp *Aboriginal Domestic Violence in Canada* (Aboriginal Healing Foundation, 2003).
78 Gorelick, above n 74 at 7.
79 James Anaya *The Situation of Indigenous Peoples in Canada* A/HRC/27/52/Add.2

is no surprise that Dawson and Dinoitzer[80] state that much of the legal research on Indigenous peoples and the criminal justice system has been undertaken in North America.[81] Despite the Aboriginal Justice programmes and policies that have been implemented, the disproportionate rate of Aboriginal offending and incarceration rates have not decreased.[82] As a result Stewart argues that governments have followed a trend towards focusing on specific areas to redress the situation, with the establishment of specialist problem solving courts for crimes committed by offenders with social problems like drug addiction.[83] The notion of healing courts has also been adopted by some jurisdictions in applying particular processes for dealing with Indigenous defendants.[84]

Spiteri argues that while First Nations people have not been able to implement a system of Aboriginal justice, it is apparent that concessions have been made within the criminal justice system to address the system's deficiencies and its inability to take into account the unique problems faced by First Nations communities.[85] These include sentence advisory committees, community mediation/ diversion programmes, sentencing panels and sentencing circles. Sentencing is an area that lends itself, at least to some degree, to the application of elements associated with the idea of Aboriginal justice. Perhaps that is why the majority of the Aboriginal Justice Initiatives in Canada deal with sentencing reflected in the changes made to the sentencing provisions of the Canadian Criminal Code. These changes were designed to address the issue of over-representation of First Nations within the sentenced prison population. Section 718.2 (e) of the Criminal Code provides that:[86]

> ... all available sanctions other than imprisonment that are reasonable in the circumstances should be considered for all offenders, with particular attention to the circumstances of Aboriginal offenders.

---

80 Myrna Dawson and Ronit Dinoitzer "Victim Cooperation and the Prosecution of Domestic Violence in a Specialised Court" (2001) 18(3) Justice Quarterly (September Issue) at 593.

81 See Human Rights Watch *Those Who Take Us Away: Policing and Failures in Protection of Indigenous Women and Girls in Northern British Columbia, Canada* (2013) for discussion on the high rates of violence against Indigenous and women and girls and the failure of law enforcement to deal effectively with this problem.

82 La Prairie, above n 53, at 258; see also Carol La Prairie "Aboriginal Over Representation in the Criminal Justice System" (April, 2002) Canadian Journal of Criminology at 181.

83 J Stewart *Specialist Domestic Violence Courts within the Australian Context* (2008) Issues Paper 10 at 4 <www.austdvclearinghouse.unsw.edu.au>.

84 At 4.

85 Melanie Spiteri *Sentencing Circles for Aboriginal Offenders in Canada: Furthering the Idea of Aboriginal Justice within a Western Framework* (2008) <www.iirp.org>.

86 Criminal Code s 718.2(e).

This supports the need to investigate the implementation of an intervention prior to sentencing. The majority decision of the Canadian Supreme Court in *Ipeelee v R* affirmed that s 718(2)(e) of the Criminal Code is:[87]

> a remedial provision designed to ameliorate the serious problem of over-representation of Aboriginal people in Canadian prisons, and to encourage sentencing judges to have recourse to a restorative approach to sentencing.

Similarly, in New Zealand s 8(i) of the Sentencing Act 2002 provides a series of principles for the judge to consider when passing a sentence including:[88]

> ... the offender's personal, family, whānau, community, and cultural background in imposing a sentence or other means of dealing with the offender with a partly or wholly rehabilitative purpose.

In light of the Supreme Court's reasoning in *Ipeelee v R*, it is contended that s 8(i) of the Sentencing Act 2002 could provide the same ameliorative impulse as s 718.2 (e) of the Canadian Criminal Code.[89] Although s 8(i) contains no express reference to Māori offenders, the inclusion of *whānau* and 'cultural background' provides an opportunity to import *tikanga* Māori and explore a proposed intervention prior to sentencing. This could include a *marae*-based forum or similar structure.

Nonetheless, developing these 'cultural' provisions within this s 8(i) limits the ability of the sentencing judge and the judiciary as an institute, to address the core problems associated with offending. This provides support for an alternative forum to meaningfully address and ameliorate the underlying reasons of offending for Māori.

Circle sentencing

Circle sentencing is an updated version of the traditional sanctioning and healing practices of Aboriginal peoples in Canada. It is a holistic, re-integrative strategy designed not only to address the criminal and delinquent behaviour of offenders, but also to consider the needs of victims, families and communities. Within the 'circle' victims, offenders, their family and friends, justice and social service personnel, and interested community residents can speak from the heart in a shared effort to uncover the event. By working together all stakeholders can identify the steps necessary to assist in healing the affected parties and prevent future crimes.

---

87 *Ipeelee v R* 2012 SCC 13 at [59].
88 Sentencing Act 2002, s 8(i).
89 Just Speak – *Māori and the Criminal Justice System Position Paper* (2012) at 35 <https://d3n8a8pro7vhmx.cloudfront.net/justspeak/pages/116/attachments/original/1479979714/JustSpeak-Maori-and-the-Criminal-Justice-System-A-Youth-Perspective.pdf?1479979714>.

The significance of the circle is more than symbolic; all circle members, including police officers, lawyers, judges, victims, offenders and community residents, participate in deliberations to arrive at a consensus for a sentencing plan that addresses the concerns of all interested parties.

In analysing Canadian circle sentencing, Ross Green observes that:[90]

> A prominent goal of circle sentencing is to promote both community involvement in conducting the circle and consensus among participants during the circle.

He also emphasises the role of Indigenous community engagement and participation in justice practices.

Circle sentencing operates within the Canadian criminal justice system, and therefore within the parameters set out by the Canadian Criminal Code. This process often takes the place of court sentencing hearings once guilt has been established.

Judge Cunliffe Barnett (1995) claimed that the term 'circle sentencing' entered legal vernacular when Judge Barry Stuart embarked upon a circle format for sentencing after realising how rigid the sentencing process was, and how it leads to the dominance of the court system over Aboriginal peoples.[91] In *R v Morin*,[92] the Judge claimed that this focus on healing and restoration was in sharp contrast to the punishment and retribution of the Canadian Justice System. Nevertheless, the practice of circle sentencing has been described by the Chief Justice Bayda of Saskatchewan Court of Appeal as:[93]

> ... part of the fabric of our system of criminal justice and ... a recognised and accepted procedure.

This discretion of the judge and the community in sentencing circles to impose non-custodial sentences paves the way for incorporating aspects of an Aboriginal justice system. This is recognised by Luke McNamara as:[94]

> ... a shift away from culturally inappropriate and unfair non Aboriginal sentencing processes towards processes that embrace a genuine respect for, and meaningful cooperation with, Aboriginal law and justice values and processes.

---

90 Ross Green *Justice in Aboriginal Communities: Sentencing Alternatives* (Canada, Purich Publishing, 1998) at 72.
91 See *R v Moses* (1992) 71 CCC (3d) 347 (Yukon Territorial Court).
92 *R v Morin* [1995] SJ No 457.
93 *R v Morin* (1995) 4 CNLR 37 at 68 (Saskatchewan Court of Appeal).
94 Luke McNamara "The Locus of Decision Making Authority in Circle Sentencing: The Significance of Criteria and Guidelines" (2000) 18 Windsor Yearbook of Access to Justice 60 at 61.

Part XXIII of the Canadian Criminal Code codifies the fundamental purpose and principles of sentencing and the factors that should be considered by the judge in determining a sentence that is fit for the offender and the offence. This enables the judge to be creative and consider alternative methods of sentencing other than imprisonment for Aboriginal offenders.

Gladue reports

In 1999 the Supreme Court of Canada released its decision on a sentence appeal from the British Columbia Court of Appeal which involved the appropriateness of a three-year jail sentence for an Aboriginal woman convicted of manslaughter in the stabbing death of her common law husband. In determining the effect of s 718(e) of the Canadian Criminal Code, the Court in *R v Gladue* stated that:[95]

> It [s. 718.2 (e)] is remedial in nature and is designed to ameliorate the serious problem of over representation of aboriginal people in prisons, and to encourage sentencing judges to have recourse to a restorative approach to sentencing.

The Supreme Court further noted that the method of analysis for determining a sentence for an Aboriginal offender must be twofold. First, the consideration of the offender's circumstances that may have been conducive to the offending, and second, the consideration of alternatives to imprisonment; and if there are no alternatives, the length of incarceration must be revisited.[96] This places a burden on the prosecutors, defence counsel and the community to provide relevant information on the accused's cultural background to the judge.[97] Often this information is presented as an aptly named 'Gladue Report'. The Supreme Court also ruled that this section only applies to non-violent and minor offending. However, Larry Chartrand notes that many Aboriginal offenders commit violent and/or serious crimes and have long criminal records.[98]

For various reasons the general academic opinion is that *Gladue* reports have failed to make a substantial impact.[99] These reasons range from the relatively

95   *R v Gladue* [1999] 1 S.C.R 688 Lamer CJ and L'Hereux-Dube, Gonthier, Cory, Iacobucci, Bastarache and Binnie JJ, at 400 and 409.
96   At 417–418 and 423.
97   See *R v Kakekagamick* [2006] OJ No 3346 (Ont CA) where the Court held that there is a positive duty on counsel to assist the sentencing judge in gathering information as to the Aboriginal offender's circumstances; see also Themla Chalifoux "A Need for Change: Cross-cultural Sensitization of Lawyers" (1994) 32 Alberta Law Review 4 at 762; K Roach and J Rudin "Gladue: The Judicial and Political Reception of a Promising Decision" (2000) July Canadian Journal of Criminology at 355.
98   Larry Chartrand "Aboriginal Peoples and Mandatory Sentencing" (2001) 39(2/3) Osgoode Law Journal 2/3 at 456.
99   Rana McDonald *The Discord Between Policy and Practice: Defence Lawyers' Use of Section 718.2(e) and "Gladue"* (University of Manitoba, 2008).

high costs in compiling such a report, the fact that the consistency of the reports are not monitored, the violence of the offending can overshadow any benefit, and the community call for race neutral advocacy.[100]

The effect of the *Gladue* decision has been incorporated within the wider justice system. For instance, in a youth bail decision,[101] and in the case of *R v Sim* where the Ontario Court of Appeal extended the reach of *Gladue* to decisions of the Ontario Review Board stating that Gladue principles are to be considered whenever the decision maker is dealing with the liberty of an Aboriginal person at any stage of the justice system.[102] In New Zealand the Bail Act 2000 contains no provision for the decision maker to take into account cultural factors when determining a bail application.[103] This approach would be welcomed in any proposed Indigenous Court.

Although it can be argued that the Gladue Reports have not assisted to reduce the disproportionate offending rates and can be perceived as the 'ambulance at the bottom of the cliff', it is suggested that this ability to consider an Indigenous approach should be extended to all aspects of the criminal justice system and not be confined to sentencing or bail applications.

Ideally this would include the training of lawyers and the judiciary to better understand the effects of domestic violence from an Indigenous perspective. The flow on from this would bring a fuller understanding of the broader causes of crime and its relationship, especially with colonisation.

The ability to apply Indigenous concepts that have been realised by an Indigenous legal system, and within the appropriate forum, is pivotal to address those areas of Aboriginal over-representation such as the incarceration of Indigenous women resulting from domestic violence issues.

Case studies

Hollow Water

The Royal Commission on Aboriginal Peoples in Canada notes an example where a First Nations community, Hollow Water, had to address persistent sexual abuse within the community.[104] In Hollow Water 75 per cent of the residents

---

100 David Milward and Debra Parkes "*Gladue*: Beyond Myth and Towards Implementation in Manitoba" (2011) 35(1) Man LJ at 84.

101 See *R v Bain* [2004] OJ No 6147 (Ont SC) on a bail review; see also *R v RRB* [2004] BCJ No 2024 (BC Prov Ct) Youth bail hearing.

102 *R v Sim* [2005] OJ No 4432 (Ont CA).

103 However, see section 7 (5) Rules as to granting bail, which states "a defendant who is charged with an offence and is not bailable as of right must be released by a court on reasonable terms and conditions unless the court is satisfied that there is just cause for continued detention". In view of *R v Sim* it could be argued that culture may account as a reason for not continuing detention.

104 Royal Commission on Aboriginal Peoples *Bridging the Cultural Divide: Aboriginal People and Criminal Justice in Canada* (Canada Communications Group, Ottawa 1996) at 159.

were victims and 35 per cent were offenders. The residents, who comprised mostly of women, developed an approach to address this situation, requiring that the offender acknowledge responsibility and over time, be accepted by the group. The offender would then be allowed to stay in the community, but subject to a 13-step process that would take five years to complete. The process is described as:[105]

> The [Community Holistic Circle Healing] is not a program or project. It is a *process with individuals coming back into balance, a process of the community healing itself* [emphasis added]. It is a process which one day will allow our children and grandchildren to once again walk with their heads high as they travel around the Medicine Wheel of Life.

Innu community of Sheshashit[106]

A non-Native offender confessed that he had committed an act of sexual abuse. He elected to be tried in the Supreme Court. He entered a guilty plea and applied for a 'sentencing circle'. After the Crown opposed the motion, an application was made for an informal 'healing circle' to take place. The Crown opposed this request, suggesting that the offender be tried by ordinary court methods. The Judge notified both counsel that they could attend.

In considering sentencing Judge O'Regan found that:

> ... [he was] cognizant of the fact that [the offender] did grow up in the community of Sheshashit and was exposed to Innu culture and thus can benefit from the community's involvement in such thing as the healing circle.

Judge O'Regan accepted the recommendations of the healing circle and imposed a non-custodial sentence. This confirms the ability of the Innu nation to develop and deliver justice based on their custom in order to meet the needs of their community. This provides fertile ground to support the implementation of an Indigenous legal system that could cater for non-Indigenous, as well as for Indigenous peoples.[107]

Specialised court –domestic violence courts

In general, domestic violence courts are designed to remove domestic violence cases from the day-to-day court process. The underlying objective is to ameliorate

---

105 Royal Commission on Aboriginal Peoples, above.
106 Wanda McAuslin "Community Peacemaking" in W McAuslin *Justice as Healing Indigenous Ways; Writings on Community Peacemaking and Restorative Justice from the Native Law Centre* (Living Justice Press, St Paul, Minnesota, 2005) at ch 6.
107 See also Sakeq Henderson *First Nations Jurisprudence and Aboriginal Rights* (Native Law Centre, Canada, 2006) for discussion on the creation of Constitutional space for the inclusion of First Nations jurisprudence.

the victims' experiences of the legal system and re-direct offenders into treatment, with the intention of providing better outcomes for victims and perpetrators, while operating within the criminal justice system. This distinguishes domestic violence courts from other problem solving courts, in that the safety of the victim and the offender's responsibility and accountability are treated equally.

In 2002 there were specialist domestic violence courts in Winnipeg, Manitoba; London, Toronto and Ottawa, Ontario; and Calgary and Edmonton, Alberta. Ontario's Domestic Violence Court is the most extensive programme in Canada. It facilitates the prosecution of domestic assault cases and the early intervention of abusive domestic situations, thereby providing better support to victims and increasing offender accountability.

An operational domestic violence court comprises an assortment of components: a Domestic Violence Court Advisory Committee, especially trained domestic violence prosecutors; Victim/Witness Assistance Program staff and interpreters; specialised evidence collection and investigation procedures by police; case management procedures to coordinate prosecutions and ensure early intervention; a Partner Assault Response intervention programme and the expanded training for police; Crown Victim/Witness Assistance Programme staff; court staff, Probation and Parole staff, and interpreters. These teams of specialised personnel work together to ensure priority is given to the safety and needs of domestic assault victims and their children. This aspect is not dissimilar to circle sentencing where circle members include a vast array of people who participate in deliberations to arrive at a consensus for a sentencing plan that addresses the concerns of all interested parties. Although it may be too soon to gauge the success or otherwise of these courts, there is good reason to be optimistic about its future. In fact, the Ontario government is currently committed to investing CA$10 million annually into the Domestic Violence Court programme.[108]

The success of the implementation and use of domestic violence courts is not confined to Canada. For instance, statistics from domestic violence courts in the United Kingdom suggest that dedicated domestic violence courts are achieving conviction rates of about 70 per cent on average.[109] This is a dramatic improvement when compared with only 46 per cent of cases being prosecuted successfully in December 2003.

In Canada there is no specialist court to address Indigenous offending related to domestic violence. There is debate that Indigenous courts are not focused on 'problem solving'; if there is a problem to be solved, it is the failure of the criminal justice system to accommodate the needs of the Aboriginal people to ensure that they are fairly treated within that system.[110] Any specialty recourse lies in the domestic violence courts within the Canadian Justice System.

---

108 See <www.ontla.on.ca>.
109 "Domestic Violence Court Success" News in Brief: *The Evening Standard* (online ed, London, 9 March 2008) <www.thisislondon.co.uk>.
110 See Western Australian Law Reform Commission *Aboriginal Customary Laws* (Discussion Paper, Report No 94, 2005) at 146.

Notwithstanding the provisions in the Indian Act (R.S.C., 1985, c. I-5) that provide for the appointment of Indigenous Justices of the Peace who have limited jurisdiction to try offences under that Act,[111] only a few have ever been appointed, and they do not have jurisdiction to apply Indigenous law. Other than the discretion of the judges at sentencing,[112] there is no direction to take Indigenous issues into consideration.

Canada – Conclusion

Indigenous women are over-represented in the Canadian penal system. The majority of Aboriginal women, which make up 30 per cent of female prisoners in Canada, are incarcerated for substance or addiction-related crimes or for excessive use of self defence in a situation of domestic violence. International bodies recommend effective access to justice for Aboriginal women.

In Canada there are no courts to adjudicate disputes on the basis of Indigenous law, such as the Navajo Tribal Courts[113] and other Indian Tribal courts in the United States of America.[114] A development in the Indian Tribal Courts in the United States establishes new laws, effective in March 2015, to restore to tribes the ability to prosecute non-Indians who commit domestic violence on the reservation.[115] However, there are some specialist courts that adjudicate disputes and sentence convicted people on the basis of Canadian law, but have Indigenous judges and are situated in places where many Indigenous people reside.[116]

The problems associated with domestic violence are multiple and complex. Responsibility for addressing such problems involves a complex array of services and agencies to provide a vast assortment of culturally appropriate services. Recognition of customary law to address Indigenous over-representation is confined to 'circle sentencing' or 'healing circles'.

111 Indian Act RSC 1985, c I-5, s 107.
112 See Criminal Code RSC 1985 c C-46, s. 718.2(e).
113 See Raymond Austin *Navajo Courts and Navajo Common Law; A tradition of Tribal Self Governance* (University of Minnesota Press, Minneapolis, 2009).
114 For example Ordinance 21 of the Hopi Indian Tribe Law and Order Code was passed in 1972 to provide for the establishment of Hopi tribal courts, a police force, judges, tribal prosecutors, and the provision of a criminal code. See Justin Richland *Arguing with Tradition: The Language of Law in Hopi Tribal Court* (University of Chicago Press, Chicago, 2008).
115 Personal academic communication with Melissa Tatum, University of Tucson, Arizona who has completed an information road show on this issue. This ability to prosecute non-Indians was also articulated during the "Conference on Indigenous Sustainability: Implications for the Future of Indigenous People and Native Nations" Arizona State University 5–7 October, 2014.
116 For example, see the Cree Court in Saskatchewan, where Gerry Morin is the Cree-speaking judge. Saskatchewan is also to establish a Dene Court. There is a second Cree Court now, with Judge Bird. See <http://www.sasklawcourts.ca/default.asp?pg=pc_div_cree_court> for full discussion of Cree Courts.

Chartrand is sceptical of s 718 (e) of the Canadian Criminal Code, arguing that the sentencing guidelines have remained the same for everyone and do little, or nothing to address offending rates.[117] He argues that the only way to reduce the high incarcerations rates of Indigenous peoples is to attack the root causes of crime. This is a view shared by Marchetti and Daly, who state:[118]

> ... any effort to address the over representation of Indigenous people in the criminal justice system must also confront a legacy of government policies and practices over the past two centuries, which systematically disadvantaged and oppressed Indigenous people.

In acknowledgment of these statistics, Canada has implemented specialist domestic violence courts. However, this does not address the over-representation of Aboriginal women in prisons for offences relating to domestic violence.

In order to address this over-representation, the Indigenous principles and the legal system that underpin circle sentencing should be extended to all levels of the criminal justice system. This is particularly so, as Marchetti and Daly note that:[119]

> ... indigenous sentencing courts have the potential to empower Indigenous communities to bend and change the dominant perspective of 'white law' through Indigenous knowledge and modes of social control, and come to terms with a colonial past.

As a result of the dissatisfaction with the mainstream criminal justice process,[120] alternative approaches to addressing criminal behaviour have been proposed, including therapeutic jurisprudence, non-adversarial justice, restorative justice and problem solving initiatives.[121]

These initiatives also include specialist or problem-solving courts such as drug courts, mental health courts, domestic violence courts and Indigenous courts. The emergence of courts that seek to incorporate traditional law and culture, such as the Gladue Reports process, alongside a number of these specialist courts, reflects a "recognition that the traditional adversarial system, in structure, style and

117 Paul Chartrand "Canada and Aboriginal Peoples: Recognition and other Constitutional and Legal Challenges" (Paper presented at a Staff Seminar, Faculty of Law, University of Auckland, 28 March 2008).
118 Elena Marchetti and Kate Daly "Indigenous Sentencing Courts: Towards a Theoretical and Jurisprudential Model" (2007) 29(3) Sydney Law Review at 443.
119 At 429.
120 Andrew Goldsmith, Mark Israel and Kathleen Daly (eds), *Crime and Justice: A Guide to Criminology* (3rd ed, Lawbook Company, Sydney, 2006) at 440.
121 For example, see Michael King, Arie Freiberg, Becky Batagol and Ross Hyams *Non-Adversarial Justice* (Federation Press, Australia, 2009) at 21; for more detail see, for example, ch 2 'Therapeutic Jurisprudence', ch 3 'Restorative Justice', ch 4 'Preventative Law', ch 5 'Creative Problem Solving', ch 9 'Problem-Oriented Courts'.

service delivery" may not be appropriate for all offenders.[122] The move is to focus on and address the underlying behaviour.[123] Whilst there is debate about whether Indigenous courts can be characterised as problem-solving due to the historical context of colonisation,[124] the move to incorporate culture in the Cree Courts of Saskatchewan or through the Gladue Reports signals philosophical changes in the criminal justice system.

It is timely to engage shifting understandings and realities that characterise the Aboriginal experience across Canada regarding issues of culture and tradition. Cultural difference arising from different traditions of conflict resolution are often central to explanations of not only why Aboriginal people clash more often than non-Aboriginal people with Canadian laws, but why the processes linked to those laws are not working for them.[125]

D Australia

As is the case in New Zealand, the Australian criminal justice system is, for the most part, the same model inherited from the British Westminster system. Since the 1980s Australia's criminal justice system has come under increasing scrutiny for failing to resolve, or indeed to reduce the perceived problem of crime.

This situation is exacerbated with the "getting tough on crime" rhetoric that has resulted in a worldwide burgeoning of prison populations.[126] In Australia between 1982 and 1998 it is estimated that the number of inmates rose by 102 per cent.[127]

Jeffries stated that drivers behind this push have included governmental failure to deal with crime and thus reduce offending rates, mangerialist drives for savings and efficiency, calls from consumer groups for their needs to be recognised, and a better court service to be provided.[128] In addition to the political, economic and

---

122 See King and others, above at 21 for more detail.
123 See Arie Freiberg "Problem-Oriented Courts: Innovative Solutions to Intractable Problems?" (2001) 11(8) Journal of Judicial Administration at 8.
124 Marchetti and Daly, above n 118; Elena Marchetti and Kathleen Daly, "Indigenous Courts and Justice Practices in Australia: Trends and Issues" (2004) Crime and Criminal Justice at 277; Law Reform Commission of Western Australia *Aboriginal Courts* (Law Reform Commission of Western Australia, Perth) at 142.
125 See Jane Dickson-Gilmore and Carol La Prairie *Will the Circle Be Broken? Aboriginal Communities, Restorative Justice and the Challenges of Conflict and Change* (University of Toronto, Canada, 2005).
126 Home Office *World Prison Population List* (Home Office, London, 2002) <www.homeoffice.gov.uk>.
127 Carlos Carcach and Anna Grant *Imprisonment in Australia: Trends in Prison Populations and Imprisonment Rates 1982–1998 Canberra* (Australian Institute of Criminology, Australia, 2000).
128 Samantha Jeffries "Transforming the Criminal Courts: Politics, Managerialism, Consumerism, Therapeutic Jurisprudence and Change" Post-Doctoral Fellow thesis (2002) <www.criminologyresearchcouncil.gov.au>.

social landscape, changing intellectual paradigms are also having a substantial impact on the criminal court practice.

This current system also consistently yields high rates of recidivism by Aboriginal and Torres Strait Islander people.[129] As the prison population and the fear of crime increases, it becomes clear that the traditional methods of delivering justice are not working, particularly for the Indigenous peoples. Indigenous Australians comprise 2.2 per cent of the population. An Indigenous Australian is 11 times more likely to be imprisoned than a non-Indigenous Australian; and in June 2004, 21 per cent of prisoners in Australia were Indigenous.[130] Family violence is also widespread. In 2002 one out of every five (21 per cent) Indigenous Australians aged 15 years and over reported that family violence was a common problem.[131] This over-representation of Indigenous Australians in prisons was brought to public attention by the 1987–1991 Royal Commission Report on Aboriginal Deaths in Custody.[132] One of the Royal Commission's main findings was that the high number of deaths of Aboriginal people in prisons was a result of the high rate of imprisonment of Aboriginal Australians rather than different treatment for Aboriginal prisoners.

The Report:[133]

> identified the history of *'domination' over Indigenous people as the underlying basis for the disadvantage* [emphasis added] … found that the *current socio-economic disadvantage stemmed from the social and economic disempowerment of Indigenous people after British arrival, the dispossession of Indigenous people from traditional lands* [emphasis added] (through violence, disease and the imposition of discriminatory policies and practices) and the subsequent erosion of Indigenous social controls, cultural identity and economic independence … found that the legacy of violence, government intervention and control had a lasting influence on Indigenous interaction with the criminal justice system … recognised, for example, a continuing hostility between police and many Indigenous communities, which affected the preparedness of some Indigenous people to identify as Indigenous when in police custody … identified a lack of faith by Indigenous people in court and corrections processes … [noted that] the Criminal justice processes, including court, sentencing and policing

129 See Human Rights Equal Opportunity Commission *Face the Facts* (2005) <www.hreoc. gov.au>.
130 Australian Bureau of Statistics *Australian Social Trends* (2008) <www.abs.gov.au>.
131 Australian Bureau of Statistics, above.
132 Royal Commission *Report on Aboriginal Deaths in Custody Final Report* (1991) <www.aus tlii.edu.au>.
133 Royal Commission into *Aboriginal Deaths in Custody, Final Report* (1991) at [1.3.7]–[1.4.20] and [1.7.6]; see further vol 2, ch 10; also [1.4]; vol 2, ch 10; vol 2, ch 13; vol 3, [21.2.4]–[21.2.5]; vol 3, [22.4]. As cited in Dennis Byles and Tai Karp *Sentencing in the Koori Courts Division of the Magistrates Court* (Sentencing Advisory Council, Melbourne, 2010) <http://www.sentencingcouncil.vic.gov.au>.

procedures, were also found to influence, or at least potentially influence, Indigenous over-representation ... determined *that court processes were culturally insensitive, intimidating and alienating for many Indigenous people. To address the high numbers of Indigenous persons in custody* [emphasis added] ... made 339 recommendations addressing the underlying causes of Indigenous disadvantage and *modifying criminal justice processes* [emphasis added].

To eliminate Indigenous disadvantage, the Royal Commission called for empowerment, the associated right to self-determination and reconciliation.[134]

Recognition of Aboriginal/Indigenous law

In 1986 the Australian Law Reform Commission completed a 10-year inquiry into processes for recognising Aboriginal Customary Law.[135] The Social Justice Commissioner made a lengthy submission to the Northern Territory Inquiry stating that:[136]

> ... there is currently a crisis in Indigenous communities. It is reflected in all too familiar statistics about the over representation of Indigenous men, women and children in criminal justice processes ... ultimately these statistics reflect the breakdown of indigenous community and family structures ... *customary law should be treated by the Government as integral to attempts to develop and maintain functional self determining Aboriginal communities* ... [emphasis added].

This Report also supported the Northern Territory Government for its statements that:

> '... in accordance with Australian and international law, Aboriginal Customary Law should be recognised consistent with universally recognised human rights and fundamental freedoms' and that it believes that 'there is much value in supporting and sustaining Aboriginal Customary Law, and that the knowledge contained in Aboriginal Customary Law can be of mutual benefit to all citizens of the Northern Territory as well as its custodians'.

The disproportionate representation of Indigenous peoples in detention centres, together with the need for a better court service against the background of changing political and intellectual paradigms, have contributed to the

134 Above at vol 1, [1.7.6]–[1.7.9]; vol 4, ch 27; vol 5, ch 38.
135 See Australian Law Reform Commission *The Recognition of Aboriginal Customary Law* (31 Sydney, 1986) <www.austlii.edu.au>.
136 Aboriginal and Torres Strait Islander Social Justice Commissioner *Submission to the Northern Territory Law Reform Committee Inquiry into the Recognition of Aboriginal Customary Law* (Human Rights Equal Opportunity Commission, Sydney, 2003) <http://www.humanrights.gov.au/legal>.

recognition of Aboriginal customary law and the establishment of Indigenous Sentencing Courts.

There are two overriding principles at all stages of development and evaluation of an Aboriginal or Torres Strait Islander Court. First, that the court is a special measure enabling Aboriginal and Torres Strait Islander peoples to enjoy their rights to equality before the law. Secondly, equal treatment before the court. Intrinsic to these two principles is the right of self-determination for the Aboriginal and Torres Strait Islander Peoples afforded by these courts, particularly as Brennan J stated:[137]

> The purpose of securing advantage for a racial group is not established by showing that the branch of government or the person who takes the measure does so for the purpose of conferring what it or he regards as a benefit for the group if the group does not seek or wish to have the benefits. The wishes of the beneficiaries for the measure are of great importance (perhaps essential) in determining whether a measure is taken for the purpose of securing their advancement. The dignity of the beneficiaries is impaired and they are not advanced by having an unwanted material foisted upon them.

The first urban Indigenous Sentencing Court was convened in South Australia in 1999 and all but one state (Tasmania) has established some type of Indigenous justice practice.[138] There are various degrees to which these fora implement Indigenous justice; these vary from a more formalised practice for sentencing Indigenous offenders to a less formalised practice, where judicial officers elicit sentence-related information from Indigenous people. Hybrid forms have also developed with the introduction of circle courts.

The doctrine of therapeutic jurisprudence has provided legitimacy and a framework for the new Indigenous courts. Problem solving courts are not a novel idea and have become increasingly common in Australia.[139] The main themes of therapeutic jurisprudence and problem solving courts include a shift of court practice away from the traditional adversarial model, a commitment to achieving offender rehabilitation, a focus on achieving tangible outcomes (i.e., reduce Indigenous over- representation), and the use of judicial authority to solve problems and change offender behaviour.[140]

---

137 *Gerhady v Brown* (1985) 57 ALR 472 at 514, 516 and 522 Australian High Court per Brennan J.
138 Marchetti and Daly, above n 118 at 416.
139 For an interesting comparison between New Zealand and Australian problem solving courts see Elizabeth Richardson, Katey Thom and Brian McKenna "The Evolution of Problem-Solving Courts in New Zealand and Australia: A Trans-Tasman Comparative" in Richard Wiener and Eve Brank (eds) *Problem Solving Courts* (Springer, USA, 2013) at 185.
140 CJR Information paper *Juxtaposition between Sentence Severity and Therapeutic Jurisprudence* (2003) as cited in "Australia's 'New' Indigenous Courts" <www.cjrn.unsw.edu.au>.

A discussion paper confirms that the evolution of Australia's 'new' Indigenous courts occurred in response to the problem of Indigenous over-representation in the criminal justice system.[141] Both the Murri (Queensland) and Koori Court (Victoria) were initiated in response to the Royal Commission into Aboriginal Deaths in Custody and subsequent undertakings (formalised Indigenous Justice Agreements) by both Queensland and Victoria to reduce Indigenous over-representation. In South Australia the Nunga Court also grew out of concerns over high rates of Indigenous offending, but did not result directly from a State Justice Agreement.[142]

Koori Court (Victoria)

The Koori Court model was established in 2002 as a direct consequence of the Victorian Aboriginal Justice Agreement.[143] The Koori Court was designed to ensure, among other things, greater Indigenous involvement in the criminal justice system and the integration of the government service provision into the Indigenous community.[144] It was described as a major initiative and was designed to minimise Indigenous over-representation in the criminal justice system through the application of mainstream law in a more appropriate way for the Koori people.[145] The Koori Court is more comprehensive than either the Nunga or Murri Court because it is enshrined in legislation. The Magistrates' Court (Koori Court) Act of 2002 provides for the establishment of a Koori Division of the Magistrates' Court and defines the jurisdiction and procedure of the Koori Division.[146]

Australian jurisdictions that have set up specialist courts to deal with the sentencing of Aboriginal peoples have yielded far lower recidivism rates.[147] Anecdotal evidence supports the findings that these courts are showing signs of success.[148] Chief Justice Wayne Martin noted that:[149]

141 CJR, above.
142 Mark Harris "From Australian Courts to Aboriginal Courts in Australia – Bridging the Gap?" (2004) 16(1) Current Issues in Criminal Justice at 26.
143 See Sentencing Advisory Council above n 133 at 8 for further discussion.
144 Mark Harris *The Koori Court and the Promise of Therapeutic Jurisprudence* (2006) 1 Murdoch University Electronic Journal of Law at 129.
145 The Office of the Attorney-General "Hull Opens Melbourne's First Koori Court" (press release, March 4, 2003).
146 See Magistrates Court (Koori Court) Act (Vic) 2002 <www.legislation.vic.gov.au>.
147 See Mark Harris *A Sentencing Conversation: Evaluation of the Koori Courts Pilot Program October 2002 – October 2004* (Victorian Department of Justice, Melbourne, 2006) at 15 <www.justice.vic.gov.au>.
148 Rachael Mazza "Deadly Yarns Launch and the Koori Court" ABC Network (online ed, Australia, 22 April 2005) <www.abc.net.au>; see also comments by Bonnie Fisher, Steven Lab, Barry Fisher in *Encyclopaedia of Victimology and Crime Prevention* (Sage Publications, 2010) at 628 where they note the complexity involved in the accurate evaluation of Koori Courts.
149 Hon Wayne Martin CJ "The Magistrates of Western Australia Annual Conference 2006" (paper presented at Annual Conference, 8 November 2006) <www.supremecourt.wa.gov.au>.

All the research that I have seen conducted on the outcomes of problem solving approaches to sentencing in Drug Courts and Domestic Violence Courts shows that they have been successful in reducing the risk of re-offending.

However, he also stated that with respect to Indigenous offending rates:

... unless and until a whole of Government approach is taken to these issues in a *conscious and deliberate attempt to restore traditional culture and lore, the over-representation of Aboriginal people in the justice system is likely to continue* [emphasis added]. However, there are things that can be done within the court system to improve the situation. Amongst them is the adoption of an approach in which Aboriginal people are given a greater sense of participation in the justice process through the adoption of sentencing processes such as those utilised in Circle Courts or Koori Courts which have been successful in other jurisdictions.

Court jurisdiction

The Koori Court Division of the Magistrates' Court[150] was established pursuant to the Magistrates' Court Act 1989.[151] In order to appear before the court, the defendant must be Aboriginal,[152] consent to the proceedings being heard in the Koori Court[153] and plead guilty.[154]

The legislation provides that the Court is to be conducted with as little formality, technicality and with as much expedition as the requirements of the legislation and proper consideration of the matters before the Court permit.[155] The proceedings must be comprehensible to the defendant, family members and other Aboriginal persons who are in attendance.[156]

The Court may regulate its own procedure.[157] The Koori Court has the power to hear all matters within the jurisdiction of the Magistrates' Court,

---

150 For discussion on general background see Elena Marchetti, Elena and Kathleen Daly *Indigenous Courts and Justice Practices in Australia* (Australian Institute of Criminology, 2004) <www.aic.gov.au>; see also K Auty and D Briggs "Koori Court Victoria: Magistrates Court (Koori Court) Act 2002" (2004) 8(1) Law Text Culture Challenging Nation 7 <www.ro.uow.edu.au> for the views of the first sitting Magistrate and first enabling Aboriginal Justice Officer; see also Sentencing Council of Australia *Report Sentencing in the Koori Court Division of the Magistrates Court* (2010) at ch 3; Department of Justice, Victoria, "Overview of the Koori Court", Brochure (2006); Department of Justice Victoria "Koori Court – A Defendant's Guide" Brochure" (2008).
151 Magistrates' Court Act (Vic) 1989, s 4D.
152 Section 4F(1)(a).
153 Section 4F(1)(d).
154 Section 4F(c).
155 Section 4D(4).
156 Section 4D(5).
157 Section 4D(6).

with the exception of sexual offences and offences against the Crimes (Family Violence) Act.[158]

In relation to sentencing, the Koori Court may consider "any oral statement made to it by an Aboriginal elder or respected person",[159] and the court may inform itself in any way it thinks fit.[160] Unlike the *marae*-based court, which is not driven by legislation, the Magistrates' Act provides for a number of persons who might be heard, including health workers, corrections officers, the victims and family members of the accused.[161]

Legislation, like the Magistrates' Court Act (Vic) 1989, provides a clear directive and certainty to the judge and those involved within the criminal justice system. It is suggested that, should any Indigenous court be established within New Zealand, similar legislative provisions should be implemented.

Victoria currently has nine Koori Courts, seven adult Courts and two Children's Courts. The adult courts are located in the rural areas of Shepparton, La Trobe Valley, Mildura, Bairnsdale, Swan Hill, Warrnambool (including a circuit to Portland and Hamilton) and the metropolitan region of Broadmeadows; the Children's Courts are located at Melbourne and Mildura. The setting of the location of the Koori Courts occurs through community consultation via the Aboriginal Justice Forum.

The Aboriginal Justice Forum is the body responsible for supervising the development, implementation and direction of Koori initiatives under the Victorian Aboriginal Justice Agreement (AJA). The Forum meets regularly to review its progress and report to the Victorian Government on Koori justice outcomes. Its key roles are to:[162]

- promote best practice approaches in program development and service delivery
- promote cross-program linkages and the development of a whole-of-government approach
- monitor and report on implementation and justice outcome data.

Elders and Respected Persons (ERPs) are recruited through advertising in local communities. The ERPs assist the court in relation to cultural and community issues, but have no role in sentencing. Unlike *kuia* and *kaumatua* from the *marae*-based courts, ERPs are statutorily appointed and are paid a sitting fee. The ERPs undergo a week-long professional training regime and ongoing professional development is available.

---

158 Section 4D(1).
159 Section 4G(2).
160 Section 4G(3).
161 Section 4G(3).
162 See Department of Justice Website for further discussion <www.justice.vic.gov.au>.

Similar to the training programme for the judiciary in New Zealand, magistrates also undergo continuing professional development. However, the Victorian scheme is quite distinct from the Māori Land Court in New Zealand, where the judges are required to be well versed in *tikanga* Māori and have an understanding of *te reo* (the Māori language). Section 7(2A) of Te Ture Whenua Māori Act 1993 provides:

> A person must not be appointed a Judge unless the person is suitable, having regard to the person's knowledge and experience of *te reo Māori*, *tikanga Māori* [emphasis added], and the Treaty of Waitangi.

A day-long training programme is conducted for magistrates who have previously presided over a Koori Court hearing, and it is recommended to all magistrates that they observe at least one full day's hearing before presiding over Koori Court. The Judicial College of Victoria conducts a biennial cross-cultural immersion programme over three days. Koori Court magistrates have three days per year set aside for meetings, in which to discuss issues pertinent to the Koori Court and to undergo further professional development.

It is acknowledged that the Judicial College of Victoria also conducts seminars in relation to Aboriginal issues and the Koori Court. In addition, the College supports the Judicial Officers' Aboriginal Cultural Awareness Committee, which is chaired by Justice Stephen Kaye of the Victoria Supreme Court.

Court procedure[163]

The Victorian model complies with the requirements of the legislation.[164] Each Koori Court has a Koori Court Officer (KCO) who prepares the list and liaises with defendants and their families, legal practitioners, prosecutors, corrections officers and service providers. The KCO ensures that any issues relating to the establishment of Aboriginality or conflict of interest are resolved before the hearing. Where appropriate, the KCO arranges services and makes referrals on behalf of the defendant.

Prior to the list commencing each morning, the magistrate meets with the KCO and the Elder and Respected Persons (ERP) who will be sitting with the magistrate later that day. The KCO provides a summary of the allegations, charges, prior convictions (if any) and any reports listed for the day with respect to each defendant. The documents are read and each case is discussed. The magistrate will explain any legal issues relating to the individual cases to the ERPs

---

163 I am grateful for the assistance and academic conversations with Magistrate Jelena Popovic and acknowledge her support with this reproduction; see also Bridget McAsey "Critical Evaluation of the Koori Court Division of the Victorian Magistrates' Court" (2005) 10 Deakin Law Review 2.

164 Magistrates' Court Act 1989 (Vic), s 4D- Koori Court.

as well as any unfamiliar terminology. The magistrate also broadly discusses what the sentencing range might be for each case.

The Magistrate will ascertain which order the ERPs wish to enter the courtroom, how the ERPs wish to be addressed, whether the ERPs wish to be introduced by the magistrate or would prefer to introduce themselves, whether they wish the persons in the courtroom to stand or remain seated upon the entrance of the magistrate and ERPs into the court room.

The Bar table is usually set up with the Magistrate, Elders, Indigenous Corrections officer, Corrections Prosecutor, Police Prosecutor, Defence Lawyer, Defendant, Defendant's family, supporter and Koori Court Officer seated around the table. Similar to the *mihi* in *marae*-based courts, each case commences with an acknowledgment of country,[165] as well as traditional owners, ancestors and elders. This is usually provided by the magistrate or by an elder. Reference is made to the court having been smoked,[166] the physical layout of the courtroom, and the artwork which is being displayed as an acknowledgment of the importance of culture and traditional beliefs; and the local Aboriginal community's approval of the Koori Court being conducted at the court house. This "redefinition" of the environment is similar to the use of the *whare nui* for *marae*-based courts.

The reference to the court having been smoked is highly significant. The smoking ceremony is conducted by an elder of the local community and involves eucalyptus leaves being lit and carried throughout the interior of the courthouse. This is similar to the smudging ceremony performed by First Nation peoples in Canada.[167] In addition to demonstrating the acceptance of the local community for the important business to be conducted in the court house, it is similar to a *karakia* for Māori. Smoking clears away bad spirits, purifies the surroundings and establishes the way for a fresh beginning.

The magistrate ascertains the defendant's consent to having the matter dealt with in Koori Court. The case then proceeds as it would normally in the Magistrates' Court; with pleas of guilty being entered, the prosecution summary of facts being read out and adopted, and any prior convictions tendered.

The legal representative commences the plea. This may be interrupted by contributions or questions from the magistrate, elders, the defendant's family, community members, police officers and prosecutors as appropriate.

The KCO advises the court of arrangements which have already been put in place and of any programmes available to the defendant. Representatives of any other support agencies are also invited to speak, as are family members and any other community members. The most powerful aspect of the proceedings is when the ERPs address the defendant.

165 Country is similar to when Māori refer to their *iwi* or tribal area.
166 Smoking is a process of lighting special native plants to cleanse the area or process.
167 See Wanda McAuslin (ed) *Justice as Healing Indigenous Ways: Writings on Community Peacemaking and Restorative Justice from the Native law Centre* (Living Justice Press, St Paul, Minnesota, 2005).

The court allows sufficient time for ERPs, family members and community members to participate fully and feel confident to speak. The magistrate can assist with this process by asking individuals directly if they wish to add anything. Often magistrates will need to remain silent and allow for quiet so that others have the chance to speak. If the victim is present, an opportunity to be heard will be provided. The defendant is asked what he/she would like to say and is encouraged to speak. The ERPs may speak to the defendant regarding his or her conduct.

The ERPs and the magistrate then confer audibly and openly at the bar table to discuss rehabilitation, community and family considerations. Conditions attached to orders may also be discussed at the table. The expertise of Community Corrections may be called upon. Everyone present in the courtroom is given the opportunity to be involved in the problem solving process.

After everyone who wishes to have input has been heard, the magistrate will announce the defendant's sentence. The defendant may again be asked to speak to ensure that he or she fully understands the nature of the sentencing order.

At both the lunch adjournment and after the last case has been heard, the magistrate, ERPs and KCO will have the opportunity for a debriefing.

Case studies[168]

Scenario 1: The Koori Court changing offending patterns

On the day of the offence, the defendant had been consuming alcohol and decided to ride his motorbike to another nearby town and back again. While driving through the town, he lost control of the motorcycle and ran onto the footpath.

The Defendant sustained minor injuries as a result of the collision and was taken by ambulance to a hospital. A sample of his blood was tested and it was subsequently found that his blood-alcohol levels were more than double the legal limit. At the time of the offence, the Defendant had been disqualified from holding a motorcycle licence, and the motorbike that he was riding at the time of the accident was not registered.

The Defendant initially denied that he had been driving the motorcycle at the time of the accident.

Charges

- Careless driving
- Exceed prescribed concentration of alcohol
- Driving whilst disqualified
- Driving an unregistered motorcycle

---

168 I am grateful to Magistrate Jelena Popovic for the reproduction of these case studies which are also cited by Harris above n 147, at 96 <www.justice.vic.gov.au>.

Sentencing considerations

It was noted that the Defendant had four previous drink driving convictions. It was revealed in the course of the proceedings that the Defendant's father-in-law had been killed in an accident, and that the Defendant had ridden his motorcycle to the scene of the accident.

The incident that led to the Defendant being charged took place on the same day. In addressing the Koori Court, the Defendant noted that, at the time of the offence, he was "out of my mind with grief". In speaking to the Defendant, one of the elders drew his attention to the fact that they were related. The elder noted that he had been through similar experiences in his own life.

ELDER: We're related. I looked you know through our family trees and stuff ... I was like you too, I mean I used to drink and I was pretty angry with myself and everybody else around me, but you know you've gotta pull yourself out of it, you get emotional.

I attended alcoholics anonymous and that helped me in lots of ways you know, I was just sort of suggesting about what he was thinking, you know, I mean you could have killed someone, kids and things like that you know, and I done the same thing, I pinched a car and rolled it and you know, but I thought about it later, I could have killed myself or I could have killed someone else.The other elder in attendance during the hearing noted that there were two laws: white law and Aboriginal law. He went on to say that he followed Aboriginal law, but that in offences like driving cars, he and the Defendant had to accept that it was the 'white law' that had to apply, even though he felt that he may well have done exactly the same thing as the Defendant in the circumstances.

The magistrate then addressed the Defendant:

I wonder if anybody's ever sat in this court as you have today and had such significant things said to them by members of their community who are such respected members. I wonder if it had ever been the case that they'd been told that those members of the community are going to support you but also tell you, you've gotta behave responsibly. Uncle — talked to you about the differences in white and Aboriginal law (and) .... Aunty — talked to you from the bottom of her heart about what she's been through ...

The Defendant was asked whether he had anything he wished to say to the elders at the conclusion of the hearing, and he said:

Like they've made sure that I've been keeping out of trouble, I've made another appointment for the drug and alcohol counselling, which I've gotta go back on Monday and I asked them if I can keep on attending so I can improve myself and suppose to say to the community and to me Elders that you know, I'm making a step, so that way I can just get on the right track, not the wrong one and by doing that I'll make sure I'm gonna not ride me motorbike.

In a subsequent media interview, the Defendant observed the impact that the Koori Court sitting had upon him. He said:

Well in the Koori Court like you feel like the size of an ant. When they talk to you, you do, you start getting a lump in your throat, you feel like you know, crying. I've cried even in there, and they make you understand, we're not above the law, and we get up and say what we have to say about ourselves, and they listen to what we say.

Scenario 2: The Koori Court and the importance of family and community in sentencing.[169]

The Defendant appeared at the Koori Court in relation to a number of charges. The first group of matters related to his driving at an excessive speed through a school area – a 40 kilometre zone. The vehicle he was driving at the time was also unregistered and had false registration plates. The second group of charges related to the actions in the early hours of a morning when he assaulted and abused two women in a nightclub. After being ejected from the nightclub, the Defendant became aggressive, took his shirt off, and abused the security personnel. A young woman, who approached him to tell him to put his shirt back on, was subsequently punched in the face.

Charges

- Intentionally causing injury (two counts)
- Assault with a weapon
- Driving while disqualified
- Use of an unregistered motor vehicle
- Fraudulently altering/using identification.

Proceedings

In this case the Defendant came from a well-known Koori family from the region. The Defendant was very keen to ensure that his father did not attend the court and had not told him of the seriousness of the charges.

The Defendant also initially refused to accept one of the elders who had been listed to sit in at the hearing, alleging that there was a history of conflict between

169 Harris, above n 147 at 101.

his family and that of the elder. As the summaries of the charges were read out, the father became quite distressed, both by the nature of the offences and by the fact that his son had received two severe beatings by unknown males after the nightclub assault.

During the course of the hearing, it was made quite clear that there was a real prospect that the Defendant might be sentenced to imprisonment for his offences.

ELDER ONE: "Cos you know I've been through a lot of things with, with drinking alcohol, nearly killed myself, you know, jumpin' off bridges and doing all them things."

ELDER TWO: "I had a good talk to [defendant's name] and I told him that these are very serious charges, and I told him that the — family were a very respectable family ... they were all the family that came over here, the [family name] came to Shepparton when things were really tough, when racism was very bad ... and they held their head up to everything ... they challenged everything that come in front of them, and they were all good sportsmen and respectable people, and I don't have to tell you any more, he knows what I said to him ... that more or less he was degradin' his grandfather and his grandmother and for what he'd done".

DEFENDANT: "I'm just ashamed of what I've done ... I've let a lot of people down and I know I've done the wrong thing. I've just got to learn by it, and so, and I apologise to youse for putting my family in pain yesterday."

FATHER OF DEFENDANT: "I'd like to first of all acknowledge the Elders as well and ... I'd just like to acknowledge and thank my other community members here of the support they've had as for, for us here and as in the (family name). And I'd also like to acknowledge the concept of the Koori Court, I think it's very, very good and, your Worship yourself, the cultural under-standing of the issues, I think you can have these sorts of processes in place but I think that it takes that kind of partnership to understand some of the things ..."

Sentence

The Defendant was placed on a Community Based Order (CBO) with conviction for twelve months, 150 hours of unpaid community work and a fine of AU $184.00.

Observation

From the initial possibility that the Defendant might be imprisoned, the Defen-dant was given a CBO. The magistrate observed, in handing down the sentence:

if you were here by yourself, standing in the back of the Court with a Magistrate hearing a submission in relation to submission, I think you'd be struggling to stay out of gaol. It's down to your community that you're not going to gaol.

This case was a clear illustration of the importance of the Koori Court process in determining the underlying facts behind the case. The facts that were subsequently revealed in the course of the hearing were invariably highly emotional and ultimately influenced the magistrate not to order a term of imprisonment.

This case also gives a strong indication of the importance of community. Even though the family no longer had such strong links with the local Koori community, they were placed in a network of shared history.

The case was also significant for the conversation that occurred between the elders and the Defendant, and the father of the Defendant and the elders. Such was the intensity of this case that the magistrate commented in closing that: "It takes a bit of courage to come in here, and it takes a lot of guts to submit yourself to your Elders and we acknowledge that too." Cases such as this one are a clear indication that the Koori Court is anything but the soft option that it is sometimes referred to.

Scenario 3 The Koori Court giving the Defendant a chance to turn their life around.[170]

The Defendant had a long history of drug use. She appeared in the Koori Court in relation to a number of incidents.

The first matter arose when the Defendant and her partner became embroiled in a dispute whilst walking along the street. The Defendant pulled a knife from her backpack and slashed her own arm. After police attended she refused to drop the knife and was holding the knife to her throat when the police intervened with pepper spray. She was then taken to the local hospital.

The second lot of charges related to an argument between the Defendant and two other persons, who she alleged had stolen some of her possessions. Upon arrival the police observed that the Defendant had a knife in her hand. She was ordered to place the knife on the ground. She complied. The Defendant was charged with using offensive language under the Summary Offences Act (Vic) 1966.

The third incident occurred when the Defendant followed another person from an office and abused her. The Defendant grabbed the victim's hair as she attempted to get into her car and struck her on the nose.

The fourth incident involved the Defendant going to a store and taking a power tool without paying. When confronted by security staff, she refused to return to the store and left the premises. After police were contacted, they visited her home address where she confessed to the theft.

The final incident involved theft of grocery items from a supermarket. The Defendant took the items from the shelves, placed them in her handbag and left

170 Harris, above at 106.

the store without paying. When confronted by a staff member, the Defendant became abusive but then agreed to hand over the stolen goods. Police subsequently arrested her in relation to this matter and she was charged with theft.

Charges

- Two counts of shoplifting
- Possession of a controlled weapon without lawful purpose
- Possession of a dangerous article
- Use of indecent language in a public place
- Possession of a prohibited weapon
- Unlawful assault

Sentencing considerations

The elders and respected persons expressed their concern at the Defendant's history of self-harm and substance abuse. There was reference to a history of sexual assault and the pain suffered by the Defendant. However, the Court also insisted that it was time for her to take responsibility for the events in her life.

ELDER: "It's really heartbreaking to see you destroy, you're trying to destroy yourself the way you do ... I hate to see youse hurt, hurting yourself. And I really do love you [defendant's name], I do love you. But, I want to see you pick yourself up and make your decisions for you."

Sentence

The Defendant was convicted and placed on a Community Based Order (CBO) for a period of 12 months, which was to include psychological counselling through the Corrections Department of Victoria. In addition, the Defendant was referred to other service providers, including a detoxification programme for her drug and alcohol problems. The Defendant entered into a nine-month residential programme to combat her substance abuse.

Observation

A remarkable feature of this Koori Court case was the manner in which the elders affirmed their love for the Defendant, but also insisted that she take responsibility for her own life. It was then possible for the Koori Court to tailor a comprehensive order that addressed the underlying problems of substance abuse and made provision for a mental health assessment. At the end of the sentencing order, after the Defendant had thanked the elders, one of them responded from around the table that she should persevere with the psychological help, even though, they noted, "it's not going to be easy". The elder concluded by saying,

"I think you're beautiful and you are ... you are a valued member of our community."[171]

In a subsequent interview, the Defendant observed that the Koori Court had been a positive experience because it gave her the chance to tell her story. She said, "It gives you the chance to tell 'em what you are and who you are and, you know, what you've been through and that."[172]

The Defendant also emphasised the fact that the elders had been there as an important part of the experience, because "they live in it, they're the same, they're Aboriginal themselves. And they understand".[173]

Evaluation of the existing Koori Courts

As with the establishment of the *marae*-based courts, the catalyst for the Koori Courts has been the disproportionate offending rates of Aboriginal peoples. Victoria was chosen as the pilot court, mainly due to the 'alarming statistics' relating to Indigenous offending in the State.[174] Since the first Victorian Koori pilot courts commenced in 2002 and 2003, there has been a keen interest in their progress and effectiveness.

Commissioned by the Victorian Department of Justice, a formal evaluation was undertaken by Dr Mark Harris of the two pilot Koori Courts in Shepparton, a regional city, and Broadmeadows, a suburb of Melbourne. The 2006 Report, titled 'A Sentencing Conversation' noted a significant reduction in recidivism rates from those two courts.[175] The rate of reoffending for participants in the Koori Court was substantially less than the recidivism rates for the general population.[176] There was also a reduction in Koori offenders breaching correctional orders and a reduction in failures to appear in court. The positive evaluation resulted in the repeal of the sunset clause that prevented the Koori Court from operating beyond 30 June 2005.[177]

It is noted that the methodologies employed by Dr Mark Harris were questioned, in particular, for counting court files rather than individual defendants; using inadequate follow-up periods; and employing an 'inappropriate comparison group'.[178] Despite this criticism, the sunset clause was repealed without opposition.

---

171   Harris, above.
172   Harris above.
173   Harris above.
174   Victoria, Parliamentary Debates, Legislative Council, 29 May 2002, 1282 (Justin Madden); Victoria, Parliamentary Debates, Legislative Assembly, 24 April 2002, 1129 (Rob Hulls) as cited in Sentencing Council of Australia, above n 150 at 3.
175   Harris, above n 147.
176   The rate from Shepparton Koori court was found to be 12.5 per cent and from Broadmeadows it was 15.5 per cent. In comparison, the recidivism rates for all Victorians was said to be 29.4 per cent.
177   Courts Legislation (Miscellaneous Amendments) Act 2005 (Vic), s 9.
178   See Jacqueline Fitzgerald "Does Circle Sentencing Reduce Aboriginal Offending?" (2008) 115 Crime and Justice Bulletin 2; Marchetti and Daly, above n 118 at 419; King and others, above n ,121 at 92.

In addition to an examination of the available statistics about offending and re-offending, the Review included a collation of questionnaires and qualitative feedback from the various parties involved in the Koori Courts. Some of the qualitative observations are reproduced below:[179]

> ... Consistent themes that emerge from the additional comments made by the defendants on their questionnaires were the importance of the role of Elders and cultural factors in their court appearance and the fact that they had the opportunity to speak and that they felt the Magistrate was listening to them. Significantly a number of the defendants indicated that they had a long prior history of involvement with the criminal justice system (ranging from 10 to 43 years) and they felt that the Court represented a significant and different justice experience for them.

The Elders were unanimous in their belief that the Koori Court had improved relations between the local Koori community and the police. However, they were less emphatic on the question of whether they thought that the court was well understood and accepted by the local non-Indigenous community; with only one replying that they thought it was accepted, while six replied that they were "not sure".[180]

In summary, the elders' questionnaire indicated that they believed the Koori Court to be a success and that their role was respected and valued by the defendants and other court personnel.[181] Significantly, they believed that the Koori Court had improved relations with the local police force, although there was less certainty as to the degree that the Koori Court was understood and accepted amongst the wider non-Indigenous community.[182]

The Report also contained 19 recommendations ranging from extending the Koori Court initiative to the provision of more Magistrates' Court locations. This would place the Koori Court on stronger financial grounds as well as extending the jurisdiction to the Children's Court.

Statistics and measures of success

One of the ongoing challenges is the collection of sufficiently accurate statistics and demographic information to inform future decisions. The Australian Bureau of Statistics defines an Indigenous person as a person of Aboriginal or Torres Strait Islander descent who identifies as an Aboriginal or Torres Strait Islander and is accepted as such by the community in which he or she lives. There are three components to the definition: descent, self-identification and community acceptance.

---

179 Harris, above n 147.
180 Harris, above n 147. See also comments by Andrew Thompson in "Elders Want Koori Court to Stay" *The Standard* (online ed, Australia, 27 April 2013).
181 Harris, above n 147.
182 Above, at 93.

As with many Māori, it is not uncommon for an Aboriginal person to not self-identify as one upon arrest. Anecdotal reasons suggest that this is due to an unwillingness to become a victim of a negative stereotype, enforced by the over-representation within the criminal justice system, and thus classified as a problem. This presents a hurdle not only when comparing Aboriginals going through Koori Courts system with Aboriginals appearing in mainstream courts, but also in ascertaining accurate rates of criminality. Nonetheless, the recent report from Victoria indicates that over the last two years there has been a reduction of sitting days in the Koori Courts.[183] Although this is not conclusive, it supports anecdotal evidence that the Koori Courts reduce recidivism rates. Deputy Chief Justice Jelena Popovic further relates that:[184]

> I met the mother of a young man whose case was heard before a magistrate and Elders at Koori Court several years ago. The young man's mother said that, as an Aboriginal person, the most significant development in Aboriginal social justice was the introduction of Koori Courts. It was her firm belief that her son's life may have taken a different turn entirely had his offending been dealt with in a conventional manner. The family had been part of the Stolen Generation and as a result, the son had not been particularly cultural before the Koori Court hearing. The hearing changed his life. For the first time in his life, the Elders connected him up to his elders and family members and he felt a sense of inclusion. Actually, he was made to feel valued by the community. The Elders told him about his family, provided him with support and reinforced community expectations. His sentence was deferred, during which period he attended Koori specific drug and alcohol counselling. He left the Court not only with a sense of identity, but of pride, purpose and belonging. He has not reoffended, has completed a trade and has a family of his own. This story encapsulates what Koori Court means to me as a magistrate. It demonstrates how powerful a culturally appropriate court process can be. The young man did not become a statistic in the substantial overrepresentation of Aboriginal persons in custody. The process connected him to his culture and community and assisted him to become a contributing member of the wider community. His response to the Koori Court had the further effect of allaying his mother's concerns about his drug and alcohol abuse and his diminished future prospects.

Magistrates' resources, court staff and training

Support for magistrates who have had previous experience working with Aboriginal peoples or receiving cross-cultural awareness training is crucial.[185] A Koori Court

183 See the Magistrates' Court of Victoria *Annual Report 2012/13* "A varied, substantial and extensive jurisdiction" 58.
184 Above, at 57.
185 Harris, above n 147, Recommendation 4.

Benchbook would ensure a level of consistency in the court process. Court Registrars and Community Corrections Officers would also be beneficial to the process.[186]

Support programmes

An Integrated Services Programme that dovetails the various programmes needed to support a person's housing, their physical, mental and educational well-being, as well as other pertinent issues in a holistic way would be beneficial. This is seen as an essential way to reduce offending patterns and behaviours – both for Koori and mainstream offenders.

Guilty plea

The possibility of extending the Koori Courts beyond hearing matters where the defendant pleads guilty is considered. As the 'success' of Koori Courts continues, the academic interest in widening this jurisdiction beyond sentencing will also increase.[187]

Offence exclusion

The report recommended continuing the existing exclusion of sexual offences and family violence crimes from the Koori Courts.[188] This area remains problematic.

Indigenous academics such as Dr Kylie Cripps expressed concern during a Court of Appeal case in which an Aboriginal man, who was serving time for violently assaulting a 15-year-old girl, received a lesser sentence. This was in part because his shaming in the Koori Court constituted an additional customary punishment.[189] This decision was in conflict with the official assurances that Koori Courts had nothing to do with customary law.

Professor Marcia Langton further commented that:[190]

> You cannot downgrade assaults on women and say it's just a minor matter… – downgrading the seriousness of violence against women. She questioned why violent Aboriginal men were offered alternative court proceedings where the men are regarded as victims.

Specialised court – domestic violence

In Australia specialised family violence courts operate in New South Wales, Victoria, Queensland, Western Australia, South Australia, Northern Territory and the

186   Above, Recommendation 5.
187   Above, Recommendations 10 and 11.
188   Above, Recommendation 12.
189   See R Guillnat "Aboriginal courts fail to deter offenders" *The Australian* (online ed, Australia, 23 October 2010) <www.theaustralian.com.au>.
190   Above.

Australian Capital Territory. In Western Australia there are customised programmes for Indigenous persons and members of other cultural groups.[191] Notwithstanding this provision, the ability of these specialised courts to consider an Indigenous legal system remains problematic.

Where the future in Australia is heading

As Chief Magistrate Ian Gray has observed, there has been a paradigm shift in sentencing in the last 10 to 20 years. Moreover, "the growing realisation that crudely punitive sentencing is not a reliable way of dealing with recidivism, has led to the introduction into courts of various modes of therapeutic and restorative justice". Koori Courts share many of the characteristics of the new form of rehabilitative sentencing that has been termed "therapeutic jurisprudence".

Clearly, the innovative approach of the Koori Court is more than just 'special treatment' or a 'soft option', but is, in fact, reflective of international trends in sentencing and legal development. What distinguishes the Koori Court, however, is the importance of the Indigenous community and the role played by the elders and respected persons. It is therefore important to distinguish the Koori Courts as more than just an example of restorative justice or therapeutic jurisprudence and recognise the Koori Courts as *sui generis*.[192] Although the Koori Courts are progressive, they have the potential to further address the raft of issues faced by Aboriginal peoples within the legal system, particularly that of power imbalance.[193]

E United States of America

Re-entry courts – specialised courts

Re-entry courts are modelled from the same principle that underpins drug courts. That is, they are designed to assist ex-prisoners to participate in a judicially supervised parole programme to promote their successful integration into the community.[194] They are specialised courts established in the United States that help to reduce recidivism and improve public safety through judicial oversight. The Hon Richard Gebelein has stated:[195]

---

191 For full discussion see Australian Government *Family Violence – A National Legal Response* (ALRC Report 114, 2010) <www.alrc.gov.au>.
192 Harris, above n 147, at 134.
193 McAsey, above n 163, at 685.
194 Terry Saunders "Re Entry Court" in Bruce Winick and David Wexler (eds) *Judging in a Therapeutic Key Therapeutic Jurisprudence and the Courts* (Carolina Academic Press, North Carolina, 2003), at 67.
195 Shadd Maruna and Thomas P LeBel "Welcome Home? Examining the 'Reentry Court' Concept from a Strengths Based Perspective" (2003) 4(2) Western Criminology Review at 92.

... drug courts have succeeded because, unlike previous failed rehabilitative efforts, the drug court movement has been able to provide a narrative of what is causing the criminal behaviour of the drug court clients and what they need to get better.

For Maruna and LeBel, the critical question about re-entry courts becomes: "... is there a similar narrative for how and why re-entry should work?"[196]

The responsibilities generally assigned to re-entry courts include:[197]

a   A review of the offender's re-entry progress and problems;
b   The ordering of offenders to participate in various treatment and reintegration programs;
c   The use of drug and alcohol testing and other checks to monitor compliance;
d   The application of graduated sanctions to offenders who do not comply with treatment requirements; and
e   The provision of modest incentive rewards for sustained clean drug tests and other positive behaviour.

Conventionally, the judiciary has no role beyond sentencing of an offender, at which point responsibility for the offender ends. In New Zealand the Department of Corrections takes over responsibility for the offender. Despite more prisoners being incarcerated and serving longer sentences before becoming eligible for parole,[198] the availability of treatment programmes in prisons in New Zealand and the USA is questionable, and programme participation among prisoners has been declining over the past decade.[199]

Countries such as the United States of America have shown that re-entry courts can assist released offenders to deal with a variety of problems that, if left unresolved, could significantly interfere with their successful re-integration into the community.[200] The long-term benefits of successful re-entry into the community are viewed as outweighing the costs associated with establishing and operating a re-entry court.

The goal of re-entry courts is to reduce recidivism and the costs of incarceration and community disrepair, thus building a safer community in the process.[201]

196   At 92.
197   Office of Justice JD Programs, Model Programs Guide *Re Entry Court* <www.dsgon line.com>.
198   Parole Act amendments now require the offenders to serve a greater proportion of their sentence before being eligible for parole, see Parole Act 2002, s 20.
199   James P Lynch and William J Sabol *Prisoner Re-entry in Perspective: Crime and Policy Report Volume 3* (The Urban Institute, Washington DC, 2001).
200   See for example discussion by Judge Terry Saunders on the Harlem Reentry Court in Winick and Wexler (eds), above n 194 at 67.
201   This is consistent with New Zealand. See *Reid v Parole Board* (CA 247/05, 29 June 2006) where the Court of Appeal held that the Parole Board's sole focus should be the recidivism risk of the individual offender.

To date, the supervision of offenders on parole has been poor.[202] These factors have given rise to a new approach to court management in which judges actively become involved in supervising the transition of the offender.

This is not a novel idea. Specialised courts such as the drug court and domestic violence courts operate in this fashion. A key component in this type of court is that the court holds the judicial authority to which offenders respond positively.[203] In addition, frequent appearances before the court with the offer of assistance, coupled with the knowledge of the predictable and prudent consequences for failure, assist the offender in the re-entry process.

A re-entry court can take various forms. A 'Case Defined' Court provides for the judge to retain jurisdiction over a case during the entire life of the sentence.[204] A 'Stand Alone' Court allows the judge to maintain exclusive jurisdiction over re-entry cases.[205] Another type involves parole boards working with the judiciary to develop quasi-courts through the use of an administrative law judge. This is similar to the situation in New Zealand where the Parole Board consists of members of the judiciary as well as community members to consider offenders for parole. All forms offer a unified and comprehensive approach to managing offenders from first appearance to incarceration and back into the community, exploring a new approach to improving offender reintegration into the community.

The goal is to establish a seamless system of offender accountability and support services throughout the re-entry process. Important elements of a re-entry court include the assessment of the offender's needs and planning for release; active judicial oversight of offenders during the period of supervised release, including the use of graduated and stringent sanctions for violation of release conditions; a broad array of supportive services with community involvement; and positive judicial reinforcement of successful completion of re-entry court goals.[206]

Procedure – an example

In February 2000 the Office of Justice Programs in the United States of America launched a re-entry court initiative to explore a new approach to improving offender re-integration into the community. One of the Delaware Superior Court re-entry pilots is the New Castle County Re-Entry Court Program, in which case managers' work with offenders to create re-entry court plans. The probation officer works closely with the community police to enhance offender monitoring.

This re-entry court process incorporates three tiers of supervision:

202 See "Report Finds Failure in Parole Management" *Newstalk ZB/One News* (New Zealand, February 17, 2009) <www.tvnz.co.nz>.
203 OJJDP Model Programs Guide *Re Entry Court* <www.dsgonline.com>
204 OJJDP, above.
205 OJJDP, above.
206 Delaware State Courts *Re Entry Courts* <www.courts.delaware.gov>.

a Phase I – participants meet weekly with the judge and probation officer
b Phase II – participants meet every fortnight for three months and, if necessary, have further status conferences with the probation officer
c Phase III – monthly status conferences are held at 30 day intervals

Case managers act as service brokers and report directly to the re-entry judge
on the appropriate services and treatment for participating offenders.

The re-entry courts are situated in the heart of the community, close to where
parolees live, receive services and work. This provides both convenience and a
familiar setting for the parolees. The period of time post release has been identified as a critical time for parolees; the provision of a quick and smooth transition
is vital.

Current (Indigenous) re-entry models

A Spanish comparison – Juez de Vigilancia Penitenciaria (JVP)

Creative initiatives from jurisdictions, such as Spain, have extended the reach of
the judiciary in re-entry courts. David Wexler has proposed that the legal structure
of Spain's JVP could be used as the foundation for a re-entry court.[207]

The JVP law in Spain was created to provide judicial watchfulness over prisoner
rights and liberties, and is responsible for monitoring the prisoner's progress
through an active treatment programme. One of the most remarkable features of
the JVP is the prisoner's active participation in the planning and execution of the
programme.[208] The JVP may impose relevant conditions on release, such as
prohibiting contact with the victim, participation in particular programmes and
periodic appearances before the JVP.[209]

The role of the JVP begins upon incarceration. Conditional release is not
automatic once the offender has served a certain length of his or her sentence,
nor does release lie in the unfettered discretion of the JVP. Conditional release
authority resides in a single judge, rather than in a multi-member board. It is not
the judge's role to recall an offender.

Although this option is somewhat underdeveloped, according to David
Wexler:[210]

> ... the enviable JVP legal structure deserves to be studied seriously by those
> in the United States and in other Anglo American legal systems contemplating
> reform of the re-entry process.

207 See Organic Law of Spain 1/1979, Art 76.
208 See D Wexler "Spain's JVP Legal Structure as a Potential Model for a Re-Entry
     Court" (2003) 7(1) Contemporary Issues in Law.
209 Above.
210 Above.

Tohono O'odham Nation

The Tohono O'odham Nation in the United States has a Law and Order Code and retains jurisdiction over many criminal offences.[211] The re-entry of these offenders is a community concern. This Law and Order Code[212] allows a tribal court to 'parole' offenders after successfully serving a portion (typically one half) of the imposed sentence.[213] Upon parole application, a tribal judge will typically grant or deny parole. Recently, the Tohono O'odham judiciary has been contemplating the use of the (tribal) Law and Order Code parole provision to facilitate and create a re-entry court where the judges would play an active role.[214] The sovereign powers and jurisdiction of the Nation lies within their boundary. This would only extend to persons outside this boundary by consent.

There are obvious issues that flow from such a proposition. These include the type of cases a re-entry court may best begin with, the nature of a judicial parole hearing, the type of preparation an offender should engage in, the kind of parole conditions that may be imposed, the role of the community and the follow up process between the offender and the judge.[215]

Navajo courts[216]

Prior to the arrival of the Spanish (1598) and the Anglo-Saxons (1846), Navajos governed themselves and resolved disputes in their own way. They lived in family groups and clans, and resolved disputes by 'talking things out'. The judges were the *hozhoji' Naat'aah*, or peace chiefs. They were leaders, chosen by community consensus because of their wisdom, spirituality, exemplary conduct, speaking ability, and skill in planning for community survival and prosperity. They mediated disputes by encouraging people to discuss their problems fully in order to reach agreed settlements and restore harmony throughout the community.

The Constitution and later federal laws granted local sovereignty to tribal nations, but not full sovereignty identifying them as 'domestic dependent nations'. The Indian Reorganisation Act 1934 was enacted to support Native American

---

211 Tohono O'odham Nation comprises of a group of Native Americans who reside primarily in the Sonoran Desert of south east Arizona and north west Mexico.

212 Tohono O'odham Law and Order Code 1.15 (5) 1994 "a person convicted of an offence and sentenced to jail may be paroled after he or she has served at least half of the particular sentence with good behaviour".

213 Bruce Winick and David Wexler "Practice Settings and Clinical Opportunities" in David Wexler (ed) *Rehabilitating Lawyers Principles of Therapeutic Jurisprudence for Criminal Law Practice* (Carolina Academic Press, North Carolina, 2008) at 313.

214 Above, at 314.

215 Above, at 316 for discussion.

216 For a similar example see also the Hopi Courts who have established both a civil and criminal jurisdiction and rely on Elders for the implementation of Hopi custom law; see Justin B Richland *Arguing with Tradition: the Language of Law in Hopi Tribal Court* (University of Chicago Press, Chicago, 2008) at 46 for further discussion.

self-government and self-management of assets. In 1953 the United States Federal Code granted full effect to Native American laws and customs, provided that they were not inconsistent with respective state laws.

Any decision by a Tribal Court was recognised by State and Federal Courts and Native tribes held exclusive jurisdiction to pass laws and prosecute within their tribal boundaries. In cases where the offender was Native American and the victim non- Native American, or for serious offences, such as manslaughter or murder, the jurisdiction of State law applied. However, if the offender and victim were both Native American, but from different tribes, the respective tribal court jurisdiction applied.[217]

Unlike European law, traditional Navajo law was based not on power, but on relationships, respect and mutual need.[218] By the early 1980s members of the Navajo Nation Council, judges and the Navajo people themselves sought to revive traditional Navajo justice methods. As part of this initiative, local judges began to apply traditional Navajo legal principles in their decisions. They did so in the English language. These decisions provided a great deal of insight into Navajo common law. According to Justice Austin:[219]

> The Navajo experience is one of going back to fundamental values. Given the disruptions of non-Indian schools ... destruction of tribal land bases ... Indians have many barriers to overcome. All those influences have eroded traditional values ... so long as Navajos preserve their language, religion, traditions and culture they retain the framework for successful modern approaches. Navajo common law is not something quaint or curious – it is alive and vibrant ... it adapts to the present and it will adapt to the future ... this is a process of going back ... back to the future.

Three foundational Navajo doctrines are *hozho* (harmony, balance and peace), *k'e'* (unity through positive values) and *k'e'i* (kinship or clan system). These concepts are equivalent to their Māori counterparts; namely, *whakapapa, whanaungatanga, rangimarie, kotahitanga* and balance – the ultimate aim for *tikanga*. These three doctrines have been incorporated by Navajo judges in a Navajo adjudicatory system that is designed for American style litigation.[220] The written decisions of the Navajo

217 See *Means v Nation* 432 F 3d 924, 933 (9th Cir 2005) where following an appeal by an Oglala-Sioux member against a Navajo Nation criminal prosecution for assault under the Navajo Nation Code the United States Supreme Court held that tribal court jurisdiction applies to all Native Americans.

218 Chief Justice (Emeritus) Robert Yazzie "History of the Courts of the Navajo Nation" (Paper prepared for the Orientation of the Judiciary Committee of the Navajo Nation, February 11 2003) <www.navajocourts.org/>.

219 Raymond Austin "ADR and the Navajo Peacemaker Court" (1993) 32(2) The Judges' Journal at 47.

220 See *In re Mental Health Services of Bizardi* 8 Nav. Rptr (Nav. Sup. Ct. 2004) where the court referred to the principle of *hozho* "bringing people in dispute back to harmony"

Courts provide information on how these doctrines provide tools for "healing" and attaining harmony within the community. In seeking answers for disproportionate rates of criminality and mental health issues, the potential answers lie not in the non-Indian system that oppressed the people, but in their own languages, philosophies and cultural practices that are intrinsic to the three underlying doctrines applied in these courts.

The Navajo Nation identifies and codifies the common law doctrines.[221] In addition, a traditional system is annexed to the modern court system to promote and facilitate the holistic use of Navajo culture, language, common law and spirituality. Unsurprisingly, restorative justice is a core responsibility of the Navajo justice system.

For example, in response to a request by the Navajo Supreme Court to review juvenile detention, the probation and peacemaking functions of the process were merged. This was to promote rehabilitation of offenders.[222] During this review many offences on the Navajo Nation were decriminalised and directed to restorative justice solutions, community participation and *nalyeeh*.[223]

A study undertaken of Navajo Peacemaking noted that "peacemaking participants show a rate of reoccurrence of the presenting problem of 29%, while those processed through the Family Court show a rate of 64%".[224] The study further suggests that "Peacemaking offers individuals and groups experiencing conflict a compelling opportunity to achieve resolution and community/family justice" and that the process offered:[225]

> a pervasive sense of fairness, experiencing higher levels of case settlement … [and] that Peacemaking allowed them to communicate their feelings much more freely and maintained the centrality … as essential to the process. These data are bolstered by the fact that many of the Peacemaking participants had previously dealt with family conflict within Family Court and had a personal basis of comparison.

as cited in Raymond Austin *Navajo Courts and the Navajo Common Law* (University of Minnesota Press, Minneapolis, 2009) at 65.

221 For example, "The Navajo Indian Nation recognise[s] common-law marriages between tribal members living on the reservation if these marriages meet the elements universally recognised as constituting a common-law marriage (agreement to be married, cohabitation, and holding out to the public as being married). Such a marriage may be validated by the Courts of the Navajo Nation upon application and submission of proof that the persons involved have entered into such a marriage and are recognised as husband and wife in their community." GN 00305.080 Navajo Tribal Common-Law Marriages <http://policy.ssa.gov/poms.nsf/lnx/0200305080>.

222 "Nábináhaazláago" Initiative Services to Youth in Detention <http://www.nava jocourts.org/Nabinahazlaago%20Files/Nabinahaazlaago.html.>

223 Above.

224 Eric Gross "Evaluation/Assessment of Navajo Peacemaking" (April 5, 2001) available also at <https://www.ncjrs.gov/pdffiles1/nij/grants/187675.pdf> at 46. Although the issue of selection bias was raised the author's fieldwork dismissed this issue.

225 At 44.

F Comparative jurisdiction conclusion

In Canada international bodies recommend effective access to justice for Aboriginal women.[226] As a way to achieve this goal, the Canadian Criminal Code supports the implementation of circle sentencing. Evidence suggests that the use of circle sentencing can contribute to lower recidivism rates.[227]

The Australian Law Reform (1986)[228] recognises the importance of customary law in addressing disproportionate offending rates. The Magistrates' Court (Koori Court) Act 2002 provides for the establishment of Koori Courts to operate during sentencing. Evidence indicates that the Koori Courts assist in issues of identity, the increase in community values and a contribution to the lowering of recidivism rates.

In the United States the concept of self-governance, a form of self-determination, is supported and has manifested in the Navajo Courts.[229] The jurisdiction of these courts is not confined to sentencing, but applies throughout the justice process. The concepts underpinning and actively employed by the Navajo Courts are similar to *tikanga* Māori.

Research indicates that circle-sentencing defendants in Canada re-offended at the same rate – 40 per cent – as Aboriginal defendants in the mainstream court system. On the other hand, Queensland's Attorney General, Cameron Dick, states the Murri Courts have better attendance, are valued by their communities and deliver culturally relevant sentences.[230]

In a review of Queensland's Murri Courts, however, it was concluded that they did not reduce Aboriginal offending.[231] This is consistent with findings from New South Wales, Victoria and Western Australia.[232] The report found that two-thirds of those appearing before these courts reoffended within twelve months. This is similar to the reoffending rate of mainstream courts.

---

226 For instance, the United Nations Declaration on the Rights of Indigenous People and also the United Nations Convention on the Elimination of All Forms of Discrimination Against Women.

227 See Carol La Prairie and Julian Roberts "Sentencing Circles: Some Unanswered Questions" (1996) 39 Criminal Law Quarterly 69 at 73.

228 Australian Law Reform Commission *The Recognition of Aboriginal Customary Law* (31 Sydney, 1986) <www.austlii.edu.au>.

229 Tribal nations are recognised as "domestic dependent nations" by the Federal Government which has established a number of laws attempting to clarify the relationship between the federal, state, and tribal governments.

230 Guilliatt, above n 189 .

231 Anthony Morgan and Erin Louis *Evaluation of the Queensland Murri Court: Final Report* (2010) Australian Institute of Criminology, Australian Government, Reports and Technical Background Paper 39, xv, where the report noted that "appearing for sentence in the Murri Court had no impact on reoffending among indigenous offenders, at least in the short term".

232 See Fitzgerald, above n 178 at 1 as cited by Elena Marchetti "Indigenous Sentencing Court Brief 5" (December, 2009) <www.indigenousjustice.gov.au>

While the recommendations of the 1986 Australian Law Reform Commission Report enjoy wide support from Indigenous communities, Indigenous customary law receives only limited recognition through the existing criminal justice system. Australia's 'new' Indigenous courts operate within the existing Magistrates' Court systems in South Australia, Victoria and Queensland. These courts are responsible for sentencing only and require offenders to admit their guilt. They can be seen as a therapeutic response to the problem of Indigenous over-representation within a more urban/mainstream location. The 'new' Indigenous courts are also said to reflect the partnership practices that were recommended in Justice Agreements between State governments and Indigenous organisations.

As in the *marae*-based courts, available research indicates some level of success, although a number of concerns have also been highlighted. These include the criticism that the new Indigenous courts are simply a European justice initiative dressed up as an Indigenous one, and do not tackle the root problems of Indigenous offending, such as the legacy of government oppression and the inter-generational effects of colonisation.[233]

In addition, these courts may place further strain on Indigenous communities that are already affected by economic marginalisation and have few social services/ resources. Ironically, the current locations of the Indigenous courts may not be suited to an urban setting and, in the case of the Nunga and Murri Courts, a lack of formalised legislation could potentially pose problems. Marchetti and Daly argue that these courts have broader aims and objectives, in that they seek to achieve a cultural and political transformation of the law.[234]

In general, these courts address minor offences. However, various issues concerning whether the court's jurisdiction should be extended to include serious offences that warranted a jury have been raised.[235] As these courts could be available to both Indigenous and non-Indigenous offenders, then theoretically, the composition of any jury should not present an issue. However, as these courts are primarily designed to address the disproportionate offending statistics of Indigenous peoples, it is suggested that any jury convened should reflect an Indigenous selection and composition. As the court is underpinned and directed by principles of healing, harmony and balance, any non-Indigenous offender should not be disadvantaged. In any event the defendant may still choose to be tried in mainstream courts.

Although some Indigenous courts indicate signs of success, it is suggested that a similar forum that is underpinned by customary law, but positioned outside the colonial justice system, may provide a way forward.

233 Marchetti above.
234 Marchetti above.
235 See for example Criminal Procedure Act 2011 ss 71–74 that provides for four categories of offences attracting Judge alone or a Jury trial. It is envisaged that the proposed model would initially be open to Category 1 offences only (minor offences), with a review if the model proves successful.

By identifying the ingredients of current initiatives from the comparative jurisdictions that have shown success and developing them further, it is suggested that the current implementation of traditional practices, such as circle sentencing, should be extended. Furthermore, a return to the concepts that underpin *tikanga* – an Indigenous legal system – is pivotal to addressing disproportionate offending and imprisonment rates among Indigenous peoples.

G A model for Māori?

In the abstract, the model of a Navajo Court is amenable to a concept of an Indigenous court for Māori. Notwithstanding this possibility, there are a few concerns.

To retain the integrity of *tikanga*, it should not be subject to codification or interpretation by the legal profession. First, there is the danger that important concepts will be lost in translation, which invariably results in some redefinition of the original concept or term.

In general, the incorporation of *tikanga* into *Pākehā* law implies a degree of acceptance and understanding of *tikanga*, which may not always be the case.

Second, the isolation of one concept or term from *tikanga* is an unnatural separation of the concept from its *tikanga* roots, its philosophical underpinnings and cultural constructs.

Third, the codification or placement of *tikanga* within mainstream legislation is only one factor to be considered amongst many others. This is also unnatural and degrading to *tikanga*.

The major problem with codifying *tikanga* is that these 'right, proper' ways of doing things are fundamentally contextual, rather than absolute. Like any other system of law, they depend on the context, including the nature of the offence, the individuals and kin groups involved, their previous transactions with each other and the particular expectations about 'proper' behaviour that have been discussed in this case.

The underlying tenets of customary law are common to all Indigenous peoples. For the First Nations Peoples of Canada:[236]

> Our traditions must be lived to be relevant, but it requires great effort to acquire and apply them. You have a choice about what laws you should follow ... those choices are strengthened when they remain connected to the earth and all we can learn from her ...

Law is most successful when it reflects the values and mores of those it serves. It is timely to now explore the concept of therapeutic jurisprudence, in particular the synergy between therapeutic jurisprudence and *tikanga* Māori.

---

236 John Borrows *Drawing Out Law* (University of Toronto Press, Toronto, 2010) at 47.

Chapter 7

Tikanga Māori and therapeutic jurisprudence

A What is therapeutic jurisprudence?

Therapeutic jurisprudence was developed out of the mental health system. American Professors Bruce Winick and David Wexler, both mental health law academics, were the pioneers of this movement. During their practice within the American health system, they conceived the idea that the operation of law and its accompanying legal processes can have a direct psychological impact on all the players, including lawyers, judges and the offender.[1] This impact could be both therapeutic or anti-therapeutic.[2] Thus, a system that is designed to help people recover or improve their mental health often backfires and has the opposite effect creating a revolving door.[3]

Therapeutic jurisprudence is a perspective that regards the law as a social force that produces behaviours and consequences.[4] Sometimes these consequences fall within the realm of what we call 'therapeutic'. At other times anti-therapeutic consequences are produced.[5] Therapeutic jurisprudence raises our attention to this and encourages us to see whether the law can be made or applied in a more therapeutic way, so long as other values, such as justice, can be fully respected.[6] For Māori, this means that the law should aspire to generate a state of *ora* (well-being) as opposed to an aggravated state of *mate* (ailing, ill). It does not trump

---

1 Bruce Winick and David Wexler (eds) *Judging in a Therapeutic Key – Therapeutic Jurisprudence and the Courts* (Carolina Academic Press, North Carolina, 2003) at 7.
2 Winick above. Also see Brian McKenna, Sandy Simpson and John Coverdale "Implementing Civil Commitment: Doing With Not Doing To" in Warren Brookbanks and Sandy Simpson (eds) *Psychiatry and the Law* (LexisNexis, Wellington, 2007) at 72.
3 Alan Feuer "The Revolving Door" in Bruce Winick and David Wexler (eds) *Judging in a Therapeutic Key – Therapeutic Jurisprudence and the Courts* (Carolina Academic Press, North Carolina, 2003) at 13.
4 Bruce Winick *Civil Commitment* (Carolina Academic Press, North Carolina, 2005) at 6.
5 See Brian McKenna and Kevin Seaton "Liaison Services to the Courts" in Warren Brookbanks and Sandy Simpson (eds) *Psychiatry and the Law* (LexisNexis, Wellington, 2005) at 449.
6 Winick and Wexler, above n 1.

other considerations or override important societal values, such as due process or freedom of speech and press.[7] Therefore therapeutic jurisprudence is the study of therapeutic and non-therapeutic consequences of the law.

Therapeutic jurisprudence is thus described as the "study of the role of law as a therapeutic agent".[8] One author offered the following definition as best capturing the essence of therapeutic jurisprudence:[9]

> ... the use of social science to study the extent to which a legal rule or practice promotes the psychological and physical well-being of the people it affects.

In this sense therapeutic jurisprudence is more of a descriptive and instrumental tool than an analytical theory.[10] It focuses on the impact of law on emotional life and psychological well-being.[11] Therapeutic jurisprudence can be thought of as a lens through which to view regulations and laws, as well as the roles and behaviour of legal actors: the legislators, lawyers, judges and administrators.[12] It is through this lens that an Indigenous legal system such as *tikanga* Māori can be implemented.

Disadvantages and criticisms

Support for therapeutic jurisprudence varies within academic circles from enthusiasm to mixed reviews. One of the early criticisms of therapeutic jurisprudence was that it was paternalistic. Perhaps this was a confusion in the title itself, which may have suggested a return to a therapeutic state.[13] The State legal system is paternalistic, so if the implementation of a therapeutic jurisprudential approach is successful in reducing Māori offending rates and those relating to domestic violence, then the positive outcome of restoring a state of *ora* would outweigh any criticism of paternalism.

In his article Judge Arthur Christean[14] outlined a number of criticisms, such as issues of due process and constitutional infringements, which are also echoed by

---

7 William Schma "Judging for the New Millennium" (2000) 37(1) Court Review.
8 Winick and Wexler, above n 1.
9 Christopher Slobogin "Therapeutic Jurisprudence: Five Dilemmas to Ponder" (1995) 1 Psychol, Pol and Law 193 at 196.
10 Warren Brookbanks "Therapeutic Jurisprudence: Implications for Judging" (paper presented at the District Court Judge's Triennial Conference, Rotorua, 1 April 2003).
11 Winick and Wexler, above n 1.
12 Schma, above n 7.
13 Dennis P Stolle and others "Integrating Preventive Law and Therapeutic Jurisprudence: A Law and Psychology Based Approach to Lawyering" in Dennis P Stolle, David B Wexler and Bruce J Winick (eds) *Practicing Therapeutic Jurisprudence Law as a Helping Profession* (North Carolina Academic Press, Durham, 2000) at 8.
14 A G Christean *Therapeutic Jurisprudence: Embracing a Tainted Ideal* (2002) The Sutherland Institute <http://www.sutherlandinstitute.org>.

David Wexler.[15] These criticisms involve the use of therapeutic jurisprudence within a specialist court setting. They include the belief that therapeutic jurisprudence puts a tremendous strain on resources and judicial collegiality, because of the 'one court, one judge' concept common to most specialised courts.

In New Zealand there is a move towards a proliferation of specialised courts.[16] A specialist judge creates consistency of response. This is pivotal to the success of the Family Violence Court, where the judge is proactive in monitoring and the success of the court hinges on consistency from the bench. In a evaluation of the Waitakere Family Violence Court, Morgan found that:[17]

> Consistency of approach among the judiciary is very important. If we have visiting judges we do whatever we can to make sure they don't go into the Family Violence Court.

Whilst this may seem to exacerbate the strain on judicial resources, the importance of specialist courts and the long-term benefits outweigh this concern.

Christean further added that therapeutic jurisprudence works against the goal of a unified court system in the direction of specialised courts. These courts operate on a different judicial philosophy from other courts within the same district. However, proponents of problem solving courts have been quick to defend critics' attempts to pick apart these new initiatives by comparing them to an "idealised vision of justice that does not exist in real life".[18]

There is also the concern that therapeutic jurisprudence undermines the separation of powers by asking the courts to fashion solutions to social problems, rather than leaving the legislature to deal with them.[19] Christean states that the line between the judicial and executive branch is blurred whenever courts become service providers, intent on achieving specific outcomes. In this regard the judge becomes part of a treatment team and assumes the responsibility for overseeing programmes sponsored by the team, thus exercising both an executive and a judicial function. Notwithstanding this criticism, it may be that therapeutic jurisprudence is being identified or conflated with drug courts or other problem-solving courts, where the judicial officer is more actively involved than are the judges in mainstream courts.

Berman has acknowledged these concerns of impartiality, including coercion, paternalism and zealous advocacy.[20] However, Berman is also an advocate for

---

15 Winick and Wexler, above n 1, at 81–85.
16 Family Court, Youth Court, Environment Court, Māori Land Court, Domestic Violence Court.
17 Mandy Morgan, Leigh Coombes and Sarah Mc Gray *An Evaluation of the Waitakere Family Violence Court Protocols* (Massey University and WAVES, Palmerston North, May 2007).
18 Winick and Wexler, above n 1, at 82.
19 Although there are sometimes blurred lines, the role of the Court is to apply the law whereas the legislature 'makes' the law.
20 Winick and Wexler, above n 1, at 81–83; see also Greg Berman "Redefining Criminal Court: Problem-Solving and the Meaning of Justice" (2004) 41 Am Crim L Rev 131.

therapeutic jurisprudence and problem solving courts, suggesting that better planning and dissemination of best practice standards can assist to allay these concerns.[21]

This occurs in New Zealand within the youth justice sector as well as in the family court jurisdiction. In a family violence court, the effectiveness of its programmes is discussed regularly between the stakeholders. Judges make policy by taking advantage of the discretion that has traditionally been afforded to them over sentencing in order to craft more meaningful sanctions, or to direct programme changes.[22]

There is merit in maintaining clear boundaries with respect to the doctrine of parliamentary sovereignty[23] and the separation of powers.[24] But in a therapeutic problem solving court, this could undermine the relational element that is necessary between the judge and the offender. By stating clear boundaries and defining roles at the outset, this problem may be overcome and the judge's position of respect maintained. In addition, therapeutic jurisprudence does not trump longstanding notions of due process or the rule of law. However, in order to work strictly within the current Westminster system, a compromise must be made.

It has been claimed that therapeutic jurisprudence compromises the objectivity and impartiality of judges. Christean argues that the collaborative process requires the judge to act as part of the therapeutic team. In doing so the judge cannot avoid unethical ex parte communications that are traditionally a serious ethical breach of the judge's role. However, such communications form a regular part of the therapeutic process.[25] When the judge becomes the enforcer of the treatment team's decisions, rather than an independent adjudicator of the facts and the law, the appearance of bias cannot be avoided. To the defendant the judge becomes one of them. On the other hand, this can also be seen to be an effort by the judge to deal more effectively and humanely with the people who come before the court.

It is also argued that the new model substitutes a judge's subjective judgment for the time honoured due process checks. This eliminates a vital check on the abuse of government power. Christean is concerned that judges cannot effectively act as impartial and detached officers to hear and rule on the competing claims of adversaries when they simultaneously function as advocates and defenders of the programmes and procedures under challenge. Beneficial intent,

---

21 Berman above; see also Kathryn Sammon "Therapeutic Jurisprudence: An Examination of Problem Solving Justice in New York" (2008) 23(3) Journal of Civil Rights and Economic Development.

22 Winick and Wexler, above n 1.

23 See Philip Joseph *Constitutional and Administrative Law in New Zealand* (Brookers, Wellington, 2014) at 515; Parliamentary Sovereignty –"Parliament enjoys unlimited and illimitable powers of legislation".

24 See Joseph, above at 199; "the doctrine identifies the executive, legislative and judiciary" it provides a check and balance system.

25 Christean, above n 14.

rather than legal soundness is seen to be the benchmark of the effectiveness of any treatment regimes that are imposed.[26]

Finally, therapeutic jurisprudence is said to abandon the role of equal justice under the law; that is, programmes are necessarily limited to those offenders who qualify rather than to all defendants who would like to participate. This implies that some defendants will be treated differently from others, depending on whether they are deemed to be worthy candidates for available programme openings. Christean suggests that difficult or resistant candidates are 'screened out' in favour of presenting a public face to a programme that may be attractive to the media and an endorsement of the programme's success. However, there would be no reason why the jurisdiction could not be widened to include all offenders once the programme becomes successful.

I acknowledge the validity of these criticisms; therapeutic jurisprudence advocates are currently addressing them.[27] Nonetheless, one should not lose sight of the aim and should bear in mind that law does not exist in a vacuum and is ever changing. If therapeutic jurisprudence has the desired healing effect, this will result in less offending. The flow on from this will be a lighter case load and a lessening strain on resources, and arguably, one justification against these criticisms.

However, according to David Wexler:[28]

> ... a therapeutic approach should be taken whenever such an approach is consistent with other values, considerations and understandings of justice, such as the rule of law.

If this is the case, it seems possible from a policy perspective that therapeutic jurisprudence can be mainstreamed. This rationalisation is not new. The mainstreaming of restorative justice into the Sentencing Act 2002 (NZ) requires the Court to take into account offer, agreement and response to make amends.[29] Also the Canadian Criminal Code 1985 directs a consideration of sanctions, other

---

26 Brookbanks, above n 10, at 9; see also Warren Brookbanks *Therapeutic Jurisprudence: New Zealand Perspectives* (Thomson Reuters, Auckland, 2015).

27 See B Arrigo "The Ethics of Therapeutic Jurisprudence: A Critical and Theoretical Inquiry of Law, Psychology and Crime" (2004) 11(1) Psychiatry, Psychology and Law at 23 for further critique; see M King "Applying Therapeutic Jurisprudence in Regional Areas in the Western Australian Experience" (2003) 10(2) Murdoch University Electronic Journal of Law; see also Winick and Wexler, above n 1; Michael King, Arie Freiberg, Becky Batagol and Ross Hyams *Non-Adversarial Justice* (Federation Press, Australia, 2009) ch 2 "Therapeutic Jurisprudence".

28 David Wexler "An Orientation to Therapeutic Jurisprudence" (1994) 20 New Eng J on Crime and Civil Confinement 259; see also Bruce Winick "The Jurisprudence of Therapeutic Jurisprudence" (1997) 3(1) Psychology, Public Policy and Law 184.

29 See John Braithwaite "Restorative Justice and Therapeutic Jurisprudence" (2000) 38 (2) CLB at 244. Restorative Justice is defined as "a process where all stakeholders involved in an injustice have an opportunity to discuss its effect on people and to decide what is to be done to attempt to heal those hurts"; Sentencing Act 2002, s 10.

than imprisonment, that are reasonable in the circumstances, with particular attention to the circumstances of Aboriginal offenders.[30]

Whilst there has been enthusiastic support for therapeutic jurisprudence, a common response is that therapeutic jurisprudence is a re-branding of previous models or a soft approach to crime. In a scathing critique, Hoffman criticised therapeutic jurisprudence as possessing a "New Age pedigree" and for being both anti-intellectual and wholly ineffective.[31] This critique fails to acknowledge the favourable evidence that drug courts have achieved in regard to keeping offenders in treatment, reducing drug use, reducing recidivism rates and saving prison costs.[32]

These criticisms should not discount the possibility that therapeutic jurisprudence may assist in reducing Māori offending rates. The commonalities between the philosophy behind therapeutic jurisprudence and Te Ao Māori will show that therapeutic jurisprudence should not be dismissed as an irrelevant and ineffective model.

Advantages and suitability

From a practical point of view, a significant advantage of therapeutic jurisprudence is that it co-exists with the existing legal system. This would answer the political arguments against a separate system for Māori. Additionally, therapeutic jurisprudence simultaneously allows for the incorporation of *tikanga* Māori. The inclusion of *tikanga* can occur, prima facie, at all levels of the criminal justice process.

Collectivity and relationality are central tenets to Māori. Therapeutic jurisprudence is asserted as being a relational based construct.[33] Te Ao Māori, like therapeutic jurisprudence, shares the idea of communitarianism or collectiveness, and the notion of *whanaungatanga* or relatedness. This move away from a rule based approach towards a principle or relational approach is consistent with Māori *tikanga*. Thus, from a conceptual point of view, therapeutic jurisprudence represents a movement away from a heavily rule based approach to one that is more collective, relational and principle based.

Therapeutic jurisprudence allows and acknowledges different conceptual frameworks. The Māori conceptual framework is at odds with the existing monocultural justice system in New Zealand. It is acknowledged that the Children, Young Persons and Their Families Act 1989 provides for concepts of support and

30 Canadian Criminal Code 1985, s 718(2)(e).
31 Morris Hoffman "Therapeutic Jurisprudence, Neorehabilitationism, and Judicial Collectivism: The Least Dangerous Branch Becomes Most Dangerous" (2002) Fordham Urban Law Journal at 2063.
32 Winick and Wexler, above n 1, at 80. Also early anecdotal evidence from the Alcohol and Other Drug Treatment Court in Auckland, New Zealand supports a reduction in recidivism rates.
33 Warren Brookbanks "Therapeutic Jurisprudence: Conceiving an Ethical Framework" (2001) 8(3) Jnl of Law and Medicine at 328.

involvement of *iwi* and *hapū* groups.[34] Section 16 of the Criminal Justice Act 1985 (now repealed) also allowed an offender's supporter to present information at sentencing relating to their ethnic or cultural background to help avoid future offending.

However, in a review of section 16 of the Criminal Justice Act 1985, now repealed and replaced by section 27 of the Sentencing Act 2002, the paucity of its use was noted.[35] There was no mandatory requirement that the offender's cultural background be considered as a mitigating factor in sentencing. The application of this section was at the discretion of the judge and the cultural information regarding an offender was but one factor to consider.[36] However, when the section was employed and the cultural background of the offender was taken into consideration, it was not uncommon for the sentence to be suspended.[37]

Notwithstanding these provisions, issues central to Māori, such as reciprocity, have no equal in the State justice system. The judge is the ultimate decision-maker under the CYPF Act 1989 and the Sentencing Act 2002.[38] So it is evident that there are differences in approach and differences in how justice should be administered between the Māori and State systems.

Therapeutic jurisprudence, like *tikanga* Māori, is a forward looking process. In comparison, the criminal justice system looks back, punishing the offender for past actions and focusing on the penalty. *Tikanga* Māori, like therapeutic jurisprudence, is not penalty orientated. It looks for the 'right' or *tika* way of doing things, ultimately resulting in a healing or restoration of balance and *ora* for the participants.

Two important issues can be drawn from this. The first is that the commonalities between therapeutic jurisprudence and *tikanga* Māori allow both systems to work in tandem. This also provides a window for the introduction of *tikanga* programmes that focus on Indigenous law as a basis to understand why the crime or

---

34 For example Part Two s 13 (d) provides that "where a child or young person is considered to be in need of care or protection, the principle that, wherever practicable, the necessary assistance and support should be provided to enable the child or young person to be cared for and protected within his or her own family, whanau, hapu, iwi, and family group".

35 Alison Chetwin, Tony Waldegrave, Kiri Simonsen with Strategic Training and Development Services and the Family Centre Social Policy Research Unit *Speaking about Cultural Background at Sentencing* (Ministry of Justice, Wellington, November 2000) <www.justice.govt.nz>.

36 Interpretation confirmed in *RS v R* [2014] NZCA 484. This 'balancing act' also occurs under the Resource Management Act 1991 when the judge in attaining the purpose of the Act considers various factors including principles of the Treaty (section 8), the concept of *kaitiakitanga* (section 7) when reaching a decision. These concepts are to be considered in a raft of many.

37 Chetwin, Waldegrave and Simonsen, above n 35; see ss 8(i) and 27 of the Sentencing Act 2002 which illustrates the intention to incorporate *tikanga* Māori into the sentencing process.

38 Section 27 of the Sentencing Act 2002 replaces section 16 of the Criminal Justice Act 1985.

hara should not be committed. Acknowledging the effect of colonialism and the law on the role of women is instrumental in understanding the true *hara* or crime that underlies domestic violence. This primarily turns on the breakdown of the *whānau*.[39]

The second issue is that the theory of therapeutic jurisprudence allows the administration of justice in the existing legal system to promote the well-being of communities, thereby empowering Māori to look after one another.[40] The challenge will be the realisation, implementation and practicality of therapeutic jurisprudence in a suitable court forum.

Addressing the criticisms for therapeutic jurisprudence from a *tikanga* perspective, the facilitator of a dispute is usually a *rangatira, tohunga, kaumatua* or *kuia*.[41] The set of principles attached to resolving disputes is supported by other principles that traditionally provided the guidelines for actions amongst individuals and groups throughout Māori society. Principles provide flexibility as to the appropriate choice of action. For this reason, Māori society is often described as 'principle based' as opposed to 'rule based'. There is less emphasis on rules, but more emphasis on principles. Thus, within a *tikanga* Māori perspective, the principle of a healing outcome would outweigh rules, such as those based on the notion of unethical ex parte communications.

Asher J viewed ex parte communications as a necessity to achieve justice.[42] However, ex parte communications with a judge can result in disciplinary actions.[43] On motions to dismiss, Judge Silvia Cartwright, sitting in the Cambodian Supreme Court, noted that ex-parte communications "create the appearance of asymmetrical access enjoyed by the prosecutor to the trial judge and for that reason alone should cease".[44]

The collectivity tenet is central to *tikanga* Māori, together with the principle of everyone being on the same level. This effectively assists to dispel the criticism of therapeutic jurisprudence that the defendant perceives the judge becoming the same as them. Further it dispels the objectivity and impartiality criticism.

Therapeutic jurisprudence, like *tikanga* Māori, is a relational ethic. In a submission on the Victims' Rights Bill to the Justice and Electoral Select Committee, the New Zealand Human Rights Commission considered that a therapeutic

---

39 Ani Mikaere "Māori Women Caught in the Contradictions of a Colonized Reality" (1994) 2 Waikato Law Review.
40 Above.
41 '*Rangatira*' is defined as a leader, '*Tohunga*' as an expert, and '*kaumatua*' and '*kuia*' as respected elders.
42 *Du Claire v M Palmer and Crown Law Office* [2012] NZHC 934 per Asher J at [105].
43 See comments made by Judge David Harvey "Social Media and the Judiciary" *NZL* (28 April, 2013).
44 Extraordinary Chambers in the Courts of Cambodia *Decision on Motions for Disqualification of Judge Silvia Cartwright* (Extraordinary Chambers in the Courts of Cambodia – Supreme Court Chambers, Cambodia, 2012) at [24].

jurisprudence model was appropriate and could be addressed through progressive amendments to the justice system.[45]

It is noted that section 9 of the Victims' Rights Act 2002 makes provision for meetings to resolve issues relating to the offence. Viewed in isolation this is similar to the provisions of a family group conference in the CYPF Act 1989 and consistent with *tikanga* Māori. Further provisions of the Victims' Rights Act 2002 include the provision for Victim Impact Statements, to be placed before the court on sentencing, which potentially offers an opportunity to seek balance for the victim and offender – the aim of *tikanga* Māori.

The programmes currently in place for Māori offenders may be stemming the tide but are not solving the problem. Over the generations the physical and spiritual move of Māori away from their *turangawaewae* (ancestral place to stand) has alienated many urban Māori from their culture. The result of this is manifested, in part, by some Māori who perceive a *marae* setting for the Te Āwhina Whānau programme, as strange as a courtroom. Consequently, the whole process is seen as having an anti-therapeutic effect. This is but one reason to support the need for an alternative system to address the disproportionate rates of Māori offending.

It is acknowledged that Te Puni Kokiri has delivered many services to Māori and advises on policy affecting Māori well-being, including Whanua Ora. Funding is also available to assist *whānau* towards greater self-reliance and self-management by building and strengthening *whānau* connections to achieve goals and aspirations.[46]

The Law Commission has noted that:[47]

> Māori should retain the right to organise as Māori, and to administer and manage their own affairs … The establishment of specific Māori services to provide access to justice would be a further indicator of progress in this outcome category.

Notwithstanding these initiatives by Te Puni Kokiri and the recommendations by the Law Commission, the statistics, which indicate that Māori are over-represented in criminal proceedings, are difficult to ignore.[48]

Therapeutic jurisprudence has encouraged people to think creatively about how to bring promising developments into the legal system. The use of tools from social sciences to promote psychological and physical well being opens the door to

45 John Galtry "Submission of the Human Rights Commission on: Victims' Rights Bill to the Justice and Electoral Select Committee" (Human Rights Commission, Wellington, March 2001) at 9 <www.hrc.co.nz>.

46 See <http://www.tpk.govt.nz/en/services/wiie>

47 Law Commission *Justice: The Experience of Māori Women* (New Zealand Law Commission, Wellington, 1999) R53, at [425].

48 See statistics noted by Department of Corrections *Over-Representation of Māori in the Criminal Justice System: An Exploratory Report* (Department of Corrections, Wellington, 2007) <www.corrections.govt.nz>.

tikanga Māori. In doing so therapeutic jurisprudence may be able to offer a vehicle that will ultimately decrease Māori offending rates. It is pertinent to note that David Wexler stated:[49]

> In many respects, the roots of this *new judicial approach can be traced back to indigenous and tribal justice systems* [emphasis added], including noteworthy examples in what today constitutes the United States, Canada, Australia, and *New Zealand* [emphasis added] … and a serious effort is now underway to learn from those systems and to introduce some of their perspectives and techniques into western judicial structures.

B Can therapeutic jurisprudence be effective for a Domestic Violence Court? Towards a *tikanga* Māori model

On average, in New Zealand, 10 children and 14 women are killed every year in domestic violence.[50] In 2013 Women's Refuge assisted 20,000 women and children in one year.[51] With regard to victimisation:[52]

– Māori women are over-represented among victims of domestic violence and are more likely to experience repeat victimisation from a partner.
– A higher proportion of Māori women than non-Māori women apply for protection orders under the Domestic Violence Act 1995.
– Māori women and children are heavy users of Women's Refuge Services. There is some evidence that Māori women do not access other services for victims at the rate that might be expected indicating a potential issue of access.

With regard to offending:[53]

– Both female and male Māori youth are far more likely to be apprehended and prosecuted than their non-Māori counterparts.
– Māori women are five times more likely to be prosecuted for an offence than non-Māori women, and Māori men are over three times more likely to be prosecuted than non-Māori men.

---

49 Winick and Wexler, above n 1, at 3.
50 Women's Refuge New Zealand Domestic Violence Statistics. <https://womensrefuge.org.nz>
51 New Zealand Police *Protection Orders and the Domestic Violence Act* <http://www.police.govt.nz>
52 Hon Lalia Harre Minister of Women's Affairs speech "Māori Women: Mapping Inequalities and Pointing Ways Forward" (Report released September 26, 2001) <www.executive.govt.nz>.
53 Above.

- Māori women commit more less serious offences, such as producing false birth certificates, than Māori men, but there are some indications that Māori women are becoming increasingly involved in all offending.
- Māori women make up over 60 per cent of the women prison population, a higher percentage than Māori men compared to non-Māori men (around 50 per cent).

With regard to establishing and maintaining sustainable families, *whānau* and communities are seriously threatened by:

- The high incidence of domestic violence experienced by Māori women.
- The disproportionately high representation of Māori women in offending.
- The significant and rising over-representation of young Māori women in the criminal justice system.
- Impacts of the offending of male partners on Māori women.
- Impacts of Māori offending on children.
- High rates of Māori reoffending.

Domestic violence is a different crime, partly because the lives of the perpetrator and the victims are usually intertwined. A domestic violence court would bring cases before a judge more quickly than in the ordinary courts. Importantly, as Rivera notes:[54]

> ... it would keep the victim working with the same judge and prosecutor; that means the victim doesn't have to repeat the story of abuse over and over, sometimes to the point of giving up.

Domestic violence

It would be valuable to look at how effectively *tikanga* ensured that Māori women and children were cared for and valued. Strong evidence from pre-European contact indicates that women and children were not hit and abused, with the exception of *taurekareka* (war captives) who had lost their *mana*.[55] According to many early European commentators, relations within the kin group were generally harmonious. Things have changed drastically since then.

It has to be said, though, that the sanctions for breaches involved actions now regarded as illegal; for example, *muru* raids, in which property was confiscated

---

54 Ray Rivera "Our View: Boise Needs New Method to Stop Domestic Violence" in Bruce Winick and David Wexler (ed) *Judging in a Therapeutic Key, Therapeutic Jurisprudence and the Courts* (Carolina Academic Press, North Carolina, USA, 2003) at 58.
55 This is from personal knowledge and teachings from my Ngapuhi tribal *kuia* (respected elder).

and the guilty party was humiliated and perhaps beaten (although they were not badly hurt) before being brought back into the kinship fold.

This section of the book suggests the application of a therapeutic jurisprudence approach as a vehicle to implement *tikanga* Māori within a specialised court setting, such as a domestic violence court, could alleviate the alarming rates of domestic violence in New Zealand. The use of therapeutic jurisprudence in a domestic (family) violence court is not a novel idea.[56] Both South Australia and Western Australian domestic (family) violence courts are inter-agency and community initiatives aimed at reducing violence in families by integrating treatment into the court process. Unlike the ordinary criminal courts, the domestic violence court seeks not only to punish and rehabilitate the offender, but also to provide support and services required by the victim after physical or psychological abuse.[57]

The current trial process for domestic violence offences has an anti-therapeutic effect on victims. The 'crime against the state' perspective on prosecution disempowers victims and closes any avenue to seek balance for both the victim and defendant. There are many negative effects from the current system that tend to fracture and permanently end relations, rather than heal or restore them to balance.

The domestic violence courts operating throughout New Zealand are problem solving courts and generally focus on the underlying behaviour of the defendant. It is acknowledged that victim support agencies are attached to these courts. However, such agencies operate quite separately and are distinct from the justice process. Acting on the input of a team of experts from the community, a problem-solving court judge orders the defendant to comply with an individualised plan, such as anger management, and then the judge (with the assistance of the community team) exercises intensive supervision over the defendant to ensure compliance with the terms of the plan.[58]

Hypothetical domestic violence court – a model

The proposed model of this section is comprised of two components. First, a 're-tuned' domestic violence court that incorporates the doctrine of therapeutic jurisprudence. Secondly, this doctrine might then support the implementation of

---

56 See Michael King "Applying Therapeutic Jurisprudence from the Bench, Challenges and Opportunities" [2003] AltLawJl 52; (2003) 28(4) Alternative Law Journal 172 <www.austlii.edu.au/au/journals/>

57 Law Reform Commission of Western Australia – Court Intervention Programs: Consultation Paper, Chapter Four Domestic and Family Violence Court Intervention Programs, at 145 <http://www.lrc.justice.wa.gov.au>. Also victims of domestic violence in Victoria may be entitled to compensation of up to $70,000, <http://victim sofcrime.com.au/domestic-violence/>. See also Victims of Crime Assistance Act 1996 (Victoria, Australia).

58 Daniel Becker and Maura Corrigan "Moving Problem Solving Courts into the Mainstream" (2002) 39(1) Court Review at 4.

tikanga in a similar way to that of circle sentencing in Canada or Indigenous sentencing courts in Australia. However, I suggest that the application of *tikanga* is extended, and applied, to the whole criminal process, not just at the sentencing phase of the justice system. Ultimately, legislative recognition will provide certainty for this process.[59]

Ideally, this would include the training of lawyers and the judiciary to better understand the effects of domestic violence and battered women's syndrome from an Indigenous perspective. The positive flow-on effect would be a broader understanding of the causes of crime and its relationship with colonisation, in particular the effect colonisation had on the position of Māori women in society and the Māori concept of property.

From a practical point of view, this model will utilise the relevant systems and frameworks already in place, including the existing court forums, *marae*, Māori Committees, and legislative provisions such as the Community Development Act 1962. Local evidence suggests that although this mechanism (Community Development Act and Māori Committees) is already in place, it is under-utilised, due in part to under-resourcing.[60]

Ideally, the judges would be Māori. However, it is acknowledged that there is a shortage of Māori judges. Considering the education and ongoing training of judges in the fields of *tikanga, te reo* and *marae* protocol, it is possible that non-Māori judges could fill the roles. However, they would need to be well versed in *tikanga* Māori. In the alternative, *kaumatua* or a panel of *kaumatua* could assist a non-Māori judge in an advisory capacity.[61] This is not novel as the Resource Management Act of 1991 provides for a similar option, even if this option is not often exercised.[62] This would allay current concerns regarding the consistency of judges in a domestic violence court and address the problem of increased workloads identified in the Australian domestic violence courts.

Procedure – tikanga *Māori* component

The jurisdiction would ideally be open to all offenders. One of the criticisms of the domestic violence court is the limitation to less serious offences[63] and the inability to deal with serious offences.[64] Whilst this concern may be warranted,

---

59 Legislative recognition of Indigenous practice is not new, see Magistrates Court (Koori Court) Act 2002.

60 For example small town 'Māori Committees' such as the Aotea Māori Committee are usurped by 'Marae Committees' primarily due to better access to funding sources.

61 Te Ture Whenua Māori Land Act 1993, s 62 – "Additional members with knowledge and experience in tikanga Māori".

62 Resource Management Act 1991, ss 252 and 269(3), which provides for the consideration of *tikanga* values.

63 For example, "failing to stop for red and blue flashing lights" classified as a Category 1 offence; see section 71 Criminal Procedure Act 2011.

64 For example, murder or manslaughter classified as a Category 4 offence; see section 74 of the Criminal Procedure Act 2011.

the practical difficulty of dealing with hardened criminals alongside first-time offenders is acknowledged.

In the initial stages, the jurisdiction could be confined to the less serious or Category 1 offences with the anticipation that, once the success of this model has been proven, the jurisdiction could be widened to include more serious offences.[65] In light of the statistics that indicate the recidivism rates for Māori are higher than any other ethnicity in New Zealand and that Māori are more likely to commit more serious offences, there is a need for an Indigenous court to eventually address serious offences.[66]

This would address the criticism of the jurisdictional limitations identified by the Australian domestic violence courts. At such time necessary provisions for security of the offender and community would need to be addressed. This model and the accompanying processes are entirely integrated. The model takes effect at the beginning of the criminal procedure, upon the arrest of the offender. The arresting officer would enquire as to whether the offender identifies himself, or herself, as Māori and advise them of the process. If the offender does not self-identify as Māori, irrespective of their appearance, then that person would fall within the general criminal justice process or in this instance, the domestic violence court.

If the offender identifies as Māori, it would be mandatory for a Māori repre-sentative or warden to be called in. It would also be mandatory for the offender to become part of the programme.[67] This is similar to the juvenile arrest process adopted by the New Zealand Police.[68] It would be helpful, but not vital, that the representative be from the legal profession. This representative would become responsible for the offender until their first court appearance.

If the offender is ostensibly non-Māori but self-identifies as Māori, this should not inhibit the offender from partaking in the process, primarily because it is a principle-based process. If successful, there should be no reason why this model ought not to be extended to non-Māori. As the statistics indicate, however, it is Māori offending and Māori victim rates that are of the greatest concern. As such, Māori offenders would need to be targeted and prioritised

The offender would be assessed within the local *marae* forum, allowing for *whānau* involvement. Initially the offender would have no choice as to which *marae*

---

65 Such as Category 2, 3 and 4 offences; see sections 72, 73, and 74 of the Criminal Procedure Act 2011 respectively.

66 See Department of Corrections, above n 48.

67 For discussion of powers for mandatory involvement to compel whanau to attend, etc and employ Māori justice practices; see Juan Tauri "Family Group Conferencing: A Case Study of the Indigenisation of New Zealand's Justice System (1998) 10 CICJ 168.

68 For comparative instances see Anne Skelton "Reforming the Juvenile Justice System in South Africa: Policy, Law Reform and Parallel Developments" Resource Material 75 (paper presented to UNAFEI 136th International Training Conference, Japan, 2007) at 43 for the discussion on the use of home based supervision as an alternative to detention upon the arrest of juveniles as a result of an amendment to the Probation Services Act <www.unafei.or.jp>.

he/she would appear.[69] In Auckland there are several "pan" *iwi marae* that cater for Māori from all different *iwi*.[70] These *marae* are typically urban based. It is envisaged that initially a "pan" *iwi marae* would be used consistent with the concept of *whanaungatanga* (kin-like reciprocal relationships).[71] The offender could then be transferred to a tribal, or *iwi* specific *marae* if he/she requested, provided that funding resources are available.

As with the Indigenous courts model, both parties would sit at eye level (*kanohi ki te kanohi*). The use of existing Indigenous fora, such as a *marae*, addresses those concerns associated with unsuitable locations, as identified by the siting of Koori Courts. The arresting warden would assist to ensure that the offender, victim and both of their families do not feel uncomfortable in such a setting. This would allow all parties to address any feelings of alienation from the process, consistent with the concept of *manaakitanga* (process of showing care, respect, kindness and hospitality).[72] Unlike actors within the mainstream criminal justice system, these actors would not be constrained by existing policies. For instance, Probation Officers are guided by the Correction Department policies.

After the 'intake' has been completed, an appropriate programme would be specified for the offender, consistent with the concept of *kaitiakitanga* (watch or guard).[73] This takes on board the success from Te Whānau Āwhina Programmes and utilises existing Youth Programmes.[74] At this point it would be crucial for the offender to understand, from a *tikanga* perspective, the nature of his or her crime, take responsibility for his or her actions, face the victim and address the need for *utu* and balance, and importantly, understand the role of women prior to colonisation. The underlying *tikanga* or cultural perspective of these programmes will address the safety needs of the victim and the future well-being of the offender. This could also include programmes to address issues such as drug and alcohol addiction. These are shortcomings of the Australian system, as identified by Stewart.[75]

For the model to be successful, this stage requires legislative promulgation, similar to the legislative provisions acknowledged by the Koori Court Act 2008 (Vic). This would provide appropriate recognition and give a clear direction to the court to follow the recommendations given.

---

69 This is similar to the Māori Focus Units in prisons where upon sentencing the offender has no choice but is allocated to an area where his protocol or *kawa* may or may not apply.

70 For example see Hoani Waititi Marae in West Auckland.

71 Richard Benton, Alex Frame and Paul Meredith (eds) *Te Mātāpunenga: A Compendium of References to the Concepts and Institutions of Māori Customary Law, compiled for Te Matahauariki Institute* (Victoria University Press, Wellington, 2013), at 524.

72 At 205.

73 At 105.

74 He Tete Kura Mana Tangata Programme for Māori violent offenders based at Nga Whare Waatea Marae in Mangere Auckland; see Department of Corrections *Judges Update Information for the Judiciary* (Issue 3, 2001) <www.corrections.govt.nz>.

75 J Stewart *Specialist Domestic Violence Courts within the Australian Context* (2008) Issues Paper 10 at 4 <www.austdvclearinghouse.unsw.edu.au>.

The current 'stopping violence' programmes used by the domestic violence court can also be undertaken in conjunction with any *tikanga*-based programme. The difference, however, is that in this model, the participation of the offender would be monitored. If, as research suggests, such programmes show no guarantees of success, this will be identified by monitoring offender participation.

Intrinsically, *tikanga*-based programmes encompass the concept of an offender taking responsibility for his/her actions. Although this directive given by the judge in domestic violence cases is often criticised, if successful, this is a shared feature between mainstream and *tikanga* judicial proceedings.

The process demonstrates direct intervention, the administration of *tikanga* Māori and the notion of Māori looking after one another. This overcomes the criticisms that are levelled at Indigenous sentencing in which Indigenous courts are not seen as adopting customary laws. Rather they are seen as using Australian criminal laws and procedures when sentencing Indigenous people while allowing Indigenous elders to participate in the process.

At this point there is room for the adoption of Moana Jackson's concept of a *marae*-based model of diversion.[76] Māori Committees established under legislation, such as the Māori Social and Economic Advancement Act 1945 and its successor the Māori Welfare Act of 1962, could easily be reconstituted as community or *marae*-based committees. These committees would then have the right to hear all charges under the Māori Community Development Act 1962, instead of processing the charges under the Domestic Violence Act 1995.[77] Its jurisdiction could also extend to cover a broader range of offences, such as those set forth in the Summary Offences Act 1981.

Where the offender is Māori, there is no conventional question of guilt. In accordance with *tikanga* Māori, if you are alleged to have committed an act or offence then you must take responsibility. The offender would enter into a *marae*-based programme.

---

76 See Moana Jackson *The Māori and the Criminal Justice System – He Whaipaanga Hou: A New Perspective: Part* 2 (Department of Justice, Wellington, 1988) – although see Courts Consultative Committee Report (1991) on He Whaipanga Hou, Department of Justice, Wellington, that recommended to the then Minister of Justice that culturally appropriate responses to Māori offending was achievable through existing state mechanisms and further recommended against transferring criminal justice-centred processes into Māori settings, especially marae settings, as cited by Juan Tauri "Reforming Justice the Potential of Māori Processes" in Eugene McLaughlin and others (eds) *Restorative Justice Critical Issues* (Sage Publications, London, 2003). The Committee was comprised of judges, lawyers and community representatives.

77 If these *marae* committees had the same standing as the New Zealand Māori Council, for the purposes of the Māori Community Development Act 1962, then these *marae* committees could collaborate with and assist Sate Departments, such as Justice and Corrections, and other organisations in the assistance of Māori in the solution of difficulties or personal problems, such as those associated with protection orders– see section 7.

There is no question of guilt or innocence, it is rather a question of *mana* and instituting a process to achieve balance. It may be that the person did not commit the offence alleged. This will be uncovered during the process and the ensuing actions or *muru* will reflect this.

If the person refuses to accept responsibility at the initial stage and disputes the allegations then a *tikanga* programme can not apply and the offender will be subject to the general court jurisdiction.

The philosophy behind this 'First Intervention Step' or 'Pre-Plea' is twofold. First, it provides for the involvement of *whānau* and implementation of *tikanga* Māori. This moves towards satisfying the call for the administration of justice for Māori and by Māori. Secondly, it recognises the fact that defendants often come before the court with problems that place them at risk of reoffending. In the case of domestic violence, the victim is also often at risk and there is a need to ensure their safety. If left without treatment, such defendants may well find themselves back before a court, having been charged with further offences while on bail. Early treatment or intervention may prevent this situation from occurring and reduce reoffending statistics while on bail.[78] This may also eliminate the jurisprudence on bail conditions and breaches thereof.[79]

Ideally, admission to this first intervention stage would be contingent upon the offender having a problem that places them at risk of offending. Also, the offender's acknowledgement of the existence of the problem, a commitment to its resolution and participation in a *marae* or other suitable programme would be required.

Upon the offender's court appearance, the judge would call for a report from the Māori representative (similar to a probation report). Taking into account the findings of the report, the judge would then assess the effectiveness of the programme and if satisfied, the offender could be returned to the community and be convicted and discharged.[80] Proposed legislation would, at this stage, provide clear directions for the judge.

Domestic violence court – therapeutic jurisprudence

It is acknowledged that there will be offenders who have not satisfactorily completed the programme for various reasons. The *marae* forum, for instance, may be alien for both the offender and the victim. The offenders, together with those who chose not to participate in the *tikanga* Māori component, would then be subject to a domestic violence court based on the doctrine of therapeutic jurisprudence. The victim, in this instance, would accordingly have recourse to support through victims support services. In May 2011, the former Minister of Justice, Simon Power,

---

78 Ministry of Justice *Trends in the Use of Bail and Offending While on Bail: 1990–1999* (Research and Evaluation Unit, Ministry of Justice, Wellington, January 2003) indicates that 21 per cent of people offended while on bail <http://www.justice.govt.nz>.

79 See *Sen v Police* [2007] NZFLR at 733 per Lang J; *Kerisiano Aeau v The Police* HC, CRI 2007-404-247, 11 September 2007, per Winkelmann J.

80 Sentencing Act 2002, s 106.

announced new initiatives for victims of serious crime, including trauma counsel-ling, discretionary grants, court attendance grants, travel assistance and a victim emergency grant.

Although that particular proposed *tikanga* programme may not have worked,[81] the judge still has the opportunity to incorporate other programmes or social sciences to assist in further treating the offender. For instance, in recognising that the offender's adverse behaviour has led to the offending, the judge could adopt a preventive approach, such as confining the offender to home detention on the days that he or she is more likely to reoffend.[82] Alternatively, for domestic violence cases, the imposition of a protection order by the court could be imposed.

The judge could also incorporate *tikanga* Māori. For instance:

- Kanohi ki te kanohi encounter (face to face or at eye level).
- Maintaining the importance of reciprocity between the offender and victim.
- Adhering to the principles used by *rangatira* such as *aroha, atawhai* and *manaaki*.

By considering the notion of *utu*, the judge could also incorporate the offender's wider family in assisting the offender to complete the programme. This is based on the understanding that *utu* may be exacted from those who have done no wrong. In this regard, *utu* can be seen as a mechanism for restoring lost *mana* – a healing tool.

The judge would take a more active role with the offender, similar to the probation or re-entry courts, by using court processes aimed at promoting reha-bilitation and crime prevention programmes. These processes would seek to facilitate the offender's participation in such programmes to maintain the offender's dignity and to promote the offender's trust.

Upon entry into the programme, the offender would sign a behavioural contract, agreeing to comply with the programme agenda.[83] The offender could also be encouraged to participate in the development of the programme. This programme could be tailored to suit the problem or offence as relevant to the offender and could be specific, such as participation in an anger management course. Part of the programme would include regular court appearances for review that would decline in regularity as progress is made.

Participants would be actively involved in the process and provide input into the programme regarding changes to be made. The judge would interact

---

81 Unlike the Youth Court, where the judge does not tend to depart from the Family Group Conference Report, the discretion would be broader here for various reasons; one being there is still another step before the General Court process would come into effect and secondly the offender would not always be a youth.

82 See Winick and Wexler, above n 1.

83 See also David Wexler "Robes and Rehabilitation: How Judges Can Help Offenders Make Good" (Spring 2001) 38(1) Court Review at 19; for discussion also see David Wexler "Therapeutic Jurisprudence: An Overview" (2000) 17 TM Cooley Review at 131.

with the offender expressing interest in his/her life and praising any progress that has been made. This would be an endeavour to establish the *tika* or correct approach.

Successful completion of the programme could be acknowledged with the award of a 'graduation certificate'. This approach is based on the ethic of care and the central tenet of therapeutic jurisprudence, given its 'relational-based' construct. The ethic of care approach is capable of offering such an alternative approach to legal problem solving, which is more overtly relational and deliberately less adversarial.[84]

Notwithstanding every effort to adhere to the tenets of therapeutic jurisprudence, it is acknowledged there will be occasions when the offender has made no progress in the programme. In such cases the programme would be terminated and the offender subjected to the jurisdiction of the general courts.

A similar model in Geraldton, Western Australia integrated therapeutic jurisprudence into a sentencing regime that showed promising results.[85] This is comparable to what happens in the drug courts, using therapeutic jurisprudence to import holistic concepts, such as transcendental meditation. This approach is based on the premise that alleviating stress-related problems of the mind, body and behaviour, as well as promoting overall growth in life, can remove the underlying causes of substance abuse and offending.[86]

Introducing a mix of *tikanga* Māori values and problem solving skills or other more mainstreamed legal practices is not a new concept. Rather, it conforms to the long-term plans to integrate problem-solving courts into established judicial systems.[87] Judge Joe Williams, the Chief Judge of the Māori Land Court, in reflecting upon the future of the Māori Land Court, proposed a model which would incorporate principles from equity and public law, mixed with *tikanga* values.[88] The changes also envisaged the inclusion of a name change and move towards a Waitangi Tribunal-like forum. This would incorporate more of a community or people's court notion. Maintaining the integrity of a *tikanga* approach within the current criminal justice process addresses the criticism levelled at Koori Courts, that they are European or non Indigenous justice dressed up as Indigenous courts and do not tackle the underlying causes of Indigenous offending.[89] The current

---

84   Brookbanks, above n 33.
85   Michael King "Geraldton Alternative Sentencing Regime: Applying Therapeutic and holistic Jurisprudence in the Bush" (Oct 2002) 26(5) Crim LJ at 260; also Michael King and Steve Ford "Exploring the Concept of Wellbeing in Therapeutic Jurisprudence: The Example of the Geraldton Alternative Sentencing Regime" (2006) 1 ELJ.
86   King, above, at 267.
87   Becker and Corrigan, above n 58, at 7.
88   Chief Judge Joe Williams "Māori Land Court" (Lecture given at the Law School, University of Auckland, Auckland, July 2003).
89   Elena Marchetti and Kate Daly, "Indigenous Sentencing Courts: Towards a Theoretical and Jurisprudential Model" (2007) 29(3) Sydney Law Review at 415.

mainstreaming of therapeutic jurisprudence within the general court system, as an evolving model, is consistent with this development.[90]

An analysis of the practicalities of government resourcing for such a model is beyond the scope of this book. Except to note that it is a problem recognised by the government, which is continually engaged in criminal law reform,[91] as well as allocating resources to reduce Māori offending.[92] If this system is shown to be effective, then the end result should contribute towards outweighing any resource or budget constraints.

Victim

Therapeutic jurisprudence can apply equally to the victim as to the offender. The focus is on the offender whose liberty is at risk. However, victims of crime also experience a negative effect on their well-being. This is often manifested in feelings of anxiety, fear and powerlessness, requiring treatment or a similar process to re-establish well-being and balance within the victim.

The victim can experience a myriad of issues, including violation, re-victimisation, a need to tell their story, loss of control, emotional distress, helplessness and post-traumatic stress. The criminal justice system may provide funding for the victim. However, victims are often treated in ways that are distressing and demeaning, with many victims finding the criminal justice system as an assault on their dignity and unfair.[93] As the prosecutor rarely consults with the victim, this contributes to feelings of helplessness.

To avoid further re-victimisation, therapeutic jurisprudence suggests that more attention and procedural information[94] be shared with the victim and adequate

90 The AODT Courts, Family Violence Courts and the Homeless Courts (Te Kooti o Timatanga Hou was established in Auckland in 2010 and aimed at defendants who have pleaded guilty, have committed on going, low level reoffending within Auckland's inner city, are homeless and/or have no fixed address, are affected by mental health concerns and/or intellectual disability, and are affected by chronic alcohol and/or substance abuse) are examples of the mainstreaming of therapeutic jurisprudence into the general court system; see K Thom, A Mills, C Meehan, and B McKenna *Evaluating Problem-solving Courts in New Zealand: A Synopsis Report* (Centre for Mental Health Research, Auckland, 2013).

91 See "Major Project to Simplify Criminal Procedure" *Law Talk* (Issue 707, 5 May 2008) at 1; see also Drivers of Crime Progress Report December 2012 Cabinet Social Policy Committee which allocated "$10 million package of initiatives to improve access to alcohol and drug assessment and treatment for offenders; significant expansion of Incredible Years and Triple P Positive Parenting programmes through health and education settings; and an extra 600 restorative justice conferences per year to achieve a total of 2,000 in 2012/13".

92 Such as the Tahua Kaihoatu Fund that is administered by Te Puni Kokiri. Te Whare Ruruhau o Meri and Tu Tama Wahine are examples of funded programmes that have a *tikanga* component.

93 Bruce Winick "Therapeutic Jurisprudence and Victims of Crime" (7 March 2008) Social Science Research Network <www.ssrn.com>.

94 See Victims Rights Act 2002, s 12; see also ss 7–11 and 12.

training by players within the criminal justice system be performed, including the police, prosecutors, corrections and the judge. This will contribute to a feeling of empowerment for the victim.

Therapeutic jurisprudence advocates that "treating victims with procedural justice can help to ameliorate their psychological stress and restore their emotional equilibrium".[95] The ability of the victim to face the offender also contributes to a feeling of empowerment and a step towards re-establishing balance. Bruce Winick notes:[96]

> Unlike the retributivist focus of many criminal justice systems, this model [therapeutic jurisprudence] gives *greater recognition to the fact that a crime has harmed the victim and upset the equilibrium of the community, and seeks to address these through victim/offender conferencing* [emphasis added] … Such victim/offender conferencing typically includes family and other support group members of both victim and offender. It provides victims an opportunity to describe to the offender the harm they experienced as a result of the crime and the feelings it produced. This sometimes provokes feelings of empathy in the offender and sometimes an apology. An acknowledgement of wrongdoing and a genuine apology can allow victims to heal. When the defendant pleads not guilty and seeks a trial to contest the charges, such victim/offender conferencing would likely be unavailing and it may not be possible to compel the defendant to participate. However, when the defendant has pled guilty and is facing a future sentencing, such conferencing with the victim might provide the defendant with an incentive to apologize and provide the victim with a healthy opportunity to express feelings.

As Māori are also disproportionately represented as victims in the criminal justice system, it is recommended that therapeutic jurisprudence principles apply equally to the victim as the offender.

The offending rates for Māori, and Māori women in particular, are disproportionately high. After an analysis of comparative jurisdictions and the judicial process for Indigenous peoples, I am proposing a model that may offer one solution to address disproportionate rates of Māori offending.

There are Māori actors within the criminal justice system including court officials, prosecutors, lawyers and judges. The Māori Language Act 1987 provides for the ability to address the court in Te Reo.[97] From July 2012 opening and closing announcements in the District, Family and Youth Courts were provided in Te Reo.[98] These provide positive steps to engage with *tikanga* Māori.

95 Winick, above n 93.
96 Above n 93.
97 Māori Language Act 1987, s 4: right to speak Māori in legal proceedings; see also Natalie Akoorie and Teuila Fuatai "Jury's Out on Compulsory Use of Māori in Court" *New Zealand Herald* (online ed, Auckland, 18 July 2012).
98 Ministry of Justice Media Release "Te Reo Introduced into District Court" (press release, 19 July 2012) <www.justice.govt.nz>.

Notwithstanding this inclusion, elements of the existing system, such as the inaccessibility of the judge to the offender, the alien court process and the lack of concern or relationship with the offender after their court appearance, have been shown to be mono-cultural and inconsistent with *tikanga* Māori.[99]

Given a criminal justice system that lacks to meaningfully appreciate the broader role that colonisation has played in contributing to the high rates of offending, the persistence of these elements has resulted in anti-therapeutic outcomes.[100]

Despite the connection between colonisation and Māori offending, courts have found that "it does not logically follow that a person is more likely to be at a disadvantage and to offend simply by virtue of his or her Māori heritage. To some such a proposition may appear offensive".[101]

Therapeutic jurisprudence as a vehicle allows:

- Māori offenders to take responsibility for their actions.
- Formal recognition of the validity and applicability of *tikanga* Māori.
- A fully integrated bicultural approach.
- Involvement of Māori through the whole process.
- Māori administering justice.
- The placing of decision-making back in the community.
- A system predicated upon *tikanga* Māori as well as Māori people.

The most important commonality between *tikanga* Māori and therapeutic jurisprudence is the recognition of collective responsibility or communitarianism, and the healing process. Therapeutic jurisprudence allows the underlying reasons for Māori offending to be addressed in a Māori way. The goal for both therapeutic jurisprudence and *tikanga* Māori is *whakahoki mauri* or restoring the balance and returning the *mauri*. This enables the offender to participate successfully in the community.

---

99 See comments by Judge Stephanie Milroy "Nga Tikanga Māori and the Courts" (2007) Yearbook of NZJ 15 where she notes "... a court setting is a really strange experience ...".

100 For instance, the raft of English law statutes did not recognise *tikanga* and custom. Māori women as property owners and equivalent to, and not the property of, men was not recognised. The replacement of extended family support structures by nuclear families is an example of the internalisation of colonial values. This breakdown of the family structure together with the alienation of Māori from their land through the Native Land Court legislation and policies have contributed to the widening the socio-economic gap between Māori and non Māori, increasing vulnerability to crime and associated drug, alcohol and poverty issues; see Jackson, above n 76; see also K Maynard, B Coebergh, B Anstiss, L Bakkerand and T Huriwai "Ki te arotu: Toward a New Assessment: The Identification of Cultural Factors which may Predispose Māori to Crime" (1999) 13 Social Policy Journal of New Zealand.

101 *Mika v R* [2013] NZCA at [12].

The model incorporates the doctrine of therapeutic jurisprudence within a court setting. It is through the vehicle of therapeutic jurisprudence that a separate Indigenous legal system – *tikanga* Māori – is incorporated. This incorporation of *tikanga* is legislated to provide greater certainty.

The high rates of Māori offending challenge both our politicians and the judiciary to implement and embrace legal systems that have shown success, but which lie outside the Westminster structure.

Indigenous courts are underpinned by therapeutic jurisprudence and offer one such option. Evaluations of Indigenous courts, suggest that they have:[102]

> ... both criminal justice aims (reducing recidivism, improving court appear-
> ance rates and reducing the over-representation of Indigenous people in the
> criminal justice system) and community building aims (providing a culturally
> appropriate process, increasing community participation and contributing to
> reconciliation). Of the criminal justice aims, only the impact of the courts on
> re-offending has been assessed.

The adoption of *tikanga* Māori and a therapeutic jurisprudential approach within a New Zealand court setting could effectively open a pathway for *tikanga* Māori to walk together with *te ture* (law) Pākehā to step towards reducing the dispropor-tionate offending rates of Māori and contribute to reconciliation and balance within the community.

Many challenges are involved in this, but it is a step in the right direction in terms of creating a new criminal justice system that incorporates the values of all members of our society.

C   An Indigenous re-entry court for Māori?

Indigenous re-entry courts are based on Indigenous legal systems. Since half of all offenders before the NZPB will be Māori, the question now becomes:

Will an Indigenous re-entry court for Māori underpinned by tikanga Māori assist Māori to re-enter the community successfully and reduce recidivism?

Proposed model

Upon the incarceration of an offender, a *kaumatua*/judge would co-ordinate, monitor and motivate the offender's progress within the correctional facility. This would require the offender to participate in various *tikanga* programmes within the correctional facility, such as the Māori Focus Units,[103] and concentrate on iden-tified areas of rehabilitation, such as drug treatment. As in the Juez de Vigilancia

---

102 Elena Marchetti *Indigenous Sentencing Courts* (Brief 5, December 2009) <www.indigen
     ousjustice.gov.au>
103 Department of Corrections *Māori Focus Units* (2009) <www.corrections.govt.nz>.

Penitenciaria programme (JVP), through periodic review hearings, the *kaumatua/*judge could help instil in the offender a vision of eventual release.[104] This could be a healing process in itself.

Ideally, this model would involve all offending, but in the early stages, it would be limited to less serious offending. The *kaumatua/*judge would be a different person from the sentencing judge, who might be viewed by the offender in a negative light, whereas the monitoring judge would be perceived to 'care' or maintain an 'ethic of care' in regard to the prisoner's rights.

Upon entry into the programme, the offender would sign a behavioural contract agreeing to comply with the programme agenda.[105] The offender could also be encouraged to participate in developing the programme and have the ability to set release conditions. The release conditions would require the taking of responsibility as a collective/*whānau*. Like the JVP, the ability to set release conditions allows for the possibility of dialogue between the court and offender, and enables a conditional release to be conceptualised as a bilateral behavioural contract, rather than a unilateral judicial fiat. Such a conceptualisation is likely to promote an offender's sense of fairness and participation, and should enhance the offender's compliance with the release conditions.

Such a programme could be 'tailor-made' to suit the problem or offence relevant to the offender, and could be specific to include *tikanga* programmes within the correctional institute that focus on anger management and other behavioural problems.

The offender's genuine involvement in correctional programmes would have a bearing on the prisoner's progress through the levels, and on their prospect of eventual release.[106]

The *kaumatua/*judge would take on a more active role with the offender by using the court processes aimed at promoting the rehabilitation of the offender or the prevention of crime. These processes would seek to facilitate the offender's participation in a programme, to maintain the offender's dignity, and to promote the offender's trust.

Part of the programme would include regular court appearances for review that would decline as progress is made. Participants would be actively involved in the court process and provide input into the programme for changes. In an endeavour to establish the *tika* or correct approach, the judge would interact with the offender, expressing interest in their life and praising any progress that has been made.

This philosophy is based on the 'ethic of care' approach and the central tenet of therapeutic jurisprudence, of it being a 'relational-based' construct. The ethic of care approach recognises, and is capable of offering, an alternative method to legal problem-solving that is more overtly relational and less adversarial.

---

104 Winick, above n 93 at 4.
105 See also Wexler, above n 83 at 18.
106 Winick, above n 93, at 6.

If parole is granted and the offender's release conditions are subsequently breached, a process of deferred revocation similar to that suggested by David Wexler could be adopted.[107] This envisages a clinical approach where the burden lies on the offender to defer revocation of parole based on a rehabilitative plan that the offender, with support and help of the collective/*whānau*. Assistance for hearing preparation would be provided by a clinic, composed possibly of law students, where advocacy could be enhanced through a therapeutic viewpoint.[108]

Although therapeutic jurisprudence may provide a window to import *tikanga* Māori concepts, the question arises as to why therapeutic jurisprudence is required? A preferred reform would be to apply *tikanga* Māori in the first instance.

---

107   David Wexler and Bruce Winick *Rehabilitating Lawyers Principles of Therapeutic Jurisprudence for Criminal Law Practice* (Carolina Academic Press, North Carolina, 2008) at 312.

108   At 314.

Chapter 8

A new vision

The similarities between *tikanga* Māori concepts and therapeutic jurisprudence suggest that *tikanga* Māori concepts are valuable and effective principles when addressing Indigenous issues. As a principle based doctrine, *tikanga* is comprised of concepts working together to achieve balance. It is premised on, and reflective of social and environmental mores. Orthodox legal systems are also reflective of social mores.

The recognition of *tikanga* and Indigenous concepts is sanctioned in instruments such as the United Nations Declaration on the Rights of Indigenous Peoples and Te Tiriti o Waitangi. Both instruments support the right of self-determination and *tino rangatiratanga*. Various jurisdictions have formalised this recognition through domestic legislation and have been manifested with the implementation of Indigenous courts, such as Koori Courts (Australia), Gladue Courts (Canada) and Navajo Courts (United States of America).

As part of this final chapter, it is timely to identify what is feasible and applicable within a New Zealand context. It is proposed that the clear directive to consider Indigenous concepts during sentencing, for instance in the Koori Courts, is extended to the arrest stage. This is similar to the proposed therapeutic jurisprudence models and the Navajo Courts. It is suggested that an extension of jurisdiction to the Māori Land Court or a formal establishment of a Tikanga Māori Court could provide such a vehicle.

A Social statistics – a catalyst

In 2006 the Te Rau Hinengaro report suggested that Māori have a higher level of mental health needs than non-Māori.[1] This is reflected in the over-representation of Māori within forensic mental health facilities.[2] Māori are also disproportionately

---

1 Joanne Baxter and others "Ethnic Comparisons of the 12 Month Prevalence of Mental Disorders and Treatment Contact in Te Rau Hinengaro: the New Zealand Mental Health Survey" (October 2006) 40(1) Australian and New Zealand Journal of Psychiatry at 905.
2 At 905.

represented in the prison population, with half the prison population identifying as Māori.[3] For Māori women the statistics are as high as 60 per cent of all women who are incarcerated. The incidence of mental illness within the criminal justice system is also disproportionately high.[4]

Taken separately, these statistics are of concern. Taken cumulatively, the statistics are tragic, indicating that an unacceptable number of Māori are within the criminal justice system, with a correspondingly higher incidence of mental illness than the rest of the population.

Both judges and solicitors, as officers of the court, lament at the continual high numbers of Māori that appear before them or they represent within the criminal justice system.[5] Irrespective of these initiatives, it is clear that an alternative forum underpinned or driven by more holistic principles, such a *tikanga* Māori, is required. This book suggests that the concepts of *tikanga* Māori be applied within a suitable forum.

Borrows suggested that:[6]

> ... both indigenous and other Canadian governments could enact legislation or undertake similar official acts that recognise and harmonise Indigenous legal traditions with the common law ... *I also suggest that Indigenous Courts, along with federal and provincial courts, could better implement Indigenous law by applying appropriate interpretive mechanisms* [emphasis added] and ensuring that at least some of those who are appointed to the bench have a knowledge of receptivity to Indigenous legal traditions ... Indigenous governments and the Canadian Parliament should pass *Indigenous law recognition legislation to facilitate the rule of law's* [emphasis added] development in Canada.

Justice Heath notes that *tikanga* Māori aligns more closely with an inquisitorial model seeking to achieve a common and mutually beneficial goal, as opposed to the current adversarial system. In proposing two avenues to incorporate Māori customary law, Justice Heath proposes that the entire judicial system could be overhauled, and either parallel systems of adjudication be developed or a stand-alone system of adjudication be created, which takes equal account of Māori

---

3   Bronwyn Morrison, Natalie Soboleva and Jin Chong *Conviction and Sentencing Offenders in New Zealand: 1997–2006* (Ministry of Justice, 2008) at 118; see also Michael Rich *Census of Prison Inmates 1999* (Department of Corrections SAS Policy Development, Wellington, December, 2000) at 43 <www.corrections.govt.nz >.

4   Baxter and others, above n 1.

5   See also comments by the Judges at the Healing Courts and Plans People, International Therapeutic Jurisprudence Conference October 9–10, First Nations Long House, Vancouver, British Columbia that also reluctantly recognise the continual high number of Indigenous offenders that appear before them.

6   John Borrows *Canada's Indigenous Constitution* (University of Toronto Press, Canada, 2010), at 181.

custom and 'European' values.[7] Second, the existing framework could be modified, thereby permitting Māori concepts and custom to operate in the appropriate circumstances.[8] Considering the first option as unlikely for a number of reasons, including the current political climate, Justice Heath considers that option two is the only politically viable solution. His Honour notes that:[9]

> While this could be seen as consigning Māori custom and values to a gap-filling role, I am more sanguine about the prospects of producing a more substantive solution.

The incorporation of Māori concepts into legislation by the government acknowledges and promotes Māori cultural identity and gives practical effect to the Treaty of Waitangi within its legislative frameworks.[10] However, there is no nexus between the passage of domestic legislation and *tikanga* Māori. The doctrine of parliamentary sovereignty does not require Parliament to consider *tikanga* Māori before passing legislation. Further, when *tikanga* is included within legislation, it is often only one factor to be satisfied or considered by the decision maker. Likewise, whether or not the definition of *tikanga* is satisfied is determined by the decision maker. Taking concepts such as *tikanga* or *kaitiaki* out of context runs the risk of mistranslation.[11]

Paul McHugh describes this process as "a conscious effort by government and Māori to move from the embattled processes of rights recognition to reconciliation".[12] This process is achieved through the development of a "sympathetic legal regime" that "accommodates the cultural disposition" of Indigenous groups.[13]

Despite the two texts of the Treaty of Waitangi, it is the English version – in which Māori cede sovereignty to the Crown – that is most often referred to. There is no impetus on the Crown to consider *tikanga* Māori from a Treaty perspective.

The monopoly of the government and its agencies interpret *tikanga* Māori in accordance with the underlying values and interests of the dominant group, rather than promoting *tikanga* Māori culture.[14] The meaning of the terms

---

7 Heath J "Problems in Applying Māori Custom Law in a Unitary State" Yearbook of NZ Jurisprudence (2010/2011) at 199.
8 At 209.
9 At 200.
10 Arnu Turvey "Te Ao Māori in a Sympathetic Legal Regime: The Use of Māori Concepts in Legislation" (2009–2010) 40 Victoria U Wellington L Rev at 531.
11 See Nin Tomas "Tangata Whenua Issues: Implementing Kaitiakitanga under the RMA" (1994) July New Zealand Environmental Reporter at 39 where Nin discusses the problems of importing Māori concepts into legislation in particular that of *kaitiaki*.
12 Paul McHugh *Aboriginal Societies and the Common Law: A History of Sovereignty, Status, and Self-Determination* (Oxford University Press, New York, 2004) at 49
13 McHugh, above, at 55.
14 Turvey, above n 10; see also Jeremy Waldron "One Law for All? The Logic of Cultural Accommodation" (2002) 59(1) Wash & Lee L Rev at 3 where he notes that the policy behind legislation can be culturally biased. He states "one law for all" ... is the

themselves become subservient to the political objectives of a government that, while sympathetic to Māori interests, is determined to steer away from the underlying questions of *tino rangatiratanga*.[15]

B Equality

Before addressing an extension of the jurisdiction of the Māori Land Court, it is important to discuss the issue of equality and whether the establishment of an Indigenous court is an anathema to equality and the rule of law, which includes the principle of 'one law for all' and the position that humans are all basically alike.[16]

Justice Heath echoes a commonly held perspective:[17]

> In my view, New Zealanders generally will not accept a system whereby different laws are applied to different classes of people ... if there are laws for Māori and other laws for other New Zealanders, what happens when the two collide? Which law prevails? Indeed, how can two legal systems founded on race and culture be justified on a principled basis?

For Māori, the *whakataukī "me haere whakamuri kia haere whakamua"*/we must journey back, or understand our past before we can move forward, is instrumental when considering the relevance of 'one law for all'.

Whilst there are competing arguments that range from, consideration of culture will result in greater differences,[18] to the call for Indigenous people to embrace self-determination and establish their own systems of governance,[19] there is an underlying need to consider the context against which the laws of New Zealand were crafted.

In the colonial era, a raft of legislation alienated Māori from their land and resources. Many early government policies were also discriminatory towards Māori. It would be disingenuous to claim that at this time the principle of equality applied when, in particular, Māori were subject to policies that resulted in land alienation. Similarly the application of "one law for all" in the criminal context is clearly not working.

inherent ally of state law, rather than an independent consideration that helps settle the issue between state law and its cultural competitors.

15 Turvey, above n 10.

16 See Jeremy Waldron "Basic Equality" (Nellco Legal Scholarship Repository, New York University Public Law and Legal Theory Working Papers, 19 December 2008) at 44. Available also <www.lsr.nellco.org> for further discussion.

17 Heath, above n 7, at 201.

18 Brian Barry *Culture and Equality: An Egalitarian Critique of Multiculturalism* (Polity Press in association with Blackwell Publishers, Cambridge, 2001).

19 See for instance Taiaiake Alfred *Peace, Power and Righteousness: An Indigenous Manifesto* (2nd ed, Oxford University Press, Oxford, 2008); see also Brad Morse "Regaining Recognition of the Inherent Right of Aboriginal Governance" in Yale Belanger (ed) *Aboriginal Self-Government in Canada: Current Trends and Issues* (Oxford University Press, Oxford, 2004).

It is superficial to claim that the recognition of Māori rights will discriminate against non-Māori before understanding the justifications for those rights.[20] Furthermore, the Human Rights Act 1993, that generally prohibits discrimination on the grounds of race, does recognise an exception for affirmative action programmes and provisions done in good faith to assist or advance persons who need assistance or advancement to achieve an equal place with other members of the community.[21]

There is usually little obstacle to a parallel or separate criminal justice system when the offender and victim are both Māori and there is no dispute as to the offender's guilt.[22] Current legislative provisions, including Sentencing Act 2002[23] and the Māori Community Development Act 1962, permit Māori committees to impose penalties on Māori for certain conduct falling within the Summary Offences Act 1981 and the CYFP Act. This provides for the inclusion of customary law or *tikanga* Māori within the justice system. The Sentencing Act further supports the use of *marae* programmes, *iwi* and *hapū* involvement.[24] Despite these incremental steps to recognise *tikanga* Māori, it is difficult to ignore the persistent disproportionate offending rates for Māori.

Justice Heath noted that:[25]

> Education and intellectual flexibility are key allies in the challenge to apply custom. Greater understanding is likely to breed confidence. With education, understanding and confidence on the part of all participants, it may be possible to find a significant place for Māori within the New Zealand judicial system. But it will be a significant challenge to do so.

It is unlikely that a right to secede or a right to external self-determination manifest in an Indigenous court will be realised for Māori. Nonetheless, a form of internal self-determination could be achieved through an extension of the existing legal forum, where the right to culture and the principles that underpin *tikanga* Māori are appreciated.

This next section will consider two possibilities: an extension of the jurisdiction of the Māori Land Court and the introduction of a 'specialist' Tikanga Court that has similarities with the current Rangatahi Court, as well as the Alcohol and

---

20 Claire Charters "Do Māori Rights Racially Discriminate against Non-Māori?" (2009–2010) 40 Victoria U Wellington L Rev 649 at 668.

21 Human Rights Act 1993, s 73.

22 Moana Jackson *The Māori and the Criminal Justice System – He Whaipaanga Hou: A New Perspective: Part 2* (Department of Justice, Wellington, 1988).

23 ection 10 – this would assume that the offender would appear before a Māori Committee and the Māori Committee could then impose actions upon the offender to compensate, apologise or 'make good the harm' this can then be taken into account by the sentencing judge.

24 Sentencing Act, ss 51(c) and 54H(c).

25 Heath, above n 7, at 212.

other Drug Treatment Court. If successful, it is proposed that like the Rangatahi Courts, the jurisdiction would be open to both Māori and non-Māori, thereby complying with the principle of 'one law for all'.

C Māori Land Court: an extension of jurisdiction or a Tikanga Court?

Various pieces of legislation, including the Native Land Court Act of 1865, sought to simplify *tikanga* Māori and 'freeze' Māori entitlements to deal with their land by requiring alienation to be made to the Crown (by sale and at time confiscation) with the approval of the early Native Land Courts. This was facilitated by assimilating native or customary title into an individualised system of land tenure and then vesting Māori land into Crown ownership.[26] This process 'fast tracked' the alienation of Māori land and had an enduring detrimental effect on Māori society and, consequently, re-defined the nature of *tikanga* Māori.

The Māori Land Court is a creature of statute with the authorisation to be a court of record under Te Ture Whenua Māori Act 1993.[27] Today the Act provides for a different philosophy. Underpinned by *tikanga* values, the preamble notes:

> … And whereas it is desirable to recognise that land is a taonga tuku iho of special significance to Māori people and, for that reason, to promote the retention of that land in the hands of its owners, their whānau, and their hapū, and to protect wahi tapu: and to facilitate the occupation, development, and utilisation of that land for the benefit of its owners, their whānau, and their hapū: And whereas it is desirable to maintain a court and to establish *mechanisms to assist the Māori people to achieve the implementation of these principles* [emphasis added].

Background

When President John Rogan of the then Native Land Court was appointed on 25 June 1864, so too were four Māori judges: Wiremu Tipene, Matikikuha, Te Keene of Orakei and Tamati Reweti. On 25 October 1864 a further seven Māori judges were appointed: Hone Mohi Tawhai, Penetana Papahurihia, Hoterene Tawatawa, Wepiha Pi, Tango Hikuwai, Riwhi Hongi and Tamatai Huingariri. It was not until 15 August 1974 that Edward Taihakurei Durie, the next Māori judge, was appointed to the bench.

26 See D Williams *Te Tango Kooti Whenua* (Huia Publishers, Wellington, 1999); see also discussion by Richard Boast "Evolution of Māori Land Law 1862–1993" in Richard Boast, Andrew Erueti, Doug McPhail and Norman F Smith (eds) *Māori Land Law* (2nd edition, LexisNexis, New Zealand, 2004) at 65 where he noted that "… difficulties associated with the management and development of Māori freehold land are not likely to be readily or easily overcome".
27 Te Ture Whenua Māori Act 1993, s 6.

Today, judges such as the Chief and Deputy Judges of the Māori Land Court, are appointed by the Governor General.[28] Furthermore, the Te Ture Whenua Māori Act 1993 provides that:[29]

> ... the person must not be appointed unless the person is suitable, having regard to the person's knowledge and experience of te reo Māori, tikanga Māori ...

Cases before the Māori Land Court can be complex and often involve *tikanga* or customary concepts. The judge will determine the conduct of the hearings that are usually held within existing court rooms in the Māori Land Court districts. Rules of *marae kawa* may be applied by the judge as considered appropriate, including a *karakia*/prayer to commence and *mihi whakatau*/greetings. *Te Reo Māori*/the Māori language is often used in court.

Since the passing of the Native Lands Act 1862, the Māori Land Court (Te Kooti Whenua Māori) and the Māori Appellate Court (Te Kooti Pira Māori) have continued in various forms under Te Ture Whenua Māori Act 1993 (TTWM Act).

The Māori Land Court has jurisdiction to hear matters relating to Māori land, including successions, title improvements, Māori land sales, and the administration of Māori land trusts and incorporations.[30] More specifically the Māori Land Court is to:[31]

- Administer and apply Te Ture Whenua Māori Act 1993 and other relevant legislation;
- Maintain the records of title and ownership information of Māori land;
- Make available Māori land information held by the Māori Land Court; and
- Facilitate Māori land administration and development through the professional delivery of services to Māori land owners, their whānau or hapū.

The TTWM Act is a comprehensive piece of legislation but does not codify all Māori land issues. The application of other statutes, such as the Income Tax Act 2007, Land Transfer Act 1952 and the Property Law Act 2007, are not excluded by the TTWM Act and it must be read in conjunction with these and other

---

28   Te Ture Whenua Māori Act 1993, s 7(1).
29   Section 7(2A).
30   See also Jeremy McGuire "The Status and Functions of the Māori Land Court" (1993–1996) 8 Otago L Rev at 125.
31   See Judge N F Smith "Māori Land Court Jurisdiction and Procedure" in Richard Boast, Andrew Erueti, Doug McPhail and Norman F Smith (eds) *Māori Land Law* (2nd ed, LexisNexis, New Zealand, 2004) at 121 for full discussion on the jurisdiction of the Māori Land Court; also Māori Land Court see <http://www.justice.govt.nz/courts/māori-land-court.>

relevant statutes.[32] The TTWM Act has been amended to include sections on the 'Jurisdiction of the Court under the Māori Fisheries Act 2004' and the 'Jurisdiction of the Court under the Māori Aquaculture Claims Settlement Act 2004'. The Court has exclusive jurisdiction to advise on disputes referred to it under the Māori Fisheries Act 2004 and the Māori Aquaculture Claims Settlement Act 2004.[33] As a court of record, the Māori Land Court's decisions are subject to judicial review.

McGuire described the Māori Land Court as:[34]

> ... a special class of administrative court designed to administer and implement policy ... It deals with a particular class of case where it is essentially an alternative to the ordinary courts.

Looking to an expanded Māori Land Court jurisdiction, as an answer an appropriate starting point to consider this possibility is noted by Joe Williams, the then Chief Judge of the Māori Land Court:[35]

> It seems to me therefore that there is a real argument for a new form of Māori Land Court – a judge sitting with two or more pūkenga or experts – adjudicating, facilitating, and mediating through issues confronting the new tribal organisations in respect of the new tribal asset. What is genuinely exciting is that the Court would be applying and developing a separate system of law – a system which is a mix of those aspects of tikanga Māori which continue to inform the lives of Māori today and those principles of the common law which have stood the test of time. A system which, as the Treaty directed, draws on the best of both worlds.

Procedure

The Māori Land Court is comprised of judges who are Māori, well versed in *tikanga* Māori and guided by a preamble that seeks to establish mechanisms to assist Māori litigants. It is proposed that in view of the recent amendments to extend the jurisdiction of the Māori Land Court, a further amendment is needed to extend the jurisdiction to include criminal and civil matters for Māori.

Criminal

The procedure would mirror the proposed model outlined in Chapter 7. Ideally, the jurisdiction would be open to all offenders with the anticipation that, after the

32 McGuire, above 30, at 125.
33 Te Ture Whenua Māori Act 1993, ss 26B and 26P.
34 McGuire, above n 30, at, 128.
35 Chief Justice Joe Williams *The Māori Land Court – A Separate Legal System?* (Occasional Paper 4, The New Zealand Centre for Public Law, VUW, July 2001) at 11.

success of this model has been proven, the jurisdiction would be widened to include more serious offences. So initially it is recommended that only the lesser offending would apply. Upon review the jurisdiction could be extended to include more serious violent offences provided for in the Crimes Act 1961.[36]

This model and the accompanying process would be entirely integrated. The jurisdiction would be open to both Māori and non-Māori as the principles applied therein are universal. Upon arrest, an advocate, warden or similar person would be contacted. This advocate would be responsible for the offender until his or her next court appearance. This is not novel. The Child and Young Persons and their Families Act, although relating to young persons and children, allows the child to be delivered to any *iwi* social service or cultural social service with the child's agreement following arrest.[37]

The offender would be assessed within the local *marae* forum, allowing for *whānau* involvement. Initially, the offender would have no choice as to which *marae* he/she would appear in,[38] but could be transferred to a tribal or *iwi* specific *marae* if he/she requested. In view of recent Treaty Settlements, the ability for *iwi* to fund and support this *marae*-based initiative within their respective area is encouraged to complement government support.

All parties, including the *kaumatua* panel and the offender, would sit at eye level or *kanohi ki te kanohi*. An advocate would assist to ensure that the offender and their families do not feel uncomfortable in such a setting and alleviate any feelings of alienation from the process. This would be consistent with the concept of *manaakitanga* – the process of showing care, respect, kindness and hospitality.[39]

During this *marae*-based phase, community members and the disputants would be encouraged to talk things through with the help of respected members of the community in order to reach a consensual agreement. The consensus of the participants is the culmination of collective decision-making. This goal is similar to the Peacemakers Court; the achievement of *hózhóji k'é náhóodleel* (peacemaking), much like the *tikanga* Māori concept of rebalancing. This step is seen to empower the community and encourage the principle of inclusivity and reciprocity.

Also during this stage, an appropriate programme would be specified for the offender, consistent with the concept of *kaitiakitanga*/watch or guard.[40] At this point it would be pivotal that the offender understands, from a *tikanga* perspective, the nature of his or her crime, take responsibility for his or her actions, face the victim, and address the need for *utu* and balance. The composition and

---

36 It is noted that the Matariki Court already considers serious violent offenders.
37 Children, Young Persons, and Their Families Act 1989, s 234 (c) (ii).
38 This is similar to the Māori Focus Units in prisons where upon sentencing the offender has no choice but is allocated to an area where his protocol or kawa may or may not apply.
39 Richard Benton, Alex Frame and Paul Meredith (eds) *Te Mātāpunenga: A Compendium of References to the Concepts and Institutions of Māori Customary Law, compiled for Te Matahauariki Institute* (Victoria University Press, Wellington, 2013), at 205.
40 Benton and others, above n 39 at 105.

underlying *tikanga* or cultural perspective of these programmes will assist in addressing the safety needs of the victim and the future well-being of the offender. Intrinsically *tikanga*-based programmes encompass the concept of the offender, taking responsibility for his or her actions.

This process recognises that defendants often come before the court with problems that place them at risk of reoffending. Any additional problems, such as drug or alcohol dependency, can be identified and the appropriate programmes recommended. If left without treatment, defendants may well find themselves back before a court, charged with further offences. For instance, early treatment or intervention may prevent this situation from occurring and reduce the statistics of offending while on bail.[41]

Upon the offender's first court appearance, the judge would call for a report from the Māori representative (similar to a probation report). Taking into account the findings of the report, the judge would then assess the effectiveness of the programme and if satisfied, the offender could be returned to the community after being convicted and discharged.[42]

Issues

Although the preamble of the TTWM clearly indicates an onus to adhere to principles of *tikanga* Māori, this is within a 'land' or civil context, not a criminal one. Incarceration is not consistent with *tikanga* Māori. Further, it is likely that a Māori Land Court judge would not be comfortable with sentencing an offender.

Currently, the Māori Land Court is not associated with Police, Corrections, Crime and Prison, and as such, does not attract the negative connotations. If the Māori Land Court was associated with such themes, the negative stigma would follow.

The Māori Land Court judges would need to be 'warranted' within this jurisdiction. Unlike the District Court, the associated court machinery and administration services would need to be established.

Civil

An extension of the Māori Land Court's jurisdiction to include civil matters, including contractual and commercial issues, may be more difficult. Like the Māori Fisheries Act 2004 and the Māori Aquaculture Claims Settlement Act 2004, the court's jurisdiction would need to be confined to the resolution of disputes in the first instance. A respective amendment may also be required in the

---

41 Ministry of Justice *Trends in the Use of Bail and Offending while on Bail 1990–1999* (Research and Evaluation Unit January 2003) indicates that 21 per cent of people offended while on bail. <http://www.justice.govt.nz>.
42 Sentencing Act 2002, s 106.

corresponding legislation to recognise the extended jurisdiction of both criminal and civil trials.

It is encouragingly noted that a special session of the Kaitaia District Court at Roma Marae in Ahipara, held in November 2014, was a New Zealand legal first where the District Court heard civil charges on the *marae*. Mr Tepania, a small-time commercial fisherman, appeared before Judge Greg Davis on six Fisheries Act charges relating to the late filing of fishing returns on six occasions between February 2012 and January 2013.[43] He also faced three more serious charges of filing a return more than a month late that carried a maximum penalty of a $100,000 fine and forfeiture of his boat. He had earlier pleaded guilty and was appearing for sentencing.

It was noted by the court that Mr Tepania was a highly regarded conservationist and community worker and was discharged without conviction and ordered to pay zero dollars in costs to the Ministry of Primary Industries.

It is noted, however, that the current purview of the Māori Land Court includes reference to provisions of the Family Protection Act 1955 and the Law Reform (Testamentary Promises) Act 1949.[44]

Both Māori and non-Māori applicants would need to apply to the court to have the matter determined. Matters or disputes concerning property, equity, contract and related civil matters that concern Māori, either as plaintiff or defendant, or the subject-matter of the proceeding, e.g., land, would fall under the jurisdiction of this new framework. If one party is non-Māori, then the other party would need to seek their consent before proceeding with an application.

The application would need to be first accepted by the Māori Land Court.[45] If the application fails, then the general jurisdiction of the District or High Court would apply. Once an application is lodged, the applicants would need to undergo mandatory mediation or arbitration prior to any court hearing. Mediation or arbitration will follow the same process as the current *marae*-based court model and be consistent with the Peacemakers Court, with the appropriate support people. These requirements would be mandatory.

During this *marae*-based phase, like a Peacemakers Court, it is envisaged that this route may be used to resolve many issues, including land use permits, validation of paternity and marriage, dissolution of marriage, correction of records, traditional adoption, guardianship, declaration of death and probate. This step is seen to empower the community and encourage the principle of inclusivity and reciprocity.

If no resolution can be reached, a court date will be set. The court process is underpinned by *tikanga* and its aim is to achieve balance – the goal of *tikanga*

---

43 *R v Te Pania* – [2015] DCR 25; see also Peter de Graf "No conviction for conservationist" (Nov 26, 2014) *Northern Advocate* <http://www.nzherald.co.nz/>.

44 Te Ture Whenua Māori Act, s 106.

45 It is acknowledged that a set of regulations and guidelines would need to be established.

Māori. Similar to that of the Navajo jurisdiction and customs, *tikanga* Māori could be employed by the judges to assist the court.

Similar to the Tribal Courts in the United States where two judges may sit, one from a state court and one from a tribal court, section 26G of the TTWM Act 1993 provides the opportunity for *kaumatua* to sit alongside the judge:[46]

> The court may, of its own motion or at the request of any party to the proceeding, appoint 1 or more additional members (not being Judges of the Māori Land Court) who have *knowledge of relevant tikanga Māori or other expertise to assist the court* [emphasis added].

Assisted by two experts, a ruling can be made within the current legislative framework.[47] Until appropriate *tikanga* is infused, and the legislation is promulgated, legal adjudicators will need to make every effort to utilise the common law principles that support *tikanga*. Appeals would be available to the Māori Appellate Court.[48]

Issues

It is anticipated that a wider civil jurisdiction would require the support of Māori and adequate resourcing. An extension to include family issues would be more consistent than criminal issues.

Currently the Resource Management Act 1991 contains provisions where the expertise of a Māori Land Court judge can be called upon when the case involves *tikanga* Māori. It may be that similar to the Environment Court when a case before, for instance, the Family Court involves *tikanga* Māori, the expertise of the MLC judges is required and called upon. It may also be that in criminal cases involving *tikanga* Māori, such as *R v Mason*, a Māori Land Court judge is requested to sit with the judge. The Law Commission foreshadows the potential use of the Māori Land Court to determine issues pertaining to burial.[49]

As the review of the TTWM is in progress, it is suggested that some of the administrative aspects of the Māori Land Court could be removed and replaced

46   Te Ture Whenua Māori Act 1993, ss 26G, 26S, 26T(4), 26U(5), 32 and 62.
47   Akin to Magistrates Court Act 1989 (VIC), s 17A: Appointment of Aboriginal Elders or Respected Persons.
48   A review of Te Ture Whenua Māori Land Act 1993 was completed in 2016. The focus of this review was to enable Māori land to be available for commercial use. See Māori Law Review "Review of Te Ture Whenua Māori Act 1993 – Select Committee report on Bill" (December 2016) <māorilawreview.co.nz>
49   Law Commission Report *Burial in New Zealand Today* (NZLC IP34) at 32, 45, 46 and 73; see also comments from Mihiata Pirini in "Law Commission looks at burial rights" 4 August 2014 Radio NZ. <http://www.radionz.co.nz/> who noted that "the (Law) commission wanted to see a judge from the Family Court and another from the Māori Land Court together to hear claims over burial rights ... the Law Commission was tweaking its original proposal so that the onus was put on having a judge from each court where there was a dispute involving tikanga and Pākehā".

with a mediation role for disputes. Such a transformation would result in the court no longer being a 'land court'. Despite this potential change of jurisdiction, it is anticipated that the underpinning concepts of *tikanga* Māori would remain.

Conclusion

It is envisaged that an extension of the Māori Land Court would include the following:

a   Expansion of jurisdiction to include civil and criminal areas; akin to the jurisdiction of the District Court;
b   Within these two areas – speciality 'courts' to hear cases on environmental, family and employment matters; and
c   Change of name to 'Te Kooti Māori'.

It is acknowledged that this would increase the workload of the judges and it is suggested that more Māori judges be appointed. But the inclusion of *kaumatua* is pivotal, particularly in youth criminal offending cases, as the *kaumatua*, through *tikanga* and *whakapapa*, is ultimately responsible for the offender. It is suggested in such cases, the *kaumatua* be afforded the *mana* to adjudicate.

As for a proposed solution, there are no hard statistics to support such an initiative. Nonetheless, the identification of serious issues, such as alcohol abuse and offending, has led to the establishment of the Alcohol and other Drug Treatment Courts. Similarly, the *marae* courts initiative was launched to address the issue of youth offending, in particular, that by Māori youth. Judges and legal counsel are well aware of the over-representation of Māori in the criminal justice system and support an initiative to address this problem.

Recent specialised courts, such as Alcohol and other Drug Treatment Court and the *marae* courts have been established as a response to social and community difficulties. Anecdotal evidence suggests that these initiatives are working. Comparative jurisdictions confirm the success of these so-called 'specialised courts'.

D Specialist 'Tikanga Māori' Court

Building on the success of the Rangatahi, Matariki, and Alcohol and other Drug Treatment Courts (AODTC), the proposed Tikanga Court, as a stand alone court, would operate in a similar way with an initial focus on criminal offending.[50] The underlying purpose of this court is to provide a forum where principles of *tikanga* can be meaningfully implemented and applied to achieve balance, healing or harmony within the individual and the community. Like the AODTC, the Tikanga Court would also focus on the root cause of the offending.[51]

50 Section 4D of the Magistrates Court Act 1989 (Vic) provides for the establishment of Koori Courts – similar provisions could be enacted.
51 See Chapter 1 'Causes of offending' section.

Procedure

The jurisdiction would be open to both Māori and non-Māori as the principles applied are universal. The process would commence upon arrest, where the offender would be offered the option to appear before a judge and two *kaumatua* at a *tikanga marae*-based court, or fall under the general jurisdiction of the District or High Court.

By choosing the option of a *tikanga marae*-based court, the defendant would need to enter a guilty plea. This reflects an important concept of *tikanga* Māori; namely, if one is charged with or alleged to have committed an act, then that person must take responsibility. This is similar to a strict liability offence under criminal law; however, assuming responsibility increases a person's *mana*.

If the offender chooses the *marae*-based option, they would then to register with a 'Marae Services'[52] facility. The Marae Services would provide all administrative assistance including compiling a court list for *marae* sittings and maintaining all files for the offenders. It is suggested that a District Court registrar be part of the Marae Services to ensure consistency between the two facilities (District Court and Marae Court). This is important, particularly if the offender chooses to opt out of the *marae* process for the general court jurisdiction.

The Marae Services would advise the offender at the time of registration of the next available date for the initial hearing, in accordance with the 'heard as soon as practicable' provision.[53] At this point a lay advocate,[54] such as a *kaitiaki*, would be assigned and become responsible for the offender. The Marae Services would then provide the file to either the lay advocate or the *marae* where the offender would remain.

The lay advocate would assist to ensure that the offender and their families are familiar with the process that lies ahead.[55] This would also include appearing with them in support (*awhi* and *manaaki*) and during the next step, the hearing at the *marae*.[56] The lay advocate would also provide support/*awhi* to the victim and their families in a similar fashion, as it is expected that the victim would also appear.

The procedure for the *marae* hearing would be similar to that of the Rangatahi Courts with a *pōwhiri, mihi, kai, korero* and *poroporoaki*. The judge would sit with two community members and preside over the hearing. Like the Rangatahi Courts, if relevant, a member from Hauora (Ministry of Health) and social support services as well as members from the community would take an active role in promoting

52 This would be similar to the service offered by the District Court.
53 New Zealand Bill of Rights Act 1990, s 23(3).
54 Section 163 CYPF Act 1989 provides for the appointment of a lay advocate. It is envisaged a similar provision could be enacted alternatively this section could be amended to include a lay advocate for a Tikanga Court.
55 Section 327 CYPF Act 1989 provides for representation of the offender's interest with a lay advocate. Again it is envisaged a similar provision could be enacted, alternatively this section could be amended to include a lay advocate for a Tikanga Court.
56 In light of the review of the role of Māori wardens, it is submitted that Māori wardens could also provide their services as a support role within a Tikanga Court.

the principle of inclusivity. This would provide support to the offender for behaviour related issues, such as mental health and anger management problems or
alcohol and drug addictions. This could also encompass an offender with
domestic violence charges who suffers from mental health issues. It is anticipated
that existing programmes could be used.

The judge, together with the two community members and support services,
will determine a suitable programme/s for the offender. With the appropriate
support of the respective programme representatives and potential supervision of
the lay advocate and/or the *marae*, the offender will commence the programmes
and then report back to the Marae Court once completed.

Upon the offender's next Marae Court appearance, the Judge and two *kaumatua*
would review the offender's progress, programme completion and also take into
account any reports from the programme leaders. At this point it could be
determined that the offender be released without conviction[57] or it may be that a
further programme is suggested to the offender for completion. If the offender has
successfully completed their programme this would be noted on his file and the
file returned to Marae Services or a similar justice depository for any future
reference should it be warranted.

Ideally, legislation similar to that of the Koori Court Act would be promulgated to
provide certainty and a clear direction for the court.

At any stage the offender should have the chance to opt for the general jurisdiction of the District or High Court. Alternatively, if the offender fails to
comply with the process, then they could be reassigned to the general District
Court process.

Similar to the Alcohol and Other Drug Treatment Court (AODTC) pilot
scheme, a Tikanga Court pilot could sit weekly at Hoani Waititi and Orakei (or
alternatively Kaikohe) as these are venues already successfully utilised by Te
Kooti Rangatahi. This could potentially cater for 100 participants each year. It is
accepted that unforeseen glitches will arise if a Tikanga Court pilot is realised.
And despite the positive nature of a Tikanga Court, a major challenge will be
finding the adequate funding and resources, particularly to support the community services. However, it is proposed that the benefits of a Tikanga Court would
outweigh the costs involved, particularly since the existing infrastructure (e.g.,
marae, social services, Corrections, judiciary) is already established.

Moreover, the District Court judges have the required judicial criminal and
trial warrants. Further, the machinery and administrative support is already in
place.

Comparative jurisdictions have found positive experiences with similar initia-
tives, although statistics show that disproportionate offending rates persist. The
Ministry of Justice recognises that culturally appropriate responses are required.
Collectively, this supports such an initiative as a Tikanga Court.

---

57 Similar to a section 106 Sentencing Act 2002.

Hypothetical example

Hemi is a twenty-year-old unemployed Māori male.

He lives at home with his mother and six younger siblings. His father, when he visits, routinely abuses Hemi's mother and siblings. Although he was the top student in his class, Hemi left school at 14 to find work and raise his siblings. Recently, Hemi has been enticed by a local gang to sell drugs.[58] However, Hemi has also become an addict, using more drugs than he can sell. To bridge the loss, Hemi decides to rob the local dairy. He is caught and charged.

For Hemi, the option of a *marae*-based court would be ideal. It would give him the opportunity to undertake the necessary rehabilitative drug programmes, and provide information and support on completing his education. This option would also provide advice to his mother regarding the ongoing abuse from his father as well as any possible housing issues. Depending on the quantity of drugs sold, and in view of the potential damage to the community, it would be suggested that Hemi engage in anti-drug treatment programmes. It would be hoped that, after the completion of these programmes, Hemi and his family will become positive members of the community.

Like the Matariki Courts, the victim's consent would not be required for acceptance into the Tikanga Court process. However, the victim would have the chance to face the offender and provide input into any programme. This could include reparation payment of the goods stolen. As offenders are often unemployed and without funds, appropriate work, such as cleaning the shop or stacking shelves, could be considered to satisfy the principle of reciprocity and balance. This situation would be preferable to a possible prison or community detention sentence with limited opportunity for rehabilitation.

Anecdotally, members of the judiciary have commented on the disproportionate representation of Māori within their courts[59] and welcomed the need to employ creative solutions to reduce recidivism rates.

A proposed Tikanga Court reflects a merging of two existing initiatives – Te Kooti Rangatahi and the Matariki Courts. This is a logical step. 'When', however, is another question.

E Conclusion

This book is concerned with, and searched for, the possibility of a new framework for Māori to ameliorate the disproportionate offending rates. Chapter 8 consolidates this research and tests the possibility of a new framework; either an

---

58 Cannabis, a class C drug.
59 For example *Mika v R* [2013] NZCA 648 at [12] where Justice Harrison notes the awareness of judges to the disproportionate offending rates for Māori and accepts that economic, social and cultural reasons contribute to this offending. However, he does also note that "the virtue of being Māori" is not a reason to be at a disadvantage.

extension of the Māori Land Court's jurisdiction[60] or a specialised Tikanga Court[61] with similarities to the AODTC and the Rangatahi Court. Like an extension to the Māori Land Court's jurisdiction, a Tikanga Court would be underpinned by important concepts, such as *manaakitanga, kaitiakitanga* and *whanaungatanga*. Further, the requirement to attain healing, harmony and balance at both an individual and community level is also intrinsic. Through drawing and building upon the positive developments of the Rangatahi Court, as well as the AODTC pilot, a Tikanga Court could empower the community with decision-making. In this sense it would be consistent with the right of self-determination.

The Māori Land Court is comprised of judges who are Māori and well-versed in *tikanga* Māori. The preamble of the TTWM Act seeks to establish mechanisms to assist Māori. Importantly, the personnel, infrastructure and legislation are already in place.

An extension to the jurisdiction of the Māori Land Court to include criminal and civil matters, together with respective amendments in corresponding legislation, would be required.[62] Until appropriate '*tikanga*-infused' legislation is promulgated, every effort to utilise the common law principles that support *tikanga* would need to be employed. A change of name to 'Te Kooti Māori' to reflect the extended jurisdiction is also proposed. It is acknowledged that a number of difficulties lie ahead. Nonetheless, the extended jurisdiction of the Māori Land Court would embrace both Māori and non-Māori applicants and would be underpinned by concepts such as healing, harmony and balance.

These proposed models recognise that a separate system may not be practical for Māori. The biggest obstacle being political will.[63] However, the meaningful implementation of *tikanga* concepts 'by Māori, for Māori' and fully supported by the community, provides an answer.

The historical and continual disproportionate statistics across all stages of the criminal justice system are notorious and unjust. Arguments based on race, unemployment, social problems, as well as those that insist we already recognise *tikanga* within our current legal system cannot ignore these continuing statistics. Returning to an Indigenous legal system is not novel. A return to the principles that underpin an Indigenous legal system – Te Ao Māori – is warranted. In

---

60 The jurisdiction of the Māori Land Court is currently to hear matters relating to successions, Title improvements, Māori land sales and the administration of Māori Land Trusts and Incorporations. The jurisdiction also includes cases under the Māori Fisheries Act 2004, Māori Commercial Aquaculture Claims Settlement Act 2004. An extension to the jurisdiction to capture criminal offending may be suggested.

61 Although phrased as a "new" Indigenous Court there are many such Courts already operating. In Canada the National Judicial Institute has provided educational courses for the Judiciary on Aboriginal Courts covering the Reality, Theory and Future of these Courts.

62 For example, the Māori Fisheries Act 2004.

63 Heath, above n 7 at 200, 211–212.

extending this approach to non-Māori, two quotes from two rangatira/leaders are advanced.

First, Justice Rothstein of the Supreme Court of Canada notes:[64]

> the goal of aboriginal ... jurisprudence should not be to separate Canadians into two camps with two competing interests but rather to unite them with the shared goal of a just peaceful and safe society ...

Second, Professor Dame Anne Salmond recommends a more balanced approach in an attempt to grapple with the following questions: "What is it to be human, what do we have in common and what divides us?"[65] Human understanding and reciprocal exchange is required. Anne Salmond notes that:[66]

> ... in New Zealand, at least, collaboration between Māori and Western knowledge seems possible. It may lead, eventually, to studies of cross-cultural encounters that do justice to the ancestors on both sides.

Finally Professor John Borrows notes that the thesis of his work[67] "'Canada's Indigenous Constitution' is that Indigenous laws can be recognized and affirmed in a Canadian legal context, and can also be justified through Western legal argumentation". He further notes that:[68]

> ... Indigenous peoples' law has been scattered by the prevailing order. It was believed to be insubstantial in comparison with the developing common law and constitutional structures ... perhaps the most promising development for the maintenance and extension of Indigenous stories comes at those moments when Indigenous law's elements mingle with the land and those of the non-Indigenous jurisprudential order

It is acknowledged that a return to an Indigenous court within a separate criminal justice system might not be practical. However, an extension of an existing forum, such as the Māori Land Court or establishing a specialist Tikanga Court to meaningfully incorporate Te Ao Māori, may indeed provide an opportunity to return to an Indigenous legal system, a return to Te Ao Māori, and a return to a *sui generis* Indigenous court.

What is now required is political will.

'He moana pukepuke e ekengia e te waka'

---

64   *R v Ipeelee* 2012 SCC 13 [2012] 1 SCR 433.
65   Anne Salmond *Between Worlds: Early Exchanges between Māori and Europeans, 1773–1815* (Penguin Books, Auckland, 1997) Salmond, at 513.
66   Salmond, above.
67   John Borrows *Drawing Out Law* (University of Toronto Press, Toronto, 2010) at xiv.
68   Borrows above at 69.

Glossary

Ariki   chief of noble birth, priest
Aroha   love, affection for others
Atawhai   foster, caring for the welfare of others
Āwhina   help
Atua   deity, god/s
Hangi   earth oven
Hapu   subdivision of a tribe, or sub tribe
Hara   crime or offence
Hee   mistake/error
Hongi   a greeting, by the pressing of noses
Hui   gathering together of people for discussion, or to socialise
Iwi   a tribe which traces descent from a common ancestor or ancestors
Kai   food
Kaitiaki   caretaker/guardian
Kaumatua   male elders
Kawa   symbol, sign, protocol
Kuia   female elders
Korero   talk/speak
Mana   prestige, authority, power or psychic force
Manawhenua   having *mana* or prestige/power over the land
Manaaki   blessing
Marae   sacred meeting place, situated within a village, traditional meeting house, area in front of the *whare*
Mauri   life force
Moko   tattoo, which can be either on the face, arms, thighs or buttocks
Mokopuna   grandchild
Muru   wipe or rub; seizing of goods to address an imbalance
Ora   well being
Pa   a village; settlement or fortified area of a tribe or sub-tribe
Pae here tangata   to bind people together
Papatūānuku   mother earth

Pākehā   person of English descent (also used in earlier times as reference to traders, settlers, missionaries)

Pono   just

Powhiri   ritual ceremony of encounter.

Rahui   prohibition; the setting aside of a place or thing for a specified time; permanent reservation of land for a specific purpose

Rangatira   leader, person of senior lineage

Rangatiratanga   leadership authority

Take   reason

Tangata whenua   literally, a person of the land or people belonging to a tribal region; hosts as distinct from visitors

Tangi   to weep, grieve, mourn or cry

Tangihanga   a ceremony of mourning

Tapu   Set aside – sacred

Tika   correct/right

Tikanga   principles, truth, customary practice

Tinana   body

Tohunga   a healer or a priest; an expert in traditional lore or a person skilled in a particular activity

Utu   revenge, recompense, reward, price, payment; repayment in goods; retribution in battle to the death

Waiata   song; to chant or to sing

Wairua   spirit, spirituality

Whakahoki mauri   restoring the balance

Whakapapa   layer – family tree

Whanau   literally – to be born or to give birth, family or an extended family

Whanaungatanga   relatedness

Whare   a house, or a dwelling

Whare wananga   a university, or a learning place

Whenua   literally – afterbirth; land, ground, earth, a country

References

Cases

New Zealand

Ashby v Minister of Immigration [1981] 1 *NZLR* 222 (CA), 128.
Attorney General v Mair [2009] *NZCA* 625, 130.
Attorney General v New Zealand Māori Council (No 2) [1991] 2 *NZLR* 147, 133.
Attorney General v Ngāti Apa [2003] *NZCA* 117; 3 *NZLR* 643, 108.
Auckland Regional Council v Holmes Logging Limited HC Auckland CRI-2009-404-3, 165.
Du Claire v M Palmer and Crown Law Office [2012] *NZHC* 934, 219.
Fuller v MacLeod [1981] 1 *NZLR* 390, 108.
Greenpeace v Minister of Energy CIV-2011-485-1897 [22 June 2012] HC Wellington, 134.
Haronga v Waitangi Tribunal and Others (SC54/2010) [2011] *NZSC* 53, 134.
Huakina Development Trust v Waikato Valley Authority & Bowater [1987] 2 *NZLR* 188; (1987) 12 *NZTPA* 129 (HC), 133.
Hunt v R [2011] 2 *NZLR* 499, 58.
Kerisiano Aeau v The Police HC, CRI 2007-404-247 11 September 2007, 228.
Latimer v R [2013] *NZCA* 562, 43.
Mika v R [2013] *NZCA* 648, 35, 233, 253.
Minister of Immigration and Ethnic Affairs v Teoh (1995) 128 *ALR* 353 (HCA), 128, 145.
Morunga v Police 16/3/04HC Auckland, CRI-2004-404-8, 106.
New Zealand Māori Council v Attorney General [1987] 1 *NZLR* 641, 146.
New Zealand Māori Council v Attorney-General [1994] 1 *NZLR* 513; [1994] 1 *AC* 466 (PC), 133.
New Zealand Māori Council v Attorney-General [1996] 3 *NZLR* 140 (CA), 128.
New Zealand Māori Council v Attorney-General HC Wellington CIV-2007-485-95, 4 May 2007, 130.
New Zealand Māori Council v Attorney-General [2008] 1 *NZLR* 318; [2007] *NZAR* 569 (CA), 134.
Ngāi Tahu Māori Trust Board v Director General of Conservation [1995] 3 *NZLR* 553, 145.
Ngāti Apa v Attorney General [2003] 3 *NZLR* 643 (CA), 52, 72, 74.
Ngāti Maru ki Hauraki Inc v Kruithof [2005] *NZRMA* 1, 126.
Nishikata v Police HC Wellington AP126/99, 22 July 1999, 18.
Paki and Ors v Attorney-General of New Zealand [2012] *NZSC* 50, 74.
Re IM [2002] *NZFLR* 846, 27.
Re Manukau HC Auckland M 1380/92, 10 June 1993, 106.
Re the 90 Mile Beach [1963] *NZLR* 461 (CA), 52.
Re The Lundon and Whitaker Claims Act 1871(1872) 2 *NZCA* 41, 114.

Reid v Parole Board (CA 247/05, 29 June 2006), 203.

R v E Hipu 1 December 1845 Supreme Court, Wellington, Chapman J., 109.

R v Mason [2012] 2 *NZLR* 695, 71, 72, 73, 74, 248.

R v Mika [2013] *NZHC* 2357.

R v Native 1 December 1847 Supreme Court, Wellington, Chapman J., 110

R v Rangitapiripiri 1 December 1847 Supreme Court, Wellington, Chapman J., 110

R v Symonds (1847) *NZPCC* 387 (SC), 73, 74, 103, 108, 127, 146.

R v Te Pania [2015] *DCR* 25, 247.

R v Toia CRI 2005 005 000027 Williams J HC Whangerei 9 August 2006, 58.

R v Wawatai [2014] *NZHC* 2374, 94, 95.

Rira Peti v Ngaraihi Te Paku (1889) 7 *NZLR* 235, 73.

RS v R [2014] *NZCA* 484, 97, 218.

Sen v Police [2007] *NZFLR* 733, 228.

Shaw v Commissioner of Inland Revenue [1999] 3 *NZLR* 154 (CA), 103.

Takamore v Clarke [2011] *NZCA* 587; [2012] 1 *NZLR* 573 (CA), 53, 72.

Takamore v Clarke [2012] *NZSC* 116, [2012] 2 *NZLR* 733, 53, 145.

Tavita v Minister of Immigration [1994] 2 *NZLR* 257; (1993) 11 *FRNZ* 508; (1993) 1
    HRNZ 30 (CA), 145.

Te Heuheu Tukino v Aotea District Māori Land Board [1941] 2 *All E.R.* 93; [1941] *NZLR*
    590, 74, 125, 127, 146.

Tutakangahau v R [2014] *NZCA* 279, 94, 96, 97, 98.

Waitemata Health v Attorney General & Ors CA [2001] *NZFLR* 1122, 27.

Wi Parata v Bishop of Wellington (1877) 3 *NZ Jur* (NS) (SC) 72, 73, 100, 101, 146.

Zaoui v Attorney-General [2004] 2 *NZLR* 339, 146.

Australia

Gerhady v Brown (1985) 57 *ALR* 472, 186.

Mabo v Queensland (No 2) (1992) 175 *CLR*, 139.

Milirrpum v Nabalco Pty Ltd (1971) 17 *FLR* 141, 261–262 (Blackburn J), 7.

Minister for Immigration and Ethnic Affairs v Teoh (1995) 183 *CLR* 273 (HCA), 128, 145.

R v Jack Congo Murrell (1836) 1 *Legge* 72, 7.

R v Wedge [1976] 1 NSWLR 581, 7.

Tuckiar v R (1934) 52 *CLR* 335, 7.

Wiks Peoples v Queensland (1996) 121 *ALR* 129, 139.

Canada

Calder v Attorney General of British Columbia [1973] *SCR* 313, 139.

R v Bain [2004] OJ No 6147 (Ont SC), 178.

R v Gladue [1999] 1 *SCR* 688, 177.

R v Ipeelee 2012SCC 13 [2012] 1 *SCR* 433, 254.

R v Kakekagamick [2006] OJ No 3346 (Ont CA), 177.

R v Morin [1995] SJ No 457, 176.

R v Morin (1995) 4 *CNLR* 37 (Saskatchewan Court of Appeal), 176.

R v Moses (1992) 71 *CCC* (3d) 347 (Yukon Territorial Court), 176.

R v RRB [2004] BCJ No 2024 (BC Prov Ct), 178.

R v Sim [2005] OJ No 4432 (Ont CA), 98, 177.

India

Vajesingji Joravarsingji v Secretary of State for India (1924) *LR* 51 Ind App 357, 127.

Latin America

Cal & Ors v the Attorney General of Belize & Anor (2007) Claim Nos 171 and 172 of 2007, Conteh CJ (Belize Sup Ct), 144, 145.
Mayagna (sumo) Awas Tingni Community v The Republic of Nicaragua ("Awas-Tingni") Inter-American Court of Human Rights No 79 (31 August 2001), 167.

United States

Means v Nation 432 F 3d 924, 933 (9th Cir 2005), 207.
In re Mental Health Services of Bizardi 8 Nav. Rptr (Nav. Sup. Ct. 2004), 207.

United Kingdom

Adeyinka Oyekan v Musendika Adele [1957] 1 *WLR* 876, [1957] 2 *All ER* 785, 52.
Brind v Secretary of State for the Home Department [1991] 1 *All ER* 720 (UK), 146.
Calvin's Case (1608) 7 Co Rep 1a, 77 *ER* 377 (Comm Pleas), 101.
The Case of Tanistry (1608) Davies 28, 80 *ER* 516 (KB), 101.
Tijani v Secretary, Southern Nigeria [1921] 2 *AC* 399, 52.

Legislation

New Zealand

Adoption Act 1955, 48.
Bail Act 2000, 94, 98, 178.
Cattle Trespass Amendment Ordinance 1844.
Children, Young Persons, and Their Families Act 1989, 38, 245.
Conservation Act 1987, 129, 147.
Constitution Act 1846, 72, 73, 108, 111.
Constitution Act 1852, 108, 111, 114, 115.
Constitution Act 1986, 112, 115, 131, 156.
Crimes Act 1961, 15, 26, 72, 91, 94, 245.
Criminal Justice Act 1985 (repealed), 42, 218.
Criminal Procedure (Mentally Impaired Persons) Act 2003, 26.
Criminal Procedure Act 2011, 15, 210, 224.
Defence Act 1909, 16.
District Courts Act 1947, 116.
Disturbed Districts Act 1869, 6, 15.
Domestic Violence Act 1995, 68, 221, 227.
Domestic Violence (Programmes) Regulations 1996, 68.
Education Act 1989, 59.
Electoral Act 1893, 33, 47.
Electoral Act 1993, 33, 34, 35.
Family Protection Act 1955, 247.
Fines for Assault Ordinance 1845, 110.

Foreshore and Seabed Act 2004, 127, 139, 149.
Historic Places Act 1993, 59.
Human Rights Act 1993, 241.
Income Tax Act 2007, 242.
Intellectual Disability (Compulsory Care and Rehabilitation) Act 2003, 27.
Intellectual Disability (Compulsory Care) Bill, 27.
Judicature Act 1908, 116.
Juries Act 1908, 33, 62.
Juries Amendment Act 1962, 62.
Land Transfer Act 1952, 243.
Law Reform (Testamentary Promises) Act 1949, 246.
Māori Affairs Act 1953, 34, 48.
Māori Affairs Amendment Act 1974 (No 73), 34.
Māori Commercial Aquaculture Claims Settlement Act 2004, 11, 253.
Māori Community Development Act 1962, 59, 227, 241.
Māori Fisheries Act 2004, 11, 244, 246.
Māori Language Act 1987, 93, 232.
The Māori Prisoners' Trial Act 1879, 16.
Māori Social and Economic Advancement Act 1945, 60, 227.
Māori Welfare Act 1962, 227.
Marine and Coastal Area (Takutai Moana) Act 2011, 139.
Marriage Act 1908, 48.
Marriage Act 1955, 49.
Mental Health (Compulsory Assessment and Treatment) Act 1992, 25, 26, 27.
Native Exemption Ordinance (No 18), 62, 109.
Native Land Act 1873, 47, 48.
Native Ordinance, 109.
New Zealand Bill of Rights Act 1990, 20, 22, 103, 115, 123, 124, 126, 250.
New Zealand Charter 1840, 108.
New Zealand Constitution (Amendment) Act 1947 (UK), 115.
New Zealand Constitution (Request and Consent) Act 1947, 115.
New Zealand Public Health and Disability Act 2000, 29, 30.
Parole Act 2002, 23, 24, 25, 203.
Property Law Act 2007, 243.
Public Works Act 1928, 57, 74.
Resident Magistrates Court Ordinance 1846, 110.
Resource Management Act 1991, 70, 129, 165, 218, 224, 248.
Sentencing Act 2002, 42, 43, 70, 77, 91, 94–98, 175, 216, 218, 228, 241, 246, 251.
State Owned Enterprises Act 1986, 129, 147.
Statute of Westminster Act 1947, 115.
Summary Offences Act 1981, 196, 227, 241.
Supreme Court Act 2003, 116, 156.
Suppression of Rebellion Act 1863, 6, 15.
Te Ture Whenua Māori Act 1993, 54, 79, 190, 242–248.
Te Urewera Act 2014, 126.
The Cattle Trespass Ordinance 1844, 72.
The Sale of Spirits to Natives Ordinance 1847, 15.
The New Zealand Settlements Act 1963, 6, 15.

Tohunga Suppression Act 1908, 49.
Treaty of Waitangi Act 1975, 9, 122, 130, 134, 147.
Tuhoe Claims Settlement Act 2014, 126.
Unsworn Testimony Ordinance 1844, 62.
Urewera District Native Reserve Act 1896, 112, 126.
Victims' Rights Act 2002, 220.
Waikato Claims Settlement Act 1995, 59.
West Coast Settlement Act 1880, 16.

Australia

Courts Legislation (Miscellaneous Amendments) Act 2005 (Vic), 198.
Magistrates' Court Act 1989 (Vic), 188–190.
Magistrates' Court (Koori Court) Act 2002 (Vic), 188, 224.
Summary Offences Act 1966 (Vic), 196, 227.

International Conventions

United Nations Convention on the Elimination of All Forms of Discrimination
Against Women, 172.
United Nations Declaration on the Rights of Indigenous Peoples, 11, 53, 134–136, 140,
    143–147, 155, 160, 167, 237.
International Covenant on Civil and Political Rights, 123, 172.
International Covenant on Economic and Social Rights, 172.
International Labour Organization Convention No. 107, 140.
International Labour Organization Convention No. 169, 138, 140.

United States

GN 00305.080 Navajo Tribal Common-Law Marriages <http://policy.ssa.gov/poms.nsf/
    lnx/0200305080>, 208.
Hopi Indian Tribe Law and Order Code – Ordinance 21, 181, 206.
Tohono O'odham Law and Order Code 1.15(5) 1994, 206.

Canada

Constitution Act 1982, 123.
Criminal Code RSC 1985 c C- 46, s 718.2(e), 181.
Indian Act RSC 1985, c I-5, s 107, 181.

United Kingdom

Constitution Act 1847 (UK), 108.
Constitution Act 1852 (UK), 108.
English Laws Act 1858, 10, 103, 108.

Latin America

Organic Law of Spain 1/1979, Art 76, 205.
Constitution of Bolivia Art 30(II)(3), 166.
New Political Constitution of the State Act 2009 (Bol), s 1(1), art 2, 144.

Russia

On Territories of Traditional Nature Use of Indigenous, Small Numbered Peoples of the North, Siberia and the Far East of the Russian Federation (7 May 2001, No 49-FZ), 112.

Books, Chapters in Books and Reports

Peter Adams *Fatal Necessity: British Intervention in New Zealand, 1830–1847* (Auckland University Press, Auckland, 1977).

S James Anaya *International Human Rights and Indigenous Peoples* (Aspen Publishers, New York, 2009).

S James Anaya *Indigenous Peoples in International Law* (Oxford University Press, New York, 2004).

S James Anaya "The Rights of Indigenous People to Self-Determination in the Post-Declaration Era" in Claire Charters and Rodolfo Stavenhagen (eds) *Making the Declaration Work: The United Nations Declaration on the Rights of Indigenous Peoples* (International Working Group for Indigenous Affairs, Copenhagen, 2009).

Taiaiake Alfred *Peace, Power and Righteousness: An Indigenous Manifesto* (2nd ed, Oxford University Press, Oxford, 2008).

Kirsten Anker *Declarations of Interdependence: A Legal Pluralist Approach to Indigenous Rights* (Ashgate Publishing, Farnham UK, 2014).

Raymond Austin *Navajo Courts and the Navajo Common Law: A Tradition of Tribal Self Governance* (University of Minnesota Press, Minneapolis, 2009).

Brian Barry *Culture and Equality: An Egalitarian Critique of Multiculturalism* (Polity Press in association with Blackwell Publishers, Cambridge, 2001).

Jean Baudrillard *Simulacra and Simulation* (translated by Sheila Glaser) (University of Michigan, Michigan, 1995).

J Baxter *Māori Mental Health Needs Profile. Summary. A Review of the Evidence.* (: Te Rau Matatini, Palmerston North, 2008) <www.matatini.co.nz>

Michael Belgrave, Merata Kawharu and David Williams (eds) *Waitangi Revisited: Perspectives on the Treaty of Waitangi* (Oxford University Press, Australia, 2005).

Richard Benton, Alex Frame and Paul Meredith (eds) *Te Mātāpunenga: A Compendium of References to the Concepts and Institutions of Māori Customary Law, compiled for Te Matahauariki Institute* (Victoria University Press, Wellington, 2013).

Judith Binney *Encircled Lands: Te Urewera* (Bridget Williams Books, Wellington, 2010).

J Binney and G Chaplin *Ngā Mōrehu: The Survivors* (Oxford University Press, Auckland, 1986).

Richard Boast "Evolution of Māori Land Law 1862–1993" in Richard Boast, Andrew Erueti, Doug McPhail and Norman F Smith (eds) *Māori Land Law* (2nd ed., , Wellington, New Zealand, 2004).

Patricia Borraz and Loreta Ferrer (ed) *Indigenous Peoples' Human Rights in Domestic Courts* (Human Rights Office of the Spanish Ministry of Foreign Affairs and Cooperation, 2013).

John Borrows *Drawing Out the Law* (University of Toronto Press, Toronto, 2010).

John Borrows *Canada's Indigenous Constitution* (University of Toronto Press, Canada, 2010).

Helen Bowen and Jim Consedine *Restorative Justice Contemporary Themes and Practice* (Ploughshare Publications, Lyttleton, New Zealand, 1999).

John Braithwaite *Inequality, Crime and Public Policy* (Routledge, London, 1979).

John Braithwaite *Crime, Shame and Reintegration* (Cambridge University Press, Cambridge, 1989).

Warren Brookbanks "Mentally Disordered Offenders" in Julia Tolmie and Warren Brookbanks (eds) *Criminal Justice in New Zealand* (, Wellington, 2007).

Warren Brookbanks *Therapeutic Jurisprudence: New Zealand Perspectives* (Thomson Reuters, Auckland, 2015).

F M (Jock) Brookfield *Waitangi & Indigenous Rights* (updated ed, Auckland University Press, Auckland, 2006).

Tom Brooking *Māori and Pākehā Relations: 1800–1860* (Ministry of Education, Wellington, 1991).

Ian Brownlie *Treaties and Indigenous Peoples* (Oxford University Press, New York, 1992)

Ian Brownlie *Principles of Public International Law* (7th ed, Oxford University Press, Oxford, 2008).

Sandra Buicerious and Michael Tonry (eds) *The Oxford Handbook of Ethnicity, Crime and Immigration* (Oxford University Press, New York, 2014).

Gale Burford and Joe Hudson *Family Group Conferencing: New Directions in Community-Centered Child and Family Practice* (Transaction Publishers, New York, 2000).

Andrew Butler and Petra Butler *The New Zealand Bill of Rights Act: A Commentary* (Wellington, 2005).

Dennis Byles and Tai Karp *Sentencing in the Koori Courts Division of the Magistrates Court* (Sentencing Advisory Council, Melbourne, 2010).

Carlos Carcach and Anna Grant *Imprisonment in Australia: Trends in Prison Populations and Imprisonment Rates 1982–1998 Canberra* (Australian Institute of Criminology, Australia, 2000).

DrSueCarswell *Family Violence and the Pro-Arrest Policy: A Literature Review* (Ministry of Justice, Wellington, December2006).

Sarah Carter "Categories and Terrains of Exclusion: Constructing the 'Indian Woman' in the Early Settlement Era in Western Canada" in Mary-Ellen Kelm and Lorna Townsend (eds) *In the Days of our Grandmothers* (University of Toronto Press, Toronto, 2006).

Antonio Cassese *Self Determination of Peoples* (Cambridge University Press, Cambridge, 1995).

Paul L A H Chartrand and Wendy Whitecloud (Commissioners) *The Aboriginal Justice Implementation Commission Report of the Aboriginal Justice Inquiry of Manitoba The Justice System and Aboriginal Peoples* (Aboriginal Justice Commission, Canada, 2001) <www.ajic.mb.ca>.

Alison Chetwin, Tony Waldegrave, Kiri Simonsen with Strategic Training and Development Services and the Family Centre Social Policy Research Unit *Speaking about Cultural Background at Sentencing* (Ministry of Justice, Wellington, November2000) <www.justice. govt.nz>.

Arthur G Christean *Therapeutic Jurisprudence: Embracing a Tainted Ideal* (The Sutherland Institute, 2002) <http://www.sutherlandinstitute.org>.

Gordon Christie "Indigenous Legal Theory" in Benjamin Richardson, Shin Imai and Kent McNeil (eds) *Indigenous Peoples and the Law: Comparative and Critical Perspectives* (Hart Publishing, Portland, 2009).

Bartolome Clavero "Cultural Supremacy, Domestic Constitutions and the Declaration on the Rights of Indigenous Peoples" in Claire Charters and Rodolfo Stavenhagen (eds) *Making the Declaration Work: The United Nations Declaration on the Rights of Indigenous Peoples* (International Working Group for Indigenous Affairs, Copenhagen, 2009).

Fiona Cram, Leonie Pihema, Kuni Jenkins and Matewiki Karehana *Evaluation of Programmes for Māori Adult Protected Persons under the Domestic Violence Act 1995* (Ministry of Justice, Wellington, June2002) <www.justice.govt.nz>.

Chris Cuneen *Conflict, Politics and Crime: Aboriginal Communities and the Police* (Allen and Unwin, Sydney, 2001).

Chris Cuneen "Colonial Processes, Indigenous Peoples and Criminal Justice Systems" in Sandra Buicerious and Michael Tonry (eds) *The Oxford Handbook of Ethnicity, Crime and Immigration* (Oxford University Press, New York, 2014).

Robert A Dentler and Kai T Erikson, "The Functions of Deviance in Groups" (1959), in Stuart H Traub and Craig B Little (eds) *Theories of Deviance* (F E Peacock Publishers, Itasca (IL), 1975).

Jane Dickson-Gilmore and Carol La Prairie *Will the Circle Be Broken? Aboriginal Communities, Restorative Justice and the Challenges of Conflict and Change* (University of Toronto, Toronto, Canada, 2005).

Sinclair Dinnen "Restorative Justice in the Pacific Islands" in Sinclair Dinnen, Anita Jowitt and Tess Newton Cain (eds) *A Kind of Meaning: Restorative Justice in the Pacific Islands* (Pandanus Books, Canberra, 2003).

Peter Doone *Hei Whakarurutanga Mo Te Ao* (Crime Prevention Unit, Wellington, 2000).

S Dunstan, J Paulin and K Atkinson *Trial by Peers? The Composition of New Zealand Juries* (Department of Justice, Wellington, 1995).

Mason Durie *Te Mana, Te Kawanatanga: The Politics of Māori Self Determination* (Oxford University Press, Melbourne, 1998).

Mason Durie *Nga Tai Matatū: Tides of Māori Endurance* (Oxford University Press, Melbourne, 2005).

Mason Durie *Mauri Ora: The Dynamics of Māori Health* (Oxford University Press, Auckland, 2005).

Mason Durie *Whaiora: Māori Health Development* (Oxford University Press, Auckland, 2006).

Mason Durie *Te Whare Tapa Wha: Māori Health Model Hauora Māori* (Ministry of Health, Wellington) <www.health.govt.nz/system>

Mason Durie "Tino Rangatiratanga" in Michael Belgrave, Merata Kawharu and David Williams (eds) *Waitangi Revisited: Perspectives on the Treaty of Waitangi* (Oxford University Press, Melbourne, Australia, 2005).

Emile Durkheim, "The Normal and the Pathological" (1938) in Stuart H Traub and Craig B Little (eds) *Theories of Deviance* (F E Peacock Publishers, Itasca (IL), 1975).

Tui Efi and others (eds) *Pacific Indigenous Dialogue on Faith, Peace, Reconciliation and Good Governance* (University of South Pacific, Samoa, 2007).

Werner J Einstader and Stuart Henry *Criminological Theory: An Analysis of its Underlying Assumptions* (2nd ed, Rowman and Littlefield, Lanham (MD)2006).

Ripeka Evans "Is the Treaty of Waitangi a Bill of Rights?" in *A Bill of Rights for New Zealand* (Legal Research Foundation Seminar, Auckland, 1985).

Alan Feuer "The Revolving Door" in Bruce Winick and David Wexler (eds) *Judging in a Therapeutic Key – Therapeutic Jurisprudence and the Courts* (Carolina Academic Press, North Carolina, 2003).

J K Fifield and A A Donnell *Socioeconomic Status, Race, and Offending in New Zealand (Research Report No 6)* (Government Printer, Wellington, 1980).

Bonnie S Fisher, Steven P Lab and Barry A Fisher *Encyclopedia of Victimology and Crime Prevention* (Sage Publications, Thousand Oaks, 2010).

Malgosia Fitzmaurice "The Question of Indigenous Peoples Rights: A Time for Reappraisal?" in Duncan French (ed) *Statehood and Self-Determination Reconciling Tradition and Modernity in International Law* (Cambridge University Press, Cambridge, 2013).

Norman Arthur Foden *New Zealand Legal History (1642 to 1842)* (Sweet and Maxwell Ltd, Wellington, 1965).

Lon Fuller *The Morality of Law* (Yale University Press, New Haven, 1969).

Jarod Gilbert *Patched: The History of Gangs in New Zealand* (AUP, Auckland, 2013).Daniel Glaser, "Criminality Theories and Behavioural Images" (1956) in Stuart H Traub and Craig B Little (eds) *Theories of Deviance* (F E Peacock Publishers, Itasca (IL), 1975).

Andrew Goldsmith, Mark Israel and Kathleen Daly (eds) *Crime and Justice: A Guide to Criminology* (3rd ed, Lawbook Company, Sydney, 2006).

Melissa Gorelick *Discrimination of Aboriginals on Native Lands in Canada: A Comprehensive Crisis* (UN Chronicle, 2007) <http://unchronicle.un.org/>.

Michael R Gottfredson and Travis Hirschi *A General Theory of Crime* (Stanford University Press, Stanford, 1990).

Ross Green *Justice in Aboriginal Communities: Sentencing Alternatives* (Purich Publishing, Vancouver, 1998).

L A Greenfeld and S K Smith *American Indians and Crime* (NCJ 173386) Department of Justice, Bureau of Justice Statistics, Washington, DC1999) <www:bjs.ojp.usdoj.gov>.

Eric K Gross *Evaluation/Assessment of Navajo Peacemaking* (National Criminal Justice Reference Centre, USA, April 5, 2001). <https://www.ncjrs.gov/pdffiles1/nij/grants/187675.pdf>

K D Harries *Crime and the Environment* (Charles C Thomas, Springfield, Illinois, 1980).Mark Harris *A Sentencing Conversation: Evaluation of the Koori Courts Pilot Program October 2002– October 2004* (Victorian Department of Justice, Melbourne, 2006).

H L A Hart *The Concept of Law* (2nd ed, Oxford University Press, New York, 1997).

Manuka Henare *Ngā Tikanga me ngā Ritenga o te ao Māori: Standards and Foundations of Māori Society Vol III* (Royal Commission on Social Policy: Future Directions, 1988).

Sakeq Henderson *First Nations Jurisprudence and Aboriginal Rights* (Native Law Centre, Saskatoon, Canada, 2006).

Berys Heuer *Māori Women* (Reed Publications, Wellington, 1972).

Richard Hill *Māori and the State Crown–Māori Relations in New Zealand/Aotearoa 1950–2000* (Victoria University Press, Wellington, 2009).

Ross Hogg "The Causes of Crime and the Boundaries of Criminal Justice" in Julia Tolmie and Warren Brookbanks (eds) *Criminal Justice in New Zealand* (, Wellington, 2007).

Institute of Judicial Studies *Youth Court Bench Book* (3rd ed, Institute of Judicial Studies, Wellington, 2008).

Moana Jackson "Changing Realities: Unchanging Truths" in Commission on Folk Law and Legal Pluralism (ed) *Papers Presented to the Congress at Victoria University of Wellington, August 1992: Volume II* (Law Faculty, Victoria University of Wellington, Wellington, 1992).

Moana Jackson *Māori and the Criminal Justice System: He Whaipaanga Hou – A New Perspective* (Policy and Research Division, Department of Justice, Wellington, 1988).

Moana Jackson "Justice and Political Power: Reasserting Māori Legal Processes" in Kayleen M Hazlehurst (ed) *Legal Pluralism and the Colonial Legacy: Indigenous Experiences of Justice in Canada, Australia and New Zealand* (Avebury, Aldershot, 1995).

Moana Jackson "Where Does Sovereignty Lie?" in Colin James (ed) *Building the Constitution* (Institute of Policy Studies, Wellington, 2000).

Shane Jones "The Bill of Rights and Te Tiriti o Waitangi" in *A Bill of Rights for New Zealand* (Legal Research Foundation Seminar, Auckland, 1985).

Philip Joseph *Constitutional and Administrative Law in New Zealand* (3rd ed, Thomson Brookers, Wellington, 2007).

Robert Joseph *The Government of Themselves: Case Law, Policy and Section 71 of the New Zealand Constitution Act 1852* (Te Matahauariki Institute Monograph Series, University of Waikato, 2002).

Just Speak *Māori and the Criminal Justice System Position Paper* (Wellington, 2012) <www.rethinking.org.nz>.

Antje Kampf *Mapping out Venereal Wilderness: Pubic Health and STD in New Zealand 1920–1980* (Transaction Publishers, London, 2007).

Ian Hugh Kawharu "A Reconstruction of Māori Text" in Michael Belgrave, Merata Kawharu and David Williams (eds) *Waitangi Revisited: Perspectives on the Treaty of Waitangi* (Oxford University Press, Melbourne, 2005).

Ian Hugh Kawharu "The Treaty of Waitangi (the text in English) by I Hugh Kawharu" in Michael Belgrave, Merata Kawharu and David Williams (eds) *Waitangi Revisited: Perspectives on the Treaty of Waitangi* (Oxford University Press, Melbourne, 2005)

Ian Hugh Kawharu *Waitangi: Māori and Pākehā Perspectives of the Treaty of Waitangi* (Oxford University Press, Ann Arbor, 1989).

Danny Keenan "Autonomy as Fiction: The Urewera Native District Reserve Act 1896" in Danny Keenan (ed) *Terror in our Midst* (Huia Publishers, Wellington, 2008).

Michael King *The Penguin History of New Zealand* (Penguin, Rosedale, New Zealand, 2003).

Michael King, Arie Freiberg, Becky Batagol and Ross Hyams *Non-Adversarial Justice* (Federation Press, Annandale, Australia, 2009).

T Knaggs, F Leahy and N Soboleva *The Manukau Family Violence Court: An Evaluation of the Family Violence Court Process* (Ministry of Justice, Wellington, 2008).

Naomi Kupuri "The UN Declaration on the Rights of Indigenous Peoples in the African Context" in Claire Charters and Rodolfo Stavenhagen (eds) *Making the Declaration Work: The United Nations Declaration on the Rights of Indigenous Peoples* (International Working Group for Indigenous Affairs, Copenhagen, 2009).

Will Kymlicka *Liberalism, Community and Culture* (Oxford University Press, New York, 1989).

Will Kymlicka *Minority Rights* (Oxford University Press, New York, 1995).

Phil Lane, Judie Bopp and Michael Bopp *Aboriginal Domestic Violence in Canada* (Aboriginal Healing Foundation, Canada, 2003).

Federico Lenzerini "The Trail of Broken Dreams, the Status of Indigenous Peoples in International Law" in Federico Lenzerini (ed) *Reparation for Indigenous Peoples International and Comparative Perspectives* (Oxford University Press, Oxford, 2008).

James P Lynch and William J Sabol *Prisoner Re-entry in Perspective: Crime and Policy Report Volume 3* (The Urban Institute, Washington DC, 2001).

Michael Lynch and W Byron Groves *A Primer in Radical Criminology* (2nd ed, Harrow and Heston, Albany (NY)1989).

Deborah Mackenzie and Holly Carrington *Monitoring Report for the Auckland Family Violence Court The First Three Months 27 March 2007–30 June 2007* (Preventing Violence in the Home, Auckland, November2007).

Elena Marchetti *Indigenous Sentencing Courts* (Brief 5) (Indigenous Justice Clearing House, Australia, 2009) <www.indigenousjustice.gov.au>

Elena Marchetti and Kathleen Daly *Indigenous Courts and Justice Practices in Australia* (Australian Institute of Criminology, Australia, 2004).

Maori Marsden "The Natural World and Natural Resources" in Charles Royal (ed) *The Woven Universe Selected Writings of Rev Maori Marsden* (Estate of Rev. Maori Marsden, Masterton, 2003).

Maori Marsden "God, Man and Universe: A Māori View" in Michael King (ed) *Te Ao Hurihuri Aspects of Māoritanga* (Reed Books, Auckland, 1992).

Gabrielle Maxwell and James Liu (eds) *Restorative Justice Practices in New Zealand: Towards a Restorative Society* (Institute of Policy Studies, Wellington, 2007).

Wanda McAuslin "Community Peacemaking" in W McAuslin *Justice as Healing Indigenous Ways; Writings on Community Peacemaking and Restorative Justice from the Native Law Centre* (Living Justice Press, St Paul (MN), 2005)

Wanda McAuslin (ed) *Justice as Healing Indigenous Ways: Writings on Community Peacemaking and Restorative Justice from the Native Law Centre* (Living Justice Press, St Paul (MI), 2005).

Rana McDonald *The Discord Between Policy and Practice: Defence Lawyers' Use of Section 718.2(e) and "Gladue"* (University of Manitoba, Winnipeg, Canada, 2008).

Morag McDowell and Duncan Webb *The New Zealand Legal System* (4th ed, , Wellington, 2006).

Fred W M McElrea "A New Model of Justice" in F W M McElrea and B J Brown (eds) *The Youth Court in New Zealand: Four Papers* (Legal Research Foundation, Auckland, 1993).

Paul McHugh *The Māori Magna Carta: New Zealand Law and the Treaty of Waitangi* (Oxford University Press, Oxford, 1991).

Paul McHugh *Aboriginal Societies and the Common Law: A History of Sovereignty, Status, and Self-Determination* (Oxford University Press, New York, 2004).

Brian McKenna, Sandy Simpson and John Coverdale "Implementing Civil Commitment: Doing With Not Doing To" in Warren Brookbanks and Sandy Simpson (eds) *Psychiatry and the Law* (, Wellington, 2007).

Brian McKenna and Kevin Seaton "Liaison Services to the Courts" in Warren Brookbanks and Sandy Simpson (eds) *Psychiatry and the Law* (, Wellington, 2007).

Hirini Mead *Tikanga Māori Living by Māori Values* (Huia Publishing, Wellington, 2003).

Hirini Moko Mead and Neil Grove *Ngā Pepeha a ngā Tīpuna* (VUP, Wellington, 2004).

Ani Mikaere "The Treaty of Waitangi and the Recognition of Tikanga Māori" in Michael Belgrave, Merata Kawharu and David Williams (eds) *Waitangi Revisited: Perspectives on the Treaty of Waitangi* (Oxford University Press, Melbourne, Australia, 2005).

Ani Mikaere "Collective Rights and Gender Issues: A Māori Women's Perspective" in Nin Tomas (ed) *Collective Human Rights of Pacific Peoples* (Indigenous Research Unit for Māori and Indigenous Education, University of Auckland, 2004).

Ani Mikaere *Colonising Myths Māori Realities He Rukuruku Wahaaro* (Huia Publishers, Wellington, 2011).

Cæcilie Mikkelsen (ed) *The Indigenous World 2013* (Eks-Skolens Trykkeri IWGIA, Copenhagen, 2013).

A Mills, K Thom, C Meehan, and M Chetty *Family Violence Courts: A Review of the Literature* (Centre for Mental Health Research, Auckland, 2013). <www.lawfoundation.org.nz>

Henry Minde "The Challenge of Indigenism: The Struggle for Sami Land Rights and Self-Government in Norway 1960–1990" in Svein Jentoft, Henry Minde and Ragnar Nilsen (eds) *Indigenous Peoples, Resource Management and Global Rights* (Eburon, Delft (Netherlands), 2003).

T Moeke Pickering *Māori Identity within the Whānau: A Review of Literature* (University of Waikato, Hamilton, 1996). <www.researchcommons.waikato.ac.nz>.

Anthony Morgan and Erin Louis *Evaluation of the Queensland Murri Court: Final Report* (Australian Institute of Criminology, Australian Government, Reports and Technical Background Paper39, 2010).

Mandy Morgan, Leigh Coombes and Sarah McGray *An Evaluation of the Waitakere Family Violence Court Protocols* (Massey University and WAVES, Palmerston North, May 2007).

Bronwyn Morrison, Natalie Soboleva and Jin Chong *Conviction and Sentencing Offenders in New Zealand: 1997–2006* (Ministry of Justice, Wellington, 2008).

Brad Morse "Regaining Recognition of the Inherent Right of Aboriginal Governance" in Yale Belanger (ed) *Aboriginal Self-Government in Canada: Current Trends and Issues* (Oxford University Press, Oxford, 2004).

Margaret Mutu *The State of Māori Rights* (Huia Publishers, Wellington, 2011).

Margaret Mutu "Constitutional Intentions: The Treaty of Waitangi Texts" in Malcolm Mulholland and Veronica Tawhai (eds) *Weeping Waters: The Treaty of Waitangi and Constitutional Change* (Huia Publishers, Wellington, 2010).

Greg Newbold *The Problem of Prisons: Corrections Reform in New Zealand Since 1840* (Dunmore Press, Wellington, 2007).

P O'Malley "The Influence of Cultural Factors on Māori Crime Rates" in S D Webb, and J Collette (eds) *New Zealand Society: Contemporary Perspectives* (John Wiley and Sons Australasia, Sydney, 1973).

Claudia Orange *The Treaty of Waitangi* (Allen & Unwin, Wellington, 1997).

Claudia Orange *Treaty of Waitangi* (Bridget Williams Books, Wellington, 2010)

Geoffrey W R Palmer *Constitutional Conversations* (Victoria University Press, Wellington, 2002).

Matthew S R Palmer *The Treaty of Waitangi in New Zealand's Law and Constitution* (Victoria University Press, Wellington, 2008).

Robert E Park, "Social Change and Social Disorganization" (1967) in Stuart H Traub and Craig B Little (eds) *Theories of Deviance* (F E Peacock Publishers, Itasca (IL), 1975).

John Paterson *Exploring Māori Values* (Dunmore Press, Palmerston North, 1992).

S Payne *Aboriginal Women and the Law* (Law and Justice Section Aboriginal and Torres Strait Islander Commission Canberra, 1993) <www.aic.gov.au>.

Amos J Peaslee *Constitutions of Nations Volume II France to New Zealand* (Brill Archive) (1956) Martinus Nijhoff, The Hague, Netherlands.

Rose Pere "To Us the Dreams are Important" in S Cox (ed) *Public and Private Worlds* (Allen & Unwin, Wellington, 1987).

Guy Powles and Mere Pulea (ed) *Pacific Courts and Legal System* (Institute of Pacific Studies University of South Pacific, Suva, 1988).

John Pratt "Assimilation, Equality, and Sovereignty in New Zealand/Aotearoa" in Paul Havemann (ed) *Indigenous Rights in Australia, Canada & New Zealand* (Oxford University Press, Auckland, 1999).

Alison Quentin-Baxter "The International and Constitutional Law Contexts" in Alison Quentin-Baxter (ed) *Recognising the Rights of Indigenous Peoples* (Institute of Policy Studies, Victoria University of Wellington, New Zealand 1998),John Rangihau "Being Māori" in Michael King (ed) *Te Ao Hurihuri: Aspects of Māoritanga* (Reed Books, Auckland, 1992).

Michael Rich *Census of Prison Inmates 1999* (Department of Corrections SAS Policy Development, Wellington, December2000).

Steve Richards *Homeless in Aotearoa: Issues and Recommendations Report for Regional Public Health* (Ministry of Health, Wellington, 2009) <www. http://nzceh.org.nz/>.

Elizabeth Richardson, Katey Thom and Brian McKenna "The Evolution of Problem-Solving Courts in New Zealand and Australia: A Trans-Tasman Comparative" in Richard Wiener and Eve Brank (eds) *Problem Solving Courts* (Springer, New York, 2013).

Justin Richland *Arguing with Tradition: The Language of Law in Hopi Tribal Court* (University of Chicago Press, Chicago, 2008).

Paul Rishworth "The New Zealand Bill of Rights" in Paul Rishworth, Grant Huscroft, Scott Optician and Richard Mahoney (eds) *The New Zealand Bill of Rights* (Oxford University Press, Auckland, 2003).

Ray Rivera "Our View: Boise Needs New Method to Stop Domestic Violence" in Bruce Winick and David Wexler (ed) *Judging in a Therapeutic Key, Therapeutic Jurisprudence and the Courts* (Carolina Academic Press, Durham (NC), 2003)

Geoffrey Robinson *Crimes Against Humanity* (3rd ed, Penguin, Melbourne, 2008).

SirClintonRoper *Report of the Ministerial Committee of Inquiry into Violence* (Ministry of Justice, Wellington, March 1987).

Royal Commission on Social Policy *The April Report: Volume II Future Directions* (Government Printer, Wellington, 1988).

Wilfrid E Rumble (ed) *The Province of Jurisprudence Determined (1832)* (Cambridge University Press, Cambridge, 1995).

Anne Salmond *The Trial of the Cannibal Dog: Captain Cook in the South Seas* (Penguin Books, Auckland, 2004).

Anne Salmond *Between Worlds: Early Exchanges between Māori and Europeans, 1773–1815* (Penguin Books, Auckland, 1997).

Terry Saunders "Re Entry Court" in Bruce J Winick and David Wexler (eds) *Judging in a Therapeutic Key* (Carolina Academic Press, Durham (NC), 2003).

Thorsten Sellin, "Culture Conflict and Crime" (1938) in Stuart H Traub and Craig B Little (eds) *Theories of Deviance* (F E Peacock Publishers, Itasca (IL), 1975).

Nan Seuffert *Jurisprudence of National Identity: Kaleidoscopes of Imperialism and Globalisation from Aotearoa New Zealand* (Ashgate, Aldershot (UK), 2006).

Alexander Simpson and others *The National Study of Psychiatric Morbidity in New Zealand Prisons: An Investigation of the Prevalence of Psychiatric Disorders Among New Zealand Inmates* (Department of Corrections, Wellington, 1999) <www.corrections.govt.nz>.

DrA I FSimpson and others *The National Study of Psychiatric Morbidity in New Zealand Prisons* (Department of Corrections, Ministry of Health and Ministry of Justice, Wellington, 1999) <www.corrections.govt.nz>.

JudgeN FSmith "Māori Land Court Jurisdiction and Procedure" in Richard Boast, Andrew Erueti, Doug McPhail and Norman F Smith (eds) *Māori Land Law* (2nd ed, , Wellington, 2004).

N Soboleva, N Kazakova and J Chong *Conviction and Sentencing of Offenders in New Zealand: 1996 to 2005* (Ministry of Justice, Wellington, 2006).

Maui Solomon "The Wai 262 Claim" in Michael Belgrave, Merata Kawharu and David Williams (eds) *Waitangi Revisited: Perspectives on the Treaty of Waitangi* (Oxford University Press, Melbourne, 2005).

P Spier *Conviction and Sentencing of Offenders in New Zealand: 1991 to 2000* (Ministry of Justice, Wellington, 2001).

Peter Spiller (ed) *A New Zealand Legal History* (2nd ed, Brookers, Wellington, 2001).

Peter Spiller *New Zealand Law Dictionary* (LexisNexis, Wellington, 2005).

Melanie Spiteri *Sentencing Circles for Aboriginal Offenders in Canada: Furthering the Idea of Aboriginal Justice within a Western Framework* (2008) <www.iirp.org>.

J Stewart *Specialist Domestic Violence Courts within the Australian Context* (Australia Domestic Violence Clearing House, Australia, 2008) Issues Paper 10. <www.austdvclearinghouse.unsw.edu.au>.

Dennis P Stolle and others "Integrating Preventive Law and Therapeutic Jurisprudence: A Law and Psychology Based Approach to Lawyering" in Dennis P Stolle, David B

Wexler and Bruce J Winick (eds) *Practicing Therapeutic Jurisprudence Law as a Helping Profession* (North Carolina Academic Press, Durham, 2000).

C Sumner (ed) *Crime Justice and Underdevelopment* (Heinemann, London, 1982).

Edwin H Sutherland, "The Theory of Differential Association" (1947), in Stuart H Traub and Craig B Little (eds) *Theories of Deviance* (F E Peacock Publishers, Itasca (IL), 1975).

Michael Taggart "Rugby, the Anti-Apartheid Movement and Administrative Law" in Rick Bigwood (ed) *Public Interest Litigation* (LexisNexis, Wellington, 2006).

Rees Tapsell "The Treatment and Rehabilitation of Māori" in Warren Brookbanks and Sandy Simpson (eds) *Psychiatry and the Law* (LexisNexis, Wellington, 2007).

Juan Tauri "Reforming Justice the Potential of Māori Processes" in Eugene McLaughlin and others (eds) *Restorative Justice Critical Issues* (Sage Publications, London, 2003).

K Thom, A Mills, C Meehan and B McKenna *Evaluating Problem-Solving Courts in New Zealand: A Synopsis Report* (Centre for Mental Health Research, Auckland, 2013).

W I Thomas and Florian Znaniecki "The Concept of Social Disorganization" (1920), in Stuart H Traub and Craig B Little (eds) *Theories of Deviance* (F E Peacock Publishers, Itasca (IL), 1975).

Samuel Timoti Robinson *Tohunga: The Revival Ancient Knowledge for the Modern Era* (Reed Publishing, Auckland, 2005).

Nin Tomas "Māori Concepts of Rangatiratanga, Kaitiakitanga the Environment and Property Rights" in David Grinlinton and Prue Taylor *Legal Aspects of Sustainable Development Property Rights and Sustainability The Evolution of Property Rights to Meet Ecological Challenges* (Martinus Nijhoff Publishers, The Hague, Netherlands, 2011).

James Tully "Indigenous Peoples and Freedom" in J Tully (ed) *Public Philosophy in a New Key* (Cambridge University Press, New York, 2008).

G B Vold *Theoretical Criminology* (Oxford University Press, New York, 1958).

Jeremy Waldron "The Cosmopolitan Alternative" in Will Kymlicka *The Rights of Minority Cultures* (Oxford University Press, New York, 1995).

Jeremy Waldron *Basic Equality* (Nellco Legal Scholarship Repository New York University Public Law and Legal Theory Working Papers 19 December2008).

Ranginui Walker *Ka Whawhai Tonu Matou – Struggle Without End* (Penguin, Auckland, 1990).

R Walter and T Bradley "Crime Statistics: 'Official' and 'Unofficial' Representations of Crime and Victimization" in R Walter and T Bradley (eds) *Introduction of Criminological Thought* (Pearson Longman, Auckland, 2005).

Alan Ward *A Show of Justice: Racial "Amalgamation" in Nineteenth Century New Zealand* (Auckland University Press, Auckland, 1995).

Gerald Waters *The Case for Alcohol and Other Drug Treatment Courts in New Zealand* (Auckland, 2011) <www.drugcourts.co.nz.

David Wexler and Bruce J Winick (eds) *Law in a Therapeutic Key* (Carolina Academic Press, Durham, 1996).

David Wexler and Bruce Winick *Rehabilitating Lawyers Principles of Therapeutic Jurisprudence for Criminal Law Practice* (Carolina Academic Press, Durham, 2008).

David Williams "Wi Parata is Dead, Long Live Wi Parata" in Andrew Erueti and Claire Charters (eds) *Māori Property Rights and the Foreshore and Seabed: The Last Frontier* (Victoria University Press, Wellington, 2007).

David V Williams *Te Kooti Tango Whenua: The Native Land Court 1864–1909* (Huia Publishers, Wellington, 1999).

H W Williams *A Dictionary of the Māori Language* (7th ed, Government Printer, Wellington, 1971).

Joe V Williams "Māori in New Zealand Law at the End of the Cooke Era – Where Have We Got To?" in Paul Rishworth (ed.) *The Struggle for Simplicity in Law: Essays for Lord Cooke of Thorndon* (Butterworths, Wellington, 1997).

Joe Williams *The Māori Land Court – A Separate Legal System?* (Occasional Paper4, The New Zealand Centre for Public Law, VUW, July2001).Robert Williams "Foreword" in Raymond Austin *Navajo Courts and the Navajo Common Law: A Tradition of Tribal Self-Governance* (University of Minnesota Press, Minneapolis, 2009).

RobertWilliamsJr *Savage Anxieties: The Invention of Western Civilisation* (Palgrave, New York, 2012)

Bruce Winick *Civil Commitment* (Carolina Academic Press, Durham, 2005)

Bruce Winick "The Jurisprudence of Therapeutic Jurisprudence" in Bruce Winick and David Wexler (eds) *Judging in a Therapeutic Key: Developments in Therapeutic Jurisprudence* (Carolina Academic Press, Durham, 1996).

Bruce J Winick and David Wexler "Practice Settings and Clinical Opportunities" in David Wexler (ed) *Rehabilitating Lawyers Principles of Therapeutic Jurisprudence for Criminal Law Practice* (Carolina Academic Press, Durham, 2008).

BruceWinick and David Wexler (eds) *Judging in a Therapeutic Key – Therapeutic Jurisprudence and the Courts* (Carolina Academic Press, Durham, 2003).

Iris Marion Young "Five Faces of Oppression" in Lisa Heldke and Peg O'Connor (ed) *Oppression, Privilege and Resistance* (McGraw Hill, Boston, 2004).

Iris Marion Young "Together in Difference: Transforming the Logic of Group Political Conflict" in Will Kymlikca *The Rights of Minority Cultures* (Oxford University Press, New York, 1995).

Journal articles

B Arrigo "The Ethics of Therapeutic Jurisprudence: A Critical and Theoretical Inquiry of Law, Psychology and Crime" (2004) 11(4) *Psychiatry, Psychology and Law*, 23.

K Auty and D Briggs "Koori Court Victoria: Magistrates Court (Koori Court) Act 2002" (2004) 8(1) *Law Text Culture Challenging Nation* 7. <www.ro.uow.edu.au>

Raymond D Austin "ADR and the Navajo Peacemaker Court" (1993) 32(2) *The Judges' Journal*, 47.

Natalie Baird "Administrative Law" [2010] *NZLJ*.

Hon JusticeDavidBaragwanath "The Evolution of Treaty Jurisprudence" (2007) 15 *Waikato Law Review*, 1.

Joanne Baxter and others "Ethnic Comparisons of the 12 Month Prevalence of Mental Disorders and Treatment Contact in Te Rau Hinengaro: the New Zealand Mental Health Survey" (2006) 40(1) *Aust N Z J Psychiatry*, 905.

Daniel J Becker and Maura D Corrigan "Moving Problem Solving Courts into the Mainstream" (2002) 39(1) Court Review, 4.

T Bennion "Ngati Hokopu ki Hokowhitu v Whakatane District Council" (2003) *Māori Law Review* July, 2.

Tom Bennion "Law and Order Maori and the Private Sector" (1996) *Māori Law Review*, 1.

Tom Bennion "Editorial" (2008) Māori Law Review, 6.

Greg Berman "Redefining Criminal Court: Problem-Solving and the Meaning of Justice" (2004) 41 *Am Crim L Rev*, 131.

John Braithwaite "Restorative Justice and Therapeutic Jurisprudence" (2000) 38(2) *CLB*, 244. Warren Brookbanks "Therapeutic Jurisprudence: Conceiving an Ethical

Framework" (2001) 8(3) *Jnl of Law and Medicine*, 328. Simone Bull "The Land of Murder, Cannibalism, and All Kinds of Atrocious Crimes? Māori and Crime in New Zealand 1853–1919" (2004) 44 *British Journal of Criminology*, 496.

Luke Birmingham "The Mental Health of Prisoners" (2003) 9(3) *Advances in Psychiatric Treatment*, 191.

P Boshier "Investing in Life: Meeting the Cost of Family Violence" (2011) *NZ Lawyer Extra*, 39.

David Carruthers "Restorative Justice: Lessons from the Past, Pointers for the Future" (2012) 20 *Waikato Law Review Taumauri*, 1.

Themla Chalifoux "A Need for Change: Cross-Cultural Sensitization of Lawyers" (1994) 32(4) *Alberta Law Review*, 762.

Claire Charters "Māori, Beware the Bill of Rights Act!" [2003] *NZLJ*, 401.

Claire Charters "BORA and Maori: The Fundamental Issues" [2003] *NZLJ*, 459. Claire Charters "Developments in Indigenous Peoples' Rights under International Law and Their Implications" (2005) 21 *NZULR*, 519.

Claire Charters "Do Māori Rights Racially Discriminate against Non-Māori?" (2009–2010) 40 *Victoria U Wellington L Rev*, 649.

Claire Charters "The Rights of Indigenous Peoples" October [2006] *NZLJ*, 335.

Larry Chartrand "Aboriginal Peoples and Mandatory Sentencing" (2001) 39(2/3) *Osgoode Law Journal*, 456. SirRobinCooke "Introduction" (1990) 14 *NZULR*, 1.

J E Cote "Reception of English Law" (1977) 25 *Alberta Law Review*, 29.

Marie Dannette "Māori and Criminal Offending: A Critical Appraisal" (2010) 43(2) *ANZ Jnl of Criminology*, 282.

Megan Davis "United Nations Reform and Indigenous Peoples" (2005) 6(14) *Indigenous Law Bulletin*.

Megan Davis "To Bind or not to Bind: The United Nations Declaration on the Rights of Indigenous Peoples Five Years On" (2012) 19 *Austl Int'l L J*, 17.

Myrna Dawson and Ronit Dinoitzer "Victim Cooperation and the Prosecution of Domestic Violence in a Specialised Court" (2001) 18(3) *Justice Quarterly* (September Issue), 593.

Matiu Dickson "The Rangatahi Court" [2011] 19 *Waikato Law Review*, 86.

Shaunnaugh Dorsett "R v E Hipu Supreme Court Wellington 1 December 1845" (2010) 41(1) *VUWLR*, 89.

Shaunnagh Dorsett "Sworn on the Dirt of Graves: Sovereignty, Jurisdiction and the Judicial Abrogation of Barbarous Customs in New Zealand in the 1840s" (2009) 30 *The Journal of Legal History*, 175.

L Duncan "Explanations for Polynesian Crime Rates in Auckland" (1971) *Recent Law*, October 1971.

Treasa Dunworth "Public International Law" [2000] *NZLR*, 217.

Eddie T Durie "Will the Settlers Settle? Cultural Conciliation and Law" (1996) 8 *Otago L Rev*, 449. Eddie Durie and Gordon Orr "The Role of the Waitangi Tribunal and the Development of a Bicultural Jurisprudence" (1990) 14 *NZULR*, 61.

Eric BElbogen, PhD and Sally C Johnson "The Intricate Link Between Violence and Mental Disorder Results From the National Epidemiologic Survey on Alcohol and Related Conditions" (2009) 66(2) *JAMA Psychiatry*.

Sian Elias "Equality Under Law" (2005) 13 *Waikato Law Review*, 1.

Karen Engle "On Fragile Architecture: The UN Declaration on the Rights of Indigenous Peoples in the Context of Human Rights" (2011) 22(1) *EJIL*, 141.

Richard Erickson "Mass Media, Crime, Law and Justice an Institutional Approach" (1991) 31(3) *Br J Criminol*, 219.

Andrew Erueti "The Demarcation of Indigenous Peoples' Traditional Lands: Comparing Domestic Principles Of Demarcation With Emerging Principles Of International Law" (2006) 23(3) *Arizona Journal of International and Comparative Law* Volume Fall 543.

Jeffrey Fagan and Sandra Wexler, "Family Origins of Violent Delinquents" (1987) 25(3) *Criminology*, 643.

Theodore N Ferdinand "The Methods of Delinquency Theory" (1987) 25(4) *Criminology*, 841.

D M Fergusson and M T Lunskey "Adolescent Resiliency to Family Adversity" (1996) 37(3) *Journal of Child Psychology and Psychiatry*, 281.

D M Ferguson, F Vitaro, L J Horwood and N Swain-Campbell "Ethnicity and Criminal Convictions: Results of a 21-Year Longitudinal Study" (2003) 36 *Australian and New Zealand Journal of Criminology*, 354.

Jacqueline Fitzgerald "Does Circle Sentencing Reduce Aboriginal Offending?" (2008) 115 *Crime and Justice Bulletin: Contemporary Issues in Crime and Justice.*

Augie Fleras "Māori Wardens and the Control of Liquor Among the Māori of New Zealand" (1981) 90(4) *Journal of the Polynesian Society*, 495.

J Forman "Why Care About Mass Incarceration?" (2010) 108 *Michigan Law Review* 1009.

Arie Freiberg "Problem-Oriented Courts: Innovative Solutions to Intractable Problems?" (2001) 11 *Journal of Judicial Administration*, 8.

Claudia Gieringer "International Law Through the Lens of Zaoui: Where is New Zealand At?" (2006) 17 *PLR*, 318.

Bruce V Harris "Law-Making Powers of the New Zealand General Assembly: Time to Think About Change" (1984) 5 *Otago LR*, 565.

Bruce V Harris "The Treaty of Waitangi and the Constitutional Future of New Zealand" [2005] 2 *NZLR*, 189.

Mark Harris "From Australian Courts to Aboriginal Courts in Australia – Bridging the Gap?" (2004) 16(1) *Current Issues in Criminal Justice*, 26.

Mark Harris "The Koori Court and the Promise of Therapeutic Jurisprudence" (2006) 1 *Murdoch University Electronic Journal of Law*, 129.

Max Harris "More on Mason Cultural Factors in Sentencing" (2013) *Māori Law Review*, Feb.

JudgeDavidHarvey "Social Media and the Judiciary" (2013) *NZL.*

HeathJ "Problems in Applying Māori Custom Law in a Unitary State" (2010 and 2011) *Yearbook of NZ Jurisprudence*, 199.

Morris B Hoffman "Therapeutic Jurisprudence, Neorehabilitationism, and Judicial Collectivism: The Least Dangerous Branch Becomes Most Dangerous" (2002) *Fordham Urban Law Journal*, 2063.

G Raumati Hook "Warrior Genes and the Disease of Being Māori" (2009) 2 *Mai Review.*
Mark Israel "Ethnic Bias in Jury Selection in Australia and New Zealand" (1998) 26 *International Journal of the Sociology of Law*, 35.

Phillip A Joseph and Gorder R Walker "A Theory of Constitutional Change" (1987) 7 *Oxford J Legal Stud*, 155.

Philip A Joseph "The Māori Seats in Parliament: A Study of Māori Economic and Social Progress" (Working Paper 2, New Zealand Business Roundtable, 2008).

Robert Joseph "Re-Creating Legal Space for the First Law of Aotearoa, New Zealand" (2009) 17 *Waikato Law Review*, 74.

Robert Joseph "Colonial Biculturalism? The Recognition & Denial of Māori Custom in the Colonial & Post-Colonial Legal System of Aotearoa/New Zealand" (paper prepared for Te Mātāhauariki Research Institute, University of Waikato FRST Project, 1998).

Robert Joseph "Historical Bicultural Developments: The Recognition and Denial of Māori Custom in the Colonial Legal System of Aotearoa/New Zealand" (LIANZ: Te Matahauriki Research Unit, Hamilton, 1998).

Robert Joseph, "Re-creating Legal Space for the First Law of Aotearoa-New Zealand" (2009) 17 *Waikato Law Review: Taumauri*, 74.

Sir Kenneth Keith "Roles of the Courts in New Zealand in Giving Effect to International Human Rights – With Some History" (1999) 29 *VUWLR*, 27.

"Major Project to Simplify Criminal Procedure" (5 May 2008) 707 *Law Talk*, 1.

Michael King "Geraldton Alternative Sentencing Regime: Applying Therapeutic and Holistic Jurisprudence in the Bush" (Oct 2002) 26(5) *Crim LJ*, 260.

Michael King "Applying Therapeutic Jurisprudence in Regional Areas in the Western Australian Experience" (2003) 10 *Murdoch University Electronic Journal of Law*, 2.

Michael King and Steve Ford "Exploring the Concept of Wellbeing in Therapeutic Jurisprudence: The Example of the Geraldton Alternative Sentencing Regime" (2006) 1 *ELJ*.

Michael King "Applying Therapeutic Jurisprudence from the Bench, Challenges and Opportunities" (2003) *Alternative Law Journal*, 172. <www.austlii.edu.au/au/journals>

Tahu Kukutai "The Problem of Defining an Ethnic Group for Public Policy: Who is Māori and Why Does it Matter?" (2004) 23 *Social Policy Journal*, December 2004

Carol La Prairie and Julian Roberts "Sentencing Circles: Some Unanswered Questions" (1996) 39 *Criminal Law Quarterly*, 69.

Carol La Prairie "The Impact of Aboriginal Justice Research on Policy: A Marginal Past and an Uncertain Future" (1999) 41(2) *Canadian Journal of Criminology*, 249.

Carol La Prairie "Aboriginal Over Representation in the Criminal Justice System" (2002) April *Canadian Journal of Criminology*, 181.

Rod Lea and Geoffrey Chambers "Monoamine Oxidase, Addiction, and the 'Warrior' Gene Hypothesis" (2007) 120 *Jnl of the NZ Med Assoc*, 1250.

Catriona MacLennan "Judge Says Domestic Violence Court Process a 'Masquerade'" (2004) 18 *Auckland District Law Society*. <www.adls.org.nz>.

Elena Marchetti and Kathleen Daly "Indigenous Courts and Justice Practices in Australia: Trends and Issues" (2004) 277 *Crime and Criminal Justice*.

Elena Marchetti and Kathleen Daly "Indigenous Sentencing Courts: Towards a Theoretical and Jurisprudential Model" (2007) 29(3) *Sydney Law Review*, 415.

Shadd Maruna and Thomas P LeBel "Welcome Home? Examining the 'Reentry Court' Concept from a Strengths Based Perspective" (2003) 4(2) *Western Criminology Review*, 91.

K Maynard, B Coebergh, B Anstiss, L Bakker and T Huriwai "Ki te arotu: Toward a New Assessment: The Identification of Cultural Factors Which may Predispose Māori to Crime" (1999) 13 *Social Policy Journal of New Zealand*, 43.

Paul Mazerolle "The Poverty of a Gender Neutral Criminology: Introduction to the Special Issue on Current Approaches to Understanding Female Offending" (2008) 41(1) *ANZ Journal of Criminology*, 1.

Bridget McAsey "Critical Evaluation of the Koori Court Division of the Victorian Magistrates' Court" (2005) 10(2) *Deakin Law Review*, 654.

Jeremy McGuire "The Status and Functions of the Māori Land Court" (1993–1996) 8 *Otago L Rev*, 125.

Paul McHugh "Court Structure" Editorial (August 2001) *NZLJ*, 261.

Luke McNamara "The Locus of Decision Making Authority in Circle Sentencing: The Significance of Criteria and Guidelines" (2000) 18 *Windsor Yearbook of Access to Justice*, 60.

Sally Engle Merry "Legal Pluralism" (1988) 22 *Law and Society Rev*, 869.

Ani Mikaere "Māori Women Caught in the Contradictions of a Colonized Reality" (1994) 2 *Waikato Law Review*, 125.

Ani Mikaere "Tikanga as the First Law of Aotearoa" (2007) 10 *Yearbook of NZJ*, 24.

Robert Miller "The Continuum of Coercion: Constitutional and Clinical Considerations in the Treatment of Mentally Disordered Persons" (1997) 74(4) *Denver University Law Review*, 1169.

Robert Miller and Jacinta Ruru "An Indigenous Lens into Comparative Law: The Doctrine of Discovery in the United States and New Zealand" (2009) 111 *West Virginia L Rev*, 849.

JudgeStephanieMilroy "Nga Tikanga Māori and the Courts" (2007) 10 *Yearbook of NZJ*, 15.

David Milward and Debra Parkes "Gladue: Beyond Myth and Towards Implementation in Manitoba" (2011) 35(1) *Man LJ*, 84.

Frank Neill "Restorative Justice: Chance to Help Clients Turn Their Lives Around" (November 2013) 831 *Law Talk*, 8.

J M R Owens "Christianity and the Māori to 1840" (1968) 2(1) *NZJH*, 18. <www.nzjh. auckland.ac.nz>.

M O'Brien "What is Cultural about Cultural Criminology?" (2005) 45 *British Journal of Criminology*, 599.

Ken A Palmer "Law, Land and Māori Issues" (1988) 3 *Canterbury Law Review*, 322.

Geoffrey Palmer "A Bill of Rights for New Zealand: A White Paper" (1985) 1 *AJHR*, A6.

Caslav Pejovic "Civil Law and Common Law Two Different Paths Leading to the Same Goal" (2001) 32 *VUWLR*, 817.

Joseph Raz "Legal Principles and the Limits of Law" (1972) 81 *Yale LJ*, 838.

Paul Rishworth "Human Rights" [2003] *NZLR*, 261.

K Roach and J Rudin "Gladue: The Judicial and Political Reception of a Promising Decision" (2000) 42 (July) *Canadian Journal of Criminology*, 355.

M Robinson "The Sealord Fishing Settlement an International Perspective" (1992) 7 *AULR*, 557.

Nicole Roughan "The Association of State and Indigenous Law: A Case Study in 'Legal Association'" (2009) 59 *UTLJ*, 135.

Kathryn Sammon "Therapeutic Jurisprudence: An Examination of Problem Solving Justice in New York" (2008) 23(3) *Journal of Civil Rights and Economic Development*.

William Schma "Judging for the New Millennium" (2000) 37(1) *Court Review*, 4.

Sandy Simpson "A Strategy that Works – Mental Health Courts" (2008) 35 *Recap Newsletter: Re Thinking Crime and Punishment in New Zealand*. <www.rethinking.org.nz>.

Christopher Slobogin "Therapeutic Jurisprudence: Five Dilemmas to Ponder" (1995) 1 *Psychol, Pol and Law*, 193.

Paul Spuhan "Legal History of Blood Quantum in Federal Indian Law to 1935" (2006) 51 *S D L Rev*, 1.

Rodney Stark "Deviant Places: A Theory of the Ecology of Crime" (1987) 25(4) *Criminology*, 893.

Mamari Stephens "Māori Law and Hart: A Brief Analysis" (2001) 32 *VUWLR*, 861.

Juan Tauri "Family Group Conferencing: A Case Study of the Indigenisation of New Zealand's Justice System" (1998) 10 *CICJ*, 168.

Juan Tauri and R Webb "A Critical Appraisal of Responses to Māori Offending" (2012) 3(4) *The International Indigenous Policy Journal*.

E W Thomas "The Treaty of Waitangi: E. W. Thomas Reviews Matthew Palmer's Book" [2009] *NZLJ*, 277.

Marc Simon Thomas "Legal Pluralism and the Continuing Quest for Legal Certainty in Ecuador: A Case Study from the Andean Highlands" (2012) 7 *Onati Socio-Legal Series*, 57.

Yvette Tinsley and Elisabeth McDonald "Is There Any Other Way? Possible Alternatives to the Current Criminal Justice Process" (2011) 17 *Canterbury Law Review*, 204.

Kiri Toki "What a Difference a Drip Makes: The Implications of Officially Endorsing the United Nations Declaration on the Rights of Indigenous Peoples" (2010) 16 *Auckland UL Rev*, 243.

Valmaine Toki "Are Domestic Violence Courts Working for Indigenous Peoples?" (2009) 35(2) *Commonwealth Law Bulletin*, 255.

Valmaine Toki "Therapeutic Jurisprudence and Mental Health Courts for Māori" (2010) 33 *International Journal of Law and Psychiatry*, 440.

Valmaine Toki "Indigenous Rights – Hollow Rights?" [2011] 19 *Waikato Law Review*, 29.

Valmaine Toki "Are Parole Boards Working or is it Time for an Indigenous Re Entry Court?" (2011) 39 *International Journal of Law, Crime and Justice*, 230.

Valmaine Toki "A Breath of Fresh, or Recycled Air – R v Mason" *NZLJ* (December2012).

Nin Tomas "Indigenous Peoples and the Māori: The Right to Self-Determination in International Law – From Woe to Go" (2008) *NZL Rev*, 639.

Nin Tomas "Tangata Whenua Issues: Implementing Kaitiakitanga under the RMA" (1994) July *New Zealand Environmental Reporter*, 39.

Andrea Tunks "Pushing the Sovereign Boundaries in Aotearoa" (1999) 4(23) *Indigenous Law Bulletin*, 15.

Arnu Turvey "Te Ao Māori in a Sympathetic Legal Regime: The Use of Māori Concepts in Legislation" (2009–2010) 40 *Victoria U Wellington L Rev*, 531.

William Tyler "Aboriginal Criminology and the Postmodern Condition: From Anomie to Anomaly" (1999) 32(2) *Australian & New Zealand Journal of Criminology*, 209.

Rod Vaughan "Judicial Makeover Opens More Doors to Wannabe Judges" *ADLSI* 6 September 2013 <http://www.adls.org.nz>

Stephanie Vieille "Māori Customary Law: A Relational Approach to Justice" (2012) 3 *The International Indigenous Policy Journal*.

Jeremy Waldron "One Law for All? The Logic of Cultural Accommodation" (2002) 59(1) *Wash & Lee L Rev*, 3.

Catherine Walsh "The Plurinational and Intercultural State: De-Colonisation and State Re-Founding in Ecuador" (2009) 6 *Kult*, 65.

Damen Ward "A Means and Measure of Civilisation: Colonial Authorities and Indigenous Law in Australasia" (2003) 1 *History Compass*, AU 049.

Hilary N Weaver "Indigenous Identity: What Is It and Who Really Has It?" (2001) 25(2) *The American Indian Quarterly*, 240.

David B Wexler "Therapeutic Jurisprudence: An Overview" (2000) 17 *TM Cooley Review*, 131.

David Wexler "An Orientation to Therapeutic Jurisprudence" (1994) 20 *New Eng J on Crime and Civil Confinement*, 259.

David B Wexler "Robes and Rehabilitation: How Judges can Help Offenders Make Good" (2001) 38(1) *Court Review*, 18.

D Wexler "Spain's JVP Legal Structure as a Potential Model for a Re-Entry Court" (2003) 7(1) *Contemporary Issues in Law*, 1.

David V Williams "Indigenous Customary Rights and the Constitution of Aotearoa New Zealand" (2006) 14 *Waikato Law Review*, 106.

David V Williams "The Foundation of Colonial Rule in New Zealand" (1988) 13 *NZULR*, 54.

David V Williams "*Queen v Symonds* Reconsidered" (1989) 19 *Victoria U Wellington Law Review*, 385.

Bruce J Winick "Therapeutic Jurisprudence and Victims of Crime" (7 March 2008) Social Science Research Network <www.ssrn.com>.

Bruce Winick "The Jurisprudence of Therapeutic Jurisprudence" (1997) 3(1) *Psychology, Public Policy and Law*, 184.

Fiona Wright "Law, Religion and Tikanga Māori" (2007) 5 *NZJPIL*, 261.

Unpublished

Jim Cameron "Plural Justice, Equality and Sovereignty in New Zealand" (unpublished paper for the Law Commission, 22 October 1997).

Stephanie Milroy "Domestic Violence: Legal Representation of Māori Women" (unpublished paper 1994).

ProfessorBradMorse Technical Report "Indigenous Provisions in Constitutions Around the World" (University of Waikato, unpublished, 2012).

Kelly Russ "Modern Human Rights: The Aboriginal Challenge" (LLM unpublished thesis, The University of British Columbia, April 2006).

Distinguished Professor DameAnneSalmond's "Brief of Evidence for the Waitangi Tribunal Wai 1040" (dated 17 April 2010, unpublished).

JudgeHeemiTaumaunu "Te Kooti Rangatahi o Hoani Waititi Ka pu te ruha, ka hao te rangatahi!" (unpublished, 2010).

Parliament and Government Materials and Reports

Australia

Aboriginal and Torres Strait Islander Social Justice Commissioner *Submission to the Northern Territory Law Reform Committee Inquiry into the Recognition of Aboriginal Customary Law* (Human Rights Equal Opportunity Commission, Sydney, 2003) <http://www.humanrights.gov. au/legal>.

Australian Government *Family Violence – A National Legal Response* (ALRC Report 114, 2010) <www.alrc.gov.au>.

Australia Law Reform Commission *Recognition of Aboriginal Laws* (ALRC Report 31, 2006)

CJR Information paper *Juxtaposition Between Sentence Severity and Therapeutic Jurisprudence* (2003) <www.cjrn.unsw.edu.au>.

Department of Justice Victoria *Overview of the Koori Court* (2006).

Department of Justice Victoria *Koori Court – A Defendant's Guide* (2008).

Human Rights and Equal Opportunity Commission *Face the Facts* (2005). <http://www. hreoc.gov.au>.

Law and Justice Fact Sheet (2010) <www.reconciliaction.org.au>.

Law Reform Commission of Western Australia *Court Intervention Programs: Consultation Paper* <http://www.lrc.justice.wa.gov.au>.

Magistrates' Court of Victoria *Annual Report 2012/13*.

Royal Commission *Report on Aboriginal Deaths in Custody Final Report* (1991) <www.austlii. edu.au>.

Sentencing Council of Australia *Report Sentencing in the Koori Court Division of the Magistrates' Court* (2010).

Victoria, Parliamentary Debates, Legislative Council, 29 May 2002, 1282 (Justin Madden)
Victoria, Parliamentary Debates, Legislative Assembly, 24 April 2002, 1129 (Rob Hulls)
Western Australian Law Reform Commission *Aboriginal Customary Laws* (Discussion Paper, Report No 94, 2005).

Canada

Human Rights Watch *Those Who Take Us Away: Policing and Failures in Protection of Indigenous Women and Girls in Northern British Columbia, Canada* (Human Rights Watch, Canada, 2013) <https://www.hrw.org/report/>
Office of the Correctional Investigator *Backgrounder: Aboriginal Offenders a Critical Situation* (2012) <www.oci-bec.gc.ca>.
Royal Commission on Aboriginal Peoples *Bridging the Cultural Divide: Aboriginal People and Criminal Justice in Canada* (Canada Communications Group, Ottawa1996)

International material

James Anaya *Report of the Special Rapporteur on the Rights of Indigenous Peoples: The Situation of Māori People in New Zealand* (2011) (A/HRC/18/XX/Add.Y).
James Anaya *The Situation of Indigenous Peoples in Canada* (2014) A/HRC/27/52/Add.2.
Eva Biaudet, Megan Davis, Mirna Cunningham and Valmaine Toki *Study on the Extent of Violence Against Indigenous Women and Girls in Terms of Article 22 (2) of the UNDRIP* (2013) Report, E/C.19/2013/9.
Megan Davis, Simon William M'Viboudoulou, Valmaine Toki, Paul Kanyinke Sena, Edward John, Álvaro Esteban Pop Ac and Raja Devasish Roy *Study on National Constitutions and the United Nations Declaration on the Rights of Indigenous Peoples* (2013) E/C.19/2013/18.
International Law Association *The Hague Conference (2010): Rights of Indigenous Peoples* Interim report.
Jim McLay statement to the Third Committee, 68th session of the United Nations General Assembly under Item 66: Rights of Indigenous Peoples 21 October 2013 (GA/SHC/4074).
Office of the High Commission of Human Rights UN Human Rights Committee: *Concluding Observations, Canada* (CCPR/C/CAN/CO/5) (2006) at [23] <www.pch.gc.ca>.
Statement of the United Nations Special Rapporteur on the Situation of the Human rights and Fundamental Freedoms of Indigenous Peoples, Professor James Anaya, upon conclusion of his visit to New Zealand, 22 July 2010 <www.ohchr.org>.
Study by the Expert Mechanism on the Rights of Indigenous Peoples *Access to justice in the promotion of indigenous peoples, restorative justice, indigenous juridical systems and access to justice for indigenous women, children and youth, and persons with disabilities* A/HRC/27/65 August 2014
Rudolpho Stavenhagen *Mission to New Zealand in United Nations Economic and Social Council, Commission on Human Rights, Indigenous Issues* (62nd session, item 15) 13 March 2006 para 85.
Special Rapporteur, Mr. José Martínez Cobo *Study of the Problem of Discrimination Against Indigenous Populations*. Final report submitted by the Introduction 30 July 1981E/CN.4/Sub.2/476 10 August 1982E/CN.4/Sub.2/1982/2, 5 August 1983E/CN.4/Sub.2/1983/21
United Nations Committee on the Elimination of Racial Discrimination: *Decision on Foreshore and Seabed Act 2004* Sixty Sixth session Decision 1 (66): New Zealand CERD/C/DEC/NZL/1.

United Nations CERD Report CERD/C/CO/18 25 May 2007 Seventieth Session 19 February–9 March 2007

United Nations Declaration on the Rights of Indigenous Peoples, GA Res 295 UN GAOR, 61st sess, 107th plen mtg, UN Doc A/Res/295 (2007).

United Nations Doc CCPR/C/21/Rev.1/Add.10 (2000); and the Convention on the Elimination of All Forms of Discrimination Against 864.

United Nations General Assembly Resolution 61/295 of 13 September 2007

United Nations High Commissioner for Human Rights "Report of the United Nations High Commissioner for Human Rights on the Activities of Her office in the Plurinational State of Bolivia" (2010) United Nations Human Rights Council A/HRC/13/26/Add.2 18 at [4] <http://daccess-dds-ny.un.org>.

United Nations Human Rights Committee, General Comment 28: Equality of Rights Between Men and Women (Article 3), 68th sess,

United Nations Permanent Forum on Indigenous Issues/2004/WS.1/3 – (New York, 19–21 January 2004).

United Nations Permanent Forum on Indigenous Issues Report 10th session (2011) E/2011/43-E/C.19/2011/14.

United Nations Report from Committee Against Torture '*Concluding observations on the sixth periodic report of New Zealand*' <https://www.hrc.co.nz/files/2814/3192/5666/CAT_Report_May_2015.pdf>

Sha Zukang "*State World's Indigenous Peoples*" ST/ESA/328 (Department of Economic and Social Affairs, Division for Social Policy and Development, United Nations, New York, 2009)

Other

Law and Justice Sectoral Objectives – No 11. Formulated in consultation with the law and justice agencies across the Fiji Islands in conjunction with the Australia Fiji Law and Justice Sector Program.

"Nábináhaazláago" Initiative Services to Youth in Detention <http://www.navajocourts.org/Nabinahazlaago%20Files/Nabinahaazlaago.html>

Decision on Motions for Disqualification of Judge Silvia Cartwright [2012] Extraordinary Chambers in the Courts of Cambodia (ECCC) (Extraordinary Chambers in the Courts of Cambodia – Supreme Court Chambers) at [24].

New Zealand

New Zealand Law Commission Reports

New Zealand Law Commission *Justice: The Experience of Māori Women* (NZLC R53, 1999).

New Zealand Law Commission *Māori Custom and Values in New Zealand Law* (NZLC SP9, Wellington, 2001)

New Zealand Law Commission *Seeking Solutions Options for Change to the New Zealand Court System* (NZLC, Preliminary Paper 52, Wellington, December 2002).

New Zealand Law Commission *Converging Currents Customs and Human Rights in the Pacific* (NZLC, SP 17, September 2006).

New Zealand Law Commission *Burial in New Zealand Today* (NZLC IP34).

Hon Peter Salmon, Dame Margaret Bazley and David Shand *Royal Commission Report on Auckland Governance* (March 2009).

Royal Commission *The Electoral System: Towards a Better Democracy* (1986).

New Zealand 1990 Commission *The Treaty of Waitangi: The Symbol of our Life Together as a Nation* (Wellington, NZ, 1989).

Parliament material

Hansard Sitting date: 04 October 2011. Volume: 676; Page: 21637.

House of Representatives *Inquiry to Review New Zealand's Existing Constitutional Arrangements* Report to the Constitutional Arrangements Committee forty seventh Parliament (August 2005) <http://www.parliament.nz/>

Human Rights Commission *Submission to the Justice and Electoral Select Committee on the Victims' Rights Bill*, 6 March 2001 <www.hrc.co.nz>.

Second Reading of the NZ Bill of Rights Bill 14 August 1985 <www.justice.govt.nz>.

Government department reports

Auditor General's report *Mental Health Services for Prisoners* (2008) <http://www.oag.govt.nz/>

Cabinet Social Policy Committee *Drivers of Crime Progress Report* (December 2012).

Courts Consultative Committee *Report of the Courts Consultative Committee on He Whaipanga Hou* (Wellington, Department of Justice, 1991).

Department of Corrections *Māori Focus Units* (2009) <www.corrections.govt.nz>.

Department of Corrections *Judges Update Information for the Judiciary* (Issue 3, 2001) <www.corrections.govt.nz>.

Department of Corrections *Over-Representation of Māori in the Criminal Justice System: An Exploratory Report* (September 2007).

Department of Corrections *Trends in the Offender Population* (2013). <http://corrections.govt.nz>

Department of Corrections *Underpinning the Department's Five-Year Strategic Business Plan is the Recognition that "To Succeed Overall We Must Succeed for Māori Offenders"* (2010) <www.corrections.govt.nz>.

Department of Corrections *Report on Tikanga Māori Programmes* (2010) <www.corrections.govt.nz>.

Department of Corrections *Tikanga based programmes share in a budget $100 million* (2009) <www.corrections.govt.nz>.

Department of Corrections *Whare Oranga Ake* (2011) <www.corrections.govt.nz>.

Department of Corrections *Māori Focus Leads to Positive Gain* (2010) <www.corrections.govt.nz>.

Department of Corrections *Men's Prison at Wiri: Facts and Factsheets* (2014) <www.corrections.govt.nz>.

Department of Corrections *McDonald (1987), Lovell and Norris (1990), Gronfors (1973), Neill (1983) studies* <http://www.justice.govt.nz/publications/global-publications/s/sentencing-policy-and-guidance-a-discussion-paper/10.-a-maori-view-of-sentencing>

Department of Corrections *Over-representation of Māori in the Criminal Justice System – An Exploratory Report* (Policy, Strategy and Research Group, Wellington, September 2007).

Department of CorrectionsMarianne Bevan and Nan Wehipeihana *Women's Experiences of Reoffending and Rehabilitation* (November 2015) http://www.corrections.govt.nz/resources/research_and_statistics/womens_experiences_of_re-offending_and_rehabilitation.html

Department of Statistics *Ethnic Diversity of Women* (2010) <www.stats.govt.nz>.

Ministerial Advisory Committee *Report on a Māori perspective for the Department of Social Welfare* (Wellington, 1988) <www.msd.govt.nz>.

Ministry for the Environment *Case Law on Tangata Whenua Consultation* (Wellington, 1999).

Ministry of Health *Services for People with Mental Illness in the Justice System: Framework for Forensic Mental Health Services* (2001) <www.moh.govt.nz>.

Ministry of Health *The Health of New Zealand Adults 2011/12* <www.health.govt.nz>.

Ministry of Health *Whakatākata Tuarua: Māori Health Action Plan 2006–2011* (Wellington, 2006) <www.health.govt.nz >

Ministry of Justice *Trends in the Use of Bail and Offending While on Bail: 1990–1999* (Research and Evaluation Unit, January 2003) <http://www.justice.govt.nz>

Ministry of Justice *Publications and Reports* (2004) <www.justice.govt.nz>.

Ministry of Justice *Evaluation of the Early Outcomes of Nga Kooti Rangatahi.* (Ministry of Justice, Wellington, 2012).

Ministry of Justice *Constitutional Advisory Panel New Zealand's Constitution: A Report on a Conversation* (He Kōtuinga Kōrero Mōte Kaupapa Ture o Aotearoa, Wellington, November 2013).

Ministry of Justice *Reoffending Analysis for Restorative Justice Cases 2008–2011* (April 2014) <www.justice.govt.nz>.

Ministry of Justice *The Family Group Conference in Youth Justice* (2014) <www.justice.govt.nz.>

Ministry of Justice *Restorative Justice* (2014) <www.justice.govt.nz >.

Ministry of Justice *Responses to Crime: Annual Review* (November 1999).

Ministry of Justice *Over-representation of Māori in Prison* (2013).

Ministry of Justice *Trends in the Use of Bail and Offending while on Bail 1990–1999* (Research and Evaluation Unit January 2003) <http://www.justice.govt.nz>

Ministry of Justice *Rangatahi Court: Evaluation of the Early Outcomes of Te Kooti Rangatahi* (Ministry of Justice, Wellington, 17 December, 2012)

Ministry of Justice *Māori Over-representation in the Criminal Justice System Strategic Policy Brief* (2009) March. <www.justice.govt.nz>

Ministry of Justice *Responses to Offending by Māori and Pacific Peoples* (1999) <www.justice.govt.nz>.

Ministry of Justice *Conviction and Sentencing of Offenders in New Zealand 1996–2005* (Wellington, 2006) <www.justice.govt.nz>.

New Zealand Police *Protection Orders and the Domestic Violence Act* <http://www.police.govt.nz>.

Statistics New Zealand *Review of Crime and Criminal Justice Statistics Report* (2009). Wellington <www.statistics.govt.nz>

Te Puni Kokiri *Rangahau Tukino Whānau Māori Research Agenda on Family Violence* (2008) <www.tpk.govt.nz>.

Te Puni Kokiri *Māori Wardens Options for Change* (2013) <www.tpk.govt.nz>.

Te Puni Kokiri *Addressing the Drivers of Crime for Māori* (Working Paper 014–2011, July 2011) <www.tpk.govt.nz>.

Women's Refuge *New Zealand Domestic Violence Statistics.* <https://womensrefuge.org.nz>

Youth Court of New Zealand *Family Group Conferences* <www.justice.govt.nz >.

Waitangi reports

He Tirohanga o Kawa ki te Tiriti o Waitangi (Te Puni Kokiri, Wellington, 2001).

Waitangi Tribunal, *Orakei Report* (Wai 9, 1987).

Waitangi Tribunal, *Muriwhenua Report* (Wai 45).

Waitangi Tribunal, *Taranaki Kaupapa Tuatahi Report* (Wai 143, 1996).

Waitangi Tribunal, *The Whanganui River Report* (Wai 167, 1999).

Waitangi Tribunal, *Contemporary Aspects of the Napier Hospital and Health Services Report* (Wai 692).

Waitangi Tribunal, *The Petroleum Report* (Wai 796, 2003).

Te Paparahi o te Raki Waitangi Tribunal Report, (Wai 1040, 2014).

Waitangi Tribunal, *The Interim Report on the National Freshwater and Geothermal Resources Claim* (Wai 2358, 2012).

Conferences and conference/seminar presentations

S James Anaya "Why There Should not have to be a Declaration on the Rights of Indigenous Peoples" 52nd International Congress of AmericanistsSevilla, Summer 2006.

David Baragwanath "Good Faith Symposium" New Zealand Māori Council v Attorney-General [1987] 1 NZLR 687 A Perspective of Counsel "In Good Faith" (Symposium, University of Otago, Dunedin, 29 June 2007).

Judge Becroft "What Causes Youth Crime and What Can We Do?" (paper presented to NZ Bluelight Ventures Inc – Conference and AGM, Queenstown, 7 May 2009) <http://www.justice.govt.nz>.

Judge Becroft "Signed, Sealed (but not yet fully) Delivered" at the Judges at the Healing Courts and Plans People, International Therapeutic Jurisprudence Conference (October 9–10, First Nations Long House, Vancouver, British Columbia, Canada).

Don Brash, National Party Leader "One Law" (Orewa Rotary Club, Auckland, 7.30pm January 27, 2004).

Warren Brookbanks "Making the Case for a Mental Health Court in New Zealand" (Paper present to 3rd International Conference on Therapeutic Jurisprudence, 7–9 June 2006, Perth, Western Australia).

Warren Brookbanks "Therapeutic Jurisprudence: Implications for Judging" (paper presented at the District Court Judge's Triennial Conference, Rotorua, 1 April 2003).

Ramy Bulan Associate Professor Director, Centre for Malaysian Indigenous Studies "Indigenous Peoples and the Right to Participate in Decision Making in Malaysia" (Discussion paper prepared for International Expert Seminar on Indigenous Peoples and The Right to Participate in Decision Making, Chiang Mai, Thailand, 20–22 January 2010).

Mark Burton, Minister of Justice "The Effective Interventions Initiatives and the High Number of Māori in the Criminal Justice System" (paper presented to Ngakia Kia Puawai, New Zealand Police Management Development Conference, November 2006).

Judge David Carruthers "Community Involvement in Treatment of Offenders Prior to Sentencing: The New Zealand Experience" (paper presented to UNAFEI 147th International Training Conference, Japan, 13 January–10 February 2010) <www.unafei.or.jp/english>.

Paul Chartrand "Canada and Aboriginal Peoples: Recognition and other Constitutional and Legal Challenges" (Paper presented at a Staff Seminar, Faculty of Law, University of Auckland, 28 March 2008).

Giselle Corradi "The Right to a Fair Trial in Legally Plural Jurisdictions: the case of Bolivia' (presentation at Human Rights and Legal Pluralism in Theory and Practice Conference 5–6 December 2014, Norwegian Centre for Human Rights (NCHR) in co-operation with the Rights, Individuals, Culture and Society Research Centre (RICS) at the Faculty of Law, University of Oslo).

Conference on Indigenous Sustainability: Implications for the Future of Indigenous People and Native Nations (Arizona State University5–7 October, 2014). http://www.sasklawcourts.ca/default.asp?pg=pc_div_cree_court for full discussion of Cree Courts).

JudgeLexdeJong "Family Violence Court Forum" (Paper presented to an Auckland District Law Seminar, Building, 9 April 2008, Auckland).

Eddie Taihakurei Durie "Address on the Declaration" (Statement given May 2010. Parliament Buildings, Wellington, New Zealand).

Arturo Escobar "Latin America at a Crossroads: Alternative Modernizations, Post-Liberalism, or Post-Development?" (Revised version of paper prepared for the Wayne Morse Center for Law and Politics and presented at the Conference "Violence and Reconciliation in Latin America: Human Rights, Memory, and Democracy"University of Oregon, Eugene, January 31–February 2 2008).

Anne Griffiths "Pluralism" (presentation to Human Rights and Legal Pluralism in Theory and Practice Conference 5–6 December 2014, Norwegian Centre for Human Rights (NCHR) in co-operation with the Rights, Individuals, Culture and Society Research Centre (RICS) at the Faculty of Law, University of Oslo).

HonLaliaHarre Minister of Women's Affairs speech "Māori Women: Mapping Inequalities and Pointing Ways Forward" (Report released September 26, 2001) <www.executive. govt.nz>.

Healing Courts and Plans People, International Therapeutic Jurisprudence Conference October 9–10, First Nations Long House, Vancouver, British Columbia.

Hon. Peggy Fulton Hora Judge of the Superior Court of California (Ret.) "Adult Alcohol and Other Drug Treatment Courts: Will They Work in New Zealand?" (Seminar given at University of Auckland, School of Law, 28 April 2011).

International Expert Seminar on Access to Justice including Truth and Reconciliation Processes (University of Columbia, New York, 27 February–1 March 2013).

Dr Peter Johnston "The NZ Department of Corrections Role and Purpose in the Criminal Justice Pipeline" (presentation to the Auckland Law Faculty, University of Auckland, Part 2 Criminal Law students October 2014).

Te Kani Kingi "The Treaty of Waitangi and Māori Health" (Te Mata o Te Tau Lecture Series, Massey University, New Zealand, 2 March 2006).

Hon Wayne Martin CJ "The Magistrates of Western Australia Annual Conference 2006" (paper presented at Annual Conference, 8 November 2006) <www.supremecourt.wa. gov.au>.

JudgeDavidMather "The Waitakere Family Violence Court: A More Focused Approach" (Paper presented, 22 October 2005, District Court of New Zealand) <www.justice. govt.nz>.

Gabrielle Maxwell "Impoverished Lives-Impoverished Childhoods: Research on Social and Economic Inequality and the Occurrence of Crime" (paper presented to the seminar Does Inequality Matter? A Policy Forum, Wellington, November 2010) <igps.victoria. ac.nz>

Ani Mikaere "Are We All New Zealanders Now? A Māori Response to the Pākehā Quest for Indigeneity" (Bruce Jessop Lecture, New Zealand, 2004) <www.d.yimg.com >.

SirGeoffreyPalmer "The Treaty of Waitangi – Where to From Here? Looking Back to Move Forward" (Presented to Te Papa Treaty of Waitangi Debate Series, 2 February 2006).

Anne Skelton "Reforming the Juvenile Justice System in South Africa: Policy, Law Reform and Parallel Developments" Resource Material 75 (paper presented to UNAFEI 136th International Training Conference, Japan, 23 May–28 June 2007) <www.unafei.or.jp>. Chief JudgeJosephWilliams "Māori Land Court" (Lecture given at the Law School, University of Auckland, 24 July 2003).

Honourable Joseph Williams Justice of the High Court of New Zealand "Lex Aotearoa: A Heroic Attempt at Mapping the Māori Dimension in Modern New Zealand Law" (presented to Harkness Henry Lecture 2013, Te Piringa Faculty of Law, University of Waikato, 7 November 2013).

Kim Workman "Redemption Denied: Aspects of Māori Over-Representation in the Criminal Justice System" (Paper presented to the Justice in the Round Conference, University of Waikato, Hamilton, 18–20 April 2011) <www.rethinking.org.nz>.

Kim Workman, Director of Rethinking Crime and Punishment, New Zealand "Restorative Justice: Victims, Violators and Community – The Path to Acceptance" (International Conference and Workshops of Restorative Justice, Human Rights and Peace Education, Chang Jung Christian University, Taiwan, 6 March 2012) <www.restorativejustice.org>.

Chief Justice (Emeritus) Robert Yazzie "History of the Courts of the Navajo Nation" (Paper prepared for the Orientation of the Judiciary Committee of the Navajo Nation, February 11 2003) <www.navajocourts.org/>.

Media – press releases

James Anaya "New Zealand: More to be Done to Improve Indigenous Peoples' Rights Says UN Expert" (2010) Office of the High Commissioner for Human Rights <www.ohchr.org>.

Natalie Akoorie and Teuila Fuatai "Jury's Out on Compulsory Use of Māori in Court" *New Zealand Herald* (online ed, Auckland, July 18 2012).

"Announcement of New Zealand's Support for the Declaration on the Rights of Indigenous Peoples" at <www.converge.org.nz>.

Australia Associated Press "A UN working group says it wants the NZ government to undertake a review of the degree of systemic bias against Māori in the justice system" April 2014. <http://www.sbs.com.au/news/article/2014/04/08/un-wants-review-maori-nz-prisons>.

Rick Barker on Drug Courts in New Zealand Labour Party "A Pilot isn't a Policy" press release, 20 October 2011 <www.scoop.co.nz>.

Chester Borrows "Action Plan the Next Step Forward for Youth Justice" 31 October, 2013 <www.beehive.govt.nz>

"Canada's Statement of Support on the United Nations Declaration on the Rights of Indigenous Peoples" (2010) at <www.ainc-inac.gc.ca>.

David Clarkson "Mob Member Wants Short Sentence for Being Māori" *Stuff.co.nz* (online ed, Auckland, 20 November 2013).

Judith Collins and Pita Sharples "Youth Māori Offending Down 32 per cent" (press release, 20 August 2013) <www.beehive.govt.nz>.

Peter de Graf "No Conviction for Conservationist" *Northern Advocate* 26 November 2014 <http://www.nzherald.co.nz/>

Justin Delacour (trans) "Interview with Ecuadorian President Rafael Correa" (North American Council on Latin America, June 18 2009) <www.ecuador-rising.blogspot.com>.

"Domestic Violence Rate Unchanged Statistics: Canada Report" *CBC News* (online, Canada, 14 July 2005) <www.cbc.ca>.

"Domestic Violence Court Success" News in Brief: *The Evening Standard* (online ed, London, 9 March 2008) <www.thisislondon.co.uk>.

"Drug Court" *Māori Television* screened Monday 1 September, 2014. https://www.maori television.com/tv/shows/pakipumeka-aotearoa-new-zealand-documentaries/S01E001/ drug-court

R Guilliatt "Aboriginal courts fail to deter offenders" *The Australian* October 23, 2010. <http://www.theaustralian.com.au/national-affairs>

DrSamHancox "'It is extremely unlikely that a single gene explains anything' in Jon Stokes 'Māori 'warrior gene' claims appalling, says geneticist" *NZH* Thursday 10 August 2006<www.nzherald.co.nz>

"Judges Doing Kaumatua's Job in Youth Courts" *Radio New Zealand* (online, New Zealand, 13 October 2011). <www.radionz.co.nz>.

"Justice groups urge government to tighten parole laws" *Radio New Zealand* (4 November 2010) <www.radionz.co.nz >.

Sipho Khumalo "Activists Berate Traditional Courts Bill" *The Mercury* (online ed, South Africa, 12 April 2012).

Kate Kenny "Māori did not give up sovereignty: Waitangi Tribunal" 14 November 2014 <http://www.stuff.co.nz/national/politics/63196127/Maori-did-not-give-up-sovereignty-Waitangi-Tribunal>

Legislative Council Minutes, Tuesday 9 July, printed in the *Daily Southern Cross*, 13 July 1844 <www.victoria.ac.nz >.

Jenny Macklin "Statement on the United Nations Declaration on the Rights of Indigenous Peoples" (2009) at <www.jennymacklin.fahcsia.gov.au>.

"Māori Wardens in Queensland under Fire" *Radio New Zealand News* (online, New Zealand, 18 July 2013) <www.radionz.co.nz >.

Rachael Mazza "Deadly Yarns Launch and the Koori Court" *ABC Network* (online ed, Australia, 22 April 2005) <www.abc.net.au>.

Ministry of Justice Media Release "Te Reo Introduced into District Court" (press release, 19 July 2012) <www.justice.govt.nz>.

New Zealand Labour Party "Barker Asks Committee to Hold Recidivism Inquiry" (press release, 15 December 2010) <www.scoop.co.nz >.

New Zealand Spectator and Cooks Strait Guardian 15 February 1845 <www.victoria.ac.nz/law/ nzlostcases>. New Zealand Law Society "First South Island Rangatahi Court for Christchurch" (24 March 2014) <www.my.lawsociety.org.nz>.

Lydia Nobbs "Just Speak exposes variation in youth prosecution rates" (2013) Aprilwww. justspeak.org

NZ Lawyer Magazine Issue 200 (25 January 2013) <www.nzlawyermagazine.co.nz>.

Mihiata Pirini "Law Commission looks at burial rights" *Radio NZ* (4 August 2014). <http://www.radionz.co.nz/>.

"Police Unhappy at Marae Sentence" *NZH* (Nov 27, 1999).

Rainforest Foundation US "Promoting Indigenous Rights Worldwide: S. James Anaya" (7 July 2009) *Blogging the Rainforest* <www.rainforestfoundationus.wordpress.com>.

"Report Finds Failure in Parole Management" *Newstalk ZB/One News* (New Zealand, February 17, 2009) <www.tvnz.co.nz>.

Jimmy Ryan "Nigel Latta Picks Lock on Prison System" (27 August 2014) <www.stuff. co.nz>

Susan E Rice "Announcement of U.S. Support for the United Nations Declaration on the Rights of Indigenous Peoples" (2010) at <usun.state.gov>.

Marty Sharp "Rangatahi Courts: A Quiet Revolution in Teen Justice" *Newswire* (online, New Zealand, October 2011) <www.newswirenz.wordpress.com>.

The Office of the Attorney-General "Hull Opens Melbourne's First Koori Court" (press release, March 4, 2003).

The Rangatahi Newsletter "Special Edition: Rangatahi Courts Hui" <www.justice.govt. nz>.

Andrew Thompson "Elders Want Koori Court to Stay" *The Standard* (online ed, Australia, 27 April 2013).

"US Senate Committee Holds Controversial Hearing on UN Indigenous Declaration" (10 June 2011) <www.bsnorrell.blogspot.com>.

"Young Māori 'More Likely' to Be Prosecuted than Pākehā" *Radio New Zealand* (online, New Zealand, 10 April 2013) <www.radionz.co.nz >.

Internet

Australian Bureau of Statistics *Australian Social Trends* (2008) <www.abs.gov.au>.

New Zealand Parliament <www.beehive.govt.nz>.

Careers NZ <www.careers.govt.nz>.

Delaware State Courts *Re Entry Courts* <www.courts.delaware.gov>.

Home Office *World Prison Population List* (London, 2002) <www.homeoffice.gov.uk>.

NZ History "Taming the Frontier" https://nzhistory.govt.nz/culture/declaration-of-indep endence-taming-the-frontier

New Zealand Parole Board policies <http://www.paroleboard.govt.nz/nzpb-policies. html>

New Zealand Parole Board *Framework Policy Covering the Development of the Board's Policies: Policy 1, Introduction* (2009) <www.paroleboard.govt.nz>.

OJJDP Model Programs Guide *Re Entry Court* <www.dsgonline.com>

Office for Disability Issues *New Zealand Disability Strategy Discussion Document: Incorporating the Treaty of Waitangi* <www.odi.govt.nz>.

Legislative Assembly of Ontario <www.ontla.on.ca>.

Statistics Canada (2010) <www.vcn.bc.ca>.

Statistics NZ <www.stats.govt.nz>.

The Elizabeth Fry Society of Manitoba, Canada "A Canadian Perspective on Addressing the Overrepresentation of Indigenous Women and Girls in the Canadian Criminal Justice System" (2009) <www.aija.org.au>.

Theories of Crime and Delinquency <http://www.sheldensays.com/theories_of_crime1.htm.>

"United Nations Declaration on the Rights of Indigenous Peoples: Adopted by the General Assembly 13 September 2007" (2007) <www.un.org>.

UNDRIP Online Public Database <http://www.ilc.unsw.edu.au/research/undrip-onli ne-public-database>

Dissertation

Samantha Jeffries "Transforming the Criminal Courts: Politics, Managerialism, Consumerism, Therapeutic Jurisprudence and Change" Post-Doctoral Fellow thesis <www. criminologyresearchcouncil.gov.au>.

Leonie Pihema "Tihei Mauri Ora: Honouring Our Voices. Mana Wahine as a Kaupapa Māori Theoretical Framework" (PhD, University of Auckland, 2001) at ch. 6 "Colonisation and the Importation of Ideologies, of Race, Gender and Class" <www.kaupa pamaori.com>.

Other resources

Simone Bull "Changing the Broken Record: New Theory and Data on Māori offending" <http://igps.victoria.ac.nz>

John Galtry "Submission of the Human Rights Commission on: Victims' Rights Bill to the Justice and Electoral Select Committee" March 2001 <www.hrc.co.nz>.

Hauauru Takiwa Te Kooti o Matariki (Report No 1210, 16 October 2012) <www.hauauru.org>.

Y Jewkes *Theorising Media and Crime*, 10–37 <http://www.sagepub.com> .

J Johnson and J Ogloff "Review of NZPB decision given on 28 June 2006 to release Graeme William Burton on Parole" (5 March 2007) <www.paroleboard.govt.nz>

Ratu Filimone Ralogaivau "Problem Solving Courts of the Fiji Islands: Blending Traditional Approaches to Dispute Resolution in Fiji with Rule of Law – The Best of Both Worlds" (July 2007). <www.aija.org.au>.

Nicola Roughan "Conceptions of Custom in International Law" <www.ssrn.com>

Johann Schiller "Crime and Criminality" Chapter 16 University of California, Davis <www.des.ucdavis.edu/faculty/>

Kim Workman "Māori Over-representation in the Criminal Justice System – Does Structural Discrimination Have Anything to Do with It?" (2007) *Rethinking Crime and Punishment* <http://www.rethinking.org.nz>

Kim Workman "Māori Over Representation in the Criminal Justice System" (2009) *Rethinking Crime and Punishment* <www.rethinking.org.nz>.

Index

For Product Safety Concerns and Information please contact our EU
representative GPSR@taylorandfrancis.com
Taylor & Francis Verlag GmbH, Kaufingerstraße 24, 80331 München, Germany

www.ingramcontent.com/pod-product-compliance
Lightning Source LLC
Chambersburg PA
CBHW050702280326
41926CB00088B/2429